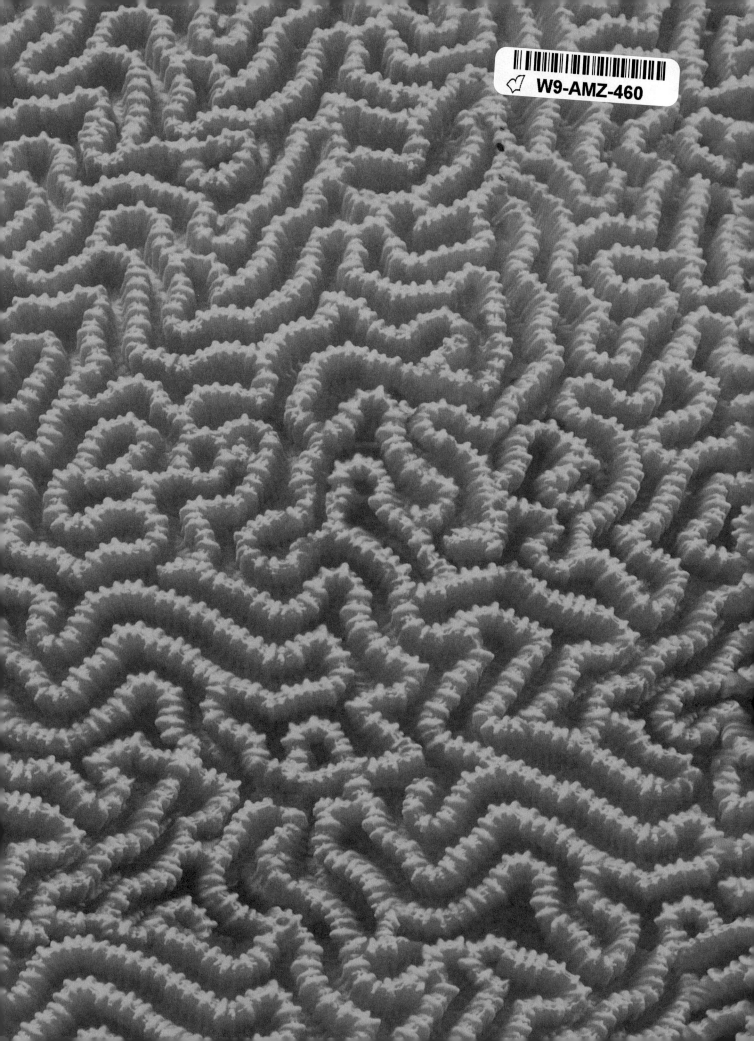

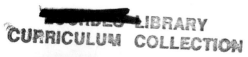

McGRAW-HILL
SCIENCE

Macmillan/McGraw-Hill Edition

Richard Moyer • Lucy Daniel • Jay Hackett

H. Prentice Baptiste • Pamela Stryker • JoAnne Vasquez

NATIONAL
GEOGRAPHIC
SOCIETY

On the Cover:

The orange-spotted coral grouper is a hearty variety of reef fish that is native to the coral reefs of the Indian and Pacific Oceans. These and other varieties of grouper are often collected as young fry or fingerlings for aquaculture purposes. The young groupers are raised on fish farms to meet the increasing demand worldwide for fish as a food source.

Mc Graw Hill **Macmillan McGraw-Hill**

New York   Farmington

Program Authors

Dr. Lucy H. Daniel
Teacher, Consultant
Rutherford County Schools, North Carolina

Dr. Jay Hackett
Professor Emeritus of Earth Sciences
University of Northern Colorado

Dr. Richard H. Moyer
Professor of Science Education
University of Michigan-Dearborn

Dr. H. Prentice Baptiste
Professor of Science and Multicultural Education
New Mexico State University
Las Cruces, New Mexico

Pamela Stryker, M.Ed.
Elementary Educator and Science Consultant
Eanes Independent School District
Austin, Texas

Dr. JoAnne Vasquez
Elementary Science Education Consultant
Mesa Public Schools, Arizona
NSTA Past President

NATIONAL
GEOGRAPHIC
SOCIETY
Washington, D.C.

The features in this textbook entitled "Invitation to Science," "Amazing Stories," and "People in Science," as well as the unit openers, were developed in collaboration with the National Geographic Society's School Publishing Division.
Copyright © 2002 National Geographic Society. All rights reserved.

The name "National Geographic" and the Yellow Border are registered trademarks of the National Geographic Society.

Macmillan/McGraw-Hill

A Division of The McGraw·Hill Companies

Copyright © 2002 Macmillan/McGraw-Hill, a Division of the Educational and Professional Publishing Group of The McGraw-Hill Companies, Inc.

Macmillan/McGraw-Hill
Two Penn Plaza
New York, New York 10121-2298

Printed in the United States of America

ISBN 0-02-280037-9 / 4

1 2 3 4 5 6 7 8 9 027 07 06 05 04 03 02 01

Teacher Reviewers

Peoria, IL
Rolling Acres Middle School
Gail Truho

Rockford, IL
Rockford Public Schools
Dr. Sharon Wynstra
Science Coordinator

Newark, NJ
Alexander Street School
Cheryl Simeonidis

Albuquerque, NM
Jackie Costales
Science Coordinator, Montgomery Complex

Poughkeepsie, NY
St. Peter's School
Monica Crolius

Columbus, OH
St. Mary's School
Linda Cotter
Joby Easley

Keizer, OR
Cummings Elementary
Deanna Havel

McMinnville, OR
McMinnville School District
Kristin Ward

Salem, OR
Fruitland Elementary
 Mike Knudson

Four Corners Elementary
 Bethany Ayers
 Sivhong Hanson
 Cheryl Kirkelie
 Julie Wells

Salem-Keizer Public Schools
 Rachael Harms
 Sue Smith,
 Science Specialist

Yoshikai Elementary
 Joyce Davenport

Norristown, PA
St. Teresa of Avila
Fran Fiordimondo

Pittsburgh, PA
Chartiers Valley Intermediate School
Rosemary Hutter

Memphis, TN
Memphis City Schools
Quincy Hathorn
District Science Facilitator

Consultants

Dr. Carol Baskin
University of Kentucky
Lexington, KY

Dr. Joe W. Crim
University of Georgia
Athens, GA

Dr. Marie DiBerardino
Allegheny University of
Health Sciences
Philadelphia, PA

Dr. R. E. Duhrkopf
Baylor University
Waco, TX

Dr. Dennis L. Nelson
Montana State University
Bozeman, MT

Dr. Fred Sack
Ohio State University
Columbus, OH

Dr. Martin VanDyke
Denver, CO

Dr. E. Peter Volpe
Mercer University
Macon, GA

Consultants

Dr. Clarke Alexander
Skidaway Institute of
Oceanography
Savannah, GA

Dr. Suellen Cabe
Pembroke State University
Pembroke, NC

Dr. Thomas A. Davies
Texas A & M University
College Station, TX

Dr. Ed Geary
Geological Society of America
Boulder, CO

Dr. David C. Kopaska-Merkel
Geological Survey of Alabama
Tuscaloosa, AL

Consultants

Dr. Bonnie Buratti
Jet Propulsion Lab
Pasadena, CA

Dr. Shawn Carlson
Society of Amateur Scientists
San Diego, CA

Dr. Karen Kwitter
Williams College
Williamstown, MA

Dr. Steven Souza
Williamstown, MA

Dr. Joseph P. Straley
University of Kentucky
Lexington, KY

Dr. Thomas Troland
University of Kentucky
Lexington, KY

Dr. Josephine Davis Wallace
University of North Carolina
Charlotte, NC

Consultant for Primary Grades

Donna Harrell Lubcker
East Texas Baptist University
Marshall, TX

Teacher Panelists

Newark, NJ
First Avenue School
Jorge Alameda
Concetta Cioci
Neva Galasso
Bernadette Kazanjian-reviewer
Toby Marks
Janet Mayer-reviewer
Maria Tutela

Brooklyn, NY
P.S. 31
  Janet Mantel
  Paige McGlone
  Madeline Pappas
  Maria Puma-reviewer
P.S. 217
  Rosemary Ahern
  Charles Brown
  Claudia Deeb-reviewer
  Wendy Lerner
P.S. 225
  Christine Calafiore
  Annette Fisher-reviewer

P.S. 250
  Melissa Kane
P.S. 277
  Erica Cohen
  Helena Conti
  Anne Marie Corrado
  Deborah Scott-DiClemente
  Jeanne Fish
  Diane Fromhartz
  Tricia Hinz
  Lisa Iside
  Susan Malament
  Joyce Menkes-reviewer
  Elaine Noto
  Jean Pennacchio
Jeffrey Hampton
Mwaka Yavana

Elmont, NY
Covert Avenue School
Arlene Connelly

Mt. Vernon, NY
Holmes School
Jennifer Cavallaro
Lou Ciofi
George DiFiore
Brenda Durante
Jennifer Hawkins-reviewer
Michelle Mazzotta
Catherine Moringiello
Mary Jane Oria-reviewer
Lucille Pierotti
Pia Vicario-reviewer

Ozone Park, NY
St. Elizabeth School
Joanne Cocchiola-reviewer
Helen DiPietra-reviewer
Barbara Kingston
Madeline Visco

St. Albans, NY
Orvia Williams

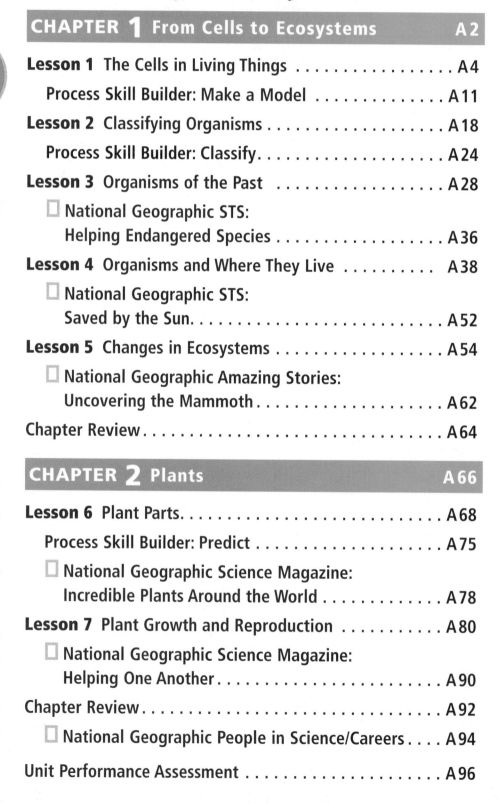

UNIT A

Life Science

The World of Living Things PAGE A1

Invitation to Science page S1

CHAPTER 1 From Cells to Ecosystems — A2

Lesson 1 The Cells in Living Things A4

Process Skill Builder: Make a Model A11

Lesson 2 Classifying Organisms A18

Process Skill Builder: Classify. A24

Lesson 3 Organisms of the Past A28

☐ National Geographic STS:
Helping Endangered Species A36

Lesson 4 Organisms and Where They Live A38

☐ National Geographic STS:
Saved by the Sun. A52

Lesson 5 Changes in Ecosystems A54

☐ National Geographic Amazing Stories:
Uncovering the Mammoth A62

Chapter Review. A64

CHAPTER 2 Plants — A66

Lesson 6 Plant Parts. A68

Process Skill Builder: Predict A75

☐ National Geographic Science Magazine:
Incredible Plants Around the World A78

Lesson 7 Plant Growth and Reproduction A80

☐ National Geographic Science Magazine:
Helping One Another A90

Chapter Review. A92

☐ National Geographic People in Science/Careers A94

Unit Performance Assessment A96

Animals as Living Things PAGE B1

CHAPTER 3 Describing Animals   B2

Lesson 1 Animal Characteristics. B4

Process Skill Builder: Observe B10

☐ National Geographic STS:
Helping Endangered Animals B12

Lesson 2 Animals Without Backbones B14

Lesson 3 Animals With Backbones B26

☐ National Geographic Amazing Stories:
Spider Giants. B38

Chapter Review B40

CHAPTER 4 Life Processes   B42

Lesson 4 Organ Systems B44

Lesson 5 Development and Reproduction B54

Lesson 6 Animal Survival. B64

Process Skill Builder: Form a Hypothesis B69

☐ National Geographic Science Magazine:
Dancing Bees. B74

Chapter Review B76

☐ National Geographic People in Science/Careers B78

Unit Performance Assessment B80

UNIT C

Earth Science

Earth and Beyond PAGE C1

CHAPTER 5 Earth's History — C2

Lesson 1 What You Can Learn from Rocks C4

Lesson 2 Clues from Fossils C16

Process Skill Builder: **Use Numbers** C23

National Geographic Amazing Stories:
Fossil Treasure Trove C26

Chapter Review C28

CHAPTER 6 Earth's Surface and Interior — C30

Lesson 3 Shaping Earth's Surface C32

Process Skill Builder: **Define Based on Observations** . . C36

National Geographic Science Magazine:
The Work of Wind and Water C40

Lesson 4 The Story of Soil C42

Lesson 5 Inside Earth C52

Chapter Review C60

CHAPTER 7 Sun, Moon, and Planets — C62

Lesson 6 Earth, the Moon, and the Sun C64

Process Skill Builder: **Interpret Data** C74

National Geographic STS:
Telescopes: Tools of Discovery C76

Lesson 7 The Solar System and Beyond C78

National Geographic History of Science:
Views of the Universe C90

Chapter Review C92

National Geographic People in Science/Careers C94

Unit Performance Assessment C96

UNIT D

Earth Science

Water and Weather PAGE D1

CHAPTER 8 Earth's Water   D2

Lesson 1 Water, Water Everywhere D4

Lesson 2 Follow the Water. D14

  ☐ National Geographic STS:
    Let It Rain! D24

Lesson 3 Motions in the Oceans D26

Lesson 4 Go with the Flow D36

  Process Skill Builder: Use Variables D44

Lesson 5 Water Please! D46

  ☐ National Geographic Amazing Stories:
    Desalination D56

Chapter Review. D58

CHAPTER 9 Earth's Weather   D60

Lesson 6 Air, Wind, and the Atmosphere D62

  Process Skill Builder: Infer. D70

  ☐ National Geographic Science Magazine:
    Endangered: Earth's Ozone Layer. D74

Lesson 7 Weather and Climate. D76

  ☐ National Geographic STS:
    Watch Out for Wild Weather!. D90

Chapter Review. D92

  ☐ National Geographic People in Science/Careers. . . . D94

Unit Performance Assessment D96

CHAPTER 10 Properties of Matter   **E2**

Lesson 1 Matter. E4

Lesson 2 Measuring Matter E14

Process Skill Builder: **Infer** E18

☐ National Geographic Amazing Stories:
Help for Landfills E24

Chapter Review E26

CHAPTER 11 Changes in Matter   **E28**

Lesson 3 What Matter Is Made Of E30

☐ National Geographic History of Science:
A Chemist Who Matter-ed E40

Lesson 4 Physical Changes E42

Process Skill Builder: **Experiment** E48

Lesson 5 Chemical Changes E50

☐ National Geographic Science Magazine:
Everything Changes E58

Chapter Review E60

☐ National Geographic People in Science/Careers E62

Unit Performance Assessment E64

Energy PAGE F1

CHAPTER 12 Forms of Energy — F2

Lesson 1 Forces, Motion, and Energy F4

Process Skill Builder: Measure F9

Lesson 2 Energy and Tools F18

Lesson 3 Heat F32

Lesson 4 Light F40

Lesson 5 Sound F52

☐ National Geographic Amazing Stories:
Circling the Globe in a Hot-Air Balloon F62

Chapter Review F64

CHAPTER 13 Electricity and Magnetism — F66

Lesson 6 Static Electricity. F68

Lesson 7 Current Electricity F76

☐ National Geographic Science Magazine:
Critical Circuits F86

Lesson 8 Electricity and Magnets F88

Process Skill Builder: Use Numbers. F97

Chapter Review F100

☐ National Geographic People in Science/Careers . . . F102

Unit Performance Assessment F104

Reference Section R1

Activities

UNIT A

Explore Activities

What Are Living Things Made Of? **A5**

How Are Organisms Classified? **A19**

How Can We Use Skeletons to Compare Organisms? **A29**

How Do Living and Nonliving Things Interact? **A39**

What Causes Ecosystems to Change? **A55**

Why Does a Plant Need Leaves? **A69**

How Does a Seed Grow? **A81**

Quick Labs

Older and Younger **A31**

Sunlight and Plants **A41**

Observe a Decomposer **A49**

The Structure of a Seed **A83**

Process Skill Builders

Make a Model: Plant and Animal Cells **A11**

Classify: Leaves **A24**

Predict: Photosynthesis Versus Respiration **A75**

UNIT B

Explore Activities

What Are Some Animal Characteristics? **B5**

What Are the Characteristics of Invertebrates? **B15**

What Are Vertebrates Like? B27

How Does Blood Travel in Fish and Amphibian Hearts? **B45**

How Do Mealworms Change As They Grow? **B55**

How Can Body Color Help an Animal Survive? **B65**

Quick Labs

Classifying Invertebrates **B23**

Classifying Vertebrates **B35**

Fool Your Senses **B51**

Heredity Cards **B62**

Process Skill Builders

Observe: Animal Symmetry **B10**

Form a Hypothesis: How Do Adaptations Help an Animal Survive? **B69**

UNIT C

Explore Activities

How Can You Interpret Clues in Rocks? **C5**

What Can You Learn from Fossils? **C17**

How Do Glaciers Scratch and Move Rocks? **C33**

What Is Soil Made Of? **C43**

What's Inside? **C53**

How Do the Sun, Earth, and the Moon Move? **C65**

How Do Objects in the Night Sky Compare in Size? **C79**

Quick Labs

Identifying Minerals **C8**

Observing Sediments **C11**

Making Molds and Casts **C19**

Rate of Flow **C48**

Earthquake Vibrations **C55**

A Comet's Tail **C87**

Process Skill Builders

Use Numbers: Dinosaur Bones **C23**

Define Terms: Flow of a Glacier **C36**

Interpret Data: Moon Phases on a Calendar **C74**

UNIT D

Explore Activities
Where Can Water Be Found? **D5**
What Makes Water Disappear? **D15**
What Makes the Ocean Move? **D27**
How Fast Does Water Flow in Soil and Rocks? **D37**
How Much Fresh Water Is Used? **D47**
What Can Air Do? **D63**
How Do Raindrops Form? **D77**

Quick Labs
Water in an Apple **D12**
Disappearing Water **D18**
Make Waves! **D32**
Make Runoffs **D39**
Wasted Water **D54**

Process Skill Builders
Use Variables: Surface Area and Evaporation **D44**
Infer: Homemade Barometer **D70**

UNIT E

Explore Activities
How Can You Identify Matter? **E5**
How Can You Measure Matter? **E15**
How Can You Classify Matter? **E31**
How Can Things Change? **E43**
What Causes the Change? **E51**

Quick Labs
Is Bigger Always More? **E10**
Comparing Densities **E20**
Mix and Unmix **E36**
Preventing Chemical Change **E55**

Process Skill Builders
Infer: Examine If Shape Affects Volume **E18**
Experiment: How Heat Energy Affects Evaporation **E48**

UNIT F

Explore Activities
How Can You Tell Something Is Moving? **F5**
What Does It Take to Move Something? **F19**
How Does Fat Keep Mammals Warm? **F33**
What Do You See When You Mix Colors of Light? **F41**
How Do Vibrations Produce Sound? **F53**
What Happens to Rubbed Balloons? **F69**
What Makes a Bulb Light? **F77**
How Is a Bar Magnet Like a Compass? **F89**

Quick Labs
Make Levers **F23**
Matter and Heat **F37**
Absorbing Light **F49**
Making Static Electricity **F71**
Conductor Test-Off **F80**
Electromagnets **F92**

Process Skill Builders
Measure: Marble Motion **F9**
Use Numbers: Reading an Electric Meter **F97**

As you study science, you will learn many new words. You will read about many new ideas. Read these pages. They will help you understand this book.

1. The **Vocabulary** list has all the new words you will learn in the lesson. The page numbers tell you where the words are taught.

2. The name tells you what the lesson is about.

3. **Get Ready** uses the picture on the page to help you start thinking about the lesson.

LESSON 2

Vocabulary

cnidarian, B17
mollusk, B20
echinoderm, B20
endoskeleton, B20
arthropod, B21
exoskeleton, B21

Animals Without Backbones

Get Ready

How big are invertebrates? Some, like ants and earthworms, can fit in the palm of your hand. Others, like the octopus shown here, can grow much larger. Some are many meters wide! How else do you think invertebrates differ from one another?

Process Skills

You classify when you place things that share properties together in groups.

B 14

Explore Activity

What Are the Characteristics of Invertebrates?

Procedure

BE CAREFUL! Be careful with live animals.

1 **Observe** Place the worm on the damp paper towel. Get a petri dish with a *planarian* (pluh·NAYR·ee·uhn) in it from your teacher. Observe each organism with a hand lens. Record your observations.

2 Gently touch the worm with your finger and the planarian with the toothpick. What do they do? Record your observations.

3 What characteristics of the praying mantis and magnified hydra do you observe? Record your observations.

Drawing Conclusions

1 **Define Based on Observations** What characteristics do you think invertebrates have? Make a list.

2 **Communicate** Compare your list with those of your classmates. Based on your observations, make a class list of invertebrate characteristics.

3 **Going Further: Classify** Think of other organisms that you would classify as invertebrates based on your observations. Make a list. Check your list as you continue this lesson.

Materials

living planarian

living earthworm

hand lens

petri dish

water

damp paper towel

toothpick

Hydra

Praying mantis

B 15

4. This **Process Skill** is used in the Explore Activity.

5. The **Explore Activity** is a hands-on way to learn about the lesson.

As you read a lesson, follow these three steps. They will help you to understand what you are reading.

1. This box contains the **Main Idea** of the lesson. Keep the main idea of the lesson in mind as you read.

2. **Before Reading** Read the large red question before you read the page. Try to answer this question from what you already know.

3. **During Reading** Look for new **Vocabulary** words in yellow. Look at the pictures. They will help you understand what you are reading.

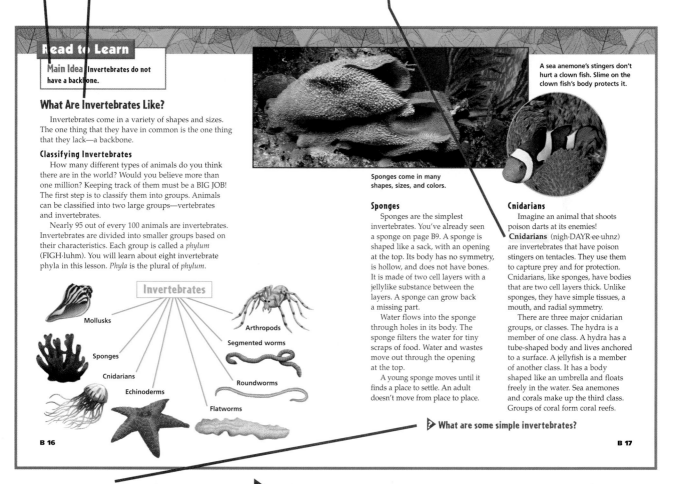

Read to Learn

Main Idea Invertebrates do not have a backbone.

What Are Invertebrates Like?

Invertebrates come in a variety of shapes and sizes. The one thing that they have in common is the one thing that they lack—a backbone.

Classifying Invertebrates

How many different types of animals do you think there are in the world? Would you believe more than one million? Keeping track of them must be a BIG JOB! The first step is to classify them into groups. Animals can be classified into two large groups—vertebrates and invertebrates.

Nearly 95 out of every 100 animals are invertebrates. Invertebrates are divided into smaller groups based on their characteristics. Each group is called a *phylum* (FIGH·luhm). You will learn about eight invertebrate phyla in this lesson. *Phyla* is the plural of *phylum*.

Invertebrates

Mollusks

Arthropods

Segmented worms

Sponges

Cnidarians

Roundworms

Echinoderms

Flatworms

B 16

A sea anemone's stingers don't hurt a clown fish. Slime on the clown fish's body protects it.

Sponges come in many shapes, sizes, and colors.

Sponges

Sponges are the simplest invertebrates. You've already seen a sponge on page B9. A sponge is shaped like a sack, with an opening at the top. Its body has no symmetry, is hollow, and does not have bones. It is made of two cell layers with a jellylike substance between the layers. A sponge can grow back a missing part.

Water flows into the sponge through holes in its body. The sponge filters the water for tiny scraps of food. Water and wastes move out through the opening at the top.

A young sponge moves until it finds a place to settle. An adult doesn't move from place to place.

Cnidarians

Imagine an animal that shoots poison darts at its enemies! **Cnidarians** (nigh·DAYR·ee·uhnz) are invertebrates that have poison stingers on tentacles. They use them to capture prey and for protection. Cnidarians, like sponges, have bodies that are two cell layers thick. Unlike sponges, they have simple tissues, a mouth, and radial symmetry.

There are three major cnidarian groups, or classes. The hydra is a member of one class. A hydra has a tube-shaped body and lives anchored to a surface. A jellyfish is a member of another class. It has a body shaped like an umbrella and floats freely in the water. Sea anemones and corals make up the third class. Groups of coral form coral reefs.

▷ What are some simple invertebrates?

B 17

4. **After Reading** ▷ This arrow points to a question. It will help you check that you understand what you have read. Try to answer the question before you go to the next large red question.

On one page in each lesson, you will find a question that practices the Chapter Reading Skill. In any chapter you will find one of these skills:

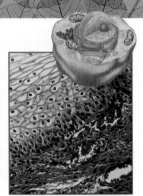

The cells of a plant have a boxlike shape. They contain chlorophyll, which gives them a green color.

Animal cells are not shaped like small boxes. They do not contain chlorophyll.

Organisms come in all shapes and sizes. Tiny flies, onion plants, great blue whales—even you—are all organisms. It doesn't matter if an organism lives in the water, on the ground, or in the tops of the tallest trees. All organisms carry out five basic life functions.

The small, boxlike structures making up the onion plant are called **cells** (SELZ). A cell is the smallest unit of living matter. In other words, cells are the "building blocks" of living things. All living things are made of cells—even you.

Although all living things are made of cells, all cells are not the same. Plant cells have a boxlike shape. Some even contain a green material called *chlorophyll* (KLAWR·uh·fil). When sunlight strikes chlorophyll, the cell can make food for the plant. Animal cells don't contain chlorophyll and are not box shaped.

READING Compare and Contrast
What is one difference between plant and animal cells?

A 7

Main idea and supporting details
The *main idea* is what the reading is about. To find the main idea:
- Answer the red question on a page.
- Look for facts that tell more about the main idea. Pictures on the page can add supporting details.

Compare and contrast
Compare means "to tell how things are alike." *Contrast* means "to tell how things are different."

Draw conclusions
A *conclusion* is a statement of what you learned by putting the facts together. To draw a conclusion:
- Make a list of the facts you read on a page.
- Write your conclusion.

Sequence of events The *sequence* is the order in which things happen. To find the sequence:
- Ask yourself: "What happened first?" Write it down.
- Then make a list of each thing that happened after that – in order.

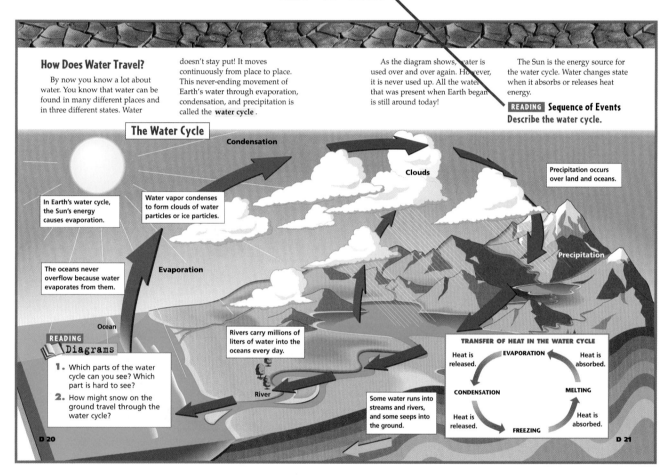

How Does Water Travel?

By now you know a lot about water. You know that water can be found in many different places and in three different states. Water doesn't stay put! It moves continuously from place to place. This never-ending movement of Earth's water through evaporation, condensation, and precipitation is called the **water cycle**.

As the diagram shows, water is used over and over again. However, it is never used up. All the water that was present when Earth began is still around today!

The Sun is the energy source for the water cycle. Water changes state when it absorbs or releases heat energy.

READING Sequence of Events
Describe the water cycle.

The Water Cycle

Condensation

Clouds

Precipitation occurs over land and oceans.

In Earth's water cycle, the Sun's energy causes evaporation.

Water vapor condenses to form clouds of water particles or ice particles.

Precipitation

Evaporation

The oceans never overflow because water evaporates from them.

Ocean

READING
Diagrams

1. Which parts of the water cycle can you see? Which part is hard to see?
2. How might snow on the ground travel through the water cycle?

Rivers carry millions of liters of water into the oceans every day.

River

Some water runs into streams and rivers, and some seeps into the ground.

TRANSFER OF HEAT IN THE WATER CYCLE

Heat is released. — **EVAPORATION** — Heat is absorbed.

CONDENSATION — **MELTING**

Heat is released. — **FREEZING** — Heat is absorbed.

D 20

D 21

Cause and effect When you read about something that happened, ask yourself: "What made it happen?"
- A *cause* makes something happen. Beating a drum is a cause.
- The thing that happens is the *effect*. The effect is the sound.

Summarize To summarize:
- Ask yourself what the page you read is about.
- State it in your own words in a sentence or two.

Reading In SCIENCE GRAPHICS

Throughout all chapters of this book, you will get information by reading graphics. Graphics are pictures that are drawn to show information.

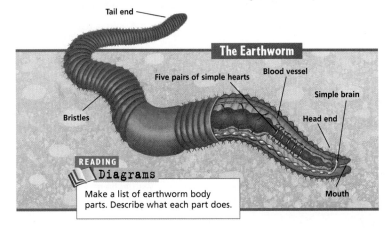

The Earthworm

Tail end

Five pairs of simple hearts

Blood vessel

Simple brain

Head end

Bristles

READING Diagrams

Make a list of earthworm body parts. Describe what each part does.

Mouth

diagrams: pictures that show how something works or is put together

graphs: lines, bars, or symbols drawn to help you compare amounts

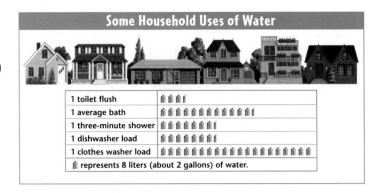

Some Household Uses of Water

1 toilet flush	
1 average bath	
1 three-minute shower	
1 dishwasher load	
1 clothes washer load	

represents 8 liters (about 2 gallons) of water.

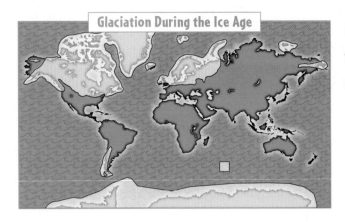

Glaciation During the Ice Age

maps: drawings that show features of places on Earth's surface

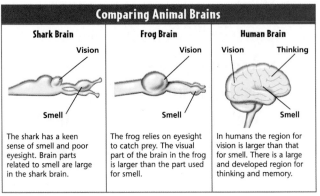

Comparing Animal Brains

Shark Brain	Frog Brain	Human Brain
Vision	Vision	Vision / Thinking
Smell	Smell	Smell
The shark has a keen sense of smell and poor eyesight. Brain parts related to smell are large in the shark brain.	The frog relies on eyesight to catch prey. The visual part of the brain in the frog is larger than the part used for smell.	In humans the region for vision is larger than that for smell. There is a large and developed region for thinking and memory.

charts: lists of information in tables with pictures

Invitation to Science

S hark! Swimmers around the world fear that word. Are all sharks dangerous? What do we really know about sharks? Find out by reading about a scientist who studies sharks. As you read, you'll learn about the **Methods of Science**, the steps a scientist follows to solve problems. You'll also see in **red** some of the skills scientists use as they follow these steps.

Dr. Eugenie Clark studies sharks, the largest fish in the ocean.

Observation

Have you ever seen sharks at an aquarium? Most people fear sharks because some kinds of sharks, such as the great white, can eat just about anything they want!

One scientist who studies sharks is Dr. Eugenie Clark. When Eugenie Clark was nine years old, her mother took her to an aquarium. Eugenie watched sharks and other fish at the aquarium almost every Saturday. When she grew up, she became a scientist. Today, Dr. Clark studies different kinds of sharks and how they behave.

Scientists gather facts and information, or data, by **observing**. They **communicate** their results by writing books and articles. Dr. Clark examined the data on sharks. She learned that there are about 400 kinds of sharks.

She also learned that most sharks are shy and swim away from people. Only about 30 kinds of sharks have ever attacked humans. More people die from bee stings than from shark attacks!

A whale shark is 15 meters long.

Question

Scientists begin studies by being curious and asking questions. They design **experiments** to try to answer their questions and test their ideas. Asking questions and testing ideas can be exciting. It can also take a long time. One question often leads to another.

A lot of people think that all sharks are dangerous. One of Dr. Clark's questions was "Are all sharks dangerous to people?"

People usually fear big sharks the most. The biggest shark of all is the whale shark. It can grow to be more than 15 meters (50 feet) long. Dr. Clark studied the whale shark carefully. She learned that the whale shark is one of the most harmless kinds of sharks.

The more Dr. Clark learned about sharks, the more curious she became. She had other questions. She wondered if sharks could learn to do things.

A reef shark is 1.5 meters long.

Hypothesis

Some scientists didn't think sharks were smart enough to learn. Dr. Clark decided to find out. To begin her study, she **formed a hypothesis**. A hypothesis is a possible answer to a question. You might think of a hypothesis as an "educated guess." However, a good hypothesis is more than just a guess.

A good hypothesis must do three things.

- A hypothesis must explain the observations.
- A hypothesis must be testable.
- A hypothesis must **predict** new findings.

You might think of a prediction as an "If . . . then . . ." statement. For example, if sharks are able to learn, then scientists should be able to teach them to do things.

Dr. Clark's hypothesis was that sharks are smart enough to be taught to do things.

Experiment

A scientific test of a hypothesis is called an experiment. A hypothesis that cannot be tested by experiments could be a waste of time.

Scientists **use variables** in their experiments. A variable is one of the things in an experiment that can be changed or controlled.

A good experiment must follow certain rules.

- An experiment must be repeatable.
- An experiment must test only one variable at a time.

Dr. Clark did many experiments to see what sharks could learn. For example, with her students she built a white, wooden target. They placed the target underwater in a big shark tank. Could a shark learn to press its nose against the target to get food as a reward? Yes! The sharks learned to do this.

Dr. Clark repeated the experiment but changed one of the variables. She gave the reward only to sharks that pressed the target and then swam to the other end of the tank. The sharks learned to do this, too.

A hammerhead shark

Conclusion

The results of a good experiment should clearly support or not support the hypothesis. What if the results do not support the hypothesis? The scientist may need to change the hypothesis or form a completely new hypothesis. Then the scientist must do new experiments to test the new hypothesis.

One day in winter, Dr. Clark set up her experiment as usual. However, this time the sharks didn't press the target. She wondered if they had forgotten everything they had learned. Her hypothesis was that sharks are smart enough to be taught to do things. Was her hypothesis wrong? More experiments were needed.

By spring she had the answer. She **measured** the temperature of the water. She learned that sharks lost interest in food when the water was cold. When the water warmed as spring approached, the sharks began to press the target for food again. Dr. Clark **inferred** that sharks could learn and had a good memory as well!

Dr. Clark **interpreted the data** to mean that sharks can learn various things. In her experiments she also proved that some kinds of sharks could tell light from dark. Some can even tell the difference between simple patterns.

A diver conducts an experiment with a shark.

Methods of Science

Here is a chart that shows the steps scientists such as Dr. Eugenie Clark follow when solving a problem in science. Scientists don't always follow the steps in the order shown.

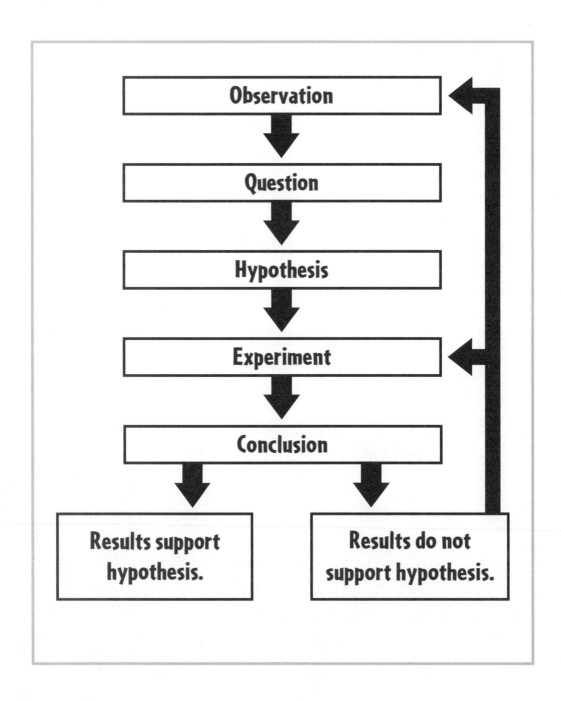

Science Process Skills

Scientists use these skills when they follow the **Methods of Science**. You will use these skills, too.

Observe to use one or more of the senses to identify or learn about an object or event

Infer to form an idea from facts or observations

Classify to place things that share properties together in groups

Measure to find the size, distance, time, volume, area, mass, weight, or temperature of an object or an event

Use numbers to order, count, add, subtract, multiply, and divide to explain data

Communicate to share information

Predict to state possible results of an event or experiment

Interpret data to use the information that has been gathered to answer questions or solve a problem

Form a hypothesis to make a statement that can be tested to answer a question

Use variables to identify things in an experiment that can be changed or controlled

Experiment to perform a test to support or disprove a hypothesis

Make a model to make something to represent an object or event

Define terms based on observations to put together a description that is based on observations and experience

Science Safety Tips

Here are some important safety rules that you should follow.

In the Classroom

- Read all directions. Make sure you understand them. When you see **BE CAREFUL!**, be sure to follow the safety rule.
- Listen to your teacher for special safety directions. If you don't understand something, ask for help.
- Wash your hands with soap and water before an activity.
- Wear safety goggles when your teacher tells you to wear them. Wear them when working with anything that can fly into your eyes or when working with liquids.
- Wear a safety apron if you work with anything messy or anything that might spill.
- Wipe up a spill right away, or ask your teacher for help.
- Tell your teacher if something breaks. If glass breaks, do not clean it up yourself.
- Keep your hair and clothes away from open flames. Tie back long hair, and roll up long sleeves.

- Be careful around a hot plate. Know when it is on and when it is off. Remember that the plate stays hot for a few minutes after it's turned off.
- Keep your hands dry around electrical equipment.
- Don't eat or drink anything during an experiment.
- Put equipment back the way your teacher tells you.
- Dispose of things the way your teacher tells you.
- Clean up your work area after an activity, and wash your hands with soap and water.

In the Field

- Go with a trusted adult—such as your teacher or a parent or guardian.
- Do not touch animals or plants without an adult's approval. The animal might bite. The plant might be poison ivy or another dangerous plant.

Responsibility

- Treat living things, the environment, and one another with respect.

UNIT

A

The World of Living Things

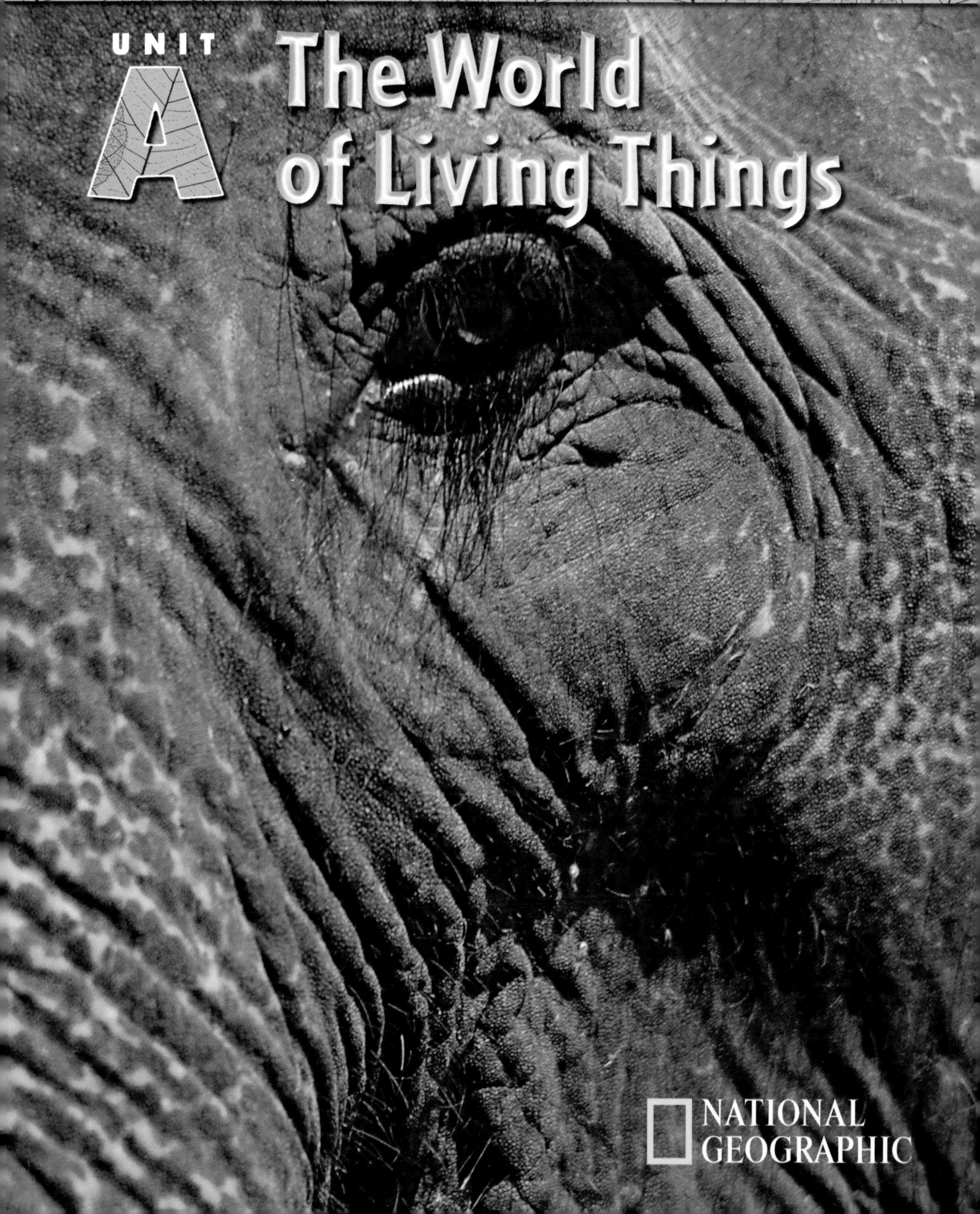

NATIONAL
GEOGRAPHIC

NATIONAL GEOGRAPHIC

LOOK!

Elephants are the largest land animals. What do elephants have in common with all living things?

The World of Living Things

CHAPTER 1

From Cells to Ecosystems. A2

CHAPTER 2

Plants A66

CHAPTER

1

LESSON 1

The Cells in
Living Things, A4

LESSON 2

Classifying
Organisms, A18

LESSON 3

Organisms of
the Past, A28

LESSON 4

Organisms and
Where They Live, A38

LESSON 5

Changes in
Ecosystems, A54

From Cells to Ecosystems

Did You Ever Wonder?

What kinds of animals live in a tidal mud flat? The
red-colored birds, called scarlet ibises, share their home
with egrets. The scarlet ibis retains its color by eating
large amounts of shrimp. How do living things interact
with their surroundings?

The Cells in Living Things

Vocabulary

oxygen, A6

organism, A6

cell, A7

tissue, A14

organ, A15

organ system, A15

Get Ready

What would you have to do to make this puppet appear to be alive? What are the differences between living and nonliving things? What do living things do? What are they made of?

Process Skill

You predict when you state possible results of an event or experiment.

Explore Activity

What Are Living Things Made Of?

Materials

onion plant

prepared slides of onion skin and leaf

hand lens

microscope

Procedure

1. **Observe** Draw the whole onion plant. Label its parts. Write down how each part might help the plant live.

2. **Observe** Ask your teacher to cut the plant lengthwise. Draw and label what you see.

3. **Observe** Look at a small section of onion skin and a thin piece of a leaf with the hand lens. Draw what you see.

4. Use the microscope to look at the onion skin and the leaf section. Use high and low power. Draw what you see.

Drawing Conclusions

1. **Communicate** What did you see when you examined the onion skin and leaf with the hand lens and the microscope? Make a table or chart.

2. How are your observations of the onion skin and leaf alike and different?

3. **Infer** What do the parts of the onion plant seem to be made of?

4. **Going Further: Predict** Do you think you would see similar structures if you observed a part of the root? How could you find out?

Read to Learn

Main Idea All living things are made up of building blocks called cells.

What Are Living Things?

Do you think you have anything in common with the onion plant? You aren't green and don't have leaves. However, you still have a lot in common with an onion.

The main thing you have in common is that you are both living things. Most living things share certain characteristics. Among them are the basic needs for food, water, a place to live, and **oxygen** (AHK·suh·juhn). Most living things use oxygen to turn food into energy. Plants need oxygen to use the food they make. Another characteristic of living things is that they are made of parts. Each part has a specific job to keep a living thing alive.

Plants, people, and other animals are all **organisms** (AWR·guh·niz·uhmz). An organism is a living thing that carries out five basic life functions on its own.

READING
Diagrams

1. How do living things get energy?

2. Why is it important that living things reproduce?

The Five Basic Life Functions

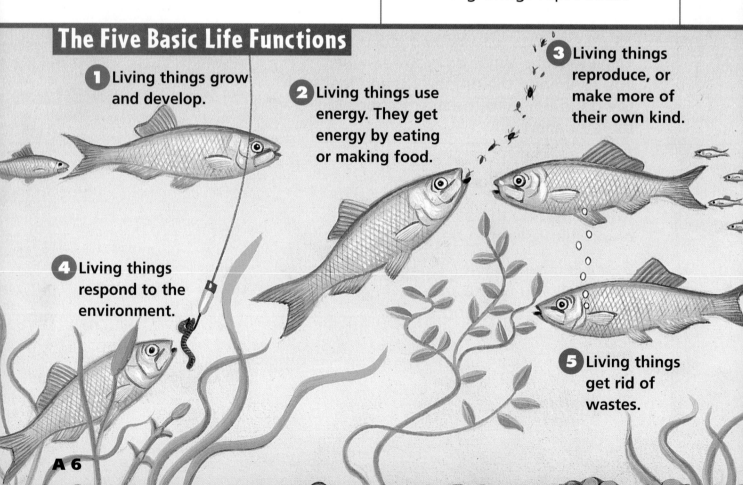

1 Living things grow and develop.

2 Living things use energy. They get energy by eating or making food.

3 Living things reproduce, or make more of their own kind.

4 Living things respond to the environment.

5 Living things get rid of wastes.

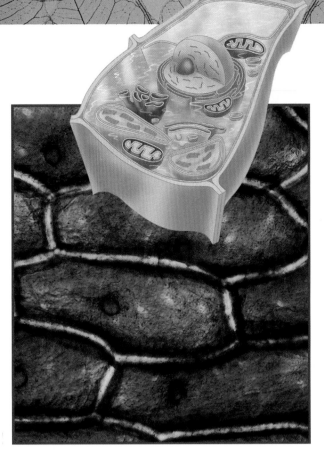

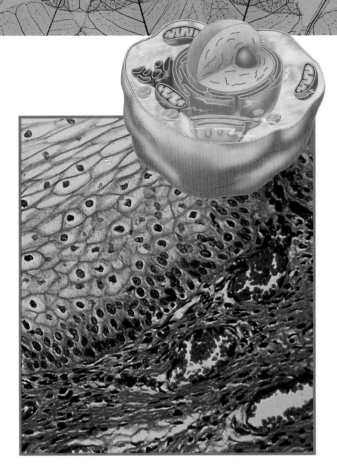

The cells of a plant have a boxlike shape. They contain chlorophyll, which gives them a green color.

Animal cells are not shaped like small boxes. They do not contain chlorophyll.

Organisms come in all shapes and sizes. Tiny flies, onion plants, great blue whales—even you—are all organisms. It doesn't matter if an organism lives in the water, on the ground, or in the tops of the tallest trees. All organisms carry out five basic life functions.

The small, boxlike structures making up the onion plant are called **cells** (SELZ). A cell is the smallest unit of living matter. In other words, cells are the "building blocks" of living things. All living things are made of cells—even you.

Although all living things are made of cells, all cells are not the same. Plant cells have a boxlike shape. Some even contain a green material called *chlorophyll* (KLAWR·uh·fil). When sunlight strikes chlorophyll, the cell can make food for the plant. Animal cells don't contain chlorophyll and are not box shaped.

READING **Compare and Contrast**
What is one difference between plant and animal cells?

A 7

How Are Plant and Animal Cells Different?

Most cells have everything they need to carry out the five basic life functions. However, plant and animal cells are not made up of all the same parts. The diagram on this page shows the major parts of a typical plant cell. The diagram on the next page shows the major parts of a typical animal cell.

Cells also contain some other parts that have specific jobs. One part is like the cell's power plant. Food is burned here to give the cell energy.

Another part of the cell is like a chemical factory. It helps make the cell's building materials.

Plant Cell

Cell wall
(SEL WAWL):
A thick, stiff structure that protects and supports the plant cell.

Mitochondrion
(migh·tuh·KAHN·dree·uhn):
The power plant of the cell. Food is burned here to give the cell energy.

Chloroplast
(KLAWR·uh·plast): The plant cell's food factory contains chlorophyll.

Endoplasmic reticulum
(EN·duh·plaz·mik ri·TIK·yuh·luhm):
The cell's chemical factory. Materials the cell needs to grow and live are made here.

Animal Cell

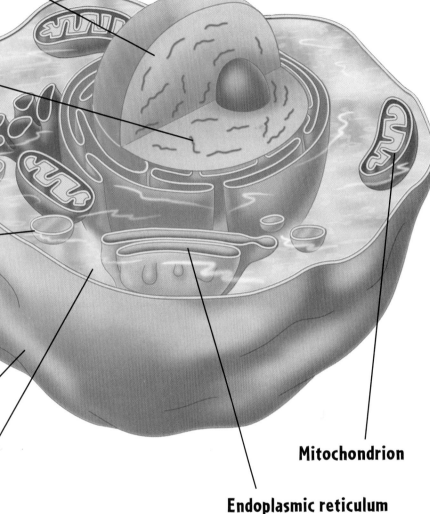

Nucleus
(NEW·klee·uhs):
One of the largest
parts of the cell. It
controls cell
activities.

Chromosomes
(KROH·muh·sohmz):
The threadlike
structures that
control an
organism's traits.

Vacuole
(VAK·yew·ohl):
A holding bin for
food, water, and
wastes. Plant cells have
one or two vacuoles.
Vacuoles are small in
animal cells. Animal cells
have more vacuoles
than plant cells.

Cell membrane
(SEL MEM·brayn):
An animal cell's thin
outer covering. In
plants it is found
inside the
cell wall.

Cytoplasm
(SIGH·tuh·plaz·uhm): The jellylike
substance that fills the cell. It is
mostly water but contains many
important chemicals.

Mitochondrion

Endoplasmic reticulum

READING
Diagrams

How are a plant cell
and an animal cell
similar and different?

▷ **What two cell parts does a plant cell
have that an animal cell doesn't?**

Can You Compare Plant and Animal Cells?

The basic differences between most plant and animal cells include their covering, color, and shape. Cells also differ depending on the types of jobs they do and the parts of the organism they make up.

How are plant cells and animal cells alike? Both are small. Both are filled with a jellylike substance. Both have outer coverings with small structures inside.

Plant cells and animal cells are different in some ways, however:
- **Covering** A plant cell has a thick cell wall covering the cell membrane. An animal cell has only the thin cell membrane.
- **Color** Most plant cells have green coloring. An animal cell does not.
- **Shape** Most plant cells have a boxlike shape. Animal cells have a wide variety of shapes. The shape of many plant and animal cells tells you about the cell's job.

▷ **Why can plants make their own food but animals can't?**

Cell Shapes

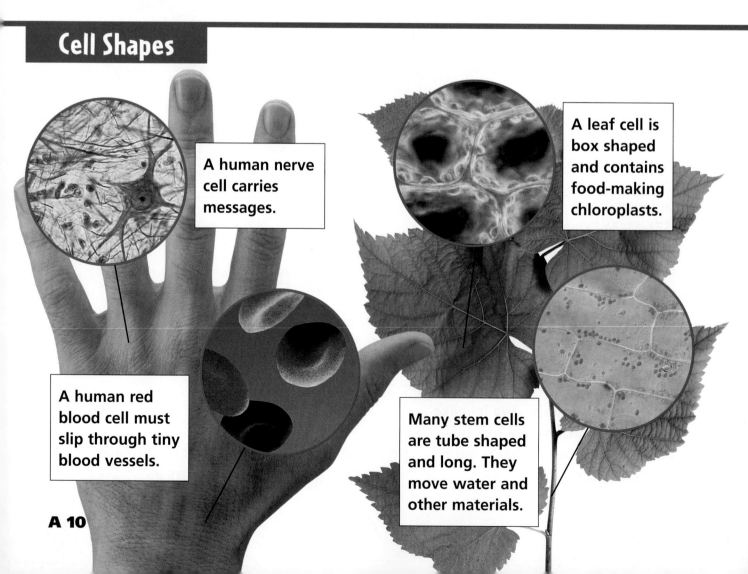

A human nerve cell carries messages.

A human red blood cell must slip through tiny blood vessels.

A leaf cell is box shaped and contains food-making chloroplasts.

Many stem cells are tube shaped and long. They move water and other materials.

Process Skill
BUILDER

Materials

prepared slide of *Elodea* leaf

prepared slide of human cheek cells

microscope

art materials and common objects to build cell models

tied plastic sandwich bags filled with light-colored gelatin (optional)

Plant and Animal Cells

Use a microscope to look at plant and animal cells. The plant cells are from *Elodea*, a freshwater plant. The animal cells are cheek cells from inside a person's mouth. Look for the cell parts you learned about. Then make models to show differences between plant and animal cells. Models are three-dimensional copies of real objects. They help you see how things are put together.

Procedure

1. **Observe** Place the slide of *Elodea* on the microscope stage. Focus through the top layers of cells using low power. Observe one cell carefully.

2. **Infer** Record your observations by making a labeled drawing. Identify the names of what you see based on what you have learned about cells.

3. Repeat steps 1 and 2 with the slide of human cheek cells.

4. **Make a Model** Decide on how you will represent each kind of cell to show its shape and parts. List the parts. Select objects you might use to show each part, such as a clear plastic sandwich bag, lima beans, or marbles. To start, you might use gelatin as the cytoplasm. Build your models. Share your results with the class.

Drawing Conclusions

1. How are your models different from the real cells you observed? How are the models like the cells you observed?

2. How might you combine parts from all the models you looked at to make the best cell model of all?

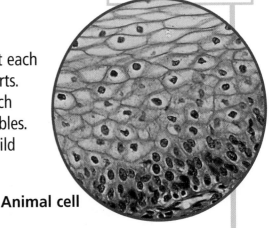

Animal cell

Plant cell

How Small Can Organisms Be?

What kinds of organisms are small enough to live in a drop of water? If you used a microscope to examine some pond water, you might see one-celled organisms like these. Some organisms are so small you need a microscope to see them. They are called *microorganisms*.

Protists

The one-celled microorganisms that live in pond water are called *protists* (PROH·tists). Do any of these microorganisms have parts that might be helpful for living in water? What are they?

Many protists are helpful. Some have chlorophyll. Like plants, they can make their own food. They are a food source for other organisms. Many feed on dead organisms in the water. Some can cause disease and illness in humans and other animals.

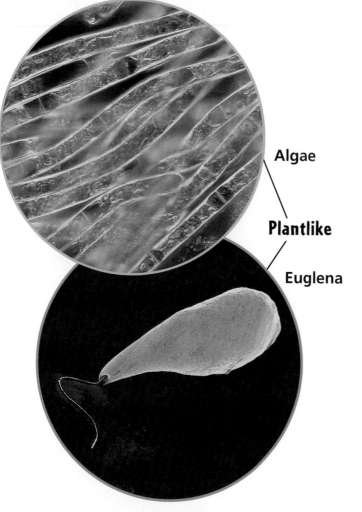

Algae

Plantlike

Euglena

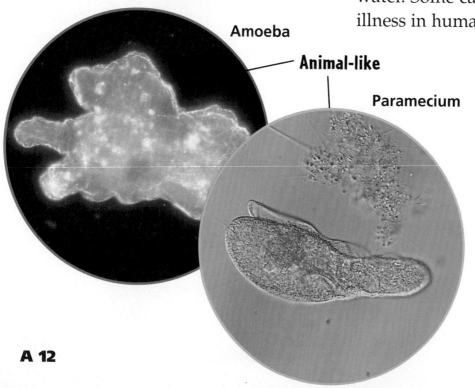

Amoeba

Animal-like

Paramecium

Algae and euglena make their own food, like plants. Amoeba and paramecia take in food, like animals.

Bacteria and Fungi

Protists are not the only microorganisms. There are some others as well. *Bacteria* (bak·TEER·ee·uh) (singular, *bacterium*) are one-celled organisms. A bacterium has a cell wall but no nucleus. The chromosomes are scattered through the cell. Bacteria do not have many cell structures. Bacteria are much smaller than most plant, animal, or protist cells. Bacteria live in many different environments.

Earth is home to a great variety of these microorganisms. Some cause illnesses, such as strep throat. Many bacteria are helpful. Some are used to make foods such as cheese and buttermilk. Some break down waste materials, such as dead plants and animals.

Have you ever eaten a mushroom or used yeast to make bread? These are two examples of *fungi* (FUN·jigh) (singular, *fungus*). Yeast is a one-celled organism. A mushroom is made of many cells. Fungi cells have a cell wall and a nucleus, like plant cells. Some cells even have more than one nucleus.

Fungi do not have chloroplasts or make food. Some fungi, such as mushrooms, absorb nutrients from dead organisms. Have you ever seen a fungus growing on a log? Along with bacteria, it is breaking down the log and absorbing nutrients from it.

▷ **What are some tiny organisms?**

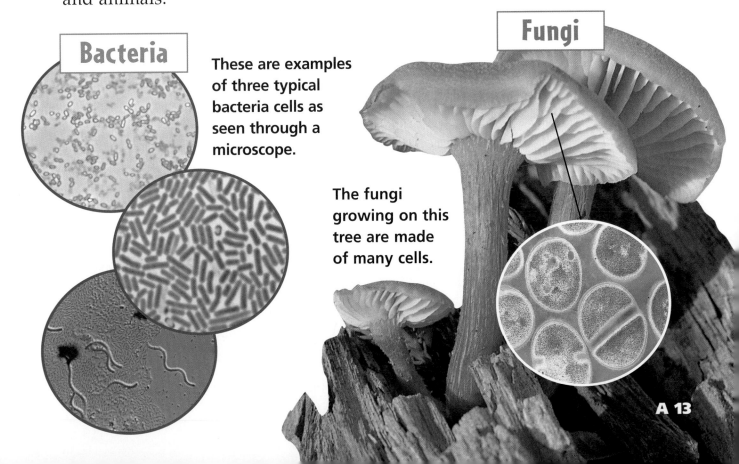

Bacteria

These are examples of three typical bacteria cells as seen through a microscope.

Fungi

The fungi growing on this tree are made of many cells.

How Is an Organism Put Together?

How are you like a euglena in a pond? A human and a euglena are both organisms. Each carries out its own life activities. However, a euglena is a one-celled organism. A human is a many-celled organism. You are made of billions upon billions of cells working together.

All animals and plants are many-celled organisms. Any animal is made of many kinds of cells. For example, you are made of blood cells, bone cells, skin cells, and many others. A plant also has different cells in its roots, stems, and leaves.

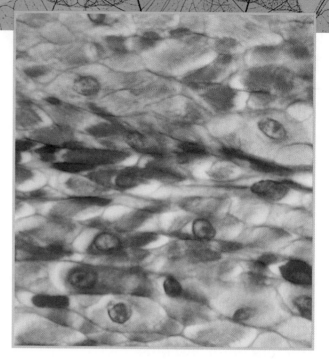

The wall of your stomach is made of muscle tissue. This tissue is made of many muscle cells working together. What job does this tissue have?

Tissues

In your body a single skin cell or blood cell does not work alone. Cells work together in groups. These groups are called **tissues** (TISH·ewz). A tissue is a group of similar cells that work together carrying out a certain job. Skin cells work together as skin tissue that covers and protects your body. Your bones contain bone cells organized into tissue that helps support your body.

Plant cells are also organized into tissues. In an onion plant, each layer of onion skin is a tissue. Tissues that make up the roots of a plant absorb water from the ground. Leaves of plants are made of tissues that help the plant make food.

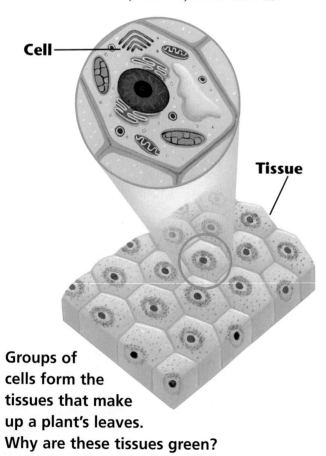

Cell

Tissue

Groups of cells form the tissues that make up a plant's leaves. Why are these tissues green?

Organs

Throughout your body, tissues are grouped together. For example, your heart contains muscle tissue, nerve tissue, and blood tissue. Your heart is an example of an **organ**. An organ is a group of tissues that work together doing certain jobs. Your heart's job is to pump blood throughout your body. Your brain is an organ. What jobs does your brain do?

Roots, stems, and leaves are organs of a plant. A leaf is an organ that makes food for the plant.

Organ Systems

A group of parts that work together forms a *system*. An **organ system** is a group of organs that work together carrying on life functions. A plant's roots, stem, and leaves are an organ system. Your digestive system is an organ system. Your digestive system contains your mouth, esophagus, liver, stomach, and small and large intestines. It breaks down food and absorbs nutrients you need to live.

▷ **What are tissues, organs, and organ systems?**

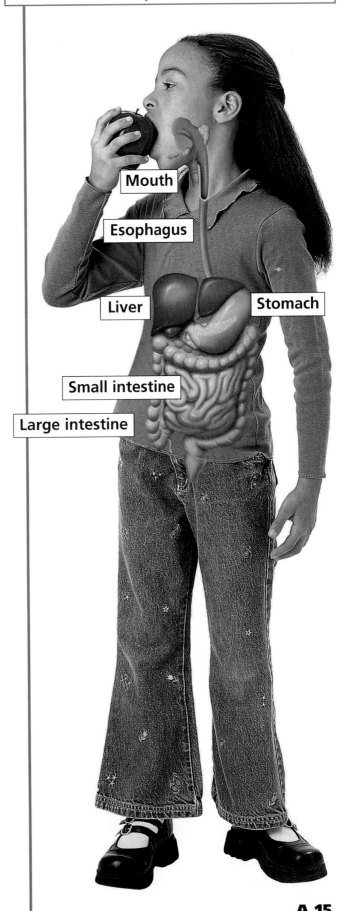

Human Digestive System

Mouth

Esophagus

Liver

Stomach

Small intestine

Large intestine

Is It Living?

Viruses (VIGH·ruhs·ez) are described as particles. They are much smaller than cells. They can't be seen with a microscope such as the one you use. They can be seen only with a very powerful microscope.

A virus is not a cell. A virus is not living. It does not have a nucleus or other cell parts. The only thing a virus contains is a "set of plans" for invading living cells.

A virus does not make or use food. It does not grow, change, or respond to its environment. The only life function a virus seems to perform is being able to reproduce.

If a virus is not living, how can it reproduce? It must use a living cell, as shown here.

▶ **Is a virus living or nonliving? Explain.**

READING Diagrams

What do you think happens after the cell bursts?

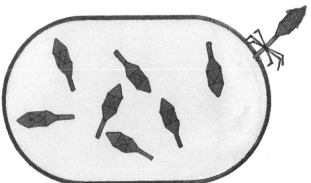

1 A virus attaches itself to a cell.

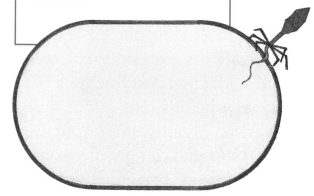

2 The virus infects the cell.

3 The virus forces the cell to make copies of the virus.

4 The cell bursts. The new viruses go on to infect other cells.

Why It Matters

Here's a riddle: What do humans, trees, and fish have in common? The answer is cells. All living things are made up of one or more cells. Not all cells are alike. That's why you are not the same as a fish or a tree.

Visit **www.mhscience02.com** to do a research project on cells.

Think and Write

1. Name any two living things. How do you know they are living?

2. The words *organism* and *organ system* both contain the word *organ*. Why?

3. What are some different kinds of microorganisms? What makes them different?

4. **Make a Model** How would a model of a plant cell be different from a model of an animal cell?

5. **Critical Thinking** Do you think viruses are a kind of microorganism? Explain.

L·I·N·K·S

MATH LINK

Compare measurements. A human intestine is about 7 meters (23 feet) long in an adult. How many times longer is that than your arm? Your leg? Your entire body? How can you find out?

LITERATURE LINK

Read *It's Alive!* to learn how living and nonliving things are different. Based on what you read, make a table in two columns. List living things in one column and nonliving things in another. Discuss why you entered each name in its column.

IT'S ALIVE!

by Billy Aronson
illustrated by Allan Eitzen

WRITING LINK

Write an explanation to a younger child. Name some robots the child may have seen in movies. Explain how robots are like living things, but are not really living.

TECHNOLOGY LINK

Science Newsroom CD-ROM Choose *That's Life* to learn how plant cells and animal cells are alike and different.

At the Computer Visit **www.mhscience02.com** for more links.

Classifying Organisms

Vocabulary

kingdom, A20
trait, A21
genus, A25
species, A25

Get Ready

Have you ever had to sort, or classify, a group of items? What were they? How did you do it?

Things such as flowers can be organized into groups. To do this, you have to decide what characteristic to use to define the groups. For example, it could be color or petal shape.

Do you think living things can be organized into groups, too?

Process Skill

You **classify** when you place things that share properties together in groups.

Explore Activity

How Are Organisms Classified?

Materials
reference
books

Procedure

1 Choose eight very different organisms that you would like to classify and learn more about. You may choose the ones you see here. Record their names.

2 What would you like to know about your organisms? Where would you look to find the information? Design a table to record the information.

3 **Classify** Try to place all of the organisms into groups. What characteristics did you use to help you make your choices?

Drawing Conclusions

1 **Interpreting Data** How many groups were formed? What were the major characteristics of the organisms in each group?

2 What organisms were placed in each group?

3 **Communicate** Make a list of the characteristics of the organisms in each group.

4 **Going Further: Classify** Test your classification system by adding a new organism. Does it fit in a group? Why or why not? If not, what changes could you make to your system so that it would fit?

Main Idea Classifying organisms helps people to study and learn about living things.

How Are Organisms Classified?

To classify organisms into large groups, scientists study many characteristics. They look at body form and how an organism gets food. They observe if it moves from place to place. They also study the number of cells, if the cells have a nucleus, and cell parts. Even an organism's blood and how the organism grows and develops before it is born are studied.

For many years scientists could not settle on a single classification system. People often used different names to describe the same organism. This often led to confusion. With time a worldwide classification system was developed. It divides organisms into large groups called **kingdoms** (KING·duhmz).

READING Charts

1. What organisms can make food? Make a list.
2. Why do you think plants and fungi don't need to move?

Classifying Organisms

Kingdom	Number of cells	Nucleus	Food	Move from Place to Place
Ancient bacteria kingdom	one	no	make	some move
True bacteria kingdom	one	no	make or obtain	some move
Protist kingdom	one or many	yes	make or obtain	some move
Fungus kingdom	one or many	yes	absorb	no
Plant kingdom	many	yes	make	no
Animal kingdom	many	yes	eat	yes

Does the organism ...	If yes, ...	If no, ...
... **have a nucleus?**	...it can be an animal, plant, fungus, or protist.	...it can be a true bacterium or ancient bacterium.
... **have many cells?**	...it can be an animal, plant, protist, or fungus.	...it can be a true bacterium, ancient bacterium, fungus, or protist.
... **eat or obtain food?**	...it can be an animal, fungus, or true bacterium.	...it can be a true bacterium, ancient bacterium, plant, or protist.
... **move?**	...it can be an animal, protist, true bacterium, or ancient bacterium.	...it can be a true bacterium, ancient bacterium, protist, plant, or fungus.

Organisms in each kingdom share basic **traits** (TRAYTS). A trait is a characteristic of a living thing. Organisms within a kingdom are similar to one another but are different from organisms in other kingdoms. The chart on page A20 shows the basic traits of organisms in each kingdom.

A chart can help you organize a lot of information. The chart on this page can help you determine what types of organisms belong in each kingdom. Simply ask the questions shown in the chart, such as "Does the organism have a nucleus?" Then read across to find the kingdoms.

READING **Compare and Contrast**
How are the six kingdoms alike? How are they different?

How Can Organisms Be Classified Further?

Mountain lions and butterflies belong to the animal kingdom even though they are very different. That is why scientists use smaller and smaller groups to further classify organisms. The smaller the group, the more similar the organisms in it are to each other.

There are seven groups into which an organism can be classified. This chart shows the groups from largest to smallest. There are fewer different kinds of organisms in each group as you move down.

▶ **What groups is a kingdom divided into?**

The sea anemone looks like a plant, but it is really an animal.

Kingdom

Members of the animal kingdom move in some way, eat food, and reproduce.

Phylum

A *phylum* is a large group within a kingdom. Members have at least one major characteristic in common, such as having a backbone.

Class

A phylum is broken down into smaller groups called *classes*. Members of this class all produce milk for their young.

Order

A class is made up of smaller groups called *orders*. Members of this order are meat eaters.

Family

An order is made up of still smaller groups of similar organisms. These groups are called *families*. Dogs, wolves, and coyotes belong to the same family.

Genus

A family is made up of organisms belonging to similar, even smaller groups. Each group is called a *genus*. Dogs and wolves belong to the same genus.

Species

The smallest classification group is a *species*. A species is made up of only one type of organism. All dogs belong to the same species.

Kingdom

Phylum

Class

Order

Family

Genus

Species

READING
Charts

1. Are there more organisms in a class or a family? How can you tell?

2. Design another chart that shows how the groups are organized. How is it different?

Process Skill
BUILDER

 **SKILL** Classify

Leaves

When you organize toys or living things into groups, you are classifying. When you classify, you organize things into smaller groups based on their traits. This skill is important not only in science. People classify things every day. Classifying helps make things easier to study and understand. To practice this skill, you will classify leaves according to different traits.

Materials

10 leaves or leaf pictures

ruler

reference books

Procedure

1. **Observe** Spread out the leaves (or leaf pictures). Observe the traits they share, such as size, color, shape, and so on. Record the traits.

2. **Classify** Choose one trait, such as color, that you recorded. Organize all ten leaves based on that trait. Draw the way your leaves are organized. You may use a chart.

3. Follow the same procedure for two other traits you recorded.

Drawing Conclusions

1. In how many different ways were you able to classify the leaves?

2. How did your classification system differ from other students' systems? In what ways were they similar?

3. Give some examples of how other things are classified. Use a kitchen, bedroom, closet, or supermarket.

4. **Infer** How do you think using a worldwide classification system might help scientists identify and understand organisms?

How Are Organisms Named?

The classification system plays a part in how each organism is named. The naming system that we use today was developed in the 1700s by a Swedish scientist, Carolus Linnaeus.

The first part of an organism's name uses that organism's **genus** (JEE·nuhs) name. Remember, a genus is a group made up of two or more very similar species. The second part of its name uses its **species** (SPEE·sheez) name. Remember, a species is the smallest classification group. Members of a species can reproduce only with each other.

For example, the genus name for a lion is *Panthera*. A number of large cats share this genus name. However, only the lion has the full name *Panthera leo*.

Using both the genus and species names lets scientists identify specific organisms.

All breeds of dogs have the same scientific name, *Canis familiaris*.

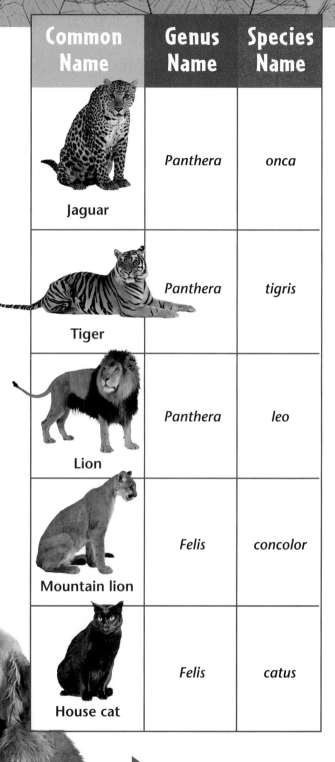

Common Name	Genus Name	Species Name
Jaguar	*Panthera*	*onca*
Tiger	*Panthera*	*tigris*
Lion	*Panthera*	*leo*
Mountain lion	*Felis*	*concolor*
House cat	*Felis*	*catus*

▶ **How do scientists name an organism?**

A 25

Have Any Organisms Never Been Classified?

Scientists have named and described about 1.75 million species on Earth so far. However, scientists are always looking for organisms that have never been described or classified. Some scientists estimate that we may be sharing the world with 5 million to 15 million species. Many of these species live in tropical rain forests.

Scientists are working to find and classify as many rain forest organisms as possible.

There are many reasons to study rain forest organisms, such as finding new types of medicines. Unfortunately, more than 50 acres of rain forest are being cleared every minute for farming and timber.

These changes affect organisms. If plants that an animal depends on for food or shelter are destroyed, the animal may die. If this continues for a long time, a species may die.

▷ **Why is it important to classify and describe organisms?**

Red-breasted toucan

Emerald tree boa

Red-eyed green tree frog

Lesson Review

Why It Matters

Classifying organisms helps people in three ways. First, it allows them to keep track of organisms. Second, classification helps people communicate by using one naming system. Finally, classification helps to organize information about organisms for further studies. Studying groups helps people see the "big picture" of how life is organized.

Think and Write

1. Name the different kingdoms. What are the key traits of organisms in each kingdom?

2. Prairie dogs are not dogs. Jellyfish are not fish. How do you think using scientific names instead of common names helps prevent misconceptions?

3. What do scientific names provide that common names do not provide?

4. **Classify** Describe how a kingdom is divided into smaller groups.

5. **Critical Thinking** How might the extinction of one organism affect others?

L·I·N·K·S

MATH LINK

Make a chart. Make a chart to classify ten organisms. What traits did you use to classify them? How many groups did you create? Did any organisms not fit into one of the groups? Explain.

LITERATURE LINK

Read *Pack Rat*, to learn about an unusual animal. Find out about some of its interesting characteristics. Try the activities at the end of the book.

SOCIAL STUDIES LINK

Find out about names and places. List at least three things that have different names in different parts of the country, for example, soda and pop. Ask adults at home for help.

WRITING LINK

Invent an organism. Think of a new kind of animal. Give it a scientific name based on its characteristics. Then write a description about what the animal does during the day, or a short story about an incident in the animal's life.

TECHNOLOGY LINK

At the Computer Visit **www.mhscience02.com** for more links.

Organisms of the Past

Get Ready

How much do we know about the great meat-eating dinosaur *Tyrannosaurus rex*? It was 14 meters (46 feet) long and 6 meters (20 feet) tall, and it weighed 8 metric tons (17,600 pounds). It walked upright on two powerful legs. How do we know this? What evidence did it leave behind?

Process Skill

You observe when you use one or more senses to identify or learn about an object or event.

Explore Activity

How Can We Use Skeletons to Compare Organisms?

Materials

ruler

pencil

paper
 or
computer
with charting
program

Procedure

1 **Observe** Compare the pictures of the skeletons on this page.

2 **Communicate** Make a chart that lists the similarities and differences. Use the computer if you like.

Drawing Conclusions

1 Write a paragraph about the similarities and differences you noticed between the skeletons.

2 **Going Further: Infer** What can be learned by comparing skeletons of present-day animals with skeletons of animals of the past?

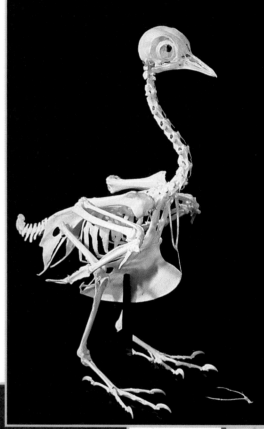

This is a skeleton of a bird.

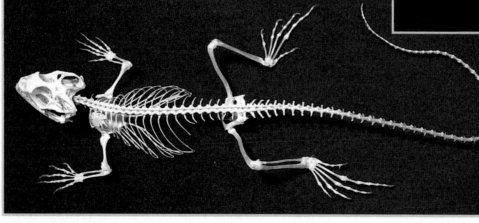

This is a skeleton of a reptile.

Main Idea Learning about the past helps us learn about the present.

How Are Skeletons Used to Compare Organisms?

A **fossil** (FAHS·uhl) is any evidence of an organism that lived in the past. Fossils are often skeletons preserved in rock. When someone discovers a new fossil, he or she might wonder, "How would the organism that made this fit into today's classification system?" He or she might compare the fossil with bones of similar animals living today.

As scientists try to learn more about an organism's past, they must consider that organisms change over time. Change in living things over time is called *evolution* (ev·uh·LEW·shuhn).

For example, using fossils of skulls, teeth, and leg bones, scientists have traced the ancestors of the modern horse back about 60 million years. The diagram on the right shows only some of the ancestors of the horse. The first ancestor was about the size of a small dog. How do the leg bones of today's horse compare with its ancestor's bones?

Another thing that we can learn is the age of a fossil compared with other fossils. This can be done by studying the rock layer in which a fossil is found.

Hyracotherium (eohippus)

Mesohippus

Merychippus

Equus

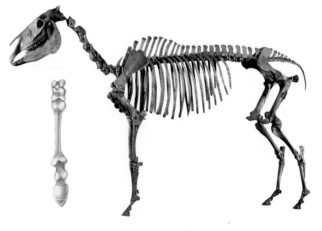

Based on fossil evidence, scientists think *Hyracotherium* (eohippus) is the ancestor of all horses. What similarities and differences do you see? How did the animals' appearance change?

How do you think studying rock layers tells you about a fossil's age? Looking at other fossils found in the same rock layer tells that the organisms lived at about the same time. The oldest fossils are in the oldest rock layers, which are at the bottom. Younger fossils are found in later, upper rock layers.

Older and Younger

1. **Observe** Cut a piece of paper into four pieces. Draw a "fossil" on each piece. Place one fossil inside the front cover of each book. Stack the books.

2. **Interpret Data** Challenge your partner to find the fossils and arrange them in order of which is "oldest" and "youngest." Record any observations you make.

3. Switch roles and repeat the activity.

4. What did the books represent?

5. Which fossil was oldest? Youngest? What evidence helped you decide?

READING **Compare and Contrast**

Fossils in layer A are younger than those in layer B. Which layer has older fossils than those in layer C?

Can Organisms That Seem Different Be Related?

What do you think the organisms on this page have in common? Do their limb bones seem similar in any way?

Even though each animal uses these bones differently, the bones are arranged in similar ways. Scientists compare limbs to understand what is similar and what is different about organisms. They can see which organisms have similar features and might be related.

Scientists use the evidence shown by limb bones when they classify organisms. Some of their findings are surprising. For example, whales are more closely related to humans than to sharks! You can see this by looking at whale flipper bones. They are much more like human arm bones than shark fins. Whales and humans are both mammals.

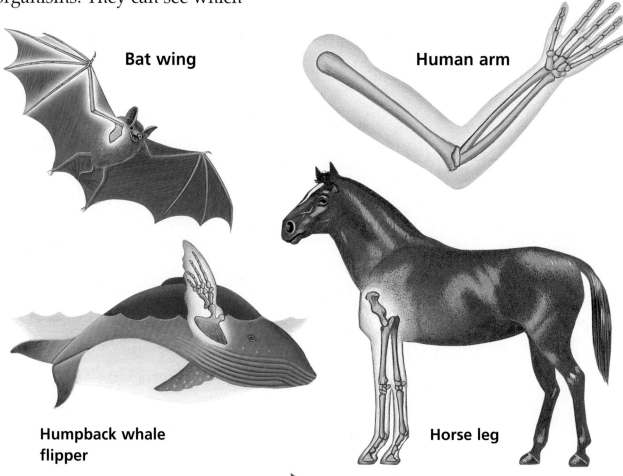

Bat wing

Human arm

Humpback whale flipper

Horse leg

▷ **What do bones of different animals tell us?**

What Are Some Other Clues?

Another clue to identifying similarities among organisms comes from before they were even born. An undeveloped animal or plant is called an **embryo** (EM·bree·oh).

Look at the embryos of a bird and a fish shown below. Each has a backbone, or a spine. They both have gill slits and a tail. These features suggest that the organisms are related. They are both vertebrates.

An embryo changes before it is ready for the world. Some features are lost in certain animals as the embryo grows. Birds do not have gill slits when they are born.

Many organisms are **extinct** (ek·STINGKT), or no longer alive on Earth. To help classify them, scientists can compare fossil embryos with each other and with modern embryos.

This blind salamander lives in deep, dark caves. It has eyes that cannot see. What conclusions can you draw about this salamander's ancestors?

Still another clue that organisms might be related can be found in "leftover" structures. Humans don't need a tail, but a human adult has a tailbone at the end of the spine. Some snakes have tiny hip and limb bones. A baleen whale has small, useless hip bones. These useless bones are clues that help classify organisms into groups. That means baleen whales are probably related to organisms that have and use those bones.

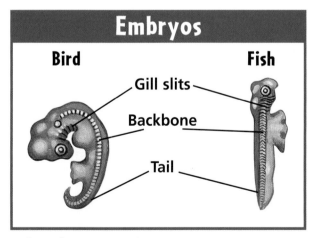

Embryos

Bird   **Fish**

Gill slits

Backbone

Tail

What do you notice as you compare these two embryos?

▶ **How can you tell if organisms are related?**

Woolly mammoth

Dodo bird

Dusty seaside sparrow

These animals are extinct.

Why Do Organisms Become Extinct?

Many organisms are extinct. Some scientists believe that 99 out of every 100 species that have ever lived on Earth are extinct.

Judging from fossils, there have been many *mass extinctions*. A mass extinction is when many different species die out at about the same time. The best-known mass extinction is that of the dinosaurs. They died out 65 million years ago, along with more than half of all other animal and plant species.

Some scientists believe that a giant comet hit Earth and caused the extinction of the dinosaurs. Walter Alvarez, along with his father, Dr. Luis Alvarez, found evidence to support the comet theory. The comet would have created great clouds of dust that blocked sunlight.

Without sunlight, plants could not have made the food they needed to survive. Without plants, plant-eating dinosaurs would have died. Without them, meat-eating dinosaurs would have died.

Other scientists believe that many huge volcanoes erupted, creating great clouds of dust. Still others think that dinosaurs spread deadly diseases as they moved about Earth. Maybe many events together caused the dinosaurs' extinction.

People play a role in extinction. People use pesticides and chemicals, destroy places where animals live, and use up resources. They also hunt and fish. This causes many species to become endangered, or in danger of becoming extinct.

▶ **How do people contribute to extinction?**

Why It Matters

In a way, learning about the past helps us learn about the present. Knowing how organisms have changed over time and who their ancestors were helps us to better understand the history of life on Earth. It also helps us classify living and extinct organisms.

Think and Write

1. What kinds of clues do fossils give about organisms of the past?

2. Is a fossil older or younger than another fossil in a lower rock layer? Explain.

3. How do embryos help identify a common ancestor of different organisms?

4. Explain some possible causes of the extinction of the dinosaurs. What are some causes of extinction today?

5. **Critical Thinking** Some snakes have tiny hip and limb bones. What does this tell you about the ancestors of snakes? What traits might you find in the group they once belonged to?

L·I·N·K·S

WRITING LINK

Interview your ancestor. People today are often interested in their past. They research family history and learn about ancestors. This helps them learn about where their families came from and how they changed over time. Make a list of questions that you would ask if you could talk to one of your relatives who lived a long time ago. For example, what would you like to ask your grandmother's grandmother?

SOCIAL STUDIES LINK

Research the condor. The condor is an endangered species. Find out more about the condor. Where does it live? Find the place on the map. What else can you find out about the condor and why it became endangered?

ART LINK

Draw a family tree. Make a family tree for an imaginary person, going back to the great-grandparents. Draw pictures of the imaginary person's relatives.

TECHNOLOGY LINK

At the Computer Visit **www.mhscience02.com** for more links.

Helping Endangered Species

Ever wish that you could help endangered animals and plants? Some kids in Hawaii did, so they found a way to help! Students at the Enchanted Lake Elementary School wanted to help as many endangered species as they could—in Hawaii and elsewhere around the world. The kids started Project Lokahi. *Lokahi* is Hawaiian for "harmony."

Many species in Hawaii had no natural enemies. Without enemies they lost their defenses over time. For example, the Hawaiian raspberry lost its thorns, and some birds lost the ability to fly.

With help from the students of Enchanted Lake, some organisms might not end up as "things of the past!"

Sea turtles need a safe place to lay their eggs.

People brought predators such as mongooses, rats, Argentine ants, and wild pigs to Hawaii from other parts of the world. These predators greatly harmed the bird and plant populations of the islands. Foreign plants also caused problems. The South American banana poka (POH·kuh) and the miconia (migh·KOH·nee·uh) are two vines that suffocated native plants.

To help endangered species, the kids set up a Web page on the Internet. There they explain which animals are in trouble and where the animals live. For example, the Web page lists the green sea turtle. At one time people hunted these turtles for their eggs, meat, and shells. Green sea turtles lay their eggs on beaches in North Carolina and other warm places.

After learning about the turtles, people might help to protect them. People might put signs on the beaches or post fliers to warn people to stay away when the turtles are laying their eggs.

Kauai

Niihau

PACIFIC OCEAN

Oahu

Molokai

Maui

Lanai

Kahoolawe

Hawaiian Islands

Hawaii

These are the islands of Hawaii.

AT THE COMPUTER

Visit **www.mhscience02.com** to learn more about endangered species.

Write
ABOUT IT

1. **What kinds of information would convince people to protect endangered species?**

2. **Why do you think kids chose the name *Lokahi* for the project?**

Organisms and Where They Live

Vocabulary

ecosystem, A40

community, A40

population, A40

habitat, A40

producer, A46

consumer, A46

decomposer, A46

food chain, A48

food web, A50

Get Ready

What types of organisms live in deserts? Deserts are the driest places on Earth. During the day some deserts sizzle at temperatures above 45°C (113°F). How do animals and plants survive in the deserts? In fact, how do living things in any environment survive?

Process Skill

You observe when you use one or more senses to identify or learn about an object or event.

Explore Activity

How Do Living and Nonliving Things Interact?

Materials

prepared terrarium container

small plants and animals

plastic spoon

ruler

water mister

grass seeds, rocks, twigs, sticks, bark, dried grass

Procedure

BE CAREFUL! Handle animals and plants carefully.

1. **Make a Model** Landscape your terrarium. Put taller plants in the back. Spread grass seed and any rocks, twigs, or other things you like.

2. If you add small animals, such as earthworms, sow bugs, and snails, add a water dish.

3. **Measure** Make a data table. Record the height of each plant. Measure the plants in two weeks, and record the data. Make a bar graph.

4. Place the terrarium in a lighted area. Avoid direct sunlight.

5. **Communicate** Draw a diagram of your terrarium. Draw arrows to show how the organisms depend on one another.

Drawing Conclusions

1. **Classify** What are the living and nonliving things in the terrarium?

2. **Infer** Why should the terrarium not be placed in direct sunlight?

3. **Going Further: Observe** Continue to maintain and observe your terrarium. Does anything unusual happen? Explain.

Main Idea Living and nonliving things depend on one another.

How Do Living and Nonliving Things Interact?

A terrarium is a model of an **ecosystem** (EK·oh·sis·tuhm). Ecosystems include both living and nonliving things. The nonliving part of your ecosystem included water, rocks, air, light, and soil. The living part of the ecosystem included the plants and animals. The study of how living and nonliving things interact is called *ecology* (ee·KAHL·uh·jee).

The living part of an ecosystem is a **community** (kuh·MYEW·ni·tee). Each ecosystem has its own community. A terrarium community can have small plants and animals. A desert community includes beautiful cacti and deadly scorpions.

Do you think the members of a community can be grouped further? Communities can be divided into different **populations** (pahp·yuh·LAY·shuhnz). A population is made of only one type of organism. Your terrarium ecosystem had populations of organisms such as snails and earthworms.

Each organism's home is called its **habitat** (HAB·i·tat). The soil is an earthworm's habitat. A whale's habitat is the ocean. A termite's habitat is a termite nest.

The diagram on page A41 will help you understand the different parts of an ecosystem.

What makes up the community in this ecosystem?

Ecosystem

A meadow

Community

The living part of an ecosystem

Populations

Frogs

Habitats

Pond   Under rocks   Soil

▷ **How is an ecosystem organized?**

QUICK LAB

FOR SCHOOL OR HOME

Sunlight and Plants

1. Your teacher will give you two identical plants. Label one plant *No Light*. Place it on a table away from a window. Water the plant. Then cover it with a paper bag.

2. Label the other plant *Light*. Place it on a sunny windowsill or near a sunny window. Water the plant.

3. **Observe** Every other day for two weeks, observe the plants. Check to make sure the plants have moist soil. Add enough water to keep the soil moist. Look for changes in the color and height of each plant.

4. Which plant looked the healthiest after two weeks?

5. What do your observations tell you about the needs of plants?

How Are Ecosystems Different?

What makes one ecosystem different from another? In many cases water is the key. A desert is very dry. Only a small number of species of plants and animals can survive with little water. A rain forest has plenty of water. That is why it can support a great variety of plants and animals.

Another resource that can affect ecosystems is sunlight. Some plants, such as cacti, grow where there is little water but plenty of sunlight. These types of plants could not grow in an area where there is little sunlight, even if there is plenty of water.

Still another resource is soil. Areas with soil rich in nutrients can support many plants. Few plants grow in areas with soil that does not have many nutrients.

The types of plants and animals that live in a particular ecosystem depend on a combination of these things. For example, a woodland forest has enough rich soil and enough water for many grasses to grow.

These plants grow in a desert. What factors affect the types of plants that grow in this ecosystem?

However, a woodland forest does not have enough sunshine for most types of grasses. Too much of the Sun's light is blocked by the trees. The forest floor is so dark that most kinds of grasses can't grow there.

Organisms Change the Environment

In all types of ecosystems, organisms cause changes. Most changes do not affect the ecosystem very much. When plants and animals move, eat, and grow, they are usually just doing their part to keep the system in balance.

Some changes can harm the environment. Too many animals in one area may use up all the food or water. Humans may harm the environment by building houses on forest or desert land.

Other changes improve and protect the ecosystem. Plants keep the soil in an ecosystem from eroding. Birds may eat insects that would harm plants in the environment. Humans protect animals by setting up wildlife preserves.

READING **Compare and Contrast**
How does a desert compare with a rain forest?

These plants grow in a rain forest. What factors affect the types of plants that grow in this ecosystem?

What Kinds of Ecosystems Are There?

Climate differences produce a variety of ecosystems. Use this diagram to learn about them.

Ⓐ Tundra
Long, dark, and very cold winters. Few trees. Ground is frozen beneath the surface.

Ⓑ Taiga
Very cold winters, cool summers. More rain or snow falls than in the tundra.

Ⓒ Grasslands
Cold winters, hot summers. More rain or snow falls than in the taiga. Rich soil.

Ⓓ Mild forest lands
Mild winters and summers. Plenty of rain or snow. Trees lose their leaves in winter.

Ⓔ Desert
Very hot days all year. Very little rain. Plants and animals adapted to conserve water.

Ⓕ Tropical rain forest
Hot and rainy all year. Poor soil. Variety of plants and animals.

A 44

READING
Diagrams

How are ecosystems determined?

Water Ecosystems

Saltwater shores
Many organisms live where the water level changes from high tide to low tide.

Freshwater rivers
Many habitats are along the shore and river bottom.

Freshwater lakes and ponds
Many habitats are at the shore, on the surface water, and under the water.

Open sea–surface
This area gets plenty of light. It is rich in nutrients and home to many populations.

Open sea–deeper down
Ecosystems change as the amount of light decreases with depth.

▶ **What ecosystem do you live in? How do you know?**

What Types of Roles Do Organisms Play?

A community works like a team. Each member of the team has its own job to do. There are three different types of team members. **Producers** (pruh·DEW·suhrz) make food. **Consumers** (kuhn·SEW·muhrz) use the food that producers make or eat other organisms. **Decomposers** (dee·kuhm·POH·zuhrz) break down wastes and the remains of other organisms.

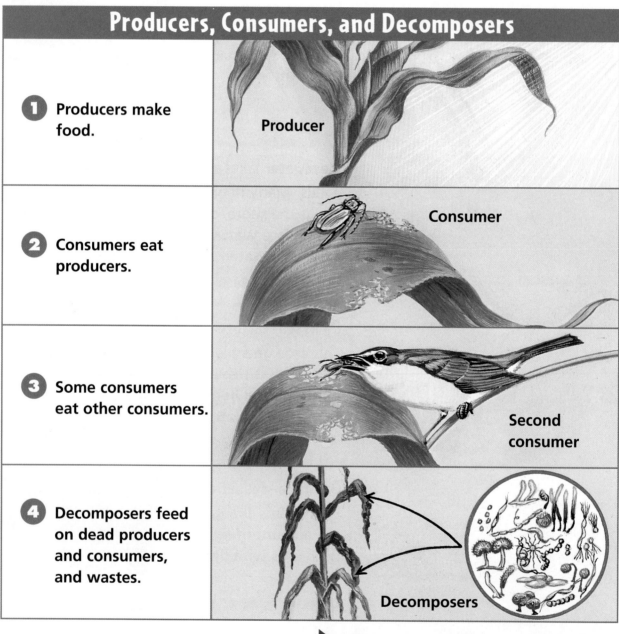

Producers, Consumers, and Decomposers

1. Producers make food.

Producer

2. Consumers eat producers.

Consumer

3. Some consumers eat other consumers.

Second consumer

4. Decomposers feed on dead producers and consumers, and wastes.

Decomposers

▶ **What are producers, consumers, and decomposers?**

What Are Producers?

How do you think you can identify a producer? You can tell most producers by their green color. The color shows that their cells have chloroplasts. Chloroplasts are the cell's "food factories" you learned about in Lesson 1. To make food, producers use water, carbon dioxide in the air, and the Sun's energy.

Producers are the "energy capturers" of the world. They capture light energy from the Sun and transform it into food. Producers use only some of the food they make. The rest is stored. Other members of the community eat producers or organisms that have eaten producers. That's how they get their food.

Producers Affect Their Environment

Producers are important to many parts of the ecosystem. Without producers there would be no way for other organisms to survive. Consumers and decomposers would not have a valuable source of energy.

Producers also affect nonliving parts of the ecosystem. Plant roots hold the soil in place. Other producers provide shelter for consumers and decomposers. Most producers contribute to the air that we breathe.

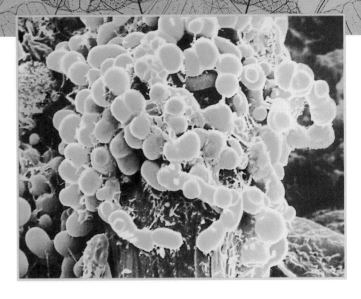

Producers include some kinds of one-celled organisms, such as these algae, and plants, such as the water grasses below.

▶ **What are two examples of producers?**

A 47

What Are Consumers and Decomposers?

Producers are only the beginning of the **food chain** (FEWD CHAYN). A food chain is the steps in which organisms get the food they need to survive. Producers make their own food. Consumers and decomposers must get food from producers or other consumers.

Consumers

Which organisms do you think were consumers in the terrarium? Organisms that eat food are consumers. Animals are consumers. So are some kinds of one-celled organisms. Consumers in the terrarium may have included insects and frogs.

To stay alive, consumers must get food from other organisms. There are three types of consumers. Consumers that eat only plants are called *herbivores*. Other consumers eat only animals. They are called *carnivores*. Consumers that eat plants and animals are called *omnivores*. Which type of consumer are you?

Decomposers

Decomposers in the terrarium may have included microorganisms such as bacteria and some kinds of fungi. They may also have included larger organisms such as worms and snails. Decomposers break down living and dead matter into simple chemicals that they use for food. The chemicals left behind by decomposers are recycled, or used over and over again. Producers use these chemicals for making food.

Have you ever seen mold? Molds are a type of decomposer that often spoils food. Where do molds grow?

This food chain shows the roles of producer, consumers, and decomposers.

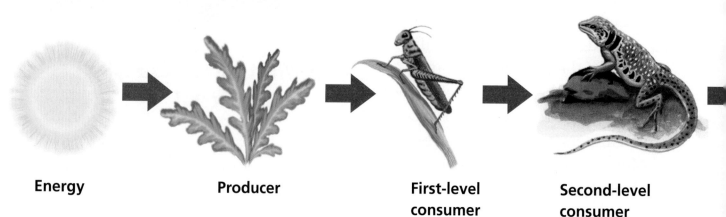

Energy   Producer   First-level consumer   Second-level consumer

In this food chain, the plant is the producer. The lizard, a second-level consumer, is eating the insect, a first-level consumer. What is the bird?

▷ **Why are decomposers so important in any ecosystem?**

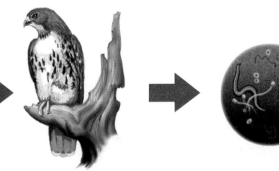

Third-level consumer   Decomposers

FOR SCHOOL OR HOME

Observe a Decomposer

BE CAREFUL! Do not open the bags after you seal them.

1. Moisten four food samples. Place each in a labeled plastic bag. Put a piece of cardboard in a bag.

2. Seal the bags, and place them in a warm, dark place.

3. Record your daily observations.

4. **Observe** On which samples did mold grow? How did it change the foods?

5. **Infer** Will molds grow on any type of material? Explain how the cardboard helped you answer this question.

READING Diagrams

1. What consumer is found in several food chains? What food chains is it a part of?

2. What might happen to this food web if the hawk dies?

What Is a Food Web?

Food chains show how energy is passed from the Sun to producers, consumers, and decomposers. In any ecosystem many food chains overlap. Different food chains may include some of the same organisms. Several consumers may all eat the same kind of plant or animal for food. When this happens, the food chains form a **food web** . A food web shows how food chains are related within an ecosystem.

Food webs in one community may be connected to food webs in another community. This makes the passage of energy even more complex.

▶ **How do food chains and food webs relate?**

Why It Matters

Producers, consumers, and decomposers all change the environment around them. Most changes do not seriously affect the ecosystem. Sometimes organisms harm the environment by destroying or using too much of a resource. People can help their ecosystem by doing their jobs and using resources carefully.

Think and Write

1. Describe how the living organisms in the terrarium interacted with the nonliving things and each other.

2. Explain the relationships among an ecosystem, community, population, and habitat.

3. Draw a diagram of an ecosystem. Include the terms *community, population, habitat, producers, consumers,* and *decomposers.*

4. What are advantages and disadvantages of organisms being part of a food web?

5. **Critical Thinking** Could an ecosystem exist without producers? Consumers? Decomposers? Explain.

L·I·N·K·S

ART LINK

Draw a food chain. Draw organisms from a prairie food chain and organisms from a desert food chain.

HEALTH LINK

Write a menu. List everything in a meal you would like to eat. Then identify each item on the menu as coming from producers, consumers, or combinations of these.

SOCIAL STUDIES LINK

Research an ecosystem. Pick an ecosystem to learn more about from the ecosystems on pages A44 and A45. Where are some places you can find this ecosystem? What plants live there? What animals? What is life like there?

TECHNOLOGY LINK

 Science Newsroom CD-ROM Choose *It's Only Natural* to learn how mushrooms thrive in the right conditions.

 At the Computer Visit **www.mhscience02.com** for more links.

SAVED BY THE SUN

Earth's living things and its ecosystems depend on the Sun. Without heat and light from the Sun, producers could not grow. Consumers and decomposers would not be able to survive. Earth would be bare, cold, and dark.

Earth is saved by the Sun's energy. The Sun sends out its energy in rays.

When the part of Earth where you live is tilted toward the Sun, the rays hit it directly. The land and water absorb lots of heat. The temperature goes up. It's summer! When your location is tilted away from the Sun, you receive indirect rays. The land and water receive less heat. The temperature drops. It's winter.

AT THE COMPUTER

Visit **www.mhscience02.com** to learn more about saving energy.

We can see some of these rays. We call them sunlight. Earth's land and water warm up when the Sun's rays shine on them. The land and water lose some of this heat into the air, warming it.

Earth is tilted on its axis. Areas facing the Sun receive direct rays from the Sun. Other areas receive indirect rays. Indirect rays provide less heat than direct rays.

Energy from the Sun is called solar energy. People can collect solar energy and use it to heat their homes. Using solar energy helps save natural resources such as coal, oil, and wood.

This home uses solar energy. Water flowing through these solar panels is heated by the Sun. The warmed water is used to heat the home.

What Did I Learn?

1. How might Earth be affected if it were not tilted on its axis?

2. Can you think of other ways people can use solar energy?

Changes in Ecosystems

Vocabulary

drought, A56

overpopulation, A57

pollution, A58

acid rain, A59

Get Ready

A desert can exist with very little rain. Grasslands require more rain. What happens to a grassland when it doesn't rain? Which organisms will be affected? A lack of rain is just one kind of change in any ecosystem. What are some others?

Process Skill

You experiment when you perform a test to support or disprove a hypothesis.

A 54

Explore Activity

What Causes Ecosystems to Change?

Materials

2 terrariums (from Lesson 4)

water mister

Procedure

1. Label one terrarium M, for moist. Label the other D, for dry. Spray only terrarium M with water. Place both terrariums in a well-lighted area, but avoid direct sunlight.

2. **Observe** Compare the terrariums every day for several days. What differences do you see?

3. **Observe** Spray terrarium D until it is moist. Wait a few days before comparing the terrariums.

4. **Communicate** Make a table to record what you observed in steps 2 and 3.

Drawing Conclusions

1. What happened to the organisms in each terrarium in step 2?

2. What happened to the organisms in each terrarium in step 3?

3. **Infer** What caused the changes in the terrariums?

4. **Infer** What happened to terrarium D in step 3? What does that tell you about ecosystems?

5. **Going Further: Experiment** Observe the terrariums for the rest of the year. See how they continue to change.

Main Idea Several things can cause changes in ecosystems.

What Causes Ecosystems to Change?

To survive within an ecosystem, organisms need many resources. The resources include water, sunlight, soil, and air. Remember, a resource is a material that helps support life on Earth. Some resources, such as water, can run out or dry up. Others, such as sunlight, never run out. Sometimes events occur that cut off or destroy a resource. An ecosystem may completely change as a result.

One event that can change an ecosystem is **drought** (DROWT). Drought is a long period of time with little or no precipitation, such as rain. During a drought, plants may turn brown and die. When plants die, the consumers that need them for food can also die. All animals need water to drink, too.

Diseases also can harm an ecosystem. One example is Dutch elm disease (DED). In the 1930s it arrived in North America in wood crates made of diseased elm wood. Over time DED spread from tree to tree. It killed more than half of all North American elm trees. Between 1945 and 1976, 43 million trees died.

DED harms more than just elm trees. The trees are home to many insects and other animals. When the trees die, these animals lose their homes. Elm trees also add to the oxygen we breathe from the air. They can prevent soil erosion, too.

These pictures show how fire, Dutch elm disease, and drought can affect an ecosystem.

Fire also can change an ecosystem. In a rain forest, all of the animals depend on trees. Many live and feed on the upper parts of the trees. These animals include monkeys, birds, and insects. How would a fire in a rain forest affect them?

Still another thing that changes ecosystems is **overpopulation** (oh·vuhr·pahp·yuh·LAY·shuhn). Overpopulation happens when an ecosystem has too many of at least one kind of living thing. In many crowded cities, people have left little space for other animals to live.

Wherever living things live, they must share water and other resources. Overpopulation reduces the resources for everyone. The plants and animals cannot find what they need to survive.

In Australia overpopulation of kangaroos has become a big problem. As people dug wells to water their cattle, kangaroos drank the water, too. At the same time, the number of dingos went down. Dingos are a kind of wild dog that hunts kangaroos. As the number of dingos went down, the number of kangaroos went up.

On farms and ranches, kangaroos compete with livestock for food and water. They also knock down fences and cause erosion. To reduce the number of kangaroos, the Australian government allows a certain number to be hunted. They are used for leather, pet food, and even human food.

▶ **What can cause changes in an ecosystem?**

An overpopulation of these kangaroos has become a problem in Australia.

How Can People Change Ecosystems?

Humans and other living things need a clean place to live. This is why **pollution** (puh·LEW·shuhn) is a problem. Pollution happens when harmful substances are added to Earth's water, air, or land.

Sometimes wastes from homes or factories are dumped into rivers, lakes, and oceans. This causes *water pollution*. Polluted water can be too dirty to use. It can be dangerous, too. Some polluted water can make living things sick. When water becomes too polluted, it can kill the plants and animals that live in it. Water pollution is a problem for everyone.

Could you use this lake for food and water? Neither could a fish!

In 1989 the oil tanker *Exxon Valdez* ran aground in Alaska's Prince William Sound. It spilled 11 million gallons of oil! The oil polluted the water and coastline for 600 miles from the ship. Many animals became ill or died. Between 300,000 and 675,000 animals were killed. Sadly, pockets of oil can still be found in the water today.

Scenes such as this are common after a major oil spill.

The oil spill also harmed the people of Alaska. In some villages people could no longer catch fish. They lost jobs and money.

Air pollution can come from forest fires or volcanoes. However, most air pollution comes from cars and factories. Burning gasoline, coal, and other fuels can pollute the air. They release compounds of sulfur and nitrogen called acids. The acids mix with water in the air and fall to Earth as **acid rain**. Acid rain can ruin lakes, forests, soils, and crops. Too much acid rain can harm many plants and animals.

Waste gases from cars, homes, and factories may join with water in the air to form *smog*. Smog hangs in the air like a cloud. It can make the air harder to breathe. It also stings the eyes. You may have heard about smog alerts. When these are issued, people who have trouble breathing in smog should stay inside.

Acid rain, smog, and trash can all pollute soil. So can chemical wastes. This is called *land pollution*. Polluted land can harm the plants and animals that live on it. Land pollution can be ugly, too. Why do you think it is important to keep land clean?

Why do you think smog occurs most often in cities?

Littering adds to pollution.

READING **Compare and Contrast**
How are smog and acid rain alike? How are they different?

How Can Humans Fight Pollution?

To keep ecosystems healthy, we must use resources wisely. Many energy sources pollute the air as we use them, so using energy wisely helps keep the air clean. Turn out lights in an empty room. Shut off televisions and radios when you are not using them. Ride in a bus or train instead of a car.

The United States government has written laws to control air pollution. One of these laws is the Clean Air Act. It sets limits on different kinds of air pollution. Laws in California are even stricter. Cars sold there must meet tough tests that help keep pollution low.

Litter is also a big problem in many places. You can help by cleaning up litter when you find it. You can also reuse things, or recycle them. Keeping the land clean helps everyone!

Water pollution is a problem in thousands of lakes, rivers, and other bodies of water. A law called the Clean Water Act is helping. It tells states to clean polluted waters and to stop further pollution. You and your family can keep water clean. Don't dump wastes that could harm the water. Don't throw things into rivers or lakes that do not belong there.

2000

1975

At one time the Chesapeake Bay was very polluted. The efforts of many people have made it a much cleaner place today.

▶ **What can you do to fight pollution?**

Why It Matters

You need clean air, clean land, and clean water to live and grow. So do many other living things. Think about the choices you make every day. Do you throw wastes on the ground or in the water? Do you use energy wisely? Do you fight pollution? Your choices affect your life and the lives around you.

Think and Write

1. What types of events can cause an ecosystem to change?

2. In what ways do people change ecosystems?

3. What causes acid rain?

4. A new factory opens in your area. Suddenly, dead fish are found in the local stream. What can you infer? How can you determine if your inference is correct?

5. **Critical Thinking** What types of things can you do every day to help prevent harmful changes in the environment?

L·I·N·K·S

WRITING LINK

Interview an adult. Write down some questions to ask a family member about a neighborhood they know. How has it changed through the years?

SOCIAL STUDIES LINK

Do research. Find out more about the Chesapeake Bay cleanup effort. What types of things did people do? What are people still doing today?

HEALTH LINK

Do research. Find out more about a contagious disease affecting humans. What can be done to help prevent it? Are there any new advances in fighting the disease?

ART LINK

Draw pictures. Draw "before" and "after" pictures describing a change or changes that you have observed in an ecosystem.

TECHNOLOGY LINK

 At the Computer Visit **www.mhscience02.com** for more links.

UNCOVERING THE MAMMOTH

In 1997 something amazing was found in the ice fields of Siberia in northern Russia. Trapped in the ice were the remains of a 20,000-year-old woolly mammoth! The body was very well preserved. It had the hair, the skin, and even the smell of a mammoth.

The woolly mammoth was a huge, furry cousin of the elephant. It stood about 4 meters (13 feet) tall and had long, curved tusks. The mammoth's thick, hairy coat kept it warm as it roamed through cold places. Most mammoths died out about 10,000 years ago, at the end of the Ice Age.

How could this amazing fossil best be studied? Researchers carefully dug a huge chunk of frozen ground containing the mammoth. The chunk weighed about 21,000 kilograms (23 tons)! A helicopter carried the chunk to an ice cave. Scientists will study the mammoth for clues about how it lived and died.

Could a woolly mammoth live again? It may be possible! Scientists are looking for special cells in the mammoth that they could clone. To clone means to make an exact copy of a living thing.

Write ABOUT IT

1. How are woolly mammoths and elephants similar? How are they different?
2. Do you think woolly mammoths can live again on Earth? If so, where might they live?

This replica of a woolly mammoth that lived in North America, Asia, and Europe is in the Royal British Columbia Museum.

Scientists uncover woolly mammoth bones at the Mammoth Site Museum in South Dakota.

AT THE COMPUTER

Visit www.mhscience02.com to learn more about mammoths and other ancient animals.

Vocabulary

Fill each blank with the best word or words from the list.

cell, A7

community, A40

extinct, A33

food web, A50

fossil, A30

kingdom, A20

organ, A15

organism, A6

organ system, A15

overpopulation, A57

producer, A46

tissue, A14

trait, A21

1. All the organisms in a population form a(n) _____.

2. If none of a kind of organism remains alive on Earth, it is _____.

3. The remains of an organism that lived in the distant past is a(n) _____.

4. A characteristic of a living thing is known as a(n) _____.

5. An organism that makes its own food is known as a(n) _____.

The smallest unit of living matter **6.** _____

↓ organized into **7.** _____

↓ organized into **8.** _____

↓ organized into **9.** _____

↓ organized into **10.** _____

11. Humans are examples of _____.

   A producers

   B consumers

   C decomposers

   D fossils

12. Molds, fungi, and bacteria are examples of _____.

   F producers

   G consumers

   H decomposers

   J herbivores

13. The largest group into which an organism is classified is the _____.

   A kingdom

   B genus

   C species

   D phylum

14. A living thing's home is called its _____.

   F trait

   G habitat

   H soil

   J food web

15. The basic needs of most living things include _____.

A food

B water

C oxygen

D all of the above

Concepts and Skills

16. Reading in Science Draw a diagram or chart that describes the relationships among producers, decomposers, and consumers.

17. Process Skills: Classify Think of something that shares some of the traits of living things but is not alive. Why is it classified as nonliving?

18. Critical Thinking Why are scientific names for living things important?

19. Product Ads Many product ads claim that the product is safe for the environment or that it helps the environment in some way. Find a product ad or label that makes such a claim. Look at laundry soaps, trash bags, or paper products. Do you think the product really does help the environment?

20. Decision Making Every year in April, the world observes Earth Day. On this day students do things to help keep Earth a healthy place to live. What could you and your friends do this Earth Day to help?

Boost your test scores!

Be Smart! Visit www.mhscience02.com to learn more.

Plants

LESSON 6

Plant Parts, A68

LESSON 7

Plant Growth and Reproduction, A80

Did You Ever Wonder?

How large can a pumpkin grow? In the year 2000, the largest pumpkin weighed in at more than 500 kilograms (1,100 pounds)! Large pumpkins like these growing on a farm in Michigan can be grown in a backyard. What do pumpkins and most other plants need to grow?

6 Plant Parts

Vocabulary

root hair, A71

epidermis, A73

stomata, A73

transpiration, A73

chlorophyll, A73

photosynthesis, A74

respiration, A74

Get Ready

In a forest thick with trees, a large group of caterpillars hatches. The caterpillars are yellow with long hairs. They will grow into large white insects called gypsy moths.

The hungry caterpillars begin to munch on the trees' leaves, especially the leaves of oaks and birches. The trees grow new leaves, but the hungry caterpillars eat those, too. After some time the trees die.

What happens to trees—and other plants—when they lose their leaves? What other parts do plants need to survive?

Process Skill

You predict when you state possible results of an event or an experiment.

A 68

Explore Activity

Why Does a Plant Need Leaves?

Procedure

BE CAREFUL! Handle scissors carefully.

1. Label the plants A and B. Use the scissors to cut all the leaves from plant B.

2. Water the soil in both plants. Place the plants in a well-lighted area, but not in direct sunlight. Do not move the plants during the experiment.

3. **Observe** Examine the plants each day for ten days. Measure any growth, and note any other changes. Record your observations in a data table like the one shown.

Observations		
Day	Plant A	Plant B
1		
2		
3		
4		

Drawing Conclusions

1. **Interpret Data** What happened to plant A? To plant B?

2. **Form a Hypothesis** Why does a plant need leaves?

3. **Going Further: Predict** What would happen if you kept plant A in a dark place?

Main Idea Plants are made up of many parts that work together. Each part helps the plant survive.

What Does a Plant Need?

Like all living things, plants have certain needs. They need air, water, energy from food, and a place to live. However, unlike animals, green plants make their own food. To make food, plants need light, water, and the gas carbon dioxide. Carbon dioxide is a gas in the air.

Plants are made up of different parts. Each part plays a role in helping a plant get or make what it needs to survive.

A plant cannot live without *leaves*. Leaves make most of a plant's food. *Roots* take in some of the materials a plant needs to make food. The *stem* carries food, water, and other materials to and from the roots and leaves. A plant needs all three parts—leaves, roots, and stem—to live, grow, and stay alive.

Geranium

Stem

Leaf

Roots

Roots

A plant's roots grow downward into the soil. You can't see roots, but they help the plant stay alive. Roots do three main tasks.

First, roots absorb water from the soil. Like all living things, plants need water to stay alive. As they take in water, roots also absorb minerals from the soil. The minerals provide nutrients a plant needs to live and grow.

Second, roots hold a plant in place. Without roots, a large plant might topple to the ground. A smaller plant might blow away in the wind.

Finally, some plants use their roots to store food. Examples include carrots, radishes, and parsnips. Many people like to eat these roots. Do you?

Two Kinds of Roots

Have you ever tried to pull a dandelion out of the ground? It is very hard to pull out the entire root.

That is because a dandelion has a single, thick root called a *taproot*.

A taproot is one of the two main types of plant roots. Dandelions, carrots, and grapevines are examples of plants with taproots. These plants send a single large root into the soil. A grapevine's taproot may grow as long as 15 meters (49$\frac{1}{2}$ feet)!

Other plants, such as grasses, have *fibrous* (FIGH·bruhs) *roots* that spread out into the surrounding soil. No one root is larger or more important than the others. Most trees have fibrous roots.

If you look closely at a carrot, you can see what look like tiny hairs. These are called **root hairs**. Root hairs are threadlike cells on a root that take in water and minerals from the soil. Most plants have root hairs.

READING **Cause and Effect**
What are three functions of roots?

Types of Roots

Taproot

Fibrous roots

Root hairs

A 71

What Do Stems Do?

A plant's stem grows above the ground. The stem carries water, minerals, and other nutrients to and from the roots and leaves. It also supports flowers, if the plant has them, and holds the leaves up to the light. Inside a stem there are several different types of tiny tubes. They act as a transportation system, moving things up and down the stem.

There are two kinds of stems. Shrubs and trees have woody stems. Woody stems provide extra support to these larger plants. In smaller plants the stems are soft, green, and bendable. Plants with nonwoody stems rely on the pressure of the watery sap in their stems for support.

▷ **What are the different things a stem does?**

Parts of a Stem

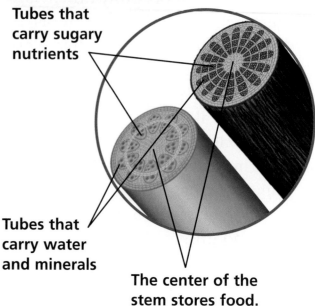

Tubes that carry sugary nutrients

Tubes that carry water and minerals

The center of the stem stores food.

READING
Diagrams

How is a woody stem different from a soft stem?

The strawberry plant has soft, green stems that grow along the surface of the ground.

What Do Leaves Do?

The leaves are the main food-making part of the plant. They use energy from sunlight to make food from water and a gas called carbon dioxide. How do you think water and carbon dioxide get into a leaf?

One thing you notice looking at a leaf are the *veins* (VAYNZ). Veins are bundles of tubes that carry food and water in stems and roots. The veins carry water to the leaf. They also take food from the leaf to the stem and roots.

If you examined a leaf under a microscope, you would see a thin layer on the leaf's top and bottom. This protective layer is called the **epidermis** (ep·i·DUR·mis). It helps keep the leaf from losing water and drying out.

On the lower epidermis are tiny openings called **stomata** (STOH·muh·tuh). Gases and water vapor pass in and out of the stomata. A plant uses its stomata to control how quickly it loses water. Any extra water exits through the stomata in a process called **transpiration** (tran·spuh·RAY·shuhn).

In the middle layer of a leaf are cells with a green substance called **chlorophyll** (KLAWR·uh·fil). Chlorophyll traps the energy from sunlight. It also gives leaves their green color.

> **What is the function of each part of a leaf?**

Sunlight

Epidermis

Vein

H_2O leaves

Air enters

Chloroplasts containing chlorophyll

Stomata

How Do Plants Make Food?

What foods did you eat today? Chances are you have eaten several plant foods. Like all living things, you need energy to survive. You eat foods to get energy. However, plants make their own food. You learned that plant leaves use the energy from sunlight to make food from water and carbon dioxide. This food-making process is called **photosynthesis** (foh·tuh·SIN·thuh·sis).

During daylight a green plant uses special leaf cells containing chlorophyll to trap sunlight. There, light energy is used to combine water and carbon dioxide from the air. The result is sugar and oxygen.

Veins carry the sugars the plant makes to all parts of the plant. These sugars give the sweet taste to fruits such as strawberries and peaches. The oxygen the plant makes goes into the air.

The plant stores food until it is needed. Then its cells use oxygen to break apart sugars. When sugars break apart, they give off energy. This process is called **respiration** (res·puh·RAY·shuhn). Respiration happens day and night. The same process releases energy in animal cells.

In many ways photosynthesis is the opposite of respiration. For example, photosynthesis stores energy. Respiration releases energy. Photosynthesis uses carbon dioxide and gives off oxygen. Respiration uses oxygen and gives off carbon dioxide.

READING Diagrams

1. Why does photosynthesis take place only during daylight?

2. How are photosynthesis and respiration similar? Different?

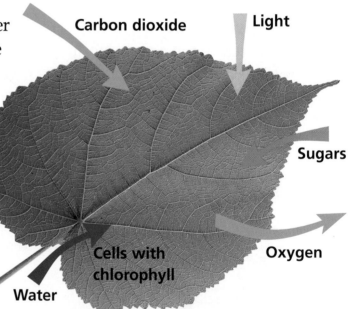

Carbon dioxide

Light

Sugars

Oxygen

Cells with chlorophyll

Water

In photosynthesis plants use the energy from light to make sugar and oxygen from carbon dioxide and water. Oxygen is released into the air.

▶ What are the products of photosynthesis?

Photosynthesis Versus Respiration

Photosynthesis gives off oxygen; respiration gives off carbon dioxide. You can observe this for yourself by placing a leaf in water. The leaf will "breathe," releasing tiny air bubbles that you can see. Which do you predict will produce more air bubbles—a leaf placed in sunlight or darkness?

Materials

2 jars

2 leaves from the same plant

water

Procedure

1 Fill each jar with fresh water. Place a leaf from the same plant in each jar.

2 Place one jar in a bright, sunny window. Place the other jar in the dark.

3 **Predict** Write down what you think will happen. On which leaf will bubbles form first?

4 **Observe** Check each leaf in five minutes, keeping a written record of what you observe.

Drawing Conclusions

1 How well did your results agree with your prediction?

2 How do your results for the leaf in sunlight compare with your results for the leaf kept in the dark?

3 **Predict** What do you think will happen if you continue the experiment for one hour? Test your prediction.

4 **Interpret Data** What do the results tell you about photosynthesis and respiration?

How Are a Cactus and an Evergreen Different?

Each fall the leaves of trees such as oaks and maples turn bright colors, then fall to the ground. During the winter the trees stay alive but are *dormant*. When trees are dormant, they save their energy for growth when warm weather returns in the spring. These trees drop their leaves to save water during the winter.

Plants such as the cactus and the evergreen have other ways to prevent water loss. This is why both the cactus and the evergreen can live in places that are too dry for other plants.

The cactus plant is designed for a hot, dry environment—the desert. Its roots spread wide to take in water from a large area. Its stem is often large and fleshy so it can store water.

Evergreens have needle-shaped leaves.

Cactus plants often have leaves that are sharp spines. This shape keeps the plant from losing too much water through transpiration. Also, the sharp spines do not allow animals to eat the plant to get water stored in the stems.

Evergreens survive in cool, dry areas. Unlike oaks and maples, these trees and shrubs keep their leaves for 1 to 18 years. Some evergreens have broad, flat leaves. Others, such as spruces and firs, have leaves that are needle shaped. The leaves of both kinds of evergreens have a thick outer layer and a coating of wax. This helps to reduce water loss.

The saguaro cactus may live for 200 years!

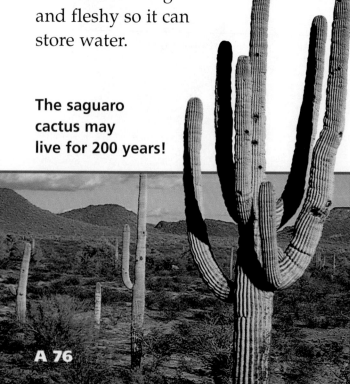

▷ **How are a cactus and an evergreen alike? Different?**

Why It Matters

We eat parts of plants all the time. Carrot roots, celery stems, and lettuce leaves may all be part of a tasty salad, soup, or stew. Without plants to make oxygen, people would not survive. We also use the woody stems, or trunks, of trees to build houses and furniture. Still other plants provide valuable medicines. Visit **www.mhscience02.com** to research a project on plants.

Think and Write

1. Why do plants have stems and leaves?

2. How does a taproot differ from fibrous roots?

3. How do the cactus and the evergreen survive in environments that are too dry for most plants?

4. Predict What would happen to a plant left in total darkness for several weeks? Explain.

5. Critical Thinking Why does a plant need both photosynthesis and respiration to survive?

WRITING LINK

Write an expository paragraph. Tell about some of the parts of plants that you use. Which ones do you use most?

SOCIAL STUDIES LINK

Do research. Choose a country. Find out more about the foods its people like to eat. Which of the foods come from plants? How do the types of plants that grow in that area affect the people's food choices?

TECHNOLOGY LINK

Science Newsroom CD-ROM Choose *Stop Before You Start* to learn about the effects of smoking cigarettes on the human body. Cigarettes are made from the leaves of the tobacco plant.

At the Computer Visit **www.mhscience02.com** for more links.

Incredible Plants Around the World

Can plants be amazing? Decide for yourself! Look at the photos, and read the captions to learn about some of Earth's most incredible plants.

This ant plant takes its name from the ants that live inside it. In return for a home, the ants leave dead insects and other waste in the plant. The decaying matter nourishes the ant plant.

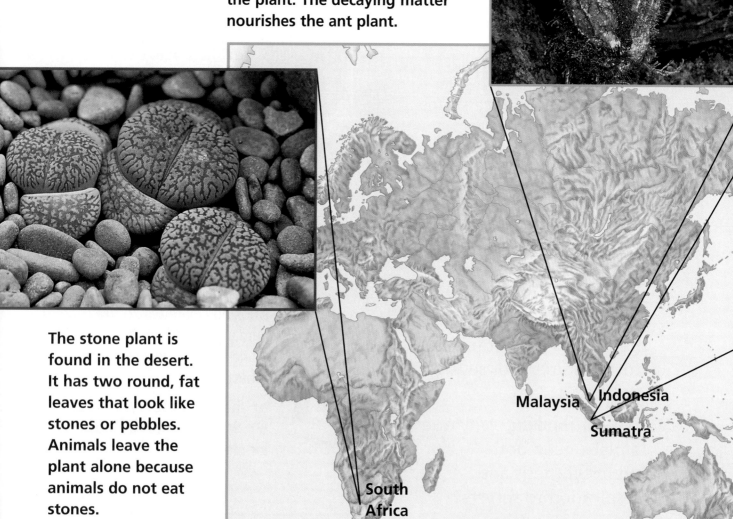

The stone plant is found in the desert. It has two round, fat leaves that look like stones or pebbles. Animals leave the plant alone because animals do not eat stones.

Malaysia
Indonesia
Sumatra
South Africa

A 78

The titan arum flower of Sumatra can grow up to three meters (10 feet) tall, yet it opens for just two days. When ready for pollination, the flowering spike heats up and smells like rotting meat. The smell attracts bees so that pollination may occur.

What Did I Learn?

1. The leaves of a stone plant look like stones. This helps the plant

A attract insects for pollination.
B keep animals from eating its fleshy leaves.
C keep cool in the hot desert.
D retain water in its leaves.

2. The spike of the titan arum flower smells like rotten meat. This helps the plant

F attract bees for pollination.
G keep hungry animals away.
H live in partnership with mosquitoes.
J nourish itself.

United States

Flies should stay away from the Venus's-flytrap! When a fly or other insect touches hairs on the plant, the leaves snap shut. The leaves' spines keep the fly from escaping. The fly becomes food for the plant.

AT THE COMPUTER Visit www.mhscience02.com to learn more about exotic plants.

A 79

Plant Growth and Reproduction

Vocabulary

seed, A82

germination, A82

pollination, A84

fertilization, A85

ovary, A85

spore, A88

Get Ready

Did you know that coconuts are the seeds of trees called coconut palms? Each seed can grow into a new coconut tree. Where do seeds come from? Do all plants go through the same stages as they grow and develop?

Process Skill

You use variables when you identify and separate things in an experiment that can be changed or controlled.

Explore Activity

How Does a Seed Grow?

Materials

2 soaked pinto bean seeds

paper towels

clear plastic cup

marking pen

water

Procedure

1. Fold a paper towel to match the height of the plastic cup. Line the cup with the paper towel.

2. Crumple another paper towel into a ball. Place it in the cup to hold the lining in place.

3. On either side of the cup, place a seed between the lining and the cup, about $\frac{3}{4}$ of the way up.

4. On either side of the outside of the cup, write Seed A near one seed and Seed B near the other.

5. **Observe** Place the cup in a sunny spot. Keep the lining moist. Observe the seeds for seven to ten days. Record your observations in a data table like the one shown.

Plant Observations		
Day	Seed A	Seed B
1		
2		
3		
4		

Drawing Conclusions

1. **Communicate** Describe the plant parts that you observed and the order in which they appeared.

2. **Interpret Data** What does a seed need to grow into a plant?

3. **Going Further: Use Variables** Try the experiment without adding water to the cup.

Main Idea Plants grow, develop, and reproduce in many ways.

How Does a Seed Grow?

A **seed** is an undeveloped plant with stored food sealed in a protective covering. The protective covering is known as a *seed coat*.

Seeds can grow into small plants when given water and light. First, roots push through the seed coat. Then, a stem and leaves start to grow. Part of each seed is food that the plants use as they begin to grow. The process of a seed sprouting into a new plant is called **germination** (jur·muh·NAY·shuhn).

A young plant that grows and develops from a seed is called a *seedling* (SEED·ling). It doesn't matter whether a seedling grows from a coconut—the world's largest seed—or a seed as small as a grape seed. All seeds develop in the same way. They grow from a seed to a seedling to an adult plant.

Most seeds, such as the peach seed shown in the diagram, swell as they take in water. The seed coat splits open. A root grows out of the seed. Then a tiny stem appears. One or two leaves grow from the stem, and the young seedling begins to grow. If conditions are right, the seedling will mature into an adult plant. Then it will be able to make its own seeds.

In some plants the time from seed to adult plant takes only days. In others it takes years. For example, a bean plant matures in just a few months. A peach seed takes several years to become a tree.

A peach falls to the ground. In time the flesh falls away. The seed is watered by the rain.

The seed sends roots into the ground. A stem and leaves grow.

The seed becomes a seedling.

Parts of a Seed

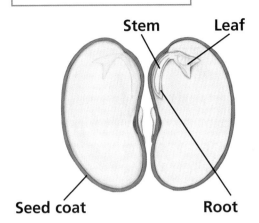

Stem Leaf

Seed coat Root

What does a seed need to germinate? First, a seed must move from the flower to a place where it can sprout. Most seeds need water and warm temperatures to germinate.

Once the seedling begins to grow, it needs the right amount of light. The leaves of the growing plant need light to make food. A seedling also needs oxygen from the air and nutrients from the soil.

READING **Cause and Effect**
What causes a seed to grow?

The seedling grows into a tree. In time it produces its own seeds to begin the cycle again.

FOR SCHOOL OR HOME

The Structure of a Seed

1. Place water-soaked bean seeds on a paper towel. The beans should have been soaked in water overnight.

2. **Observe** Carefully pull apart the two halves of the seed. Examine each half with a hand lens.

3. **Communicate** Draw a picture of the seed parts you observed.

4. Which part of the seed is the seed coat? Which part is the source of the root, stem, and leaves?

5. **Infer** Where does the seed store its food?

A 83

How Do Seeds Form and Grow?

In most plants, seeds are made in flowers. The seeds of flowering plants are formed when a male sex cell joins with a female sex cell.

Male sex cells are found in *pollen* (PAHL·uhn). Have you ever brushed up against a flower and come away with a yellow or orange powder on your arm? This powder is pollen. Pollen is produced by a part of the flower that is known as the *anther* (AN·thuhr).

Female sex cells, the eggs, are in a part of the plant known as the *pistil* (PIS·tuhl). The transfer of a pollen grain to the pistil is called **pollination** (pahl·uh·NAY·shuhn). Pollination can take place when pollen is carried from a flower's anther to its own pistil or to another flower's pistil.

Look at the diagram. Find the anthers and pistils. Then use the diagram to help you trace the steps of pollination.

Unlike many other living things, plants cannot move from place to place. How do you think pollen from one plant reaches another? Plants rely on insects, birds, mammals, wind, or water to help with pollination.

Insects and other animals are attracted to the bright colors and sweet smells of some flowers. They feed on the pollen or a sugary food called nectar that flowers make. They may pick up some pollen on their bodies. If the animals then visit another flower of the same kind, the pollen may rub off onto its pistil.

Other flowering plants rely on the wind to blow pollen from one plant to the next. Some water plants use the water to carry their pollen to other plants.

Pollination

Anther

Pistil

Pollen

READING

Diagrams

1. What part of a flower makes pollen? What part makes the eggs?

2. Where does the pollen land during pollination?

Bees help pollinate flowers.

After pollination the next step in the formation of a seed is **fertilization** (fur·tuh·luh·ZAY·shuhn). Fertilization is the joining of a female sex cell and a male sex cell into one cell, a fertilized egg.

After pollen reaches the pistil, a pollen tube starts to grow. The pollen tube grows down the flower into the **ovary** (OH·vuh·ree). The ovary is a structure containing egg cells. It is the ovary that grows to form a protective fruit.

The pollen tube grows until it reaches an egg. The male sex cell then travels down the pollen tube and combines with the egg. The plant egg is now fertilized.

A seed develops from a fertilized egg cell. Look at the photo of a bean seed. Can you find the beginnings of a root, stem, and leaves? Together, this part of the seed is called the embryo.

Inside each seed is an embryo and a food source. When the time is right, the embryo uses the food to begin to grow its first root, stem, and leaves. A new plant develops.

Embryo

▷ **What is pollination? Fertilization?**

In fertilization the male sex cell travels down the pollen tube and combines with the egg to form a fertilized egg.

Fertilization

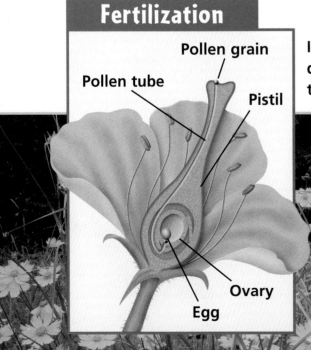

Pollen grain

Pollen tube

Pistil

Ovary

Egg

How Are Seeds Carried Away?

Once a seed forms, it needs a place to grow. The best chance it has for survival is to be in its own space, away from the parent plant.

If the parent plant and plants like it are too close, the larger plants block sunlight from reaching the seedling. They also soak up the water and nutrients the seedling needs from the soil.

That is why a plant's best chance to grow is for the seed to be carried away, or dispersed, from the parent.

Seeds disperse in different ways. Some plants scatter their own seeds. The protective, fleshy fruits explode to shoot their seeds away from the parent plant. Other seeds are carried by the wind or water. For example, dandelion seeds have a "parachute" of feathery hairs. They are light enough for the wind to carry them long distances.

Many seeds are carried by animals. The fleshy fruit may attract animals that eat the seeds along with the fruit. The seeds may fall to the ground as the animals eat the fruit. If the seeds are eaten, the animals will pass them out in their droppings. The seeds may also hitch a ride on an animal's fur or feathers and fall off in some new place.

What ways of seed dispersal do these pictures show?

1 The apple tree grows to adult size.

2 The apple tree grows flowers. Bees pollinate the flowers.

3 The plant egg is fertilized.

4 The seeds begin to grow. The ovary grows into an apple.

5 The fruit falls off the tree and decays.

6 A deer eats the fruit and spreads the seeds through its waste.

7 Seedlings grow from the seeds, far away from the parent plant.

READING Diagrams

What are the steps in the life cycle of a flowering plant?

The Life Cycle of Flowering Plants

Did you know that more than $\frac{8}{10}$ of all green plants have flowers? The purpose of a flower is to make seeds that grow into new plants.

However, the steps from flower to seed to a mature plant are not easy. First, the parent plant must make its own male and female sex cells. Then, the male cell in the pollen must combine with an egg to make a seed.

The new seed must travel to a place away from the parent plant. Its new home must have the light, water, nutrients, oxygen, and warm temperatures that the seed needs to germinate and grow. Then, the young seedling must live long enough to produce new seeds.

Most plants make many more seeds than will ever become adult plants. In this way, at least some of the offspring will survive to continue the plant's life cycle.

▶ **How do animals help flowering plants?**

Do All Plants Grow from Seeds?

Some plants do not have flowers, nor do they produce seeds. Plants such as mosses and ferns use **spores** (SPAWRZ).

A spore is a cell in a seedless plant. Like a seed, a spore can grow into a new plant. Remember, a seed is produced by one male and one female sex cell, often from different plants. Spores are different. They have no sex cells. Each spore is produced by just one plant.

The moss plant has two separate stages to its life cycle. In the first stage, it produces spores. The moss spores grow into moss plants that have male branches and female branches.

Spores grow in spore cases. These tough little cells can live through a drought or extreme temperatures.

In the second stage, the male branches produce male sex cells. The female branches make female sex cells. One male and one female sex cell combine to make a fertilized egg.

The fertilized egg grows into a thin stalk with a spore case on top. When the spore case opens, the spores are released. Spores that land on damp ground may grow into new moss plants, and the cycle begins again.

▶ **What are spores?**

From a distance mosses look like thick carpets of green. Up close you can see their thin, green leaflike structures.

LINKS

Why It Matters

Imagine pizza without the tomato sauce or the wheat crust. A flowering plant produced both the tomato and the wheat. What about strawberries, peaches, walnuts, peas, or corn on the cob? The fruits and seeds of plants are often good to eat. However, these plant parts are valuable to us as more than food sources. Without them, plants would not be able to make new plants. We also would not have the food and oxygen we need to survive.

Think and Write

1. What are the three main stages in a plant's life cycle?

2. What are pollination and fertilization?

3. Briefly describe or draw the life cycle of a flowering plant.

4. How are a seed and a spore alike? Different?

5. **Critical Thinking** Why do plants need animals?

ART LINK

Make a painting. Look at the flower paintings of American artist Georgia O'Keeffe (1887–1986). Try creating your own flower painting or drawing in the style of this famous painter.

WRITING LINK

Write a story. Tell it from a seed's point of view. Include how the seed traveled to its current spot, what happens as it begins to grow, and the kind of plant that it grows into.

LITERATURE LINK

Read *Discovering the Secrets of Nature* to get an inside view of nature photography. Think about places you'd want to visit and plants and animals you'd like to record. Try the activities at the end of the book.

HEALTH LINK

Do research. A healthful diet includes foods that come from plants. Research Food Guide Pyramid. Identify the foods in the pyramid that come from plants. Share your findings with your classmates.

TECHNOLOGY LINK

At the Computer Visit **www.mhscience02.com** for more links.

HELPING ONE

Could there be life on Earth without plants? Without animals? Even if there could, how would one survive without the other?

Plants provide most of the food animals eat. Animals also use trees and other plants for shelter. Humans make medicines from plants.

The coloring of some animals makes them blend in with the plants around them. Some animals use plants to hide and store food. Plants even produce oxygen for animals to breathe!

Plants do a lot for animals, but many plants need animals, too. When bees fly from flower to flower, they pollinate flowers. As a bee feeds, pollen grains stick to its body. Then when the bee flies to another flower, it deposits some pollen there. The pollen helps form seeds so new flowers can grow!

Some animals eat fruits of plants but can't digest the seeds. These are later passed through the body and deposited somewhere else. Other seeds cling to an animal's fur and fall off later in some other area. If plant seeds just fall, a garden becomes too crowded for every plant to grow. Animals help put seeds where they'll have a chance to grow.

Some plants need animals as food! The leaves of a Venus's-flytrap snap shut to catch insects that land. The bladderwort traps insects in pouches on its underwater branches!

This deer hides behind plants for safety.

ANOTHER

Write ABOUT IT

1. Why do you think some plants need insects for food?
2. How do humans help plants spread their seeds around?

AT THE COMPUTER

Visit www.mhscience02.com to learn more about the relationships of plants and animals.

This insect is caught by a Venus's-flytrap

Chapter 2 Review

Vocabulary

Fill each blank with the best word from the list.

chlorophyll, A73
fertilization, A85
germination, A82
ovary, A85
photosynthesis, A74

pollination, A84
respiration, A74
seed, A82
stomata, A73
transpiration, A73

1. Plants release water through the process of _____.

2. In a flower the egg is created in the _____.

3. Flowers make _____ which can grow into new plants.

4. When a male and female sex cell join together, _____ occurs.

5. The green chemical called _____ helps plants perform photosynthesis.

6. A plant breaks sugars apart for energy in a process called _____.

7. Plants lose water through leaf openings called _____.

8. A seed sprouts into a new plant in a process called _____.

9. Plants make and store food through the process of _____.

10. When a pollen grain meets a pistil, _____ occurs.

Test Prep

11. The part of the plant that carries water from the roots to the leaves is the _____.

    A ovary
    B spore
    C stem
    D root hair

12. A leaf's main job is to _____.

    F reproduce
    G pollinate
    H protect
    J make food

13. Seeds may be carried away from a parent plant by _____.

    A sticking to an animal's fur
    B blowing in the wind
    C an animal eating it
    D all of the above

14. To make food, plants need to take in a gas called _____.

   F water

   G carbon dioxide

   H oxygen

   J helium

15. The job of roots is to _____.

   A make food

   B absorb water and nutrients

   C gather sunlight

   D attract insects

Concepts and Skills

16. **Reading in Science** Why do plants need water, air, and sunlight? Explain how these things help the plant stay alive.

17. **Product Ads** Ads for cereal and bread sometimes use the words *whole grain* and *fiber*. What do these words mean? Why might whole grains and fiber be good for you? Research the answers.

18. **Decision Making** The Amazon rain forest is home to many animals. It also is a source of Earth's oxygen. However, much of it is being cleared for homes and farms. What do you think should be done?

19. **Critical Thinking** You share the world with a countless number of plants. What would your life be like if there were no plants?

20. **Process Skills: Predict** Look at different vegetables. You may choose a potato, a stalk of celery, a head of lettuce, a tomato, or other vegetables. For each vegetable, predict the plant part from which it came. What did you base your predictions on?

Boost *your test scores!*

Be Smart! Visit www.mhscience02.com to learn more.

Dr. Clifford W. Houston
Bacteriologist

Remember the last time you stayed home sick with a sore throat? Maybe your doctor gave you a special medicine to help you feel better. If so, bacteria were the likely cause of your sore throat. Bacteria cause many illnesses in people and other animals.

Dr. Houston is a bacteriologist—a scientist who researches and studies bacteria. Dr. Houston has always been curious about living things. When he was in elementary school, he created his own ant farms and studied how ants live.

Today, Dr. Houston studies different bacteria and how they cause disease. Many different kinds of bacteria cause illness. This means that we need different medicines to fight them.

One of the tools Dr. Houston uses is a powerful microscope. This microscope makes pictures of bacteria several hundred times larger than their real size. By learning how bacteria live and grow, Dr. Houston can help find the vaccines to prevent them from causing disease. Dr. Houston likes the challenge.

Dr. Houston uses a microscope to study bacteria, such as this streptococcus.

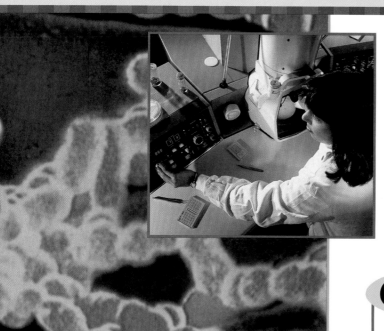

Scientist using an electron microscope to study bacteria

Write ABOUT IT

1. What is one of the most important instruments a bacteriologist uses? Why?
2. Why are different medicines required to fight bacteria?

Careers IN SCIENCE

Veterinarian

If you're interested in helping animals, you may want to be a veterinarian. A veterinarian is a doctor for animals.

To become a veterinarian, you need a degree from a veterinary medical school. This takes about four years after finishing college.

Veterinarians often work in their own office or with others in an animal hospital. Veterinarians do more than treat sick animals. Some work on farms, and some work in laboratories doing research. For those who love animals, a veterinary career can be very rewarding.

You can use the Internet or library resources to find out more about this career.

AT THE COMPUTER

Visit www.mhscience02.com to learn more about careers.

Ecosystem Poster

Your goal is to make a poster about an ecosystem of your choice.

What to Do

1. Research a rain forest, a desert, an ocean, or another ecosystem of your choice.

2. Find answers to these questions:

- Where on Earth is the ecosystem?
- What is the ecosystem like?
- What plants and animals live there?
- Is the ecosystem changing? If so, how?

3. Make a poster that shows the information you found out. Include pictures and words. Display the poster in the classroom.

A Plant Book

Your goal is to make a book that shows the life cycle of a plant.

What to Do

1. Choose a plant. Research the plant and its life cycle.

2. Draw a picture of the plant at different stages of its life cycle. Use a different sheet of paper for each picture. Draw at least four stages. Label the parts of the plant that you can name.

3. Add captions to the pictures.

4. Make a cover and table of contents for the book. Be sure to include a title. Staple or glue the pages together.

UNIT
B

Animals as Living Things

NATIONAL GEOGRAPHIC

Animals as Living Things

CHAPTER 3

Describing Animals B2

CHAPTER 4

Life Processes B42

LOOK!

Young ostriches must grow a lot to become adults. Why do you think young ostriches stay close to their parent?

CHAPTER

LESSON 1

Animal
Characteristics, B4

LESSON 2

Animals Without
Backbones, B14

LESSON 3

Animals with
Backbones, B26

Describing Animals

Did You Ever Wonder?

Is there such a thing as a "free ride"? For these
cattle egrets there is. The birds are riding on black
rhinoceroses. They help the rhinos by cleaning the
rhinos' backs of insects. This provides the birds
with a source of food. In Africa these rhinos are
endangered and many efforts are being made to
protect them. What do animals need to survive?

Animal Characteristics

Vocabulary

vertebrate, B8

invertebrate, B8

symmetry, B8

Get Ready

How would you describe animals? Think about any animals you know. Think about your pets or your friends' pets. Have you seen any animals in a zoo? Have you read any books about animals? Don't forget that you are an animal, too. What types of characteristics, or traits, do all animals have in common?

Process Skill

You infer when you form an idea from facts or observations.

Explore Activity

What Are Some Animal Characteristics?

Materials

clear container with aquarium water

water snail

goldfish or guppy

fish food

ruler

Procedure

BE CAREFUL! Handle animals with care.

1. Obtain a container with a fish and a snail in it.

2. **Observe** Record the shape and approximate size of both animals. Describe how each animal moves and any other observations that you make.

3. Add a few flakes of fish food to the beaker. What do the animals do? Record your observations.

4. What does the fish eat? The snail?

Drawing Conclusions

1. **Observe** What body parts does each animal have? How do they use these parts?

2. Compare how the fish and the snail move. Is movement an advantage for the animals?

3. **Infer** Do you think the fish and the snail are made of one cell or many cells? Why?

4. **Communicate** What are some characteristics that the fish and the snail have? Make a list. Compare your list with other groups' lists. Make a class list.

5. **Going Further: Infer** How are you similar to the fish and the snail? How are you different?

Main Idea Animals have many characteristics, including being able to move and to eat.

What Are Animals Like?

Here are some of the characteristics that all animals have in common.

Animals are made of many cells.

- Each cell has a nucleus and a cell membrane.
- Animal cells do not have a cell wall or chlorophyll, like plants.
- Different cells have different jobs. Bone cells support and protect. Nerve cells carry messages.

Animals reproduce.

- Some animals have thousands of offspring, or young, in their lifetimes. Others have only a few.
- Many animals care for and protect their offspring.

Animals move in some way.

- Most animals move during some time of their life.
- Animals move by walking, running, flying, gliding, crawling, and swimming.
- Animals move to find food, escape danger, find mates, and find a new home.

Animals grow and change.

- Some animals change form as they grow.
- Some animals just grow larger.

Animals eat food.

- Animals cannot make their own food, as plants do.
- They get food by eating plants or other animals.
- Animals digest food for energy.
- Animals use oxygen to turn their food into energy.

Some animals change form as they grow older. A caterpillar is an early stage in the life of a moth.

All living things need energy to stay alive. Animals get energy from food. A food chain shows how energy flows among a group of organisms. An ecosystem can have many different food chains. Combined, they form a food web. A food web shows how food chains in an ecosystem are related.

READING Outline

What do all animals have in common?

A Food Chain

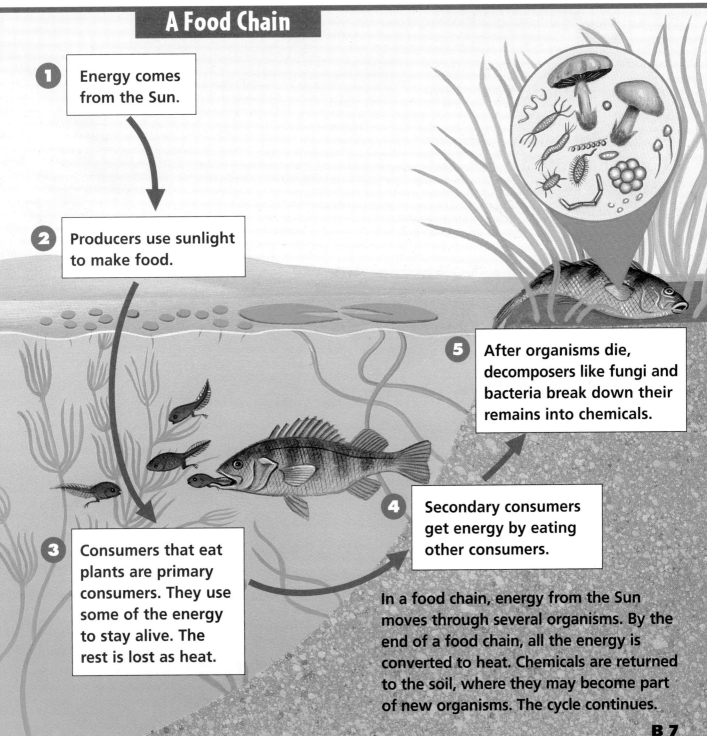

1 Energy comes from the Sun.

2 Producers use sunlight to make food.

3 Consumers that eat plants are primary consumers. They use some of the energy to stay alive. The rest is lost as heat.

4 Secondary consumers get energy by eating other consumers.

5 After organisms die, decomposers like fungi and bacteria break down their remains into chemicals.

In a food chain, energy from the Sun moves through several organisms. By the end of a food chain, all the energy is converted to heat. Chemicals are returned to the soil, where they may become part of new organisms. The cycle continues.

B 7

How Are Animals Different?

All animals have many characteristics in common. They are made of cells, they reproduce, they move in some way, they grow and change, and they eat food.

However, animals are also different in many ways. One major difference is having or not having a backbone. An animal with a backbone is called a **vertebrate** (VUR·tuh·brayt). An animal without a backbone is called an **invertebrate** (in·VUR·tuh·brit). You will learn more about vertebrates and invertebrates later in this chapter.

Symmetry

Another difference among animals is the way their body parts match up around a point or central line. This is known as **symmetry** (SIM·uh·tree). To study symmetry, fold a picture of an animal to match body parts. Body parts with symmetry match up as mirror images when they are folded over.

Some animals have no symmetry. One example is a sponge, the simplest kind of invertebrate. No matter how you might fold a sponge, its body parts do not match up.

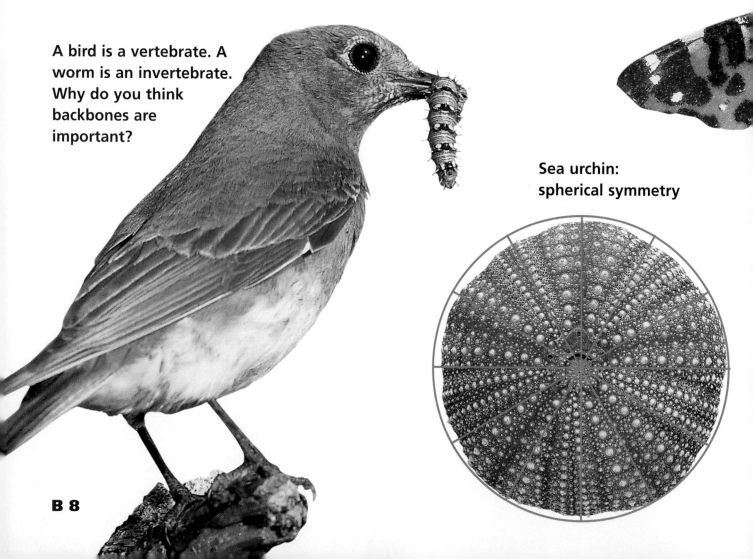

A bird is a vertebrate. A worm is an invertebrate. Why do you think backbones are important?

Sea urchin: spherical symmetry

An animal with *radial* (RAY·dee·uhl) symmetry has body parts that extend outward from a central point. You could fold a sea star through its center five ways and it would match up.

An animal with a sphere-shaped body, like a sea urchin, has *spherical* (SFER·i·kuhl) symmetry. You could fold a sea urchin any way through its center and it would match up.

An animal with *bilateral* (BIGH·LAT·uhr·uhl) symmetry has only two sides that are mirror images. You could fold a butterfly only one way through its center to have it match up. Organisms with bilateral symmetry have a definite front end, back end, upper side, and lower side. Vertebrates and some invertebrates have bilateral symmetry.

▷ **How are these animals different?**

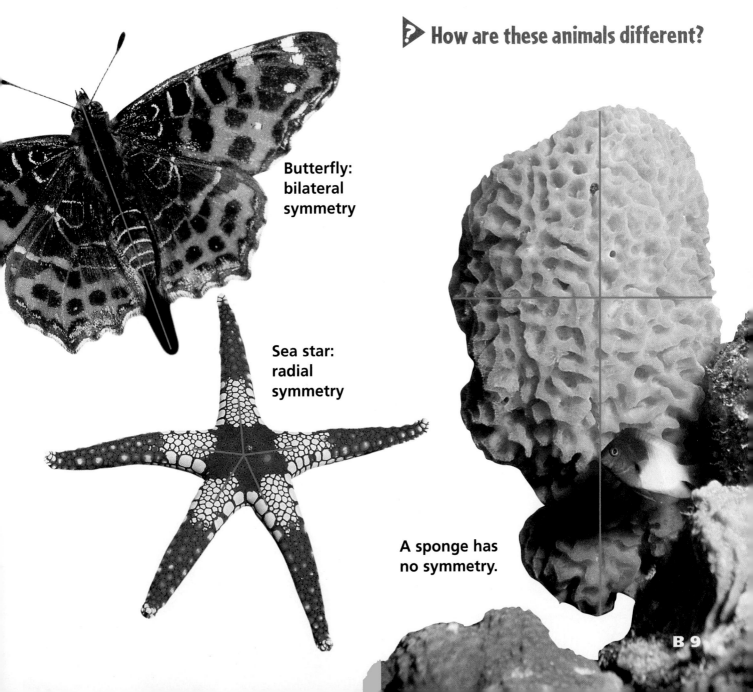

Butterfly: bilateral symmetry

Sea star: radial symmetry

A sponge has no symmetry.

B 9

Process Skill
BUILDER

Animal Symmetry

A scientist's most important job is to *observe*, meaning to look closely. When you observe carefully, you often see things that you didn't know were there. You can practice your observation skills by looking for symmetry in different animals.

Procedure

1 **Observe** Determine whether each animal shown has no symmetry, spherical symmetry, radial symmetry, or bilateral symmetry.

2 **Classify** Record your observations in a chart.

Drawing Conclusions

1 Which animal or animals have radial symmetry? Bilateral symmetry?

2 Which animal or animals have spherical symmetry? No symmetry?

3 **Infer** Does an animal with radial symmetry have a front end and a back end? Explain.

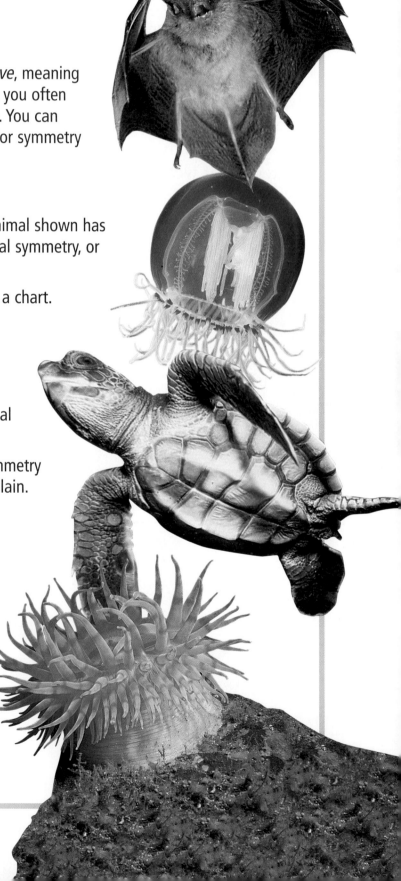

Why It Matters

Identifying an animal isn't always an easy task. The organism to the right looks like a cross between a horse and a salad! In fact, it's a fish. Its wavy spines and leaflike appearance help conceal it on the seabed where it feeds. How might the fish's appearance help it survive?

Think and Write

1. What characteristics do all animals have?

2. What is the difference between a vertebrate and an invertebrate?

3. Compare radial symmetry and bilateral symmetry.

4. Observe What do you observe about yourself that shows you are an animal?

5. Critical Thinking What do you think would happen if one organism was removed from a food chain?

ART LINK

Draw a picture. What if you discovered a new organism? Draw a picture of this organism. Label the features you think are important for identifying it.

WRITING LINK

Write a paragraph. Is there anything unusual about your newly discovered organism? Describe where it lives, how it moves, and what it eats.

MATH LINK

Draw a diagram. What kind of symmetry does your own body have? Draw a diagram that shows how you could fold your body so each half matched up.

LITERATURE LINK

Read *The Polar Bear and the Jaguar* to learn about two animals who live in very different homes. Then try the activities at the end of the book.

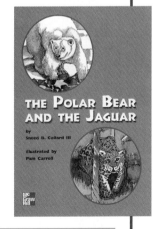

THE POLAR BEAR AND THE JAGUAR
by Sneed B. Collard III
illustrated by Pam Carroll

TECHNOLOGY LINK

At the Computer Visit **www.mhscience02.com** for more links.

HELPING ENDANGERED ANIMALS

What are those creatures gliding through the water? They're manatees. These mammals spend their days slowly munching grasses in the water. That's why manatees are also called "sea cows!"

Unfortunately, people hunted the manatee. Its tough hide was used for making shoes and leather shields. Oil from its body was burned in lamps. Its bones had many uses, and the animal could be eaten.

In the United States, most manatees live in the waters off Florida. Manatees are endangered. Trash in the water can choke and kill them. Fishing nets trap them. Boat propellers scar or kill them.

Many manatees are identified by their scars. Some are equipped with radio transmitters so researchers can track them. When researchers find sick or injured manatees, they nurse them back to health.

The California condor is one of the largest flying birds in the world. It has a wingspan of about 2.5–3.1 meters (8–10 feet). Once thousands of these graceful giants soared over the wilds of the American West. Now much of that territory has been developed. Hunting and poisoning by pesticides also pushed the condor close to extinction.

Sadly there are only about 150 California condors alive, most of which are in captivity. In the early 1980s, scientists began capturing condors to protect them from extinction. Condors have been born under the watchful eye of scientists. A few have been released in the wild.

Write ABOUT IT

1. What is killing manatees today?
2. Why would it be important to track manatees and condors?

AT THE COMPUTER

Visit www.mhscience02.com to learn more about endangered animals.

A falcon puppet is used to feed orphan birds.

Animals Without Backbones

Vocabulary

cnidarian, B17

mollusk, B20

echinoderm, B20

endoskeleton, B20

arthropod, B21

exoskeleton, B21

Get Ready

How big are invertebrates? Some, like ants and earthworms, can fit in the palm of your hand. Others, like the octopus shown here, can grow much larger. Some are many meters wide! How else do you think invertebrates differ from one another?

Process Skills

You classify when you place things that share properties together in groups.

Explore Activity

What Are the Characteristics of Invertebrates?

Materials

living planarian

living earthworm

hand lens

petri dish

water

damp paper towel

toothpick

Procedure

BE CAREFUL! Be careful with live animals.

1. **Observe** Place the worm on the damp paper towel. Get a petri dish with a *planarian* (pluh·NAYR·ee·uhn) in it from your teacher. Observe each organism with a hand lens. Record your observations.

2. Gently touch the worm with your finger and the planarian with the toothpick. What do they do? Record your observations.

3. What characteristics of the praying mantis and magnified hydra do you observe? Record your observations.

Drawing Conclusions

1. **Define Based on Observations** What characteristics do you think invertebrates have? Make a list.

2. **Communicate** Compare your list with those of your classmates. Based on your observations, make a class list of invertebrate characteristics.

3. **Going Further: Classify** Think of other organisms that you would classify as invertebrates based on your observations. Make a list. Check your list as you continue this lesson.

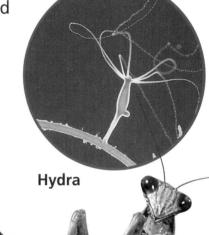

Hydra

Praying mantis

What Are Invertebrates Like?

Invertebrates come in a variety of shapes and sizes. The one thing that they have in common is the one thing that they lack—a backbone.

Classifying Invertebrates

How many different types of animals do you think there are in the world? Would you believe more than one million? Keeping track of them must be a BIG JOB! The first step is to classify them into groups. Animals can be classified into two large groups—vertebrates and invertebrates.

Nearly 95 out of every 100 animals are invertebrates. Invertebrates are divided into smaller groups based on their characteristics. Each group is called a *phylum* (FIGH·luhm). You will learn about eight invertebrate phyla in this lesson. *Phyla* is the plural of *phylum*.

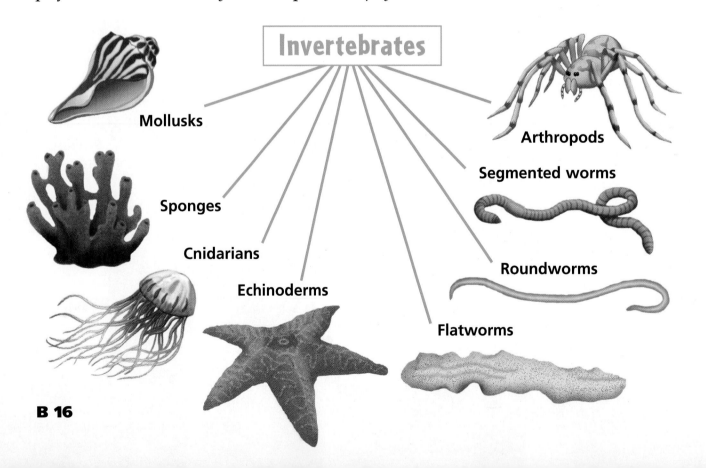

Invertebrates

Mollusks

Arthropods

Segmented worms

Sponges

Cnidarians

Roundworms

Echinoderms

Flatworms

A sea anemone's stingers don't hurt a clown fish. Slime on the clown fish's body protects it.

Sponges come in many shapes, sizes, and colors.

Sponges

Sponges are the simplest invertebrates. You've already seen a sponge on page B9. A sponge is shaped like a sack, with an opening at the top. Its body has no symmetry, is hollow, and does not have bones. It is made of two cell layers with a jellylike substance between the layers. A sponge can grow back a missing part.

Water flows into the sponge through holes in its body. The sponge filters the water for tiny scraps of food. Water and wastes move out through the opening at the top.

A young sponge moves until it finds a place to settle. An adult doesn't move from place to place.

Cnidarians

Imagine an animal that shoots poison darts at its enemies! **Cnidarians** (nigh·DAYR·ee·uhnz) are invertebrates that have poison stingers on tentacles. They use them to capture prey and for protection. Cnidarians, like sponges, have bodies that are two cell layers thick. Unlike sponges, they have simple tissues, a mouth, and radial symmetry.

There are three major cnidarian groups, or classes. The hydra is a member of one class. A hydra has a tube-shaped body and lives anchored to a surface. A jellyfish is a member of another class. It has a body shaped like an umbrella and floats freely in the water. Sea anemones and corals make up the third class. Groups of coral form coral reefs.

 **What are some simple invertebrates?**

How Are Worms Classified?

Flatworms

Worms are classified into several phyla. You will learn about three of these phyla.

A planarian is a type of flatworm. Flatworms are more complex than cnidarians or sponges, but they are the simplest worms. They have flat, ribbonlike bodies with a head and a tail. Their bodies have bilateral symmetry and are three cell layers thick.

One group of flatworms includes the planaria. Worms in this group live in fresh water and eat food with a mouth. Undigested food and wastes pass through the mouth, too. Another group includes parasites. They have no mouth or digestive system, and live and feed inside the bodies of other animals. They absorb digested food in the host's intestines.

An *Ascaris* can grow to 40 centimeters (16 inches) long. It can also lay up to 200,000 eggs a day!

Roundworms

Roundworms have a slender, rounded body with pointed ends. The *Ascaris* (AS·kuh·ruhs), hookworm, and vinegar eel are typical roundworms. Some roundworms, such as the *Ascaris* and hookworm, are parasites. They cause illness in people and other animals. About 2,500 species of roundworms are parasites of plants and animals. Others, such as the vinegar eel, do not depend on one particular organism for food or a place to live. They can live on land and in water.

Roundworms are more complex than flatworms. They have a one-way digestive system. In a one-way system, food comes into the body through one opening. Waste leaves through another opening at the opposite end of the animal's body.

A tapeworm is a parasite that can live in many host animals, including people!

Segmented Worms

Have you ever seen or touched an earthworm? Earthworms, sandworms, and leeches are in the phylum of segmented worms.

Segmented worms have bodies that are divided into sections called segments. They have a three-layer body and bilateral symmetry. They have a digestive system with two openings. Food enters through the mouth. Wastes leave through an opening at the other end of the body.

The best-known segmented worm is the earthworm. An earthworm has a head end and a tail end. Every segment of its body, except for the first and last, has four pairs of tiny bristles. These bristles help the earthworm move through the soil.

An earthworm has complex organ systems that keep it alive. Blood is pumped through blood vessels by five pairs of simple hearts. Nerves give the worm information about its surroundings.

▷ Why is an earthworm classified in a different group from a tapeworm?

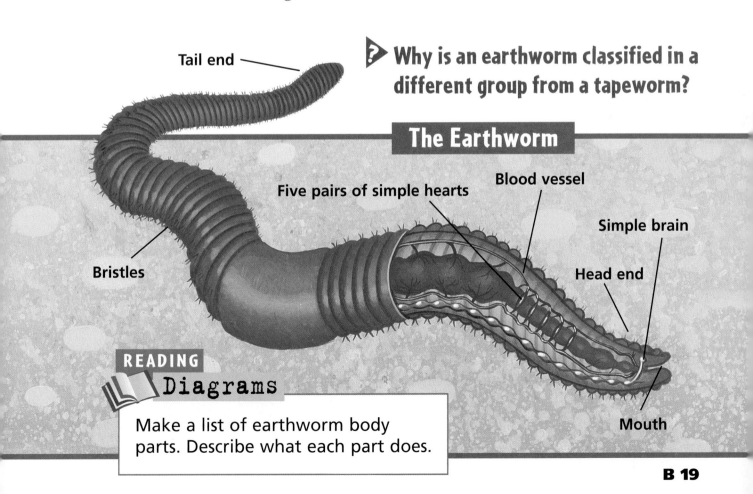

Tail end

The Earthworm

Blood vessel

Five pairs of simple hearts

Simple brain

Bristles

Head end

Mouth

READING Diagrams

Make a list of earthworm body parts. Describe what each part does.

What Are Some Other Invertebrates?

Mollusks

Do you have a seashell collection? Most seashells come from **mollusks** (MAHL·uhsks). Mollusks are soft-bodied invertebrates. Some, such as snails and slugs, live on land. Others, such as clams, oysters, and squids, live in water. Most mollusks have bilateral symmetry and many organ systems.

Mollusks have many different kinds of shells. Snail-like mollusks have one shell. Clamlike mollusks have two shells. The group that includes octopuses and squids has lost its shell.

Echinoderms

Have you ever seen a sea star? It is an **echinoderm** (i·KIGH·nuh·durm). Echinoderms are spiny-skinned animals. You can identify most echinoderms by their star design and spiny skin. Echinoderms include sea stars, sand dollars, sea cucumbers, and sea urchins.

Echinoderms have an internal supporting structure called an **endoskeleton** (en·doh·SKEL·i·tuhn). Usually the endoskeleton has many protective spines. Many echinoderms move and grab things with tiny tube feet. Each tube foot is powered by suction.

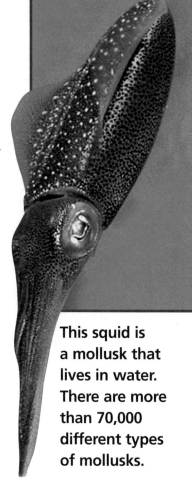

This squid is a mollusk that lives in water. There are more than 70,000 different types of mollusks.

The sea star uses its arms and tube feet to pry open the oyster. Then it turns its own stomach inside out. It sticks its stomach out to digest the oyster.

Arthropods

The largest invertebrate phylum is **arthropods** (AHR·thruh·pahdz). It is also the largest of all animal phyla. Arthropods live almost everywhere on Earth. Scientists think there are more than a million arthropod species!

Arthropods have jointed legs and a body that is divided into sections. Some arthropods breathe with gills. Others have an open-tube breathing system.

Arthropods have a hard skeleton on the outside of their bodies called an **exoskeleton** (ek·soh·SKEL·i·tuhn). It protects them and keeps them from drying out. Exoskeletons are made of a light but tough material called *chitin* (KIGH·tin). An exoskeleton does not grow, but is shed in a process called *molting*.

There are more arthropods than all other types of animals combined! You will learn about four main arthropod classes—arachnids (uh·RAK·nidz), centipedes and millipedes, crustaceans (krus·TAY·shuhnz), and insects.

▷ **What is the largest animal phylum?**

Scorpions feed on spiders and insects. Their sting can be dangerous to people and deadly to many small animals.

Arachnids

Include: Spiders, mites, scorpions, ticks, daddy-longlegs

Head: No antennae

Legs and Body: Four pairs of legs, two-section body, up to eight eyes

Home: A wide variety of habitats

Food: Most arachnids are hunters, mainly eating insects.

Special Features: Many arachnids are poisonous, including some spiders and scorpions. Some arachnids, such as spiders, can spin webs to trap their food.

Fact: Not all spiders are dangerous. Many are helpful to people. They eat insects and other pests.

B 21

What Are Some More Arthropod Groups?

Crustaceans

Include: Crabs, lobsters, shrimp, barnacles, crayfish, sow bugs

Head: Jawlike structures for crushing food and chewing; two pairs of antennae for sensing

Legs and Body: Ten or fewer legs, including claws. The body has sections.

Home: Some live in ocean or fresh water. A few live on land.

Food: Dead animal remains, seaweed, other leftovers

Special Features: Crabs and lobsters can have huge claws. One claw is often much bigger than the other. They use claws to fight and to scare off predators.

Facts: Many people enjoy eating shrimp, crabs, and lobsters. Crustaceans are also important foods for larger ocean animals.

Lobsters can live 50 years and grow to lengths of 60 centimeters (2 feet) or more.

Centipedes and Millipedes

Include: Centipedes, millipedes

Legs and Body: Centipedes: usually less than 100 legs. Millipedes: more than a hundred legs. Both have long, thin, segmented bodies.

Home: Under rocks, in rotting wood and other dark, damp places

Food: Centipedes eat worms, slugs, and insects. Millipedes eat plants.

How to Tell Them Apart: Centipedes have one pair of legs per segment and can move quickly. Millipedes have two pairs of legs per segment and move slowly.

Facts: Although *centi-* means "100," most centipedes have only 30 legs. Some have poison claws. A millipede's legs move in a wavelike motion.

Scolopendra (skah·luh·PEN·druh) centipedes can grow to a length of 30 centimeters (1 foot)!

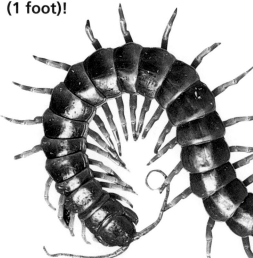

B 22

Insects

Include: Beetles, flies, bees, ants, mosquitoes, butterflies, dragonflies, fleas, termites, many others

Head: One pair of antennae

Legs and Body: Three pairs of legs; one or two pairs of wings; three body sections: head, thorax, abdomen

Home: Land, air, and fresh water

Food: Other animals and plants

Special Features: A special tube system for breathing; compound eyes made of hundreds of lenses

Facts: There are more different kinds of insects than there are all other kinds of animals. The first insects lived about 350 million years ago.

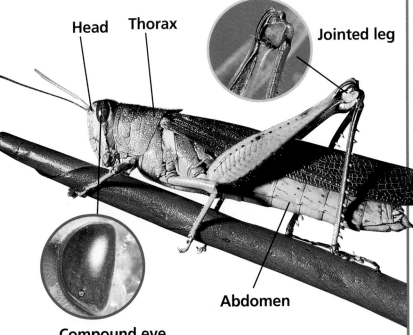

Head   Thorax   Jointed leg

Abdomen

Compound eye

READING Outline
What are three arthropod groups?

FOR SCHOOL OR HOME

Classifying Invertebrates

1. **Observe** Use clues in each picture to identify the type of invertebrate.

2. **Communicate** Make a table to show how you classified each picture. List key characteristics for each phylum.

3. How do you know the phylum that each animal belongs to?

What Invertebrates Live in Coral Reefs?

Imagine an animal that forms its own island! Corals do. Coral is made by colonies of polyps. Each polyp looks like a tiny sea anemone. For protection polyps build cup-shaped skeletons around their bodies. When polyps die, the skeletons remain. After many years they pile up. A coral reef or island forms.

Coral reefs contain invertebrates of almost every size and shape. A typical reef will have anemones, prawns, worms, lobsters, sea stars, jellyfish, and giant clams. Reefs also have more than 2,000 different kinds of fish—many with brilliant colors and unusual shapes. Coral reefs are among the richest communities on Earth.

Coral reefs are delicate. Coral needs warm, clean water to grow. Unfortunately, many coral reefs are threatened by pollution, souvenir hunters, ships, and boats. People take chunks of a coral reef as souvenirs. Ships crash into reefs. Small boats damage reefs with heavy anchors. It may take hundreds of years for the damaged reef to grow back.

What can we do to help protect coral reefs? We can stop pollution, boat carefully, not buy coral souvenirs, and learn more about reefs.

▷ **What types of invertebrates live in the Great Barrier Reef?**

The Great Barrier Reef, located near Australia, is about 2,000 kilometers (1,240 miles) long.

Why It Matters

Between 90 and 95 of every 100 animal species are invertebrates! Invertebrates are important because they are a food source for other animals. People also depend on them for many things. We eat clams, shrimp, and lobsters. Earthworms help enrich soil. This helps plants grow. Coral reefs protect islands and provide homes to animals. Water-absorbing sponges have many uses.

Even chitin is useful! Most people are not allergic to chitin. That is why it is often used to make contact lenses, artificial skin, and thread for stitches!

Think and Write

1. What is an invertebrate? How can you identify invertebrates?

2. How are segmented worms different from other worms?

3. What is an echinoderm? Give an example.

4. What threatens coral reefs? How can reefs be saved?

5. **Critical Thinking** How are all invertebrates alike? How are they different?

L·I·N·K·S

SOCIAL STUDIES LINK

Research a reef. Find the Great Barrier Reef on a map or a globe. Research what types of invertebrates make up the Great Barrier Reef.

ART LINK

Draw a picture. Draw a close-up picture of an invertebrate. Exchange pictures with a partner. Try to identify the animal and its phylum.

WRITING LINK

Write an expository paragraph. What if all invertebrates suddenly disappeared? How do you think this would affect life on Earth?

MATH LINK

Make a chart. Show the eight phyla of invertebrates. Give an example of an animal in each phylum.

TECHNOLOGY LINK

At the Computer Visit **www.mhscience02.com** for more links.

Animals with Backbones

Vocabulary

cold-blooded, B28

warm-blooded, B28

amphibian, B31

reptile, B32

mammal, B34

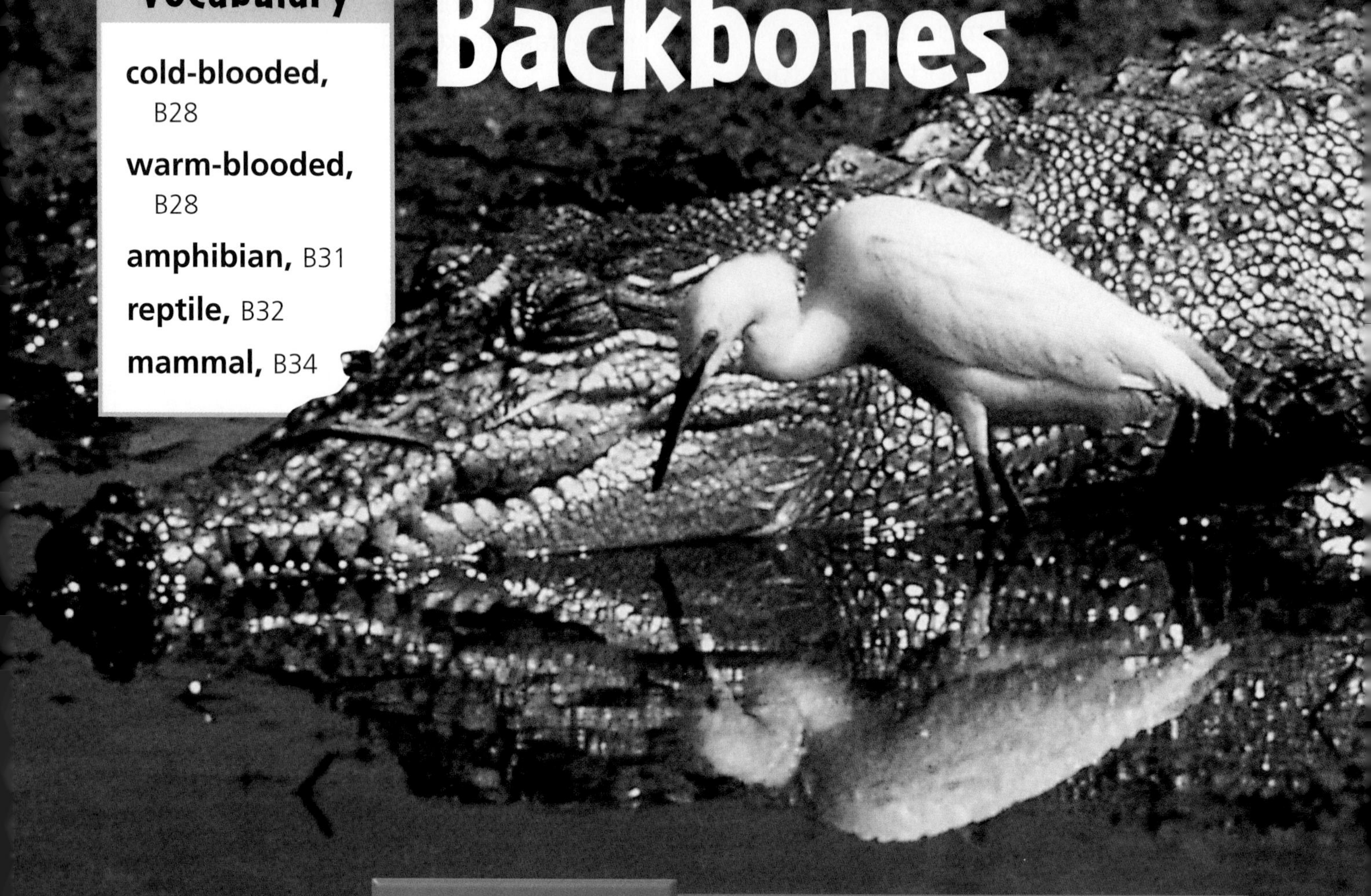

Get Ready

Did you know that you are classified into the same large group as fish, toads, snakes, birds, and rabbits? What could you all possibly have in common?

All these animals have a backbone. They are classified into a large group known as vertebrates. However, these animals are also very different from one another. These differences are used to make smaller groups.

Process Skill

You classify when you place things that share properties together in groups.

Explore Activity

What Are Vertebrates Like?

Procedure: Design Your Own

BE CAREFUL! Handle animals with care.

Observe As you observe each animal, look for answers to these questions. Record your observations. If you like, you can record sounds or take photographs to better observe these animals.

a. Where does it live—in water, on land, or both?

b. What color is it?

c. What kind of outer covering does it have?

d. What body parts does it have?

e. Do you see eyes, ears, nostrils, or other sense organs?

f. How does it move?

Drawing Conclusions

1 What major characteristics did you observe in each animal?

2 What are the main differences between a fish and a frog?

3 What are the major differences between a bird and a hamster?

4 **Going Further: Classify** Which animal in this activity are you most like? Why do you think so?

Materials

goldfish

frog

chameleon, turtle, or lizard

parakeet

hamster, gerbil, or guinea pig

hand lens

camera (optional)

tape recorder (optional)

Main Idea Having a backbone gives animals many advantages.

What Are Vertebrates Like?

Although vertebrates have very different characteristics, they all have a backbone that is part of their endoskeleton.

An endoskeleton has two important jobs. First, it supports the body. It also protects the soft inner organs.

Classifying Vertebrates

The animal kingdom is divided into many invertebrate phyla and one chordate phylum. Vertebrates are part of the chordate phylum.

Vertebrates are divided into the seven classes shown below. They are also classified by how they control body temperature.

Fish, amphibians, and reptiles are **cold-blooded**. A cold-blooded animal gets heat from outside its body. Its body temperature changes with the temperature of its surroundings.

Birds and mammals are **warm-blooded**. Their body temperature doesn't change much. They use the energy from food to keep a constant body temperature.

■ Cold-blooded
■ Warm-blooded

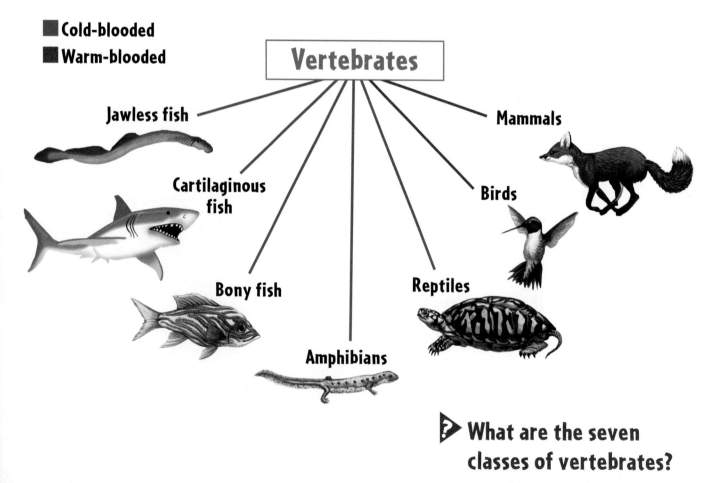

Vertebrates

Jawless fish

Cartilaginous fish

Bony fish

Amphibians

Mammals

Birds

Reptiles

▷ **What are the seven classes of vertebrates?**

What Do Fish Have in Common?

There are three classes of fish—jawless fish, *cartilaginous* (kahr·tuh·LAJ·uh·nuhs) *fish*, and bony fish. All fish have several characteristics.

- Fish are cold-blooded vertebrates that live in fresh or salt water.
- Fish have streamlined bodies and gills for breathing.
- Gills take oxygen out of water. They also get rid of carbon dioxide.

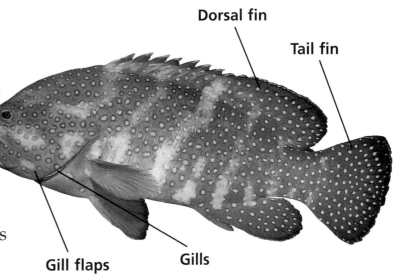

Dorsal fin

Tail fin

Gill flaps

Gills

A typical fish

▶ **In what ways are all fish alike?**

Jawless Fish

What do you notice about the eel-like animals shown here? They do not look much like other fish! These fish are jawless fish.

Jawless fish are soft and slimy. Instead of jaws they have powerful suckerlike mouths. A jawless fish uses its mouth to attach itself to another animal. It uses a horn tooth to cut a hole. Then it slowly sucks out the fluids and insides of the animal.

Jawless fish include lampreys and hagfish. These fish have no scales and unusual fins. Their bodies have a rubbery skeleton made of cartilage. Cartilage is a tough, flexible tissue. Your outer ears are made of cartilage.

Lampreys are jawless fish. Most lampreys live in fresh water.

What Other Kinds of Fish Are There?

Cartilaginous Fish

The major characteristic of a cartilaginous fish is a skeleton made entirely of cartilage. Cartilaginous fish also have movable jaws, fins, and tough, sandpaper-like skin.

These fish include rays, skates, and sharks. Sharks are keen hunters. They can smell blood in the water from many meters away. With their razor-sharp teeth, sharks can tear apart prey in seconds. Most sharks, however, do not attack people. They feed on small fish and invertebrates.

Bony Fish

Have you ever gone fishing? If you ever caught a fish, it most likely was a fish from this class. Bony fish are the largest vertebrate class. They have jaws and skeletons made of bone. More than 21,000 different kinds of bony fish swim both in the ocean and in fresh water.

What makes bony fish so successful? Tough, overlapping scales protect their skin. Gill flaps protect their gills. Fins help the fish steer in the water.

Bony fish have different body plans. Predator fish have sleek bodies and powerful muscles. Reef fish have box-shaped bodies that fit in small spaces. Bottom dwellers are flat. Eels have snakelike shapes to fit into tight spaces.

The cichlid (SIK·lid) fish keeps its eggs in its mouth until the fish hatch. What type of advantage does this give the young fish?

▷ **What is the largest vertebrate class?**

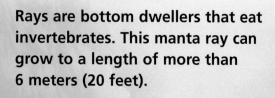

Rays are bottom dwellers that eat invertebrates. This manta ray can grow to a length of more than 6 meters (20 feet).

What Do Amphibians Have in Common?

Have you ever seen a frog, toad, or salamander? If you have, how would you describe it? Frogs, toads, and salamanders are **amphibians** (am·FIB·ee·uhnz). An amphibian is a cold-blooded vertebrate that spends part of its life in water and part of its life on land.

Amphibians start out their lives in the water. A tadpole is a young frog. It has gills and fins. It cannot live on land because it has no lungs or legs. Over time the tadpole turns into a frog. It loses its gills and breathes through lungs and its skin. It also loses its fins and grows legs.

Although adult frogs live mostly on land, they are never far from water. An amphibian's skin will dry out without water. That is why amphibians live in wet or damp places.

▷ **What are three examples of amphibians?**

Frog

Toad

Salamanders are also amphibians.

What Do Reptiles Have in Common?

Do you think that a snake has a slimy skin? Some people think that **reptiles** (REP·tuhlz) such as snakes are slimy. In fact, reptile skin is dry. Reptiles have skin with scales or larger plates. Strong, waterproof skin helped reptiles become the first vertebrate group to live on land.

Reptiles are cold-blooded animals with a backbone and an endoskeleton. They have several traits that help them live on land. They breathe with lungs. Their skin keeps water from escaping out of their body. Their eggs are tougher than amphibian eggs. All of these traits helped reptiles become successful on land.

Reptiles can be classified into four smaller groups, called orders. There are four main reptile orders—tuataras (tew·uh·TAHR·uhz), turtles, lizards and snakes, and alligators and crocodiles.

▶ **Do reptiles have slimy skin?**

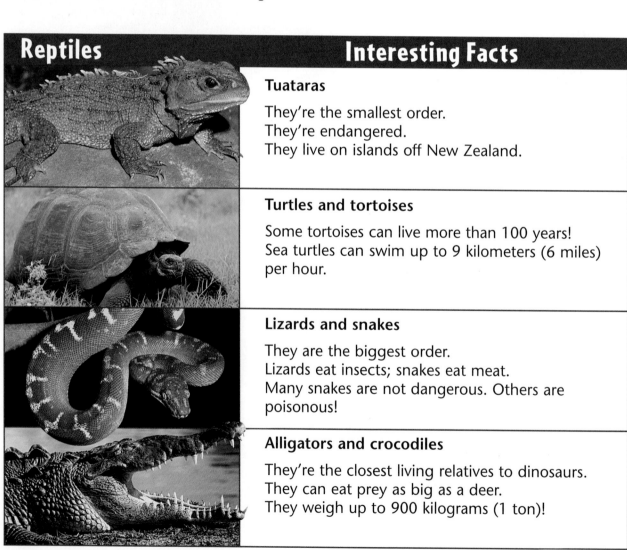

Reptiles	Interesting Facts
	Tuataras They're the smallest order. They're endangered. They live on islands off New Zealand.
	Turtles and tortoises Some tortoises can live more than 100 years! Sea turtles can swim up to 9 kilometers (6 miles) per hour.
	Lizards and snakes They are the biggest order. Lizards eat insects; snakes eat meat. Many snakes are not dangerous. Others are poisonous!
	Alligators and crocodiles They're the closest living relatives to dinosaurs. They can eat prey as big as a deer. They weigh up to 900 kilograms (1 ton)!

What Do Birds Have in Common?

Birds are vertebrates with several distinct characteristics. They have feathers. Feathers are light but very warm. They have beaks and no teeth. Birds have two legs with clawed feet. They have scales on their feet, like reptiles. Birds are warm-blooded like you. Unlike you, birds lay eggs with strong shells. Most birds sit on their eggs to keep them warm until they hatch. All birds have wings, and most birds can fly. Their bodies are designed for flight. Bird bones are light and thin. Bird lungs and flight muscles are powerful.

▶ **What is a bird?**

Birds	Interesting Facts
	**Swift** A swift flies very well. Some swifts spend almost all their lives in the air! Swifts have tiny, weak legs but strong feet. They eat insects with their short, wide beaks.
	Hawk A hawk has a strong, hooked beak and legs with sharp talons. These body parts help it catch and eat mice, snakes, and other small animals. Hawks live all over the world.
	Flamingo A flamingo's long legs and webbed feet help it wade in shallow water. To eat, it bends its long neck and fills its big beak with water. Then it filters the water for tiny pieces of food.
	Penguin A penguin cannot fly. On land it waddles on short, stocky legs. In water, however, it swims very well. Penguins live in cold places and eat fish or other water animals.
	Ostrich The ostrich is the largest living bird. Its eggs can weigh up to 30 grams (about 3 pounds)! Its powerful thighs and thick toes help it run quickly over grasslands.

What Do Mammals Have in Common?

Did you know that you are a **mammal** (MAM·uhl)? Mammals are the highest class of vertebrates. All mammals are warm-blooded and have hair. They can live in almost every kind of habitat. They can also learn! Female mammals produce milk to feed their young.

There are three basic groups of mammals.

Mammals That Lay Eggs

One group of mammals lays eggs. Only two members are alive today. They are the duckbilled platypus and the spiny anteater. Unlike most mammals, they have no teeth. The platypus has a muzzle like a duck's beak. The anteater has a tiny mouth with a sticky tongue.

The cheetah is the fastest animal on land.

A horse will rear on its back legs when startled. A horse kick can be deadly!

These platypus young hatched from eggs.

Although dolphins live underwater, they do not have gills. They come to the surface to breathe air.

Mammals with Pouches

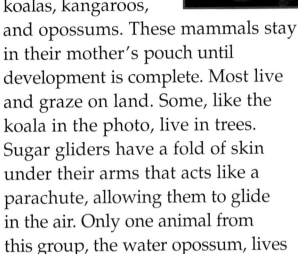

Another group of mammals has pouches. It includes koalas, kangaroos, and opossums. These mammals stay in their mother's pouch until development is complete. Most live and graze on land. Some, like the koala in the photo, live in trees. Sugar gliders have a fold of skin under their arms that acts like a parachute, allowing them to glide in the air. Only one animal from this group, the water opossum, lives in water.

Mammals That Develop Inside

The largest group of mammals contains those that develop inside their mothers' bodies. These mammals include cats, horses, whales, bats, mice, apes, and humans—just to name a few! Rabbits are born after 30 days. Rhinoceroses are born after over a year!

After the young are born, they need to stay close to their female parent for milk. Adults also may protect the young from danger. As the young grow, they are better able to take care of themselves.

READING Outline
What are the characteristics of the three groups of mammals?

QUICK LAB

FOR SCHOOL OR HOME

Classifying Vertebrates

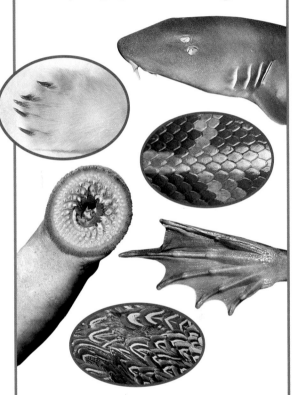

1. Classify Use the clues in each picture to help you classify each animal.

2. Communicate Make a table to show how you classified each picture.

3. How do you know which class each animal belongs to?

How Can Animals Help People?

Sometimes people have a disability, get ill, or become sad. When people have troubles, animals can often help.

The photograph below shows Duffy. Duffy is part of a program called Pet Partners. Every week Duffy and other Pet Partners go to hospitals and other places. Their job is to help people who are sick, sad, or lonely to feel better.

Specially trained dogs often help a person who is blind. These dogs wear a harness with a handle. The person holds onto the handle and lets the dog guide them safely.

People who use a wheelchair often have trained dogs to help them, too. The dogs can help pull the wheelchair when the person gets tired. They can fetch things the person needs, such as glasses or a book. They also give lots of love.

Certain types of monkeys are also trained to help disabled people. They can act as a second pair of hands for someone who has trouble doing things without help.

Duffy wears a special uniform. He has a blue harness and a special badge that says, "I am a visiting dog."

Many animals are raised for food, clothing, or other products. Cows, sheep, and even goats give milk that people drink or make into cheeses. People use the wool from animals like sheep, llamas, and alpacas to make yarns. The yarns are used to knit blankets and sweaters, or are woven into fabrics. Certain animals are eaten for food by people who choose to eat meat.

Can you think of other ways animals can help people? Can you think of some ways people can help animals?

▶ **Why do you think it is important to respect animals?**

L·I·N·K·S

Why It Matters

Most invertebrates are small. Many vertebrates are very large, like the rhinoceros, the great white shark, and the polar bear. This is no coincidence. Backbones and endoskeletons give animals support. This support allows vertebrates to grow to very large sizes. You can learn much more about animals on the Internet. Visit **www.mhscience02.com** to do a research project on animals.

Think and Write

1. How are vertebrates different from invertebrates?

2. What is the difference between the three types of fish?

3. How can a Pet Partner help people?

4. Compare the three groups of mammals.

5. **Critical Thinking** A newt looks like a lizard, but it is an amphibian. What traits must a newt have?

LITERATURE LINK

Read *Penguins: Birds That Swim* to learn more about these fascinating creatures. Write about how they are different from most birds and how they are like them.

MATH LINK

Solve a problem. The humpback whale can weigh up to 36 metric tons (40 tons). How many pounds is that? Now find out how much you weigh. How many times heavier than you is the heaviest humpback whale?

SOCIAL STUDIES LINK

Do research. What animals live in your neighborhood? Pick a completely different kind of place, and research what kinds of animals live there. Compare the two groups of animals. Could an animal in your neighborhood live in the other neighborhood?

TECHNOLOGY LINK

At the Computer Visit **www.mhscience02.com** for more links.

Spider Giants

What's that creeping through the South American jungle? It's a Goliath bird-eating spider, the world's biggest tarantula. It's big enough to cover a dinner plate! It eats not only birds, but lizards, mice, and other small animals.

A Goliath does not spin a web to catch its prey. Instead, it pounces on its victim and bites it with poisonous fangs. The poison kills the animal and softens its insides. The spider then sucks the juices out of the dead animal's body.

A Goliath uses its body hairs to sense movements nearby. The hairs also aid in defense. When attacked, a Goliath shoots out hairs from its stomach. The hairs can stick to an attacker and irritate its skin.

There are more than 800 different kinds of tarantulas in the world. Luckily, they're not all as big as the Goliath!

Close-up look at a Goliath's fangs

Write ABOUT IT

1. How does a Goliath spider kill its prey?
2. How does a Goliath spider defend itself?

This Goliath bird spider is from South America.

AT THE COMPUTER

Visit www.mhscience02.com to learn more about spiders and other animals of South America.

Chapter 3 Review

Vocabulary

Fill each blank with the best word or words from the list.

amphibian, B31   **mollusk,** B20

arthropod, B21   **reptile,** B32

cold-blooded, B28   **vertebrate,** B8

endoskeleton, B20   **warm-blooded,**
B28

exoskeleton, B21

invertebrate, B8

1. An animal that has a constant body temperature is called
_____.

2. One example of a soft-bodied invertebrate is a(n) _____.

3. An animal with a backbone is called a(n) _____.

4. A cold-blooded vertebrate that lives on land and in water is a(n) _____.

5. The hard covering that protects an invertebrate's body is a(n) _____.

Use the words in the vocabulary list to describe these animals. Some words may be used more than once.

6. _____
7. _____
8. _____

9. _____
10. _____
11. _____

Test Prep

12. One reason mammals are different from reptiles is because mammals _____.

A have a backbone

B are warm-blooded

C are cold-blooded

D do not live in water

13. All birds are able to _____.

F swim

G fly

H eat seeds

J lay eggs

14. Which of these animals is a vertebrate?

 A octopus

 B snake

 C snail

 D coral

15. Which of these animals is an arthropod?

 F turtle

 G frog

 H sponge

 J ant

16. The body of a starfish has _____.

 A radial symmetry

 B spherical symmetry

 C bilateral symmetry

 D no symmetry

Concepts and Skills

17. **Reading in Science** Explain the difference between a food chain and a food web.

18. **Product Ads** The Happy Pet Company wants you to design a terrarium for iguanas. What would you put in the terrarium, and why?

19. **Scientific Methods** What if you discovered two animals that you had never seen before? They look very different but are similar in many ways. How could you tell if they were in the same phylum? Write down all the different ways you would compare and contrast them.

20. **Critical Thinking** All very large invertebrates, such as the octopus, live underwater. Explain why these large invertebrates could not live on land.

21. **Process Skills: Observe** Look at the pictures of the animals in this chapter. Make a chart that shows the classification of ten different animals. Choose animals from different phyla.

Boost *your test scores!*

Be Smart! Visit www.mhscience02.com to learn more.

CHAPTER
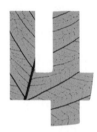
4

LESSON 4

Organ Systems, B44

LESSON 5

Development and
Reproduction, B54

LESSON 6

Animal Survival, B64

Life Processes

Did You Ever Wonder?

Does the tomato frog actually eat tomatoes?
No. It feasts primarily on invertebrates in
the wild. In captivity it feeds mainly on
crickets. Tomato frogs live in swampy areas
of Madagascar. When tomato frogs are
younger, they have yellow backs and dark
legs. How do living things function?

Organ Systems

Vocabulary

circulatory
  system, B46

respiratory
  system, B47

excretory
  system, B47

digestive
  system, B49

nervous
  system, B50

skeletal system,
  B52

muscular
  system, B52

Get Ready

How do a fish and a frog compare? Think about their bodies and where they live. A frog breathes with lungs instead of gills. It has limbs instead of fins. It can live both on land and in water. Do you think a frog has organs and organ systems that are more complex than a fish's?

Process Skill

You observe when you use one or more senses to identify or learn about an object or event.

B 44

Explore Activity

How Does Blood Travel in Fish and Amphibian Hearts?

Procedure

1. Label each small cup "atrium." Label each large cup "ventricle."

2. **Make a Model: Fish Heart** Tape the paper circle with one flap over the top of one ventricle. Center the top of an atrium over the flap in the circle. Tape it to the paper.

3. Label one straw "From gills and body." Place it in the hole in the bottom of the atrium. Label another straw "To gills and body." Place it in the hole in the bottom of the ventricle. Draw the model.

4. **Make a Model: Amphibian Heart** Tape the paper circle with two flaps over the top of a ventricle. Center the top of an atrium over each flap. Tape the cups to the paper.

5. Label one straw "From body." Place it in the hole in the bottom of the right cup. Label another straw "From lungs." Place it in the hole in the bottom of the left cup. Label the third straw "To lungs and body." Place it in the hole in the paper between the two small cups. Draw the model.

Drawing Conclusions

Going Further: Observe How are the fish heart and the amphibian heart alike? Different?

Materials

5 straws

two 7-oz cups, each with a hole in the bottom

three $3\frac{1}{2}$-oz cups, each with a hole in the bottom

2 paper circles with flaps

5 labels

marking pen

tape

Model fish heart

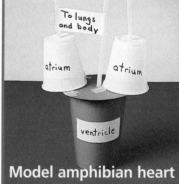
Model amphibian heart

How Do Blood and Air Travel?

Blood is a liquid tissue. Blood carries food, oxygen, and water to the body's cells and removes wastes from cells.

The heart is the main organ that makes up the **circulatory system** (SUR·kyuh·luh·tawr·ee SIS·tuhm). Its job is to move blood through the body.

Sponges and cnidarians don't have a circulatory system. Materials move in and out of each thin body layer. Insects and other invertebrates have open circulatory systems. The heart bathes tissues in blood, which slowly drains back to the heart.

All vertebrates have a closed circulatory system. So do some invertebrates, such as earthworms. Blood travels through tubes called blood vessels.

A fish heart has two parts, or chambers. It allows blood carrying wastes and oxygen to mix. An amphibian heart has three chambers.

Mammals have hearts with four chambers, like the one shown below. They do not allow blood carrying waste gas, colored blue, to mix with blood carrying oxygen, colored red.

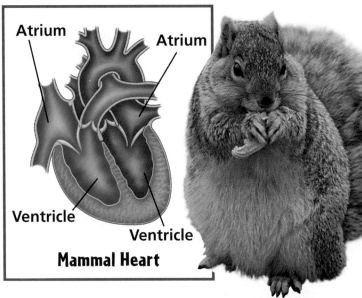

Atrium   Atrium

Ventricle   Ventricle

Mammal Heart

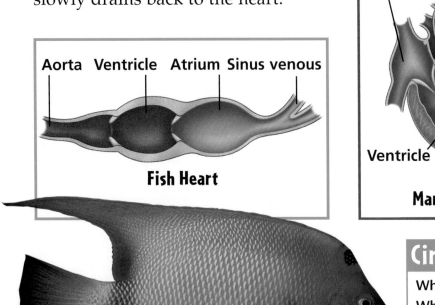

Aorta Ventricle Atrium Sinus venous

Fish Heart

Circulatory System Facts

What: Heart, blood, blood vessels

Where: Throughout body

Jobs: Bring food, water, and oxygen to cells; remove waste

Who has it: All but sponges, cnidarians

Types: Open (many invertebrates), closed (vertebrates)

How Animals Get Oxygen

Cells need the oxygen carried by blood to get energy from food. The **respiratory system** (RES·puhr·uh·tawr·ee SIS·tuhm) brings oxygen to the blood and removes the waste gas carbon dioxide.

Most invertebrates don't have a specialized respiratory system at all. Their bodies usually are small. Gases can easily move in and out of tissues, even through their skin. An insect's exoskeleton has holes connected to tubes. These bring oxygen to different tissues.

Larger, more complex animals need a respiratory system. Each has one well designed for its body and where it lives. Fish and young amphibians have gills that exchange gases with the water. Adult amphibians breathe through both their skin and lungs.

How Liquid Wastes Leave the Body

Liquid wastes, created when cells break down chemicals, are removed by the **excretory system** (EK·skri·tawr·ee SIS·tuhm). Simple animals have simple systems. More complex animals, such as reptiles and humans, have two waste-removal organs called *kidneys* (KID·neez). They filter wastes from blood. The liquid waste is stored in the *bladder*, and then leaves the body.

Like many other small animals, earthworms take in air directly through their skin.

Respiratory System Facts

What: Lungs, gills, skin
Where: Open to outer air
Jobs: Bring oxygen into body, remove waste gases from body
Who has it: Vertebrates, large invertebrates, insects
Works with: The circulatory system to move gases in and out

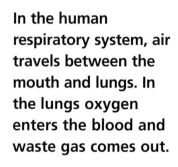

Air in

Lungs

In the human respiratory system, air travels between the mouth and lungs. In the lungs oxygen enters the blood and waste gas comes out.

▷ **What does blood do?**

Human Respiratory System

How Do Animals Take In and Digest Food?

Unlike plants, which make their own food, all animals must take in food for the energy they need to survive. The ways animals get food depend on their bodies and where they live.

An octopus and squid both have bodies made up of a head and tentacles. They use their tentacles to capture and kill the animals they eat.

A sea star has arms lined with tube feet. The tube feet provide powerful suction to move the sea star and pry open clam and mussel shells. The sea star then turns its stomach inside out between the open shells to break down and eat the animal inside.

Birds use their beaks to eat food. Some birds eat only seeds and fruits they pluck from trees and shrubs. Other birds eat meat. They use strong claws to catch and hold onto their food, which they tear into pieces with their beaks. Many meat-eating birds pluck fish out of the water, other birds from the air, or animals from the ground. Then they fly to a safe place to eat.

Lobsters and crabs have claws, too. Although they are different in shape from bird claws, they also are used to capture and hold foods.

Many frogs and lizards use long, sticky tongues to catch insects and other small animals. Many can move their tongues so fast you can hardly see it happen!

An osprey uses its strong claws to catch and hold onto a fish.

Claws help a crab capture a sea urchin.

Gotcha! The toad has used its sticky tongue to catch its next meal.

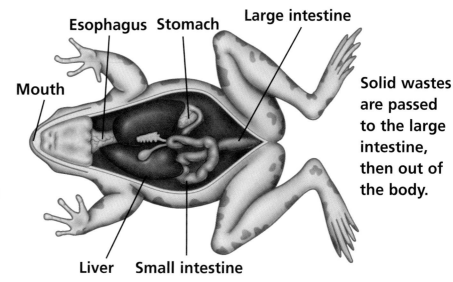

Frog's Digestive System

Esophagus   Stomach   Large intestine

Mouth

Food passes through the parts shown here. The stomach churns and mixes food. The liver adds chemicals to the small intestine, where food is broken down further and absorbed. Solid wastes pass through the large intestine and out of the body.

Solid wastes are passed to the large intestine, then out of the body.

Liver   Small intestine

Before body cells can use food for energy, it must be broken down. That is the job of the **digestive system** (di·JES·tiv SIS·tuhm).

In simple animals like sponges and cnidarians, cells along the body walls break down food into small particles. These cells transfer the particles to cells in the body.

Other simple invertebrates, like some flatworms, have a digestive system with one opening. Food enters through the mouth. Wastes and undigested food leave through the same opening.

A segmented worm has a digestive system with two openings. Food enters through the mouth. Wastes exit through the other end of the body.

Birds do not chew food. A muscular organ called a *gizzard* (GIZ·uhrd) stores pebbles that grind

food before it enters the rest of the system.

A frog's digestive system is even more complex. Study the diagram. How does a frog take in and digest its food?

Digestive System Facts

What: Teeth, saliva, esophagus, stomach, intestines, liver, glands
Where: Hollow tube through body
Job: Break down food
How: Chewing, grinding, squeezing, chemicals
Types: One or two openings
Who has it: Vertebrates, most invertebrates
Works with: Circulatory system

READING **Main Idea and Supporting Details What is the digestive system? What are some of its parts?**

How Do Animals Sense Changes?

How do animals sense changes in their world and control their organ systems? The **nervous system** (NUR·vuhs SIS·tuhm) is the body's master control system. A nervous system is made of nerve cells joined to form nerves. More complex animals have a brain and some or all of the senses—sight, taste, hearing, touch, and smell.

Simple animals have simple nervous systems. More complicated animals have more complicated nervous systems. Vertebrates have the most complex nervous systems.

The structure of an animal's nervous system relates to its lifestyle. Compare the parts of the brain related to the senses of sight and smell in these three organisms.

Comparing Animal Brains

Shark Brain

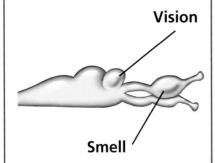

Vision

Smell

The shark has a keen sense of smell and poor eyesight. Brain parts related to smell are large in the shark brain.

Frog Brain

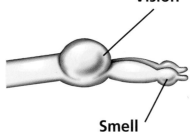

Vision

Smell

The frog relies on eyesight to catch prey. The visual part of the brain in the frog is larger than the part used for smell.

Human Brain

Vision

Thinking

Smell

In humans the region for vision is larger than that for smell. There is a large and developed region for thinking and memory.

Nervous System Facts

What: Nerve cells, spinal cord, brain

Where: Body network

Jobs: Control the senses; control muscles, breathing, heart rate, and many other body functions

Who has it: Vertebrates and almost all invertebrates

Special Sense Organs

Many animals have specialized sense organs that collect information about their surroundings. For example, a bat makes a series of clicking sounds, then listens for echo patterns when the clicks bounce off objects. Using echoes, it can find prey in the dark.

A snake's forked tongue collects tiny odor particles. These particles tell where prey or enemies are. The pictures show two more sense organs.

Lateral line

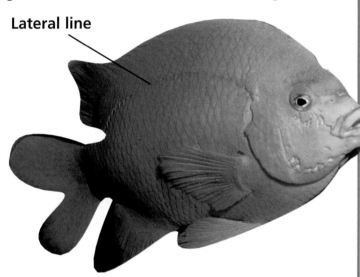

Cells along a fish's lateral line have tiny hairs. Waves in the water move the hairs. This helps the fish detect prey or enemies.

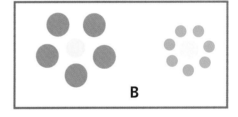

An insect eye has many lenses. Insects see light and movement in several directions, but not a clear image.

QUICK LAB

FOR SCHOOL OR HOME

Fool Your Senses

1. **Observe** Look at drawing A. What do you see?

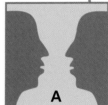

A

2. **Observe** Study the center circles in drawing B. Which is larger?

B

3. **Measure** Measure each center circle. Which is larger?

4. **Infer** Can your eyes fool you? Explain.

▷ **Why are sense organs important for an animal's survival?**

How Do Animals Move?

A vertebrate's bones form its **skeletal system** (SKEL·i·tuhl SIS·tuhm). Bones are living tissues. Minerals make bones hard. The skeletal system supports the body and protects body organs. It works with the **muscular system** (MUS·kyuh·luhr SIS·tum) to allow a vertebrate to move. The muscular system is made of the body's muscles. Muscles are tough tissues that can move.

How do invertebrates move? Almost all invertebrates that can move have some kind of muscle tissue. Muscles in an earthworm shorten and stretch to move the body.

In vertebrates muscles produce movement by shortening and

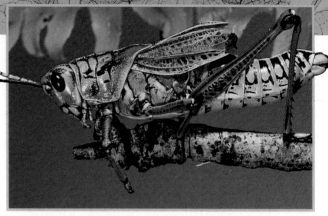

Muscles work in pairs to bend a joint, such as the joint in the middle of a grasshopper's leg. When one muscle shortens, it pulls on the joint. The other muscle in the pair relaxes and gets longer.

pulling on bones. Vertebrates use bones and muscles together to move in different ways. Powerful muscles allow a fish to wriggle back and forth as it swims. A snake uses its muscles to slither along. Its bones are designed to wriggle as its muscles shorten and relax.

Birds have powerful muscles in their chests. Some use them to fly at incredible speeds. A racing pigeon can fly at speeds of 177 kilometers (110 miles) per hour.

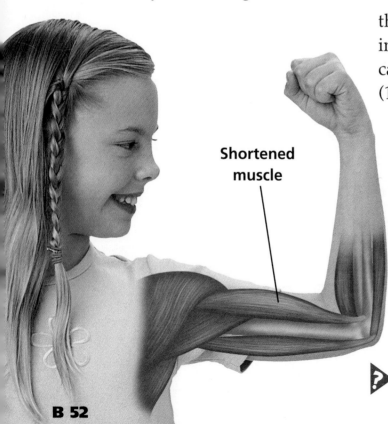

Shortened muscle

Muscular and Skeletal Systems Facts

What: Bones, muscles, cartilage
Where: Entire body
Jobs: Support, protect, move
Types: Exoskeleton and endoskeleton
Who has it: Vertebrates and some invertebrates
Works with: Nervous system

▶ **What do bones and muscles do?**

L·I·N·K·S

Why It Matters

Everything you do depends on organ systems. Think what happens when you kick a ball. Your nervous system sees the ball and sends a message to kick. Your circulatory system moves food and oxygen from your digestive and respiratory systems to your foot. Then your skeletal and muscular systems kick the ball! Stay healthy, and your body will keep working for you.

Think and Write

1. Name and describe the function of seven body systems. Which system controls all of the others?

2. Compare open and closed circulatory systems.

3. Describe three different ways that animals take in food.

4. Compare senses in three different animals.

5. **Critical Thinking** How are body systems different from one animal group to another? Which animals have simple body systems? More complex systems?

WRITING LINK

Write a paragraph. What if you could shrink to take a tour of one of your body systems? Describe which system you would choose and why.

ART LINK

Draw a picture. Describe what your tour of one of your body systems would be like. Draw pictures to add to your description.

MATH LINK

Measure your exercise. Work with a partner. Count how many times each of you breathes while you rest in a chair for a minute. Then take turns doing jumping jacks or running for one minute. Time your breathing again. Compare your results.

TECHNOLOGY LINK

Science Newsroom CD-ROM Choose *At Arm's Length* to learn more about how your muscles work.

At the Computer Visit **www.mhscience02.com** for more links.

Development and Reproduction

Vocabulary

metamorphosis, B56

life cycle, B58

life span, B59

reproduction, B60

heredity, B62

Get Ready

What do you observe about these kittens? They have fur of different colors and patterns. However, they all have the same body size and shape. How do you think they will change as they grow?

Process Skill

You infer when you form an idea from facts or observations.

Explore Activity

How Do Mealworms Change As They Grow?

Materials

jars containing food and mealworms in different stages of development

3 hand lenses

3 rulers

Procedure: Design Your Own

BE CAREFUL! Handle animals with care.

1. As a group, choose a Mealworm Observation Station that your teacher has set up. Each station has three jars labeled A, B, and C.

2. **Observe** Break into smaller groups. Each small group should observe the animals in one jar. Record your observations. Share your observations with the other members of your larger group.

3. Record any questions you have about mealworms and how they change and grow. How could you find the answers?

4. **Experiment** Design simple experiments to find out more about the mealworms. Do they prefer light or dark places? Damp or dry places?

5. **Observe** Make observations of the animals every few days. Record your observations.

Drawing Conclusions

1. **Communicate** Describe the stages of mealworm development.

2. Use your drawings to arrange the stages in the order in which you think mealworms develop.

3. **Going Further: Infer** How does the way a mealworm grows differ from how other animals like cats and dogs grow?

Main Idea Animals develop and reproduce in many different ways.

What Is Metamorphosis?

Most young animals look like smaller copies of their parents. Puppies look like small dogs. Chicks look like small birds. They grow larger as they grow older. However, other young animals don't look like their parents at all.

Certain animals, like mealworms, go through big changes during their development. This process is called **metamorphosis** (met·uh·MAWR·fuh·sis), meaning "a change in body form." There are two types of metamorphosis— complete and incomplete. Insects such as mealworms and butterflies go through complete metamorphosis.

Complete Metamorphosis

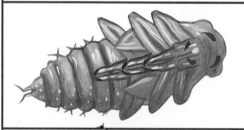

1 Egg Stage
An adult mealworm is known as a grain beetle. After mating, a female grain beetle lays eggs.

2 Larva Stage
A wormlike *larva* (LAHR·vuh) hatches from each egg. A larva is a young organism with a form different from its parents. After hatching, a larva begins to eat.

3 Pupa Stage
A larva becomes a *pupa* (PYEW·puh). Many changes take place in this stage. Adult tissues and organs form.

4 Adult Stage
An adult grain beetle is completely unlike its larva. It has a smooth body, wings, and six legs.

Insects such as grasshoppers, termites, and damselflies go through incomplete metamorphosis. Metamorphosis allows animals to specialize. Larvae and nymphs specialize in eating and growing. Adult animals specialize in breeding. They come to a new environment where their eggs have a better chance of surviving.

▶ **How do nymphs differ from larvae?**

Metamorphosis

Complete stages	Incomplete stages
1. Egg 2. Larva 3. Pupa 4. Adult	1. Egg 2. Nymph 3. Adult
Time: several weeks	**Time** up to 2 years
Who does it: wasps, ants, bees, flies, beetles, fleas, butterflies, moths	**Who does it:** bugs, mayflies, dragonflies, grasshoppers, cockroaches, termites

Incomplete Metamorphosis

3 Adult Stage
The damselfly nymph molts several times until it becomes an adult.

2 Nymph Stage
The young damselfly, called a *nymph* (NIMF), hatches from an egg. A nymph is a young insect that looks like an adult. The damselfly *nymph* lives in water and has gills. After many weeks it comes out of the water. Soon it sheds its skin, or molts. Small wings appear.

1 Egg Stage
A female damselfly lays her eggs on a reed underwater.

READING
Diagrams

How do mealworms and damselflies change as they grow?

How Do Animals Reproduce?

The life cycle of every animal includes **reproduction** (ree·pruh·DUK·shuhn), the making of offspring. There are different ways animals can reproduce.

Budding and Regeneration

Simple invertebrates, like sponges and cnidarians, can reproduce by *budding*. A bud forms on the adult's body. It slowly develops into a new animal. After some time the bud breaks off. Each animal then continues its own life cycle.

In *regeneration* (ri·jen·uh·RAY·shuhn), a whole animal develops from just a part of the original animal. Sponges and planaria reproduce through regeneration.

Both budding and regeneration produce *clones*. A clone is an exact copy of its parent. Its traits, or characteristics, are identical to the traits of its parent.

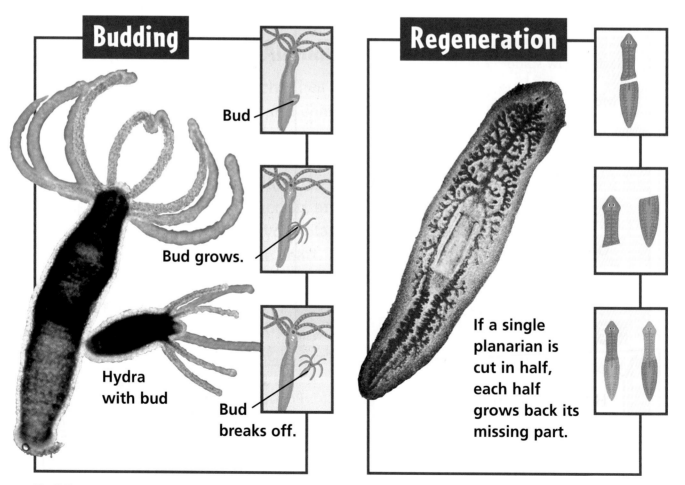

Budding

Bud

Bud grows.

Hydra with bud

Bud breaks off.

Regeneration

If a single planarian is cut in half, each half grows back its missing part.

Turtles are reptiles that lay eggs in protective shells. When an egg cell joins with a sperm cell, fertilization takes place. This produces a new organism.

Fertilization

Another type of reproduction requires cells from two parents. The female cell is called an egg. The male cell is called a *sperm*. Their offspring are not clones. They are similar to their parents but not identical. These offspring are new individuals. They have traits from both parents.

Do you think an egg can become a new organism by itself? In most cases it cannot. Neither can a sperm. To reproduce, an egg and a sperm join. This joining is called *fertilization* (fur·tuh·luh·ZAY·shuhn). This produces a developing animal called an *embryo* (EM·bree·oh). An embryo can grow to become a new organism, with traits from both parents.

Some animals lay eggs. Egg-laying animals include most invertebrates, reptiles, amphibians, birds, fish, and a very few mammals. In most cases the embryo grows inside a protective shell. The embryo uses stored food in the egg to develop. After maturing, the offspring hatches into a newborn animal.

All but a few mammals give birth to live young. One mammal that lays eggs is the platypus.

READING Main Idea
What are three ways that animals reproduce?

Comparing Reproduction

	Budding and Regeneration	Fertilization
Parents	1	2
Male and female	no	yes
Clones	yes	no
Offspring traits	same as parent	mixed
Egg and sperm	no	yes

QUICK LAB

FOR SCHOOL OR HOME

Heredity Cards

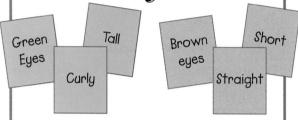

Green Eyes Tall Curly Brown eyes Short Straight

1. Cut three cards from each paper. Pink cards represent the female, blue cards the male.

2. Write a trait for "Hair," "Eye color," and "Height" on one set of cards. Make sure the traits on the other set are different.

3. Match cards to make "offspring." Each offspring needs one card for each trait.

4. Continue matching cards to create offspring. Give each a number. Record the traits in a table.

5. **Observe** How many different offspring did you get?

6. **Predict** How many offspring would you get with eight cards?

How Are Traits Passed to Offspring?

The passing of traits from parent to offspring is called **heredity** (huh·RED·i·tee). Offspring inherit traits from both parents.

When an egg and a sperm join, the traits they carry are mixed like a deck of cards. The offspring ends up with a mixture of traits. Some traits come from the father. Other traits come from the mother.

Farmers learned long ago that they could choose and mate, or breed, animals with desirable traits. They bred sheep with longer hair or corn with many juicy ears on one stalk.

▶ **How do farmers use heredity?**

A cow raised for its milk

A sheep bred for longer, thicker hair

L·I·N·K·S

Why It Matters

Where are you in your life cycle right now? You are probably in the childhood stage. In a few years, you'll reach adolescence, then adulthood. What challenges lie ahead for you? What dangers and opportunities? Knowing about life cycles can help you identify some of the problems that lie ahead and plan for a better future. What plans do you have for your adolescent years? What can you do now to help you achieve your goals?

Think and Write

1. What is the difference between a life cycle and a life span?

2. Compare complete and incomplete metamorphosis.

3. What is heredity?

4. How is budding different from fertilization?

5. **Critical Thinking** Do you think that animals should be bred to develop specific traits? Why or why not?

WRITING LINK

Write a plan. What would you like to accomplish in your adult years? Why? Write a plan for how you would like to achieve your goals.

ART LINK

Make a collage. Find pictures of animals and their young. Clip them from magazines, or copy them from books or the Internet. Arrange the pictures into a collage. Add words to explain how young compare with their parents.

HEALTH LINK

Write a paragraph. The average human life span has increased a lot since the 1800s. Back then, it was only 35 or 40 years. Why do you think people now live twice as long? List some reasons.

TECHNOLOGY LINK

Science Newsroom CD-ROM Choose *Don't Bug Me* to learn how to tell butterflies and moths apart.

At the Computer Visit **www.mhscience02.com** for more links.

Animal Survival

Vocabulary

camouflage, B66

adaptation, B66

mimicry, B68

inherited behavior, B70

instinct, B70

learned behavior, B71

Get Ready

Have you ever played hide-and-seek? Where did you hide? How did you cover yourself up? The insect in this picture is also hiding. Why might larger animals have trouble seeing it?

Process Skill

You predict when you state possible results from an event or experiment.

Explore Activity

How Can Body Color Help an Animal Survive?

Materials

colored toothpicks

plastic bag or shoe box

label or piece of masking tape

marking pen

Procedure

1. Label your bag or box with your name. This is your "nest." Use it to hold all the toothpick "worms" that you collect.

2. **Observe** Follow the rules given by your teacher to capture the worms. Record the rules. Also record any observations that you make while collecting the worms.

3. **Communicate** When you are done, record your results in a bar graph like the one shown.

Drawing Conclusions

1. Which color worms were easiest to see? Why?

2. Which color worms were hardest to see? Why?

3. If you were to become a toothpick worm, what color would you want to be? Why?

4. **Going further: Predict** Colors help certain animals blend in with their surroundings. Why do you think some animals have bright colors? How could you find out?

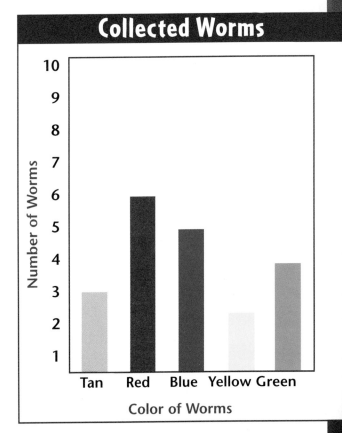

Collected Worms

Number of Worms (vertical axis: 1–10)

Color of Worms: Tan, Red, Blue, Yellow, Green

What Are Adaptations?

An animal's color can help it blend into its surroundings. Blending due to color is called **camouflage** (KAM·uh·flahzh).

In the early 1800s, dark peppered moths were rare in England. Light moths were common. Then factories polluted England's air in the late 1800s. Suddenly dark moths outnumbered light moths.

Why do you think that happened? Dark moths stood out on light-colored trees. Birds could spot them

You can see the leaf mimic among dark-colored leaves, but in nature the insect is the same color as the leaves.

easily and ate them. Then pollution slowly darkened the trees. The light moths stood out and were eaten.

Look at the picture above. That isn't a leaf—it's an insect! Its body resembles its environment very closely. This is *protective resemblance* (pruh·TEK·tiv ri·ZEM·bluhns). The fact that an animal resembles something else protects it.

Camouflage and protective resemblance are examples of **adaptations** (ad·uhp·TAY·shuhnz). Adaptations are traits that help organisms survive.

Light and dark peppered moths.

Body adaptations are called physical adaptations. Physical adaptations help animals survive in their environments. Here are just a few physical adaptations.

- **Gills and Fins** They allow fish to breathe and swim underwater.

- **Fur** Thick white fur helps a polar bear blend in with its snowy home. It also keeps the bear warm.

- **Legs** The long legs of the horse help it run fast.

- **Neck** A giraffe's long legs and neck allow it to reach leaves high up in trees, where other animals can't reach.

- **Shell** A hard outer shell protects a turtle's soft body parts.

- **Trunk** A trunk helps an elephant grasp things, and feed itself.

- **Bright Color** The bright red body of a male cardinal helps it attract a mate. In other animals bright colors tell predators to stay away. They have learned the animal is poisonous!

Animal adaptations happen naturally. The peppered moths didn't choose to be dark or light. The birds simply ate the light-colored moths because they were easier to see on the dark trees. Only an adaptation that helps an animal survive is likely to become common.

This giraffe can reach leaves high up in trees.

READING Main Idea
What are three animal adaptations?

What Is Mimicry?

Monarch butterflies have an important adaptation that helps them survive—they don't taste good. Predators spit out monarch butterflies if they eat them. Monarch butterfly bodies contain a poison that they get from feeding on the milkweed plant.

Most predators stay away from monarch butterflies. They recognize the bold, bright coloring. Predators also stay away from the viceroy butterfly. The viceroy is not poisonous, nor does it taste bad. However, it looks very similar to the monarch. Most predators won't take a chance eating it.

The viceroy butterfly is protected by **mimicry** (MIM·i·kree). Mimicry occurs when one organism imitates another. What advantage does mimicry give animals?

How did the viceroy come to resemble the bad-tasting monarch? At one time there probably was a variety of viceroy butterflies. The ones that looked like monarchs survived. The ones that looked less like monarchs got eaten. As time passed, the viceroys that looked more and more like monarchs survived.

▶ **How does mimicry help the viceroy butterfly survive?**

Viceroy butterfly

Monarch butterfly

Process Skill
B U I L D E R

How Do Adaptations Help an Animal Survive?

Every science experiment begins with a hypothesis. A hypothesis is a statement you can test. "Dogs like big bones best" is a hypothesis. You could test this hypothesis by giving dogs different-sized bones.

In this activity you will design two different kinds of animals— a super predator and an animal that is skilled at avoiding predators. Then form a hypothesis about how their adaptations would help each animal in different situations.

Procedure

1. What traits should your predator have? Record them. Describe how these traits would help the animal.

2. Do the same for your avoider animal.

3. **Communicate** Make a table like the one shown for each animal. Fill in each category that applies. Add any extra categories that you need.

4. **Make a Model** Make models or colored drawings of your animals. Label all the features of your animals. Tell how they function.

5. **Form a Hypothesis** How would these features help the animal survive?

Drawing Conclusions

1. **Communicate** What are the animals' most important features? How would they use these features?

2. Review your hypothesis. How could you test it?

3. **Predict** Predict what would happen if you could test your hypothesis.

Materials

modeling clay

construction paper

drawing materials

Animal Name _____	
Predator ☐	Avoider ☐
Food _____	
Enemies _____	
Environment _____	
Trait	**How It Helps**
Length	
Weight	
Shape	
Coloring	
Pattern	
Skin	
Arms	
Legs	
Tails	
Fins	
Eyesight	
Hearing	
Smell	
Strength	
Quickness	
Intelligence	

How Do Animals Behave?

Physical adaptations help animals survive. Other kinds of adaptations involve behaviors, or actions.

One type of behavior is not learned. It is an **inherited behavior** (in·HER·it·uhd bi·HAYV·yuhr). The simplest inherited behavior is a *reflex* (REE·fleks). A reflex is automatic, like scratching an itch.

Complicated inherited behavior is called **instinct** (IN·stingkt). Instincts are patterns of behavior, like spinning a web and building a nest. The behavior is complicated, but automatic. The spider and bird do not think about what to do, they just know.

When salmon swim thousands of miles to mate and lay eggs, they are *migrating* (MIGH·grayt·ing). Migration is an instinct. Animals migrate for three main reasons. First, they avoid cold weather. Second, they find new food supplies. Third, they find a safe place to breed and raise their young.

How do migrating animals find their way? Many birds navigate by the Sun and the stars. Other migrators may use magnetic "compasses" inside their bodies.

Surviving a cold winter is hard. Some animals struggle to find food. Others *hibernate* (HIGH·buhr·nayt), or sleep through the winter. True hibernation is a deep sleep. All body processes slow down. Body temperature can drop to just above freezing. Mice and bats are true hibernators.

Bears and chipmunks do not sleep as deeply. Their body temperatures drop, but their heartbeats remain high. They can wake up in an emergency.

The dormouse is a true hibernator. It loses up to half its body weight while hibernating.

Some animal behaviors are inherited. Others aren't. Behavior that is not inborn is called **learned behavior**. Animals learn through experience and change their behavior. Learning starts with a need, such as food, protection, and escaping predators. All animals do not learn in the same way.

- **Learning to Ignore** At first a frog jumps at moving shadows. Later it doesn't. It has learned that the shadow is not a threat.
- **Copying** Newborn ducks follow their female parent wherever she goes. They copy her to learn to find food.
- **Learning from Experience** At first a rat is unsure of where to go in a maze. After many trips the rat learns to find its way from experience.
- **Using Two Unrelated Things** A trainer shouts, "Up!" If the dolphin jumps, the trainer gives it a fish. At first the dolphin gets a fish every time it jumps. After a while it jumps simply because the trainer shouts, "Up!"

Almost all learning involves some form of trial and error. For example, the rat in the maze makes mistakes but learns from them. After a while it can find its way through the maze.

A program called Helping Hands trains monkeys, then places them

This monkey helps its owner live a better life. It is a companion and a helper.

with people who have trouble moving their bodies. What do Helping Hands monkeys do? They open books and fetch snacks. They change radio and TV stations. They perform dozens of tasks quickly and easily.

Many animals are trained to help people. Dogs can be trained to help the blind. Horses are trained to carry people on their backs.

▷ **What are some of your inherited behaviors and learned behaviors?**

How Can Quick Responses Help Animals Survive?

Many types of animals have special behaviors that help them survive. For example, when a squid senses danger, it squirts a dark, inky liquid at an attacker. The liquid blinds the attacker for a short time and lessens its sense of smell. This allows the squid to make a quick getaway.

A puffer fish has a body covered with sharp, hard spines. When attacked or scared, the puffer fish inflates its body to look like a ball. This pushes the sharp, hard spines outward.

Another prickly animal is the porcupine. It has specialized hairs called *quills*. About 30,000 hard, sharp quills with barbed ends cover a porcupine's body and tail. When the porcupine is attacked, the hairs stand up to protect the animal's body. Also, a porcupine can slap an attacker with its tail, sending painfully sharp quills into the attacker's body.

Puffer fish

Have you ever smelled a skunk? A skunk protects itself by spraying a terrible-smelling liquid at attackers. This liquid is also very painful when it gets into the eyes.

Some animals use their outer body coverings as a shield. An insect called a sow bug can roll itself into a ball. Its hard outer covering protects it from enemies. Two types of mammals, armadillos and pangolins, have hard protective plates. Like sow bugs, they roll into a ball to protect themselves.

Armadillo

Porcupine

▷ **What quick responses do these animals use to survive?**

Why It Matters

Understanding adaptations helps us learn how animals survive. It also makes us more aware of our own adaptations—our hands, feet, eyes, nose, ears, and tongue to name a few. Your greatest adaptation of all is your brain. It can produce more learned behavior than any other organism. In fact, you are using it right now—to learn! Visit **www.mhscience02.com** to do a research project on animal adaptations.

Think and Write

1. How is camouflage different from mimicry? How do both help animals survive?

2. What is an instinct?

3. Describe how a dog might learn to open the cabinet where its food is kept.

4. Form a Hypothesis How might having a bright color help a bird survive?

5. Critical Thinking A sheepdog is an expert at herding sheep. Do you think this is learned or inherited behavior? Why?

L·I·N·K·S

LITERATURE LINK

Read *Why Tortoise Has a Shell* to learn how Tortoise found a way to protect and shelter herself. Try the activities at the end of the book.

WRITING LINK

Write a paragraph. Choose an adaptation you would like to have. Why would you choose that adaptation? How would it help you in your life?

SOCIAL STUDIES LINK

Research bears. Research where brown bears and polar bears live. Explain how their appearance is related to their environment.

TECHNOLOGY LINK

Science Newsroom CD-ROM Choose *A Change for the Better* to learn how beaks help birds obtain food.

At the Computer Visit **www.mhscience02.com** for more links.

Dancing Bees

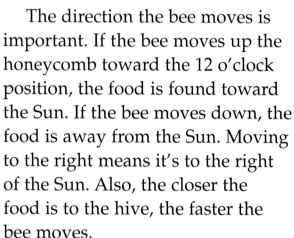

Most types of honeybees collect nectar, the sweet juice of a flower, and pollen. When one bee finds a good source of pollen and nectar, it flies back to its hive to tell all the others.

How do you think some types of honeybees communicate this information? Scientists have been studying honeybee communication for a long time. They observed that bees perform a special type of "waggle" dance. Even the Greek philosopher Aristotle, who lived from 384 to 322 B.C., observed honeybee dances!

Scientists have used a variety of experiments to learn how bees communicate with each other. After a bee finds a flower, it first fills its honey sac with nectar and returns to the hive. There it performs a special dance. As the bee walks in a figure eight, it stops from time to time to shake, or waggle, its body.

The direction the bee moves is important. If the bee moves up the honeycomb toward the 12 o'clock position, the food is found toward the Sun. If the bee moves down, the food is away from the Sun. Moving to the right means it's to the right of the Sun. Also, the closer the food is to the hive, the faster the bee moves.

For a long time, scientists thought that bees communicated only by dancing. They now know that some bees also use sounds created by beating their wings. Through experiments, they found that dancing alone doesn't communicate the food's location. The other bees didn't look for the food. However, when the bees were allowed to hear the correct sounds from the dancer's beating wings, they flew straight to the food. Who would have thought that bees can hear!

Write ABOUT IT

1. How do bees communicate with each other?

2. How does a bee tell other bees in the hive that food is found toward the Sun?

AT THE COMPUTER

Visit **www.mhscience02.com** to learn more about bees.

Chapter 4 Review

Vocabulary

Fill each blank with the best word or words from the list.

adaptation, B66
camouflage, B66
circulatory system, B46
excretory system, B47
heredity, B62
instinct, B70

learned behavior, B71
life cycle, B58
nervous system, B50
respiratory system, B47

1. The organ system that removes liquid wastes is called the _____.

2. The stages of an animal's growth and change are part of its _____.

3. Organisms use _____ to blend with their surroundings.

4. The system that moves blood through the body is the _____.

5. All body systems are controlled by the _____.

6. The passing of a trait from parents to offspring is _____.

7. A pattern of behavior that an animal is born with is called a(n) _____.

8. Species have often survived changing environments through _____.

9. Some animals take in gases through their skin, and lack a(n) _____.

10. When a dog plays dead, it is showing a(n) _____.

Test Prep

11. The system that carries oxygen to body cells is the _____.

  A circulatory system
  B respiratory system
  C excretory system
  D digestive system

12. Which animal goes through metamorphosis?

  F mealworm
  G chicken
  H snake
  J fish

13. A robin's beak helps it to catch worms. Its beak shape is a(n) _____.

   A adaptation

   B instinct

   C learned behavior

   D mimicry

14. When a bear hibernates, it _____.

   F eats food

   G catches fish

   H climbs trees

   J does none of these things

15. Which of these processes helps species become more diverse?

   A regeneration

   B respiration

   C fertilization

   D budding

Concepts and Skills

16. **Reading in Science** Name three adaptations that help animals survive. Describe how these adaptations help the animals.

17. **Decision Making** Humans can decide what to learn and how to learn it. What would you like to learn, and why? Discuss the ways you learn something new.

18. **Process Skills: Form a Hypothesis** Most birds build nests, where they live and raise their young. Does a bird learn how to build nests, or is it an instinct? Form a hypothesis. Then design an experiment to answer this question.

19. **Safety** Why is it important to handle living animals carefully?

20. **Critical Thinking** Compare how camouflage and mimicry protect an animal. Use examples in your answer.

Boost *your test scores!*

Be Smart!
Visit www.mhscience02.com
to learn more.

People in Science

Dr. Coretta Patterson
Veterinarian

Do you have a pet? What do you do when it gets sick? Sometimes it's hard to tell when animals are sick. They can't tell you exactly what's wrong. Sometimes you know they're sick, but you don't know what to do. That's when you need to take your pet to the veterinarian. A veterinarian, or vet, is a special doctor just for animals.

There are different kinds of vets. Some treat small animals like dogs and cats. Some treat large animals like the horses and cows on a farm. Some do not treat animals at all but do veterinary research in a laboratory.

Dr. Coretta Patterson is a veterinarian at Michigan State University College of Veterinary Medicine. She has wanted to become a vet since she was a child and spent summers on a family farm in Alabama. Veterinarians must attend veterinary school for about four years after completing college. Dr. Patterson received her doctorate of veterinary medicine from the University of Illinois.

Dr. Patterson treats animals at the university's animal clinic.

Her usual duties include checkups, blood tests, dental work, and shots—ouch! She gets help from her nurse and technician. A veterinary technician is an assistant. Technicians go to school for about two years to get their degree. They assist vets in many ways, but they are not doctors.

Dr. Patterson also teaches classes for future vets. She enjoys teaching because it allows her to encourage students to pursue a meaningful profession. She loves her job because she feels she's making a real difference!

Write ABOUT IT

1. Describe two different kinds of work veterinarians do.
2. How do you think being a veterinarian is different from being a physician?

AT THE COMPUTER

Visit www.mhscience02.com to learn more about careers.

Careers IN SCIENCE

Here are some different types of careers related to the study of veterinary medicine. You can use the Internet or library resources to find out more about these careers.

- veterinary technician
- naturalist
- zoologist
- biologist
- physician

This veterinarian works on a leopard at the zoo.

Animal Pages

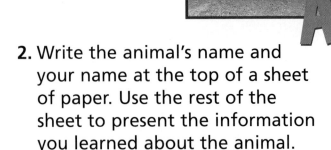

Your goal is to make a page for a book about animals.

What to Do

1. Choose an animal to research. Find answers to the following questions:

- How is the animal classified?
- What is the animal's body like?
- Where does the animal live?
- Where does it fit in a food chain or food web?
- Is the animal endangered?

2. Write the animal's name and your name at the top of a sheet of paper. Use the rest of the sheet to present the information you learned about the animal. Include words and pictures.

3. With your classmates, staple or tape the pages together to make a book. Include a cover and a table of contents.

Animal Tale

What to Do

Write a story or play about an animal or group of animals. The point of view could be that of someone studying animals or that of the animals themselves.

Your story or play should answer at least one of these questions:

- How does an animal change as it grows?
- How does it use adaptations to stay alive?
- What happens when its habitat changes or is destroyed?

The Claw of the Tiger by Mary B.

Earth Science

UNIT C

Earth and Beyond

NATIONAL GEOGRAPHIC

NATIONAL GEOGRAPHIC

LOOK!

Today, this part of Colorado is rocky and dry. Do you think it was different millions of years ago?

Earth and Beyond

CHAPTER 5

Earth's History C2

CHAPTER 6

Earth's Surface and Interior C30

CHAPTER 7

Sun, Moon, and Planets C62

LESSON 1

What You Can Learn from Rocks, C4

LESSON 2

Clues from Fossils, C16

Earth's History

Did You Ever Wonder?

Can wood really turn to stone? Petrified wood, or wood turned to stone, was formed more than 225 million years ago. These trees in the Petrified Forest National Park in Arizona are thought to have been in a great flood. Over the years, sediment and rock seeped into the wood. Can petrified wood tell us about Earth's history?

What You Can Learn from Rocks

Vocabulary

mineral, C6

igneous rock, C9

sedimentary rock, C10

relative age, C11

metamorphic rock, C12

rock cycle, C13

Get Ready

What do you see in this picture? You see rocks! This is Bryce Canyon in Utah. The canyon walls are made of layers of rocks.

Rocks have interesting stories to tell. What do you think you could learn from rocks?

Process Skill

You infer when you form an idea from facts or observations.

Explore Activity

Materials

5 different rock samples

hand lens

How Can You Interpret Clues in Rocks?

Procedure

1. **Observe** Carefully observe each rock. Describe and record its properties. Observe the rock's color, hardness, texture, and shininess. Is it made of smaller particles that you can see? Does it have any layers?

2. **Observe** Use a hand lens to observe each rock sample. Record your observations.

3. **Communicate** Compare your observations with those of your classmates. Make a class list of all the properties you observed.

Drawing Conclusions

1. **Infer** Which rocks may have formed from sand or gravel? What evidence supports your answer?

2. **Infer** Which rock may have formed on an ocean bottom? What evidence supports your answer?

3. Compare samples. How are they alike? How are they different?

4. **Going Further: Infer** How do you think the samples formed? Why do you think so?

Main Idea Rocks, which form in many ways, hold clues about Earth's past.

How Do You Interpret Clues in Rocks?

Have you ever noticed how rocks come in different colors, shapes, and sizes? Rocks are solid materials that make up the outer layer of Earth. *Geologists* (jee·AHL·uh·jists) study the properties of rocks to tell how the rocks may have formed.

One way to study a rock is to look for **minerals** (MIN·uhr·uhlz) in the rock. Rocks are made of minerals. Minerals are naturally occurring substances that are neither plants nor animals. Minerals are the building blocks of rocks.

For example, granite is a rock found in many areas. It is made of several minerals, as shown below. If you find a rock with these minerals in it, you have found granite.

How can you identify minerals? You can become a mineral detective. Each mineral has properties you can use as clues. One property of minerals is color. Look again at the piece of granite shown below. What is the color of each mineral in the granite?

However, color is not always a useful property. A mineral may come in several colors. Mica, for example, can be silvery or black. Quartz can be white, pink, or purple. What's more, both mica and quartz may be colorless. Another reason color is not always a useful property is that two or more minerals may have the same color.

Mica (MIGH·kuh)

Quartz (KWARTS)

Feldspar (FELD·spahr)

Hornblende (HAWRN·blend)

Granite

Granite is a rock made of several minerals. How are the minerals different?

Pyrite is brassy yellow but has a greenish-black streak.

Diamond is the hardest mineral. It looks glassy.

Galena has a metallic luster. You can scratch it with a copper penny.

Talc is the softest mineral. It looks greasy.

A mineral detective looks for properties other than color.

- You can tell some minerals by the way light bounces off them. This property is called *luster*. Some minerals are shiny like a new metal pan or coin. Other minerals are not shiny. They may look dull, glassy, or even "greasy."
- Another clue comes from rubbing a mineral gently but firmly on a *streak plate*. You often see a streak that's the same color as the mineral surface. However, pyrite is a yellow mineral. When you rub it on a streak plate, you see a thin trail of black powder. What a clue!

- Another clue is how hard a mineral is. The harder it is, the less likely it will be scratched. Test a mineral's hardness with three testers—a fingernail, a copper penny, and an iron nail.

A soft mineral, such as talc or mica, can be scratched by all three. Calcite is a harder mineral than mica. It cannot be scratched by a fingernail. It can be scratched by a copper penny. A harder mineral, such as fluorite, can be scratched by an iron nail. Many minerals, such as quartzite, are too hard to be scratched by any of the testers.

READING Summarize What are three ways to tell minerals apart?

QUICK LAB

Identifying Minerals

1. Use tools and this table to identify each mineral sample. Write the properties and names.

2. Which properties helped you most to identify each mineral?

How Do Minerals Split?

Some minerals split easily along flat surfaces. For example, mica splits easily into thin sheets. Galena (guh·LEE·nuh) splits along flat surfaces in three directions. The result is a cube. Many minerals break unevenly, such as quartz and talc.

Some minerals have special properties. For example, magnetite is attracted by a magnet. The table below lists the different properties of some minerals.

▷ How can you tell galena from quartz?

Mineral Identification Table

Mineral	Color	Luster	Streak	Hardness	Other
Galena	silver gray	shiny like a metal	gray	scratched by copper and iron	splits into cube shapes
Pyrite	brassy yellow	shiny like a metal	greenish-black	not scratched by testers	looks like gold; breaks unevenly
Quartz	colorless, white, pink, purple	glassy	white	not scratched by testers	breaks unevenly
Mica	colorless, silvery, brown	may look glassy	white	scratched by fingernail	splits into thin sheets
Talc	pale green, white	pearly, dull, greasy	white	scratched by fingernail	flakes or crumbles easily
Feldspar	yellow, white, gray, red, brown	glassy, pearly	white	not scratched by testers	splits easily in two directions
Hornblende	green, black	glassy	brown, gray	not scratched by testers	splits easily in two directions
Calcite	colorless, white	glassy	white	scratched by copper and iron	splits in three directions

What Are Igneous Rocks?

Geologists can tell rocks apart by the minerals that are in the rocks. They also look to see how large the minerals or grains in a rock are. Large grains give rocks a coarse or rough texture. Smaller grains give rocks a fine texture.

Geologists also see how the grains fit together. Are the grains closely locked together, or do they stand out like separate pieces?

By checking these properties, geologists can tell how rocks formed. They classify rocks into three main groups based on how they formed.

Many rocks are classified as **igneous** (IG·nee·uhs) **rocks** . The word *igneous* means "fire-made." An igneous rock is formed from hot, molten rock material that has cooled and hardened.

This molten material may cool and harden below or above Earth's surface. Below the surface this molten material is called magma. Because it is below the surface, magma may cool and harden slowly over time. The slower it cools, the larger the mineral grains can become. The result is a rock with coarse texture. Granite is an example.

Magma tends to rise upward toward Earth's surface. If it reaches the surface before it hardens, it can escape through volcanoes or cracks. Magma that reaches the surface is called lava.

Lava cools quickly as it is exposed to air. As a result the minerals do not have a chance to form large grains. The grains are small, producing rocks with a fine texture. *Basalt* (buh·SAWLT) is an example of this type of rock. Some of these rocks may have tiny holes that are the result of escaping steam and gases.

Sometimes lava can cool so quickly that mineral grains do not have time to form. The rocks that result are volcanic glass.

▷ **How do igneous rocks form?**

Three Main Igneous Rocks

Granite is a coarse-grained rock.

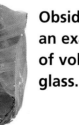
Obsidian is an example of volcanic glass.

Basalt is a fine-grained rock.

Four Examples of Sedimentary Rocks

Rock salt

Shale

Limestone

Conglomerate

What Are Sedimentary Rocks?

Did you ever see rocks that looked like bits of sand glued together in a clump? Such rocks are classified as **sedimentary** (SED·uh·men·tuh·ree) **rocks** .

There are several types of sedimentary rocks. One type is formed from smaller bits of rock that become pressed or cemented together. They start out as small, broken-down pieces of rock carried by water, wind, or ice. In time the pieces are dropped off in other places in layers.

Deposited rock particles and other materials that settle in a liquid are called *sediments* (SED·uh·muhntz). With time the weight of new layers of sediments packs together the layers on the bottom. The sediments change to rock as air and water are squeezed out of the layers.

Sandstone is an example of this type of sedimentary rock. It is made up of grains of sand that have been cemented together. Conglomerate is made up of larger pieces cemented together. Shale is made up of fine mud particles cemented together.

Some sedimentary rocks are made up of substances that were once part of living things. Shells and skeletons of dead sea animals build up in layers on the ocean floor. Eventually they become cemented together. They may form a kind of limestone.

In some cases certain minerals become dissolved in the waters of lakes and small seas. When the water evaporates, the minerals are left behind as sediments. Rock salt and some kinds of limestone are formed this way.

▶ **How do sedimentary rocks form?**

How Do Sediments Form Layers?

Sediments, like bricks in a wall, are laid down in time order. Those at the bottom are laid down first. Those at the top are laid down last. Time order tells us about age. While we cannot always give the age of something in units of time—such as years—we can give its **relative age**. Relative age is age expressed by words such as older, oldest, younger, and youngest. It describes the age of something compared with the age of another thing.

For example, in this drawing layer A is the oldest. Layer D is the youngest. Layer B is younger than layer A but older than layers C and D.

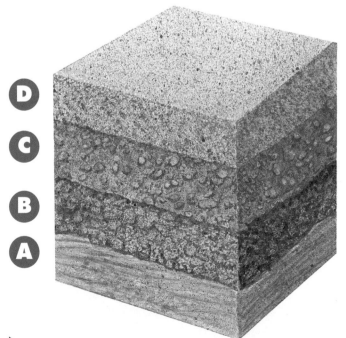

D
C
B
A

▶ **How can you tell the relative age of a sedimentary rock?**

FOR SCHOOL OR HOME

Observing Sediments

BE CAREFUL! Wear goggles.

1. Make a Model Put some gravel and sand in a jar of water. Cover it with a lid. Shake the jar. Set it aside.

2. Observe How many layers formed? Which layer settled first? Last?

3. Infer How does this illustrate the formation of sedimentary rocks?

What Are Metamorphic Rocks?

In a way, some rocks result from being cooked. They are classified as **metamorphic** (met·uh·MAWR·fik) **rocks** . The word *metamorphic* means "changed in form." A metamorphic rock is a rock that has been changed by heat, pressure, or both. Before the change the rock may have been any kind of rock, even another metamorphic rock.

Heat from nearby rising magma can cause a chemical change in the minerals making up a rock. The weight of rocks stacked on top of a rock builds up pressure that can cause the rock to change.

Geologists classify metamorphic rocks into two groups. In one group pressure causes minerals to spread out in bands. The rocks can break

This Greek horse head is made of marble. Marble is a metamorphic rock that forms from limestone.

apart along these bands. One example of this type of rock is *gneiss* (NIGHS). It can form when granite or shale is heated under pressure.

Rocks classified in the other group of metamorphic rocks do not have bands of minerals. They do not break in layers. Marble is one example of this type of rock. Marble forms when limestone is heated under pressure.

▷ **How do metamorphic rocks form?**

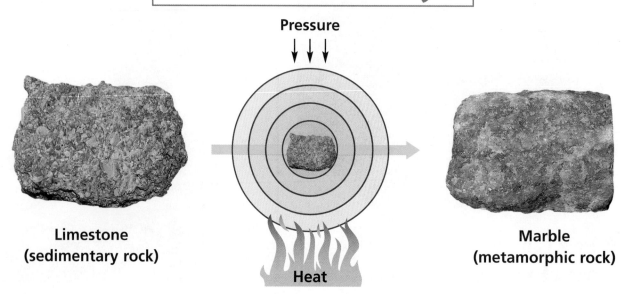

How Rocks Can Be Changed

Pressure

Limestone
(sedimentary rock)

Heat

Marble
(metamorphic rock)

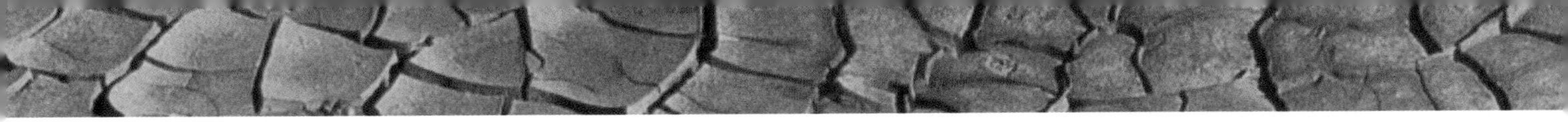

How Do Rocks Change?

Rocks are always changing. All rocks are part of the **rock cycle**. The rock cycle is a never-ending process by which rocks are changed from one type into another. A cycle is something that happens over and over again.

▶ **What is the rock cycle?**

How the Rock Cycle Works

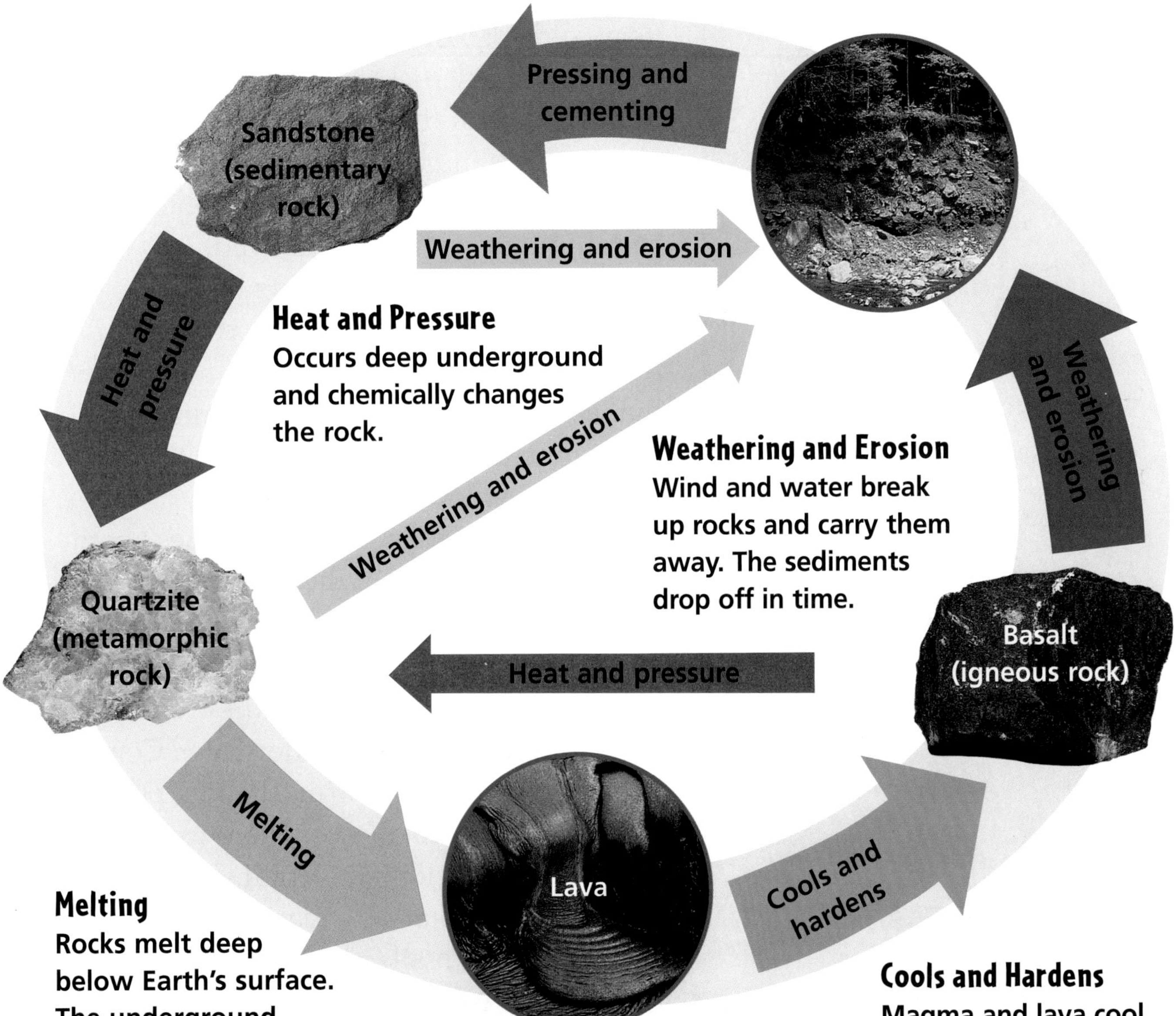

Pressing and cementing

Sandstone (sedimentary rock)

Weathering and erosion

Heat and pressure

Heat and Pressure
Occurs deep underground and chemically changes the rock.

Weathering and erosion

Weathering and Erosion
Wind and water break up rocks and carry them away. The sediments drop off in time.

Weathering and erosion

Quartzite (metamorphic rock)

Heat and pressure

Basalt (igneous rock)

Melting

Lava

Cools and hardens

Melting
Rocks melt deep below Earth's surface. The underground melted rock is called magma.

Cools and Hardens
Magma and lava cool into hardened rock.

READING
Diagrams

What causes a sedimentary rock to become a metamorphic rock?

C 13

What Can You Learn from Rock Layers?

Did humans ever have to fight off dinosaurs or saber-toothed tigers? How do we know? Rock layers contain *fossils* (FAHS·uhlz). A fossil is any trace, mark, or remains of an organism at least 10,000 years old. Usually, it has been preserved in sedimentary rock. Scientists study the relative ages of rocks and fossils to learn about extinct organisms. Based on this evidence, they have concluded when certain plants and animals lived.

For example, all dinosaurs became extinct before any saber-toothed tigers or humans appeared on Earth. We now know that all rocks with dinosaur remains are older than all rocks with saber-toothed tiger or human remains.

Rocks and fossils give many clues about what Earth was like in the past. Most limestones are formed of materials deposited in the oceans. Regions where limestone occurs were probably once underwater. Corals live only in warm, shallow parts of the ocean. Places where we find rocks with fossil coral were once tropical areas covered by shallow seas. Fossil ferns in polar regions tell us these areas were once warmer than today.

Fossils provide evidence of plants and animals that lived in the past. They also provide clues about what Earth was like in the past.

▷ **What do fossils tell about the past?**

L·I·N·K·S

Why it Matters

Rocks occur everywhere on or near Earth's surface, and we use them in many different ways. Pieces of rock are mixed into cement used to build things. They are also mixed with asphalt used to pave roads. Some rocks, such as marble, are used to make beautiful sculptures. By studying rocks and rock layers, scientists have explained what they think Earth was like in the past.

Think and Write

1. List five properties of minerals.

2. Name the three main groups of rocks. Describe how the rocks in each group form.

3. How could you find the relative age of a sedimentary rock.

4. How might pieces of an igneous rock become a sedimentary rock?

5. **Critical Thinking** Imagine you are climbing a mountain and you discover a fossil of a fish! What does this mean?

MATH LINK

Solve a problem. Ted has samples of five minerals, as shown in the bar graph. What is the total mass of Ted's samples?

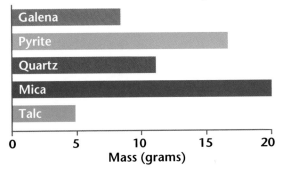

Mass of Mineral Samples

Mass (grams)

WRITING LINK

Write a story. Someone in the story should use a rock or mineral from this lesson, or try to identify it.

ART LINK

Make rock art. Find some rocks, stones, or pebbles. Use them to make a sculpture, a necklace, a mosaic, or other work of art.

LITERATURE LINK

Read *Rocks Don't Just Sit There* to learn how rocks go through many changes. Try the activities at the end of the book.

TECHNOLOGY LINK

At the Computer Visit **www.mhscience02.com** for more links.

Clues from Fossils

Vocabulary

imprint, C18

mold, C18

cast, C19

amber, C20

Get Ready

What do you think happened in the picture? Like a detective, you can use clues to figure out what took place. The tracks are your clues. Who do you think made them?

Process Skill

You interpret data when you use information that has been gathered to answer questions or solve a problem.

Explore Activity

Materials
footprint
puzzle

What Can You Learn from Fossils?

Procedure

1 **Observe** Carefully study the footprints. Look for clues in the sizes and types of prints. Think about which were made first, next, and last.

2 **Communicate** Discuss the evidence with your partner. How can you work together to interpret it?

3 Record the story you think the prints tell.

Drawing Conclusions

1 **Infer** How many animals made the tracks? Are all the animals the same kind? How can you tell?

2 **Infer** Were all the animals moving in the same direction? How do you know? Which came first? Next? Last?

3 How does your story compare with those of your classmates? On what points do you agree? Disagree? Be prepared to defend your interpretation.

4 **Going Further: Interpret Data** Create another footprint puzzle. Challenge a classmate to figure out the story the footprints tell.

What Can You Learn from Fossils?

Scientists use clues from fossils to learn about the past. By studying fossils they can learn about past events, past environments, and past organisms.

For example, scientists studied the fossil footprints shown in the picture. From them they learned that dinosaurs did not drag their tails. They saw only footprints and no signs of dragged tails.

How Fossils Form

What happens when a plant or animal dies? The soft parts quickly decay or are eaten. Hard parts, such as bones, teeth, and shells, last longer. They are more likely to become fossils.

Most fossils are found in sedimentary rocks. The remains are gently and rapidly buried by sediments. They may become fossils if they remain undisturbed as the sediments become rocks.

Sometimes a shallow print or impression is the only evidence of a plant or animal that once existed. Fossils of this kind—such as animal tracks, body outlines, leaf prints, and grooves made by tiny fish bones—

From fossil evidence such as these dinosaur tracks, scientists determined that dinosaurs did not drag their tails as they walked.

are called **imprints**. An imprint is a mark made by pressing.

Shells often leave behind fossils known as **molds**. A mold is a hollow form with a particular shape. A mold forms when water seeps into the rocks where a shell is buried. The water eventually dissolves the

shell. This leaves a hollow space where the shell once was. The hollow space, often clearly showing the outside features of the shell, is a mold.

Another type of fossil is known as a **cast** . A cast is something that is formed or shaped in a mold. A cast forms when minerals slowly accumulate in a mold and fill it. The minerals take the shape of the original shell and form a copy. If you have ever made gelatin in a shaped cup, you can understand the difference between molds and casts. The cup is a mold. The hardened gelatin is a cast.

READING **Summarize** **What are three kinds of fossils?**

At left is a mold of a fern leaf. At right is a cast of the leaf. What features of the fern can you see?

FOR SCHOOL OR HOME

Making Molds and Casts

1. **Make a Model** Coat a shell with petroleum jelly. Then firmly but gently press the shell into the clay.

2. Carefully remove the shell from the clay. Fill the clay with plaster of Paris.

3. When the plaster has dried, remove it from the clay.

4. Which is the mold? Which is the cast? How are they similar and different?

5. What shell characteristics can you see in the mold? In the cast? Record your observations.

What Are Some Other Ways Fossils Form?

Imprints, molds, and casts are some types of fossils. Organisms of the past were also preserved in other interesting ways.

Sometimes entire insects became trapped in sticky sap oozing from certain trees. The trapped insects were preserved as the sap hardened into **amber** (AM·buhr).

Sometimes entire animals were preserved by being frozen. Mammoths are relatives of modern elephants. Fossilized mammoths have been found in ice and frozen ground in the northern parts of Asia and North America. Bones, hair, skin, flesh, and even internal organs have been preserved.

Many fossils have been discovered in tar pits. Saber-toothed tigers, camels, mammoths, and other animals became stuck in tar pits and died. Their flesh decayed, while their bones sank. The bones were preserved as the tar around them hardened. Rancho La Brea in California is famous for fossils in its tar pits.

Sometimes animal remains are preserved as mummies. They slowly dried out in hot, dry regions like deserts. These fossils have changed little since they formed.

Examples of Fossils

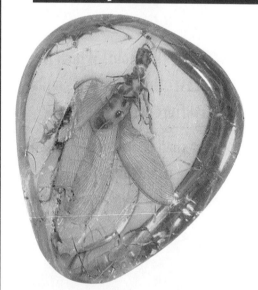

This insect was trapped as sap oozed down a tree. Today it is a perfectly preserved fossil in amber.

This plant left behind a carbon film that shows many details. What observations can you make about the plant?

Plants and animals that decay slowly may leave behind a thin film of the element carbon. Carbon films of ferns, leaves, and fish often show detailed outlines.

Parts of plants and animals, especially wood and bones, may also be preserved by being *petrified* (PET·ruh·fighd). *Petrified* means "turned to stone."

How do you think bones become petrified? Bones have a hard, compact outer layer. Inside is a spongy layer with connected openings, or pores. When a bone is buried, minerals may slowly seep into the pores and fill them. When this happens, the bone is partly petrified. The fossil still has the original bone material. Later the bone itself may be dissolved and replaced by minerals. The bone is then completely petrified.

The woody parts of plants are preserved in the same way as completely petrified bones. Minerals filled the hollow spaces and also replaced all the once-living parts.

> **? How could a whole animal become a fossil?**

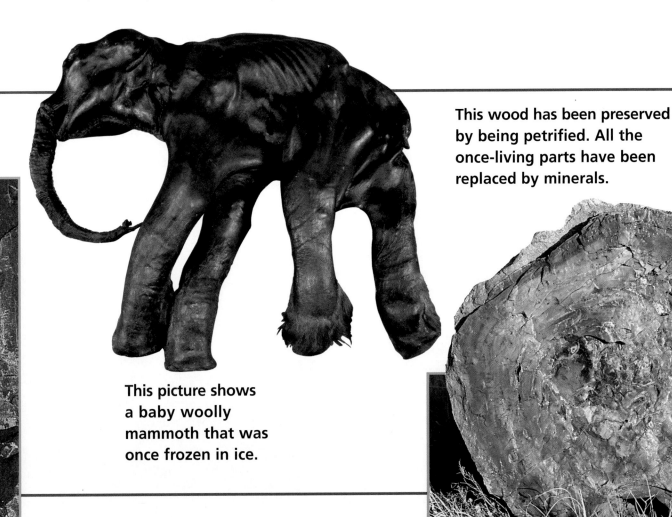

This picture shows a baby woolly mammoth that was once frozen in ice.

This wood has been preserved by being petrified. All the once-living parts have been replaced by minerals.

What Happens Once Fossils Are Found?

Fossils represent only a very small part of all the plants and animals that lived in the past. Most organisms die without leaving a single trace. Even hard parts, such as bones, are usually scattered, broken, and mixed. Complete skeletons are rare, lucky, and exciting finds.

Collecting is the first step. Workers at fossil sites carefully remove the skeleton, bone by bone, from the rock. Each bone is wrapped in plaster to prevent damage. Each is carefully labeled and sent to a museum or university.

The next step is removing the last bits of rock from the bones. People use tools to file and pick away the rock. They also soak the bones in a liquid that dissolves rock.

The prepared specimens are then ready for study or display.

The next step is assembling the bones. Sometimes they are put on display in museums. Metal rods and wires are often used to hold up a skeleton so it appears to be standing. Sometimes gaps are left where bones are missing. Sometimes missing bones are replaced by artificial bones. Fossil bones used in exhibits are usually coated with shellac or varnish to help protect them.

Some fossils are stored safely for further study. Casts are used in the exhibits, not the real fossils. Models may be made to show what an extinct animal probably looked like when it was alive.

▷ **How do fossils displayed in museums compare with those in the ground?**

A lot of work goes into a display of a fossilized dinosaur skeleton.

Dinosaur Bones

Footprint size gives a good idea of overall size and height. Scientists have determined that the length of a footprint is generally equal to one-quarter the length of the hind-leg bone of the animal that made it. The length of the bone gives a good idea of the animal's overall size.

Procedure

1 Collect Data This table gives the footprint length of six adult dinosaurs. Copy the table.

2 Use Numbers Determine how to calculate the lengths of the hind-leg bones. Complete column C.

3 Rank the dinosaurs in order of probable overall size. Write 1 for the largest and 6 for the smallest in column D.

Drawing Conclusions

1 Interpret Data Which dinosaur probably had the largest hind-leg bone? The smallest?

2 Which two dinosaurs were probably close in size? The most different in size?

A	B	C	D
Name of Dinosaur	Length of Footprint	Probable Length of Hind-Leg Bone	Probable Rank in Overall Size
Triceratops	15 inches ($1\frac{1}{4}$ feet)		
Tyrannosaurus	30 inches ($2\frac{1}{2}$ feet)		
Stegosaurus	18 inches ($1\frac{1}{2}$ feet)		
Velociraptor	6 inches ($\frac{1}{2}$ foot)		
Compsognathus	3 inches ($\frac{1}{4}$ foot)		
Ultrasaurus	78 inches ($6\frac{1}{2}$ feet)		

This fossil shows an animal that had a weak jaw and flat teeth. Was this animal a meat eater or a plant eater?

What Other Clues Do Fossils Provide?

Fossils also give information about the age of organisms when they died. Annual-growth rings in petrified wood tell the age of fossil trees. Similar footprints of different sizes tell if organisms were young or old.

Fossils also give many clues about the characteristics of organisms. Footprint size is a clue to an animal's size. Distances between footprints may tell whether an animal was walking or running. Footprints also tell if an animal walked on two or four legs.

What types of clues would tell you what animals ate? Meat eaters usually had strong jaws with many pointed teeth. Plant eaters usually had weaker jaws with flat or peglike teeth. Fossilized stomach contents can tell what an animal ate.

Fossils can also tell about past environments. Fossilized aquatic organisms tell where rivers, lakes, or oceans once existed. Fossils also tell that parts of the world were once colder or hotter than they are today. Fossil ferns tell that an area had a warm or hot, moist climate. Fossil evergreen leaves tell that an area was cool.

> ## ▷ What are three things you can learn from fossils?

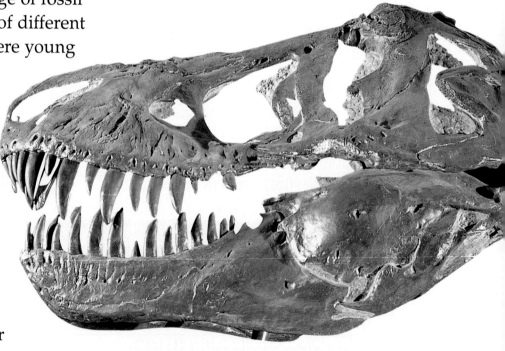

This fossil shows an animal that had a strong jaw and many large, sharp teeth. Was this animal a meat eater or a plant eater?

L·I·N·K·S

Why It Matters

Fossils tell how life on Earth has changed over time. The fossil bones of a dinosaur are very different from those of animals today. All we know about dinosaurs comes from studying fossils.

Museums are great places to see fossils and learn more about them. You can also study fossils on the Internet. Visit **www.mhscience02.com** to do a research project on fossils.

Think and Write

1. What can you learn from animal tracks and footprints?

2. Describe how imprints, molds, and casts are formed.

3. What are two ways that whole organisms from the past have been preserved?

4. Use Numbers A fossil of an adult dinosaur foot measures 69 centimeters. About how long would its hind-leg bone have been?

5. Critical Thinking Why are most fossils found in sedimentary rocks?

WRITING LINK

Write a story. Include a fossil in your story. Describe the fossil and the plant or animal that made it.

ART LINK

Model imprint fossils. Roll modeling clay into a thin layer. Press a pencil, eraser, or other object into the clay. Trade models with a classmate. See if you can guess what made the imprint.

SOCIAL STUDIES LINK

Research fossil finds. What fossils have been found in your state? Look at library books or the Internet for the answer.

TECHNOLOGY LINK

Science Newsroom CD-ROM *Choose Time Will Tell* to learn more about rocks and fossils.

At the Computer Visit **www.mhscience02.com** for more links.

Fossil Treasure Trove

Fossils are not found everywhere. Some places in the world, however, are full of fossils. In the Gobi, a desert in central Asia, scientists are finding hundreds of fossils. Many are complete skeletons of dinosaurs that lived 80 million years ago!

Why are there fossils in this desert? Long ago, the Gobi was a very different place. Plenty of rain fell there, making it a good home for plants and animals.

Some dinosaurs nested in low, marshy areas. During heavy rains, sandy mud from higher ground washed down. The mud covered and killed the animals. Over time the mud turned to sandstone, and the bones within turned to fossils. Changes above ground turned the land into a desert.

Fossils teach us about ancient life. They also can show how Earth has changed over the years. How do you think Earth will change in the future?

A scientist finds a dinosaur skeleton in the Gobi.

This is a dinosaur skeleton of a Protoceratops.

AT THE COMPUTER

What Did I Learn?

1. Eighty million years ago, the weather in the Gobi was

   A hot and dry.
   B cold and icy.
   C more rainy than today.
   D less rainy than today.

2. Below the Gobi's surface, dinosaur bones changed into

   F sandstone.
   G mud.
   H sand.
   J fossils.

Chapter 5 Review

Vocabulary

Fill each blank with the best word or words from the list.

amber, C20   mineral, C6

cast, C19   mold, C18

igneous rock, C9   relative age, C11

imprint, C18   rock cycle, C13

metamorphic   sedimentary
  rock, C12   rock, C10

1. A(n) _____ is a mark made by pressing.

2. Rocks are made of _____.

3. Hardened tree sap, called _____ can make insect fossils.

4. A rock's position within rock layers can tell its _____.

5. A(n) _____ is a hollow space in a rock where a plant or animal once was.

6. Minerals that seep into hollow spaces in rock might form a(n) _____.

7. Rocks change from one form to another in an endless process called the _____.

Sediments	press into →	8. ___.
Melted rock or lava	cools into →	9. ___.
Any rock	heat and pressure change to →	10. ___.

Test Prep

11. The best way to identify a mineral sample is to _____.

    A observe its color and luster

    B scratch it with different materials

    C streak it on a plate

    D do all of the above

12. Rocks near the opening of a volcano are likely to be _____.

    F igneous rocks

    G sedimentary rocks

    H metamorphic rocks

    J rocks not a part of the rock cycle

13. Fossils are most likely to be found in _____.

   A igneous rocks

   B sedimentary rocks

   C metamorphic rocks

   D rocks not a part of the rock cycle

14. Fossils have taught us a lot about dinosaurs, but NOT their _____.

   F sizes

   G foot shapes

   H skin colors

   J diets

15. Which of these body parts is LEAST likely to become a fossil?

   A feather

   B bone

   C shell

   D tooth

Boost *your test scores!*

Be Smart! Visit www.mhscience02.com to learn more.

Concepts and Skills

16. **Reading in Science** Describe three ways that fossils can form.

17. **Process Skills: Use Numbers** A dinosaur leaves a footprint 10 inches long. About how long is its hind-leg bone? Hint: See page C23.

18. **Critical Thinking** You have two mineral samples. Both are yellow and soft, like gold. Are they the same? Are they gold? Explain.

19. **Decision Making** You have been hired to build a new factory. As you dig into the ground, you discover what you think is a dinosaur fossil. What would you do next? Who might agree with your decision? Disagree?

20. **Scientific Methods** You are given a sample of calcite and one of quartz. What could you do to tell them apart? Hint: See page C8.

CHAPTER

6

Earth's
Surface and Interior

LESSON 3

Shaping Earth's Surface, C32

LESSON 4

The Story of Soil, C42

LESSON 5

Inside Earth, C52

Did You Ever Wonder?

Was the 1989 Oakland, California earthquake the biggest earthquake ever? On the Richter scale, the scale used to measure earthquakes, the biggest earthquake of the 20th century occurred in Chile on May 22, 1960. It registered a 9.5 out of 10. The 1989 California earthquake measured 7.1. What causes earthquakes?

Shaping Earth's Surface

Vocabulary

glacier, C34

terminus, C35

moraine, C35

glacial till, C35

erratic, C37

outwash plain, C37

Get Ready

Do you know what an iceberg is? Icebergs are large pieces of glaciers that break off and float away. They are very dangerous to ships because only their tips can be seen above the water's surface.

What is a glacier? How does it change Earth's surface?

Process Skill

You experiment when you perform a test to support or disprove a hypothesis.

Explore Activity

How Do Glaciers Scratch and Move Rocks?

Materials

paper towel

clean ice cube

ice cube made with sand or gravel

aluminum foil

wood scrap

Procedure: Design Your Own

1. **Form a Hypothesis** Look at the two ice cubes. Which do you think will cause more changes as it moves across a surface? Record your answer, which is a hypothesis. Explain why you think it is correct.

2. **Experiment** Design an experiment to test your hypothesis. Use only the materials that your teacher provides. Record the results.

3. **Observe** Place the ice cubes on a folded paper towel. Allow them to melt. Observe and record what they leave behind.

Drawing Conclusions

1. How did each ice cube feel as you rubbed it over a surface?

2. **Interpret Data** Did the observations support your hypothesis? Explain.

3. Describe what was inside each ice cube.

4. **Going Further: Infer** Imagine a huge mass of ice moving across the land. How might it change the land?

Main Idea Glaciers can change Earth's land.

What Do Glaciers Do?

A **glacier** (GLAY·shuhr) is a large mass of ice and snow that moves over land. Glaciers form when more snow falls in winter than melts in summer. With time the snow collects in layers. The weight of the upper layers turns the lower layers into ice.

How do glaciers move? The weight of the snow and the force of gravity cause the layers to "creep" or flow downhill. Heat from friction and from Earth below may melt some of the bottom layer of ice. The thin layer of water that forms helps the glacier move.

Glaciers also contain *rock debris* that includes boulders, rock fragments, gravel, sand, and soil. Glaciers pick up rock debris as they move.

Most debris is found at the bottom and along the sides of a glacier. These are places where glaciers come in contact with solid rock below the soil. This rock is known as bedrock. Debris often creates deep scratches in the solid bedrock.

Parts of a Glacier

READING

Diagrams

List and describe the parts of a glacier.

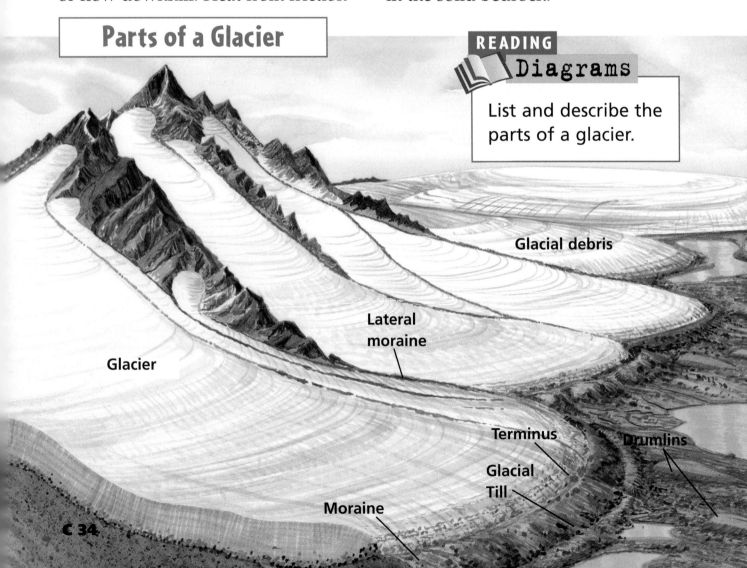

Glacier

Lateral moraine

Glacial debris

Moraine

Glacial Till

Terminus

Drumlins

Rock debris collects at a glacier's **terminus** (TUR·muh·nuhs). The terminus is the end, or outer margin, of a glacier. The terminus moves forward when a glacier grows and backward when it shrinks.

When a glacier melts, the rock debris is left behind. Rock debris deposited by glaciers forms features called **moraines** (muh·RAYNZ).

Moraines are made up of **glacial till** (GLAY·shuhl TIL). Glacial till is an unsorted mixture of rock materials deposited as a glacier melts. Rock materials that make up till vary greatly in size, from large fragments to fine clay. An oval mound of till is called a *drumlin* (DRUM·lin).

Glaciers leave distinctive features on Earth's surface. They act like giant bulldozers, pushing and piling up anything in their paths. As glaciers move, they loosen and scrape away broken rocks, sometimes even plucking out giant blocks of bedrock. Loosened material from valley walls also falls into glaciers. This leaves steep cliffs and circular basins.

Rock fragments in the ice act like sandpaper. They grind away the bedrock. They may carve deep, parallel scratches. They can smooth and polish the rock below.

The general effect of erosion by continental glaciers is to flatten and round the land. However, some types of glaciers carve out valleys, making them deeper and U-shaped.

READING **Draw Conclusions**
How can glaciers change the land?

This is an example of a U-shaped valley.

Process Skill
BUILDER

SKILL Define Terms

Flow of a Glacier

What do we mean when we say that a glacier flows? In this activity you will make and observe a model to see how glacial ice flows. Then you will be able to define glacial ice flow based on your experiences and observations.

Procedure

BE CAREFUL! Wear goggles.

1 **Make a Model** Place a spoonful of the cornstarch mixture on a piece of waxed paper. This represents a glacier. Record what happens.

2 **Observe** Place another spoonful on top of the first. This represents new snow. Record what happens.

3 Sprinkle some of the sand mixture in a 3-cm band around the edges and on top. Mark the edges of the sand on the waxed paper.

4 **Observe** One at a time, add four more spoonfuls of the cornstarch mixture. Each time, mark how far the glacier moves and the sand's position.

5 **Observe** Flip the glacier over onto another piece of waxed paper. Measure and draw the bottom.

Drawing Conclusions

1 **Explain** Did the sand mixture sprinkled on top in step 3 eventually reach the bottom?

2 **Interpret Data** What do you think happens when a real glacier moves over rocks and boulders?

3 **Define Terms** Define *glacial ice flow*.

Materials

goggles

prepared cornstarch mixture

mixture of sand, gravel, and soil

waxed paper

metal spoon

ruler

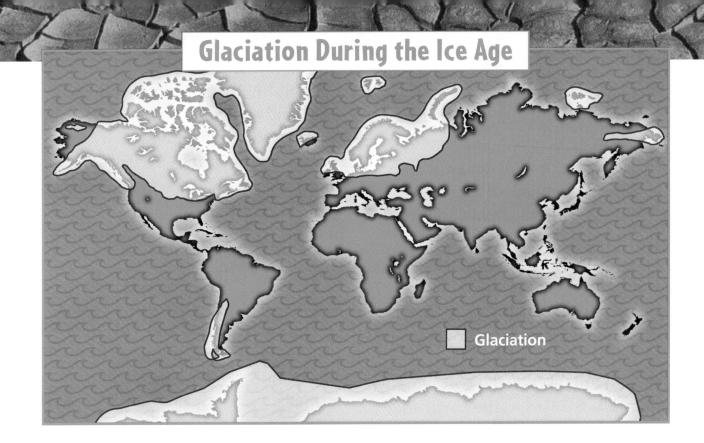

Glaciation

Did Glaciers Exist in the Past?

Scientists have learned about glaciers of the past by studying present-day glaciers and their features. You have read about some of these features, such as scratched bedrock, and U-shaped valleys. Other glacial features include erratics and outwash plains. **Erratics** (i·RAT·iks) are isolated boulders left behind by a glacier. **Outwash plains** are gravel, sand, and clay carried from glaciers by melting water and streams. They are deposited over large areas.

Glacial features are found today far from where glaciers now exist. They are evidence that glaciers once covered much larger parts of the world than they do today. Periods of very cold temperatures and many glaciers are called ice ages. During the ice ages, vast ice sheets as thick as several kilometers covered as much as one-third of Earth's surface. Temperatures were very low. Snowfall was heavy. Only places far from the glaciers were even slightly warm. As more and more water became ice, the oceans were greatly reduced in size.

Periods of warmer weather existed between ice ages. They are known as interglacial periods. Some scientists think that we are now in an interglacial period. They also believe that far in the future, Earth will undergo another ice age.

▷ **What is an ice age?**

What Other Forces Shape Earth?

Glaciers are not the only things that slowly change Earth's surface. Other agents of erosion include wind, waves, running water, and gravity.

As wind blows across Earth's surface, it picks up small particles of dust, soil, and sand. With time, exposed rocks and soil are worn down by the particles as if rubbed by sandpaper. When the wind finally slows down or stops, the particles drop to the ground, often far from where they were picked up.

Gravity and running water caused these rocks to move down the hillside.

Pounding waves break up rocks, coral, and shells into smaller pieces. As the pieces rub against each other, they grind down into particles. Waves also carry these materials away from the shore and drop them in other places. With time, waves can change a coastline.

Running water, such as streams, rivers, and flowing rainwater, picks up and carries particles of rock and soil. As these particles move, they may eventually cut a valley in the bedrock.

Running water may drop particles far from where they were picked up. When they settle at a river's mouth, they form a delta.

How do you think gravity can shape Earth's surface? Gravity causes any loose materials such as rocks, boulders, soil, water, and glaciers to move from a higher place to a lower place. Gravity can also cause landslides and mudflows.

Landslides occur when rocks and other materials are shaken loose by an earthquake or heavy rain. Mudflows typically occur after a heavy rain, when the soil can no longer absorb water.

▷ **How do gravity and water change Earth's surface?**

L·I·N·K·S

Why It Matters

Glaciers once covered much of Canada and parts of the United States. Most of them have melted away, but they changed the land in many ways. They carved valleys, scratched rocks, and dropped rocks as they passed.

Glaciers also show us what happens when snow and ice build up. Does it snow in the winter where you live? If so, be glad that the snow melts in the spring! Visit **www.mhscience02.com** to do a research project on glaciers.

Think and Write

1. What is a glacier?

2. What happens in ice ages?

3. In what ways can glaciers change the land?

4. Define Terms Describe glacial flow. Compare how glaciers and water flow.

5. Critical Thinking The people of Iceville are worried about a nearby glacier. They are thinking of building a large fence to keep it in place. Do you think their idea will work? Explain.

WRITING LINK

Write a story. How could people live during an ice age? Write a story that takes place during an ice age.

SOCIAL STUDIES LINK

Read a map. Look for glaciers on a map of the United States. Which states have glaciers? Are glaciers near any parks, towns, or cities?

MATH LINK

Solve a problem. In 1990 a glacier was 400 meters away from a road. Every year since then, it has moved about 7 meters closer to the road. At this rate, when will it meet the road?

TECHNOLOGY LINK

Science Newsroom CD-ROM Choose *A Moving Experience* to learn more about how glaciers change the land.

At the Computer Visit **www.mhscience02.com** for more links.

The Work of

Wind AND

Is erosion always a bad thing? Millions of people who've marveled at the view at Arizona's Grand Canyon don't think so! Over millions of years, the Colorado River carved out this beautiful canyon that is 1.6 kilometers (1 mile) deep. What a great use of water erosion!

Rainfall can create rivers. As rain flows downhill, it cuts into the soil. In time it can produce a deep canal or canyon. The water wears away river banks, and soil and rocks are slowly deposited on the sides. This creates a flat plain where the river begins to curve. Much of the soil and rocks a river carries is dropped off on the inside of the curves, where the flow is the slowest.

Wind can wear away the surface of soft rocks, especially in dry areas like deserts. Strong winds pick up bits of sand and gravel that beat against the hillsides. This erosion can create unusual shapes in the rocks. Some look like faces!

Wind can also cause dust storms in drought areas. Without enough rain the topsoil dries up and becomes loose. If strong winds blow across the land, they pick up the soil and carry it miles away. This is wind erosion.

These rocks were shaped by erosion.

Water

What Did I Learn?

1. The Grand Canyon was created by

A dust storms
B earthquakes
C waterfalls
D erosion

2. Dust storms are likely to strike

F drought areas
G rainy places
H canyons and valleys
J riverbanks

AT THE COMPUTER Visit **www.mhscience02.com** to learn more about erosion.

The Story of Soil

Vocabulary

humus, C44

horizon, C45

topsoil, C45

subsoil, C45

soil profile, C45

pore space, C48

permeability, C49

Get Ready

Why do we need soil? As every farmer knows, crops need soil to grow. Farmers take good care of soil to make it last year after year. Without soil, we would have no food to eat. What do you think makes soil so special?

Process Skill

You observe when you use senses to identify an object.

Explore Activity

What Is Soil Made Of?

Materials

3 types of soil

hand lens

eye dropper

water

newspaper

paper towels

3 sharp pencils

Procedure

1 Spread the newspaper on a desk or table. Place a soil sample on each paper towel. Put the paper towels on the newspaper.

2 **Observe** Use a pencil to push around the soil a little bit. Observe each sample with the hand lens. Record your observations of each soil sample.

3 **Classify** Use the pencil tip to classify the particles of each sample into two piles—pieces of rock and pieces of plant or animal material.

4 **Observe** Put four drops of water on each sample. After a few minutes, check which sample leaves the biggest wet spot on the newspaper.

Drawing Conclusions

1 **Infer** What kinds of materials make up each soil sample?

2 How do the particles you sorted in each soil sample compare by size? By color?

3 **Observe** Describe the properties you observed of each sample.

4 Which sample absorbed the most water? How can you tell?

5 **Going Further: Infer** What do you think soil is made of? How do you think it is made?

Main Idea Over time, processes in nature change bedrock into soil.

What Is Soil Made Of?

Soil begins to form when bedrock is broken apart into small pieces of rock and minerals. Rain, ice, wind, freezing, and thawing can do this. Chemical changes can do it, too.

What else breaks apart rocks? Plants and animals that live in small rock pieces help break them apart further. As plant roots grow downward, they pry apart rocks.

Burrowing animals, such as earthworms and ants, create tunnels between rock pieces. Some of these tunnels fill with air and water. Water expands as it freezes, further breaking apart the rocks.

Bacteria and fungi also help create soil. They decompose dead plants and animals for energy. The leftover plant and animal matter is called **humus** (HYEW·muhs). Humus becomes mixed with the rock pieces. Finally, a material that can be called soil is produced. Soil is a mixture of tiny rock particles, minerals, humus, water, and air.

How Soil Forms

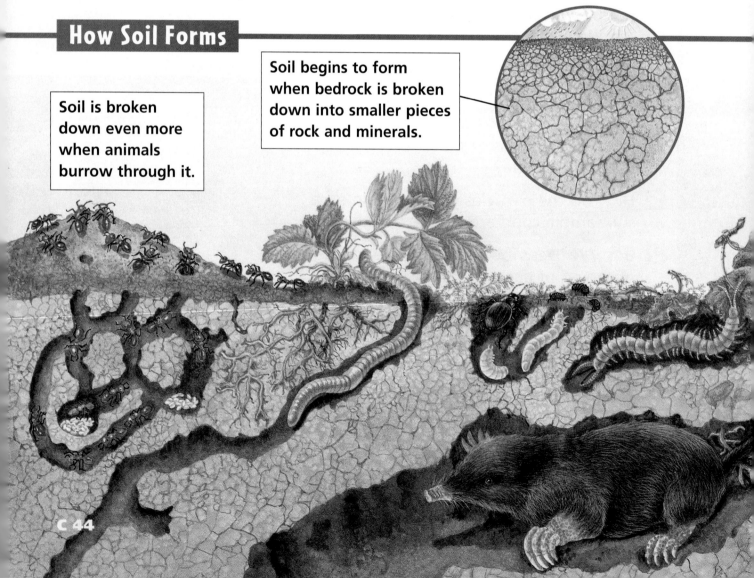

Soil is broken down even more when animals burrow through it.

Soil begins to form when bedrock is broken down into smaller pieces of rock and minerals.

Soil takes a long time to form. It may take hundreds to thousands of years for one inch of soil to form.

As soil forms, different layers result. A layer of soil differing from the layers above and below it is called a **horizon** (huh·RIGH·zuhn). Soils typically have three horizons. From the top down, they are A, B, and C. Each horizon has certain characteristics.

The A horizon is made up of **topsoil**. Topsoil is the top layer of soil. It is rich in humus and minerals. Topsoil is usually dark in color. Most plants grow here. Many organisms live here, too.

The B horizon is known as **subsoil**. Subsoil is normally a fairly hard layer. It is made of clay particles and minerals that have filtered down from the A horizon. It is usually light in color. Sturdy plant roots may grow down into the B horizon.

The C horizon is made up of coarse material broken down from the underlying bedrock. It is typically beyond the reach of plant roots.

The soil horizons make up a **soil profile**. A soil profile is a vertical section of soil from the surface down to bedrock.

▷ **What are three soil horizons?**

Soil Profile

A horizon: topsoil

B horizon: subsoil

C horizon: broken-down bedrock

Bedrock

READING

Diagrams

Which horizon in soil is the narrowest?

How Are Soils Alike and Different?

There are dozens of different kinds of soils, each with its own set of properties. The properties include texture, composition and thickness, mineral content, and the place it formed.

Soil with a lot of clay has a fine texture.

Silty soil has a medium texture.

Sandy soil has a coarse texture.

Texture refers to the size of the particles making up the soil. Sandy soil, for example, has a coarse texture. Soil with a lot of silt, or fine minerals, has a medium texture. Soil with a lot of clay has a fine texture. Most soils are mixtures of particles of several different sizes.

The composition and thickness of soils depend on several factors. They include the kind of bedrock from which the soils are formed, organisms, climate, steepness of the land, and time.

The kinds of minerals and rock fragments that make up different soils vary with the bedrock. The amount of humus depends on the kinds and numbers of organisms in the region. High temperatures and heavy rainfall cause rock to break down into soil quickly.

Farmers often add fertilizers to soil. This replaces minerals that were washed away or used up by crops.

Soil that forms on steep slopes is usually quite thin because it is eroded quickly. Where soil is eroded, new soil begins to form as bedrock is exposed at the surface.

Time is another important factor that determines soil thickness. Usually soil that is left alone becomes thicker over time.

Soils also differ based on the minerals they contain. The minerals in soil depend on the minerals found in the bedrock from which it was formed. Soil formed from limestone has minerals different from soil formed from granite.

Soil in one area may have more or less mineral content than soil in another area. The amount of minerals in soil depends on how much water passes through the soil. Water can dissolve and wash away minerals. Plants also use minerals as nutrients to make their own food. Areas with many plants may have few minerals in the soil.

Water, wind, or ice can erode soil, or move it from place to place. When eroded soil is deposited in other places, it is called transported soil. Minerals in transported soil may be quite different from those found in the bedrock below. This is a good clue that the soil has not always been there. Large parts of the central United States are covered in soil that was eroded by glaciers or wind.

Water passes through some soils more quickly than through others. The rate at which water travels through soils is another way in which soils differ.

READING **Draw Conclusions**
How can soil change over time?

QUICK LAB

FOR SCHOOL OR HOME

Rate of Flow

1. **Make two containers like the one shown at right. Put sandy soil in one container. Hold the container over a measuring cup. Slowly pour 1 cup of water over the soil, and start timing.**

2. **Measure** When water drops begin to "hang," record the total time. Determine the amount of water left in the soil. Record your findings.

3. **Repeat with the clay-rich soil in the other container.**

4. **Through which soil did the water pass more quickly? Which soil allowed more water to pass?**

5. **Interpret Data** Can you relate your findings to soil texture?

How Does Particle Size Affect Water Flow?

On page C46 you learned that sandy soil has a coarser texture than clay-rich soil. Does it surprise you that water flows through sandy soil more quickly than through clay-rich soil?

Remember that soil is made up not only of rock particles, minerals, and humus but also of water and air. Even in tightly packed soil, there are spaces between the solid materials. The spaces between soil particles are called **pore spaces** . Water and air fill these spaces.

As water travels through a soil's pore spaces, the soil acts like a filter. It filters certain pollutants out of the water as the water passes through.

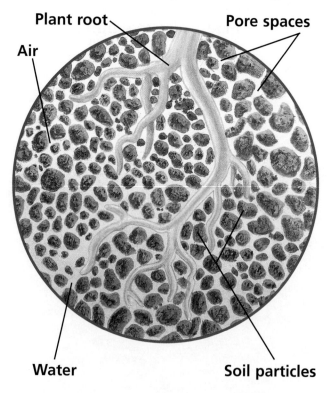

Plant root

Pore spaces

Air

Water

Soil particles

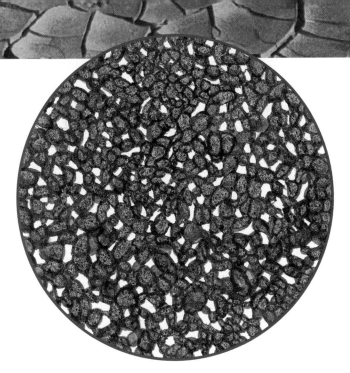

The small particles of a fine soil are packed together tightly. This type of soil has small pore spaces.

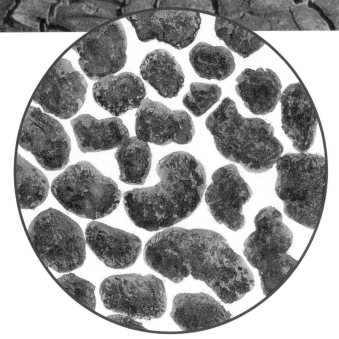

The large particles of a coarse soil are not packed together tightly. This type of soil has large pore spaces.

Materials with pore spaces are said to be *porous* (PAWR·uhs). Coarse-grained soils such as sandy soils have numerous pore spaces. That is because the larger particles are not packed together as tightly as smaller particles. This creates larger pore spaces through which water travels quickly.

The size of pore spaces and the way in which the pore spaces are connected affect **permeability** (pur·mee·uh·BIL·i·tee). Permeability is the rate at which water can pass through a porous material. Soils through which water passes quickly have a high permeability. Sandy soils have a high permeability. The larger particles are packed loosely together, holding little water.

Importance of Soil Permeability

Soil permeability is important to plants that live on land. Therefore, the type of soil in which plants grow is important. Coarse soil is very porous. It absorbs water quickly. Water moves downward quickly. It often travels to depths beyond the reach of plant roots. It dissolves minerals in the topsoil and carries them along with it.

How do you think fine soil affects a plant? While fine soil is porous, it is not very permeable. Water soaks into it slowly. It may remain in the pore spaces for a long time. The soil layers in which plant roots grow may become soaked. The plants drown from too much water.

▷ **Why is soil permeability important?**

Why Is Soil Important?

Without soil, few things would live on Earth. Soil supports the growth of plants on land. Plants use carbon dioxide, water, energy from the Sun, and nutrients in soil to make food. Plants, in turn, provide food for other organisms. Some animals eat plants directly. Others eat animals that eat plants.

Farmers who grow food crops must take good care of soil. Soil supplies the crops with water and nutrients such as nitrogen, potassium, and phosphorus. It also supports the crops' roots.

Land is often cleared of its natural vegetation to make it available for farming. Soon dramatic changes may take place in the soil. For example, when tropical forests are cut down, the soil is broken up and exposed. It becomes more permeable, and minerals are dissolved and carried downward. In a short time, the soil is unable to support plants.

Soil is also important in other ways. It filters pollutants out of water. We build houses, cities, and roads on it. We plant grass, flowers, and trees in it.

▶ **Why do you need soil?**

In a very short time after a rain forest is cleared, the soil is unable to support plants.

Why It Matters

Soil supplies us with food and filters our water. Soils are also living systems, providing homes for many organisms.

Soils are sensitive to changes in water, temperature, and human activity. That is why many people work to protect the soil. Soil scientists learn about soils and work to help conserve them. Some work with farmers to help them manage the soils in their fields.

Think and Write

1. What is soil made of?

2. Is soil different at different depths below the surface? Explain.

3. What are pore spaces? What do they hold?

4. List two reasons why soil is important.

5. **Critical Thinking** Sam grows tomatoes on his land year after year. Each year he gets fewer and smaller tomatoes than the year before. Why do you think this is happening? What do you think Sam should do?

L·I·N·K·S

SOCIAL STUDIES LINK

Research crops. Choose four states from different parts of the country. Find out what the soil is like in each state and what crops are grown there. Present your report to your teacher or classmates.

MUSIC LINK

Write a song. Your song should teach a lesson about soil or show why soil is important. Write new words to a familiar tune, or make up a new tune.

LITERATURE LINK

Read *Do You Feel Earth Moving?* to learn about soil, glaciers, and earthquakes. When you finish reading, look at the land in your own neighborhood. How is it changing? Try the activities at the end of the book.

HEALTH LINK

Make a list. Write down five healthful foods you eat that are grown in soil. Find out the three main nutrients in each of these foods. Do the five foods have nutrients in common? What might this mean?

TECHNOLOGY LINK

At the Computer Visit **www.mhscience02.com** for more links.

Inside Earth

Vocabulary

earthquake, C54

fault, C56

seismic wave, C56

crust, C58

mantle, C58

outer core, C58

inner core, C58

Get Ready

What lies under Earth's surface? Although they have tried, people have never dug holes deep enough to get to Earth's center. Still, scientists have learned a lot about Earth's interior. How do you think you can learn about something you cannot see?

Process Skill

You predict when you state possible results of an event or an experiment.

Explore Activity

What's Inside?

Procedure: Design Your Own

1 What kinds of observations can you make about the objects in the containers? Make a plan with your group. Outline different things you can test. Record your plan.

2 **Observe** Make your observations. Be sure you do not damage the containers. Each group member should have a turn with each container. Record all the observations.

3 **Interpret Data** Study your data. What clues do your observations provide?

Drawing Conclusions

1 **Infer** What do you think is in each container? Include a diagram or model that supports your observations.

2 **Communicate** Present your observations for each test. Explain how they support your conclusions.

3 **Going Further: Predict** Prepare a container like the ones used in this activity. Put one or more objects inside it. Exchange containers with a partner. Predict what is inside the container.

How Can We Learn About Earth's Interior?

How far down into Earth do you think you could dig? Would the bottom of your hole be near Earth's center? Not even close!

The deepest wells and mines extend only a relatively short distance into the bedrock that makes up Earth's outer layer. Even deeply eroded canyons barely scratch Earth's surface. The Grand Canyon is almost 2 kilometers (about 1 mile) deep. However, this distance is small compared with the total distance from Earth's surface to its center. That distance is about 6,400 kilometers (4,000 miles)!

Scientists learn about Earth by studying **earthquakes** (URTH·kwayks). Earthquakes are movements or vibrations in Earth. They are caused by the release of stored energy in Earth's outer layer. This release of energy causes sudden shifts of rock as well as other kinds of changes.

Scientists "feel" and "listen to" Earth by using instruments called *seismographs* (SIGHZ·muh·grafs). A seismograph detects, measures, and records the energy of earthquake vibrations.

A seismograph is an instrument that measures the energy of earthquake vibrations. Earthquake vibrations can cause extensive damage, such as the collapse of concrete buildings.

Imagine the world as an apple. Imagine the apple's skin to be like the Earth's crust. The Grand Canyon and the deepest wells and mine shafts would not even extend through the apple's skin. They provide information only about Earth's very thin, rocky outer layer.

Scientists have spent many years trying to answer the question of what lies below Earth's thin surface. They certainly can't cut Earth open to observe what is there. Earthquakes give scientists valuable information about the other layers of the Earth. Scientists must depend on information obtained in several different ways, such as from earthquakes. They then combine and interpret the information to come up with an answer.

▷ **What is an earthquake?**

Earthquake Vibrations

1. Spread out some newspaper to absorb splashed water. Place a pan of water on the newspaper.

2. Observe Take turns dropping a marble into the water from a height of about 15 cm (6 in.). Shine a flashlight on the water to see more clearly. Record your observations of the wave patterns.

3. Communicate What wave pattern did the marble create?

4. Infer How do you think this pattern might relate to the way earthquake vibrations travel?

What Causes Earthquakes?

Pressure within Earth can cause rocks in its outer layer to break. If the rocks found along a break move, the break is called a **fault** (FAWLT). The place where the movement begins is called the *focus*. The focus may lie as far as 700 kilometers (450 miles) below Earth's surface. When an earthquake begins, pressure from within Earth causes rocks along faults to move and break. As they move, energy is released as vibrations. These vibrations are called **seismic waves** (SIGHZ·mik WAYVZ), or earthquake waves.

In what direction do you think seismic waves travel? Seismic waves travel out from the focus in all directions. As seismic waves move through Earth and along its surface, they are felt as shakings and vibrations.

▷ **What are seismic waves?**

Earthquake Features

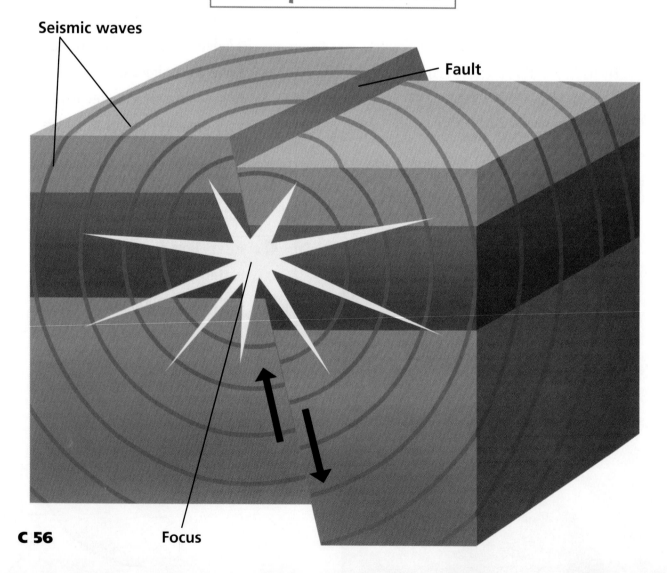

Seismic waves

Fault

Focus

What Can We Learn from Earthquakes?

The farther waves travel away from the focus, the weaker they become. Seismographs in different places record the strength of the waves. Very weak waves at great distances from the focus can be detected. The printed record made by a seismograph is called a *seismogram* (SIGHZ·muh·gram).

By comparing seismograms scientists can track waves and determine their speed and direction of travel. They can also learn about Earth's interior. That is because there are different kinds of seismic waves, and they travel at different speeds.

READING **Draw Conclusions**
How can seismograms teach us about Earth's interior?

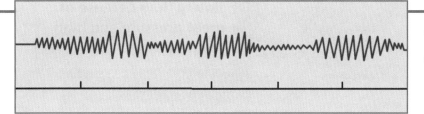

This seismogram was recorded during a weak earthquake.

This seismogram was recorded during a strong earthquake. How are the two seismograms similar? Different?

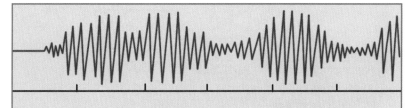

Types of Seismic Waves

Primary waves. Also called P waves, these are the fastest seismic waves. They are the first to arrive at a distant point. P waves can travel through solids, liquids, and gases.

Secondary waves. Also called S waves, they travel slower than P waves. They arrive later at a distant point. S waves travel only through solids.

Surface waves. Also called L waves (long waves), these are the slowest waves of all. They are felt at the surface as they slowly move the ground up and down, and from side to side. These waves cause the damage that often comes with an earthquake.

Waves travel at different speeds through solids, liquids, and gases. By studying waves from earthquakes, scientists infer what Earth is like on the inside.

What Is Earth's Structure?

The diagram shows the locations and characteristics of Earth's layers.

READING
Diagrams

Which layer is the thickest? Which is the thinnest?

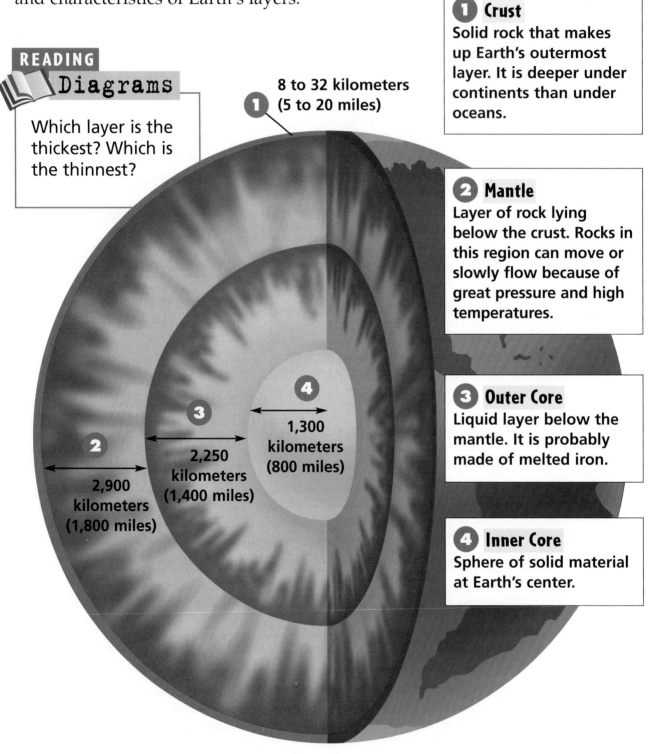

8 to 32 kilometers (5 to 20 miles)

1

2 2,900 kilometers (1,800 miles)

3 2,250 kilometers (1,400 miles)

4 1,300 kilometers (800 miles)

1 Crust
Solid rock that makes up Earth's outermost layer. It is deeper under continents than under oceans.

2 Mantle
Layer of rock lying below the crust. Rocks in this region can move or slowly flow because of great pressure and high temperatures.

3 Outer Core
Liquid layer below the mantle. It is probably made of melted iron.

4 Inner Core
Sphere of solid material at Earth's center.

▶ **What are Earth's four layers?**

Why It Matters

Scientists use instruments to predict when an earthquake might occur. A gravity meter tells scientists about the rise and fall of the land surface. A strain meter measures how much rocks expand and contract. A tilt meter measures changes in the tilt of the surface of Earth. A creep meter measures how much the land moves along a fault. This information may help scientists warn people of a possible earthquake.

Think and Write

1. What is a seismograph?

2. What causes an earthquake?

3. Compare Earth's crust with its interior.

4. What is Earth's thinnest layer? What is its thickest?

5. **Critical Thinking** How can studying seismic waves teach us about Earth's interior?

L·I·N·K·S

WRITING LINK

Write a story. Imagine you are traveling to the center of Earth! Write a story about your adventure. Be sure to include a description of each layer you travel through. Discuss problems with this journey and how they might be solved.

SOCIAL STUDIES LINK

Research an earthquake. Over the past 100 years, strong earthquakes have struck Japan, Mexico, and the western United States. Prepare a report on a strong earthquake. Present it to your teacher or classmates.

LITERATURE LINK

Read *Laura and the Great Quake* to learn about a girl who lives through an earthquake in Italy. Try the activities at the end of the book.

MATH LINK

The Earth's crust is about 20 km thick. Using the information on page C58, figure out how many times thicker the inner core is than the crust.

TECHNOLOGY LINK

At the Computer Visit **www.mhscience02.com** for more links.

Chapter 6 Review

Vocabulary

Fill each blank with the best word or words from the list.

crust, C58   **mantle,** C58

fault, C56   **outer core,** C58

glacier, C34   **permeability,** C49

horizon, C45   **topsoil,** C45

inner core, C58

1. Soil develops in layers called _____.

2. A huge, moving mass of ice and snow is called a(n) _____.

3. A layer of soil is also called a soil _____.

4. Earthquakes occur along a split in Earth's crust called a(n) _____.

5. _____ is the soil layer richest in humus.

6. How fast water travels through soil is a measure of a soil's _____.

Earth's outer layer: **7.** _____

8. _____

9. _____

Earth's center: **10.** _____

Test Prep

11. A large, lone rock dropped by a glacier is a(n) _____.

  A mantle

  B morraine

  C erratic

  D glacial till

12. Humus comes from _____.

  F bedrock

  G heavy rainfall

  H dead plants and animals

  J clay soil

13. The Grand Canyon reaches into Earth's _____.

  A crust only

  B crust and mantle

  C crust and outer core

  D crust, mantle, and outer core

14. During the Ice Age, glaciers covered _____.

  F only the areas near the poles

  G about half of North America

  H all of Earth

  J only Earth's oceans

15. The center of a seismic wave is called the _____.

A fault

B focus

C morraine

D seismogram

Concepts and Skills

16. Reading in Science Describe how scientists used data from earthquakes to infer the structure of Earth.

17. Product Ads Many products claim to help gardens grow. Design an experiment to see how well the product works.

18. Critical Thinking We did not live during the Ice Age, and we have not visited the center of Earth. How can we infer what this time and this place was like?

19. Decision Making You are a farmer with a big problem. Insect pests are killing your wheat crop! You could use *Blammo*, a new product that kills the pests. However, it might damage the soil for next year. Would you use *Blammo*? What further information might help you decide?

20. Process Skills: Define Based on Observation What if the water in a garden forms puddles and doesn't soak in? What do you think the soil in the garden is like? Why do you think so?

Boost *your test scores!*

Be Smart!
Visit www.mhscience02.com
to learn more.

CHAPTER

7

LESSON 6
Earth, the Moon, and the Sun, C64

LESSON 7
The Solar System and Beyond, C78

Sun, Moon, and Planets

Did You Ever Wonder?

Where did Earth's Moon come from? Some planetary scientists believe that the Moon was formed when an object collided with Earth about 4 billion years ago. The debris from the massive collision started orbiting Earth. Earth and the Moon are part of the solar system. What other objects belong to the solar system?

Earth, the Moon, and the Sun

Vocabulary

rotate, C66

axis, C67

revolve, C68

orbit, C68

crater, C71

Process Skill

You infer when you form an idea from facts or observations.

Get Ready

If you call someone in Asia this afternoon, you might get a very grouchy "Hello." It will be the middle of the night there! Every minute of every hour, darkness is falling somewhere on Earth. At the same time, morning occurs somewhere else. What causes this cycle of day and night?

Explore Activity

How Do the Sun, Earth, and the Moon Move?

Materials

lamp without a shade

75- or 100-watt bulb

extension cord

craft-foam ball

Procedure

1. **Observe** Look at the pictures that show the ways the Moon appears from Earth at night.

2. **Make a Model** Create a model of the Sun, Earth, and the Moon. Let the lamp be the Sun. One partner should hold the ball to model the Moon. The other partner should represent Earth.

3. **Experiment** Turn out the lights in the room. Turn on the lamp. Do not move the lamp. Experiment with different positions to try to model the different ways the Moon looks in the pictures.

4. **Make a Model** Again let the lamp be the Sun. This time let the ball be Earth. Do not move the lamp. Demonstrate and explain what you think causes day and night on Earth.

Drawing Conclusions

1. What causes the Moon to look different to us on Earth from night to night?

2. Why does Earth have day and night?

3. **Infer** Why are the patterns of day and night and changes in the Moon's appearance predictable?

4. You can model day and night on Earth by keeping the ball still and moving the lamp. This is not an accurate model. Why?

5. **Going Further: Infer** How are the Sun, Earth, and the Moon positioned when the Moon looks largest?

Main Idea Earth moves around the Sun. The Moon moves around Earth.

How Do the Sun, Earth, and the Moon Move?

How can it be afternoon where you live and the middle of the night in Asia? The answer is that Earth moves.

A long time ago, people thought that Earth stood still while the Sun traveled around it each day. It's easy to see why they thought the Sun moved. Every day the Sun seems to rise and set.

Today we know that the Sun doesn't move around Earth. It is Earth that moves around the Sun. As Earth moves around the Sun, it also spins, or **rotates** (ROH·tayts). It is Earth's rotation that causes day and night.

If you spin around, you see different parts of the room go by. Likewise, as Earth rotates, you see different parts of space. During the day the part of Earth where you live faces the Sun. As Earth rotates, that part of Earth moves away from the Sun. Soon it faces dark outer space. It is now night where you live.

The rotation of Earth changes day into night and night into day. One complete rotation of Earth takes 24 hours, or one whole day.

The movement of Earth and the Moon also causes the Moon to look different at different times. You will learn more about the Moon later in this lesson.

As Earth rotates, the Sun appears to rise, as shown here, and set.

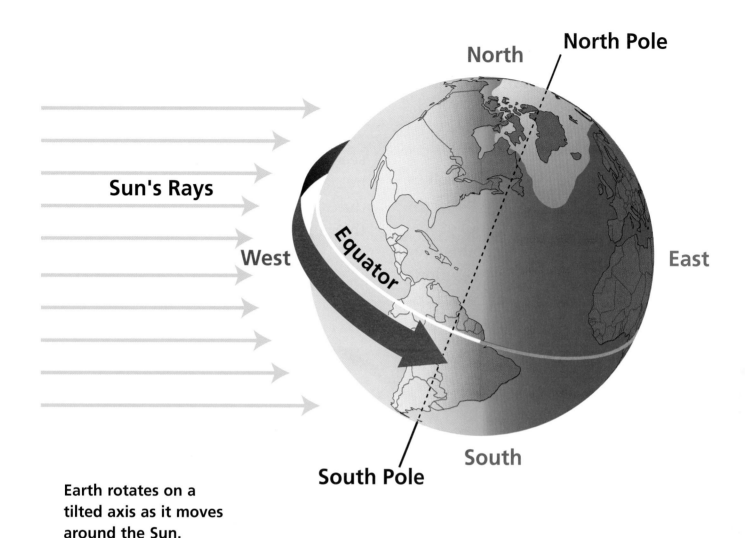

North

North Pole

Sun's Rays

West

Equator

East

South Pole

South

Earth rotates on a
tilted axis as it moves
around the Sun.

You can't feel Earth's rotation, but standing on Earth is like riding a giant top. The diagram above shows Earth's rotation. The imaginary line drawn from the North Pole to the South Pole is Earth's **axis** (AK·sis). An axis is a real or imaginary line that a spinning object turns around. As Earth rotates, it turns about its axis just as a top spins about its axis.

However, unlike a spinning top, Earth's axis is tilted. Earth is tipped at an angle of 23.5°. Some scientists think that long ago, Earth was hit by a large object, such as a big chunk of rock and dust. The object pushed Earth onto its side. Earth stayed tilted.

▶ **How can it be daytime in one city and nighttime in another?**

Why Are There Seasons?

Earth not only spins on its axis, it also **revolves** (ri·VAHLVZ) around the Sun. To revolve is to move in a circular or nearly circular path around something else.

Earth's trip around the Sun takes $365\frac{1}{4}$ days, or one year. As Earth travels on this journey, it moves in an **orbit** (AWR·bit). An orbit is the path a revolving object moves along. Earth's orbit is shaped like an *ellipse* (i·LIPS), or flattened circle.

As Earth revolves around the Sun, it keeps spinning on its axis. The fact that Earth's axis of rotation is tilted, and not straight up and down, produces an important effect—seasons! Autumn, winter, spring, and summer all result from Earth's revolution on its tilted axis.

How does Earth's tilt create seasons? Look at the diagram below. As Earth revolves around the Sun, its axis is always tilted in the same direction.

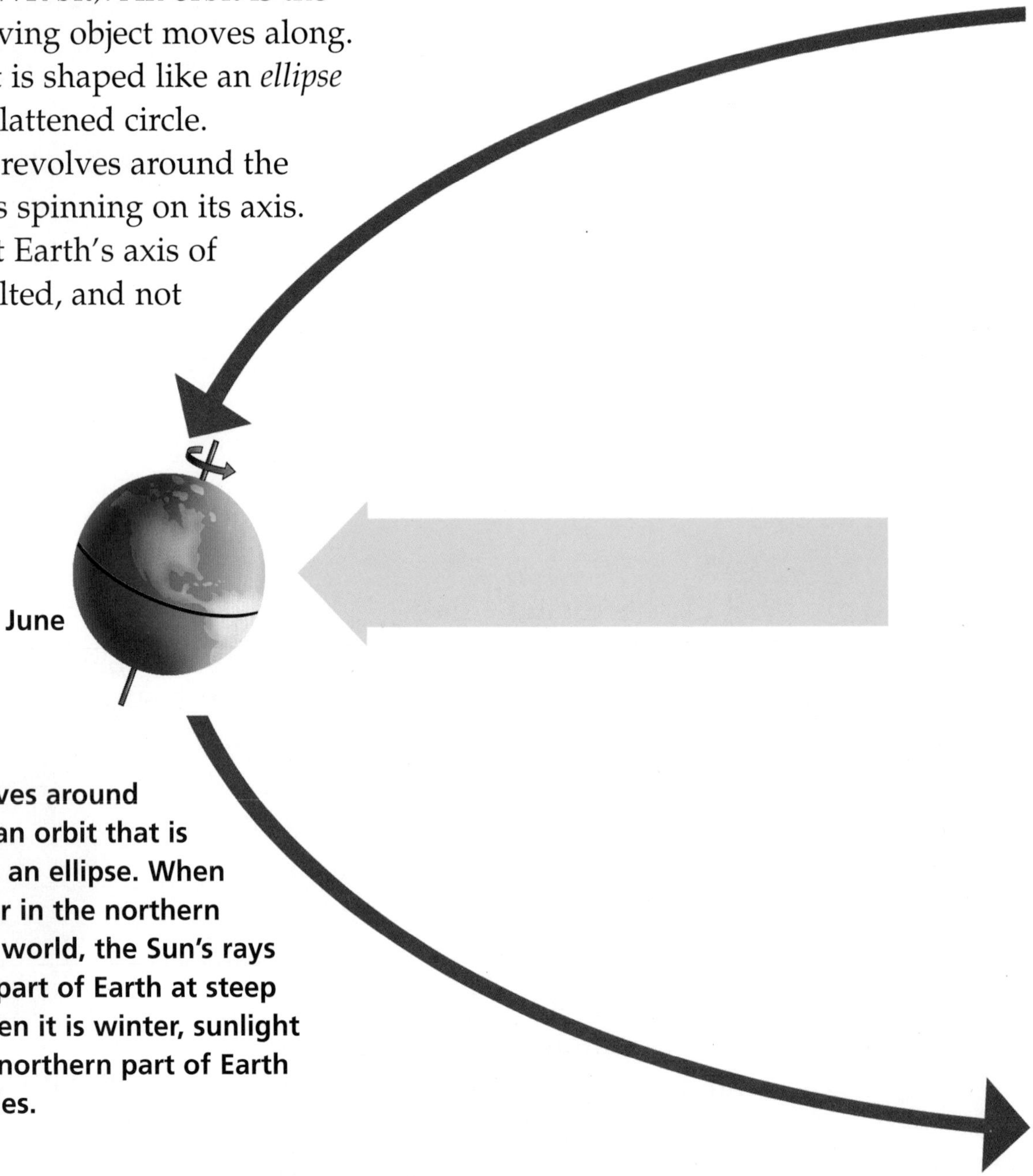

June

Earth revolves around the Sun in an orbit that is shaped like an ellipse. When it is summer in the northern part of the world, the Sun's rays strike that part of Earth at steep angles. When it is winter, sunlight strikes the northern part of Earth at low angles.

In June the North Pole tilts toward the Sun. The Sun's rays strike the northern half of Earth at steep angles. It is summer there.

However, in December the North Pole tilts away from the Sun. The Sun's rays strike the northern half of Earth at low angles. The rays are more slanted than they were in summer. It is winter in the northern part of the world.

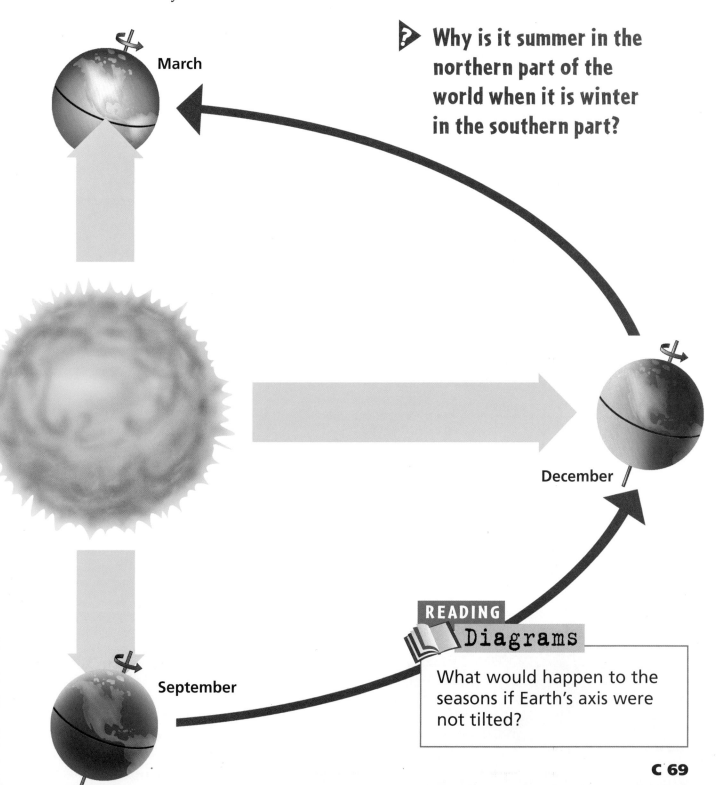

March

December

September

▶ **Why is it summer in the northern part of the world when it is winter in the southern part?**

READING
Diagrams

What would happen to the seasons if Earth's axis were not tilted?

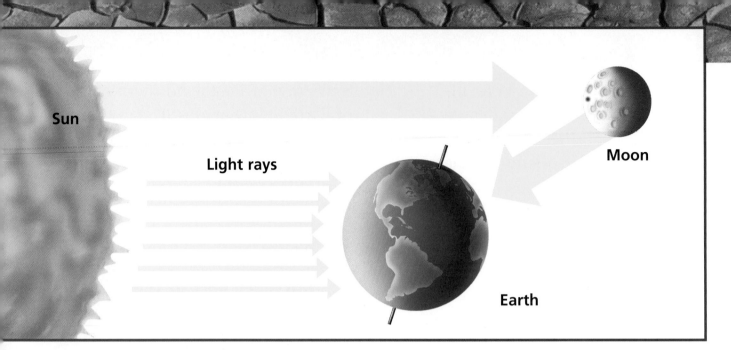

Sun

Light rays

Moon

Earth

The Moon does not make its own light. It reflects light from the Sun onto Earth.

How Do the Moon and Earth Compare?

The Moon is the biggest and brightest object in the night sky. Is it really as big as it appears? In fact, the Moon is smaller than stars and planets. It looks so big and bright because it is Earth's closest neighbor in space. It is about 384 thousand kilometers (240 thousand miles) away.

The Moon is about one-fourth as wide as Earth. If the Moon were the size of a tennis ball, Earth would be the size of a basketball. Not only is it smaller than Earth, but it has less mass, too. Gravity on the Moon is weak compared with Earth because of this.

Gravity is the force that holds things on the ground and determines how much they weigh. Gravity is six times stronger on Earth than on the Moon. If you stepped on a scale on the Moon, you'd weigh only one-sixth of your weight on Earth.

The moonlight we see from Earth is really light from the Sun. Sunlight strikes the Moon and reflects onto Earth.

The Moon is Earth's nearest neighbor in space. This is why it looks as big and as bright as it does.

The Moon travels in an orbit, just as Earth does. Earth revolves around the Sun, and the Moon revolves around Earth. However, the Moon's trip around Earth takes only about 28 days. This is much shorter than the year-long journey of Earth around the Sun.

What the Moon Is Like

The Moon is dusty and lifeless. There is no air or liquid water. Daytime is so hot that a person's blood would boil! At night the Moon is much colder than any place on Earth. It has mountains, large flat plains, and a huge number of **craters** (KRAY·tuhrz). A crater is a hollow area, or pit, in the ground. Ancient volcanoes may have formed some of the Moon's craters. However, most of the craters were made by chunks of rock and metal from space crashing into the Moon.

The first missions to the Moon used robots and spacecraft without astronauts. In the 1960s and 1970s, *Apollo* missions sent astronauts to the Moon six times. The astronauts wore spacesuits to protect themselves. They collected data and samples. After these missions, Moon exploration slowed because it is expensive. Some unmanned missions continue today.

What does the future hold? Maybe someday we will build a space station on the Moon! People would live and work there for months at a time.

Apollo mission astronaut David R. Scott walked on the Moon. The Moon's surface is dusty and covered with craters.

READING Cause and Effect
Why do visitors to the Moon need to wear spacesuits?

What Makes the Moon Look Different?

You look up in the sky one night and see a beautiful round Moon. A week later the Moon seems smaller and has a new shape. In another week you can barely see the Moon at all. What's going on?

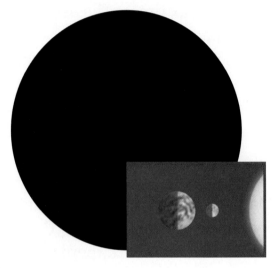

1 New Moon
The Moon is between the Sun and Earth. You can't see the lighted half of the Moon.

2 Crescent Moon
The lighted side of the Moon begins to show. The Moon is waxing, meaning the part you see is growing larger.

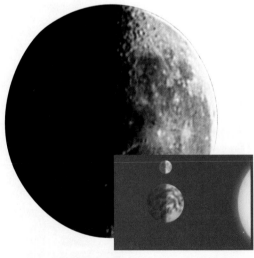

3 First Quarter Moon
The Moon is a quarter of the way around Earth. This is sometimes called a half Moon.

4 Gibbous Moon
A gibbous (GIB·uhs) Moon is almost full.

Half of the Moon always faces toward the Sun and the other half is in darkness. As the Moon travels around Earth, we see different amounts of its lighted half. That makes the Moon appear to change shape. These different shapes are called *phases*. It takes about 29 days for the Moon to show all of its phases.

5 Full Moon
The Moon is now halfway around Earth. You can see all of its lighted side.

6 Gibbous Moon
The Moon is waning, meaning the part you see is getting smaller.

7 Last Quarter Moon
The Moon is three-quarters of the way around Earth.

▶ **What causes the Moon's phases?**

8 Crescent Moon
The lighted side has almost disappeared. Soon a new Moon will begin the cycle again.

Process Skill BUILDER

Moon Phases on a Calendar

When you interpret data, you use information from a picture, a table, or a graph. A calendar is a type of table. Each icon in this calendar tells you what phase the Moon will be in for that day. Interpret the data in the calendar to answer the following questions.

Procedure

1 Communicate Make a table that shows how many times each phase of the Moon appears in the month shown on this calendar.

2 Make another table listing each phase of the Moon discussed on pages C72 and C73. Next to each phase, write the day of the month that phase occurs for the month shown on this calendar.

SEPTEMBER						
Sunday	Monday	Tuesday	Wednesday	Thursday	Friday	Saturday
		1	2	3	4	5
6	7	8	9	10	11	12
13	14	15	16	17	18	19
20	21	22	23	24	25	26
27	28	29	30			

3 Interpret Data On which day or days was there a new Moon? A first quarter Moon? A gibbous Moon?

4 Interpret Data Were there any days this month that had the same phase of the Moon? If so, what were they?

Drawing Conclusions

1 Observe What pattern do you see in the phases of the Moon for this month?

2 Interpret Data Find a calendar that shows the phases of the Moon. Compare the month shown in this activity with one month in your calendar. How are the phases of the Moon similar? Different?

L·I·N·K·S

Why It Matters

Since early times people have wanted to know why there are seasons, day and night, and phases of the Moon. Ancient cultures told many stories. Today we have learned a great deal about Earth, the Moon, and the Sun. We have even visited the Moon! You may not be able to visit the Moon in person just yet. Instead, visit **www.mhscience02.com** to do a research project on the Moon.

Think and Write

1. Why can it be day where you live and night in Asia?

2. How long does it take Earth to make one rotation? One revolution?

3. How does Earth's axis affect seasons?

4. Interpret Data What shape is the Moon? Why does it appear to change shape?

5. Critical Thinking How would your life be different if you lived in the southern half of Earth?

ART LINK

Draw a picture. On a large piece of paper, draw a picture of Earth orbiting the Sun. Show where Earth is during winter, spring, summer, and fall. On your diagram, draw pictures of things that happen during each season, such as what the weather is like and what sports you play.

MATH LINK

Solve a problem. In one second, Earth moves about 30 kilometers (19 miles) in its orbit around the Sun. How far does Earth move in one minute?

WRITING LINK

Write a poem. What do you think about when you gaze at the Moon? Would you like to visit there? What do you think your trip would be like? Write a poem or story about Moon travel, from blast-off to touchdown.

TECHNOLOGY LINK

At the Computer Visit **www.mhscience02.com** for more links.

TELESCOPES:
Tools of Discovery

In the 1600s the Italian scientist Galileo improved a telescope and used it to explore space. He discovered craters on the Moon, spots on the Sun, four moons of Jupiter, and many stars.

Today, scientists study space with many kinds of telescopes. Some work like magnifying glasses. They use curved pieces of glass, or lenses, to make objects look bigger. Other telescopes use curved mirrors to enlarge the images of objects.

Clouds and city lights make it hard to see through telescopes. This is why many telescopes are located in clear, deserted areas or on mountaintops.

One of the best places for a telescope is in space itself. The Hubble telescope orbits Earth outside the atmosphere. It takes pictures of the solar system and beyond, into deep space. The Hubble doesn't have to look through Earth's atmosphere.

The Hubble telescope was launched in 1990. It has taken pictures of galaxies in deep space.

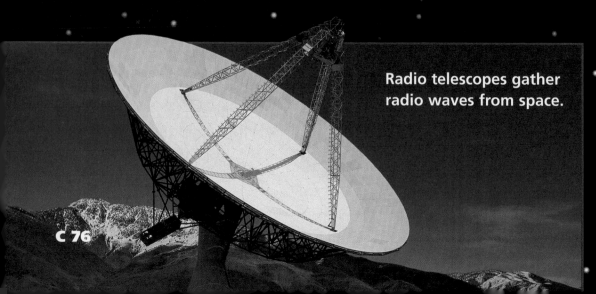

Radio telescopes gather radio waves from space.

Large lens

Path of light

Eyepiece

This photo of Saturn was taken with a telescope.

The large lens in this telescope gathers light from stars. A small double-lens eyepiece magnifies the image.

It can see objects in space much more clearly than telescopes on Earth.

Objects in space produce signals other than visible light. Special telescopes can detect radio waves, X rays, or infrared waves. Telescopes have come a long way since the first time Galileo used one to gaze at the Moon!

AT THE COMPUTER

Visit www.mhscience02.com to learn more about telescopes.

What Did I Learn?

1. The Hubble telescope is located in

A Italy.
B orbit around the Moon.
C orbit around Earth.
D a distant galaxy.

2. Today, a telescope can detect

F light only.
G radio waves only.
H X rays only.
J many different kinds of signals.

The Solar System and Beyond

Vocabulary

star, C80

planet, C81

solar system, C81

asteroid, C86

comet, C86

meteor, C86

constellation, C88

Get Ready

Where are we? It's no place on Earth! This is the surface of the planet Mars. Humans have not yet visited Mars. However, we have sent spacecraft there. Cameras sent back pictures such as this one. You can see Mars in the sky on some nights. It looks like a small dot of light. Why do you think Mars looks so small when seen from Earth?

Process Skill

You make a model when you make something to represent an object or event.

Explore Activity

How Do Objects in the Night Sky Compare in Size?

Materials

colored craft paper

sheets of newspaper

meterstick

metric ruler

marker

scissors

Procedure

BE CAREFUL! Handle scissors carefully.

1 **Measure** Study the table. Compare diameters of different objects in the night sky. The diameter is the distance across the middle of a circle or sphere.

2 **Make a Model** Cut a paper circle 1 cm across to model Earth. Measure and cut paper circles to model each object listed in the table. If you cannot make the model Sun large enough, make it as large as possible. Label each object.

3 **Classify** Arrange the objects in a way that lets you compare their sizes.

Drawing Conclusions

1 Compare the sizes of the Moon, the Sun, and the planets.

2 How can the Moon and the Sun look the same size in our sky?

3 **Infer** The Sun is an average-sized star. Why do other stars look so much smaller than the Sun?

4 **Going Further: Make a Model** Research the sizes of the other planets that orbit the Sun. Cut paper models of the right sizes to represent them. Assemble all the circles into a model of the Sun and its planets.

Comparing Diameters	
Object	**Size** (in Earth Diameters)
Earth	1
Moon	$\frac{1}{4}$
Mars	$\frac{1}{2}$
Saturn	$9\frac{1}{2}$
Jupiter	11
Sun	109

Main Idea Earth is part of a system that includes the Sun, planets, and other objects.

Why Is the Sun a Star?

Here's a riddle: What star do you see only in the daytime? Answer: The Sun! Our Sun is a **star**. A star is a hot, glowing sphere of gases that gives off energy.

The Sun is an average star in many ways. It is medium-sized.

It looks bigger and brighter than any other star only because it is much closer to Earth.

The Sun and other stars are not solid like the ground under your feet. Instead, they are made of gases. One important gas in the Sun is hydrogen. This is the Sun's fuel. The Sun uses hydrogen to make heat and light energy. It gives off so much energy that it warms and lights Earth, millions of kilometers away!

This sentence may help you remember the order of the planets from the Sun in our solar system: My Very Excellent Mother Just Served Us Nine Pizzas.

Sun

Uranus

Mars

Venus

Jupiter

Neptune

On a clear night, you can sometimes see a **planet** in the sky. Planets are *satellites* of the Sun. A satellite is an object that moves in orbit around another, larger body. From Earth planets can look like stars in the night sky. Planets are not stars, however. They are smaller and cooler than stars. Also, like the Moon, planets cannot make light.

The Sun, Earth, eight other planets, their moons, and smaller objects make up the **solar system** .

Each planet rotates on an axis and revolves around the Sun. However, the planets have many differences. They rotate at different speeds. A day on Earth is 24 hours long, but a day on Venus is 243 Earth days long. The planets revolve around the Sun at different speeds, too. One year on Pluto lasts about 250 Earth years.

▷ **What makes up our solar system?**

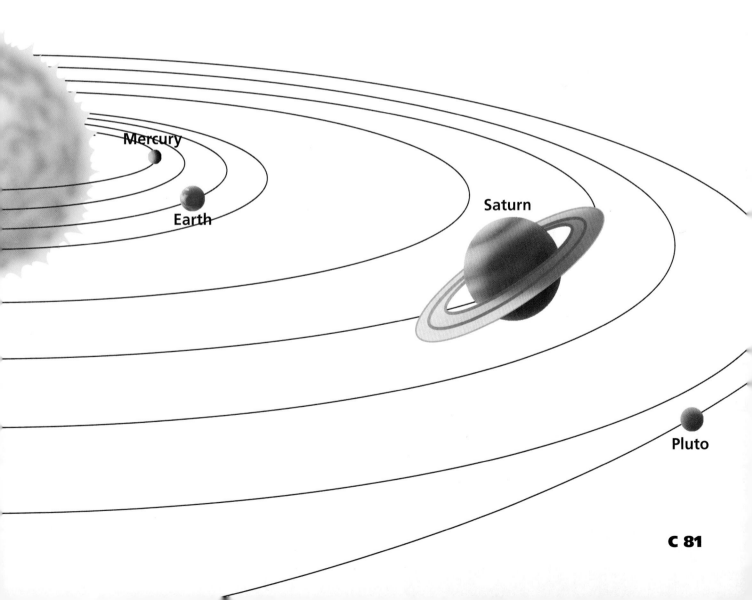

What Are the Inner Planets?

Mercury, Venus, Earth, and Mars are called the *inner planets*. They are the closest planets to the Sun. They are warmer and smaller than the other planets. All of them are made of solid, rocklike materials. In their early years, they were constantly struck by other objects in space. As a result, craters cover their surfaces. The inner planets have few, if any, satellites.

Mercury, the closest planet to the Sun, is a lot like Earth's Moon. It has a very hot side and a very cold side. There is no water and very little air.

Venus is almost the same size as Earth, but the two planets are very different. Like Mercury, Venus has no water. However, it does have an atmosphere. Its atmosphere is made up mostly of carbon dioxide. This gas covers Venus like a thick blanket. It traps heat, making Venus the hottest planet in the solar system.

Earth is the only planet that we know supports life. Earth's atmosphere keeps it from getting too hot or too cold. Also, Earth has water and oxygen. These things make Earth the special, life-supporting member of the solar system.

Mars is smaller than Earth but has two moons. Its thin atmosphere is mostly carbon dioxide. Strong winds create large dust storms. Mars is known as "the red planet" because of its reddish surface. Craters and inactive volcanoes cover most of the surface. One of Mars's volcanoes is the highest known mountain in the solar system. It is more than two kilometers ($1\frac{1}{2}$ miles) high!

 **How does Earth compare with the other inner planets?**

The Inner Planets

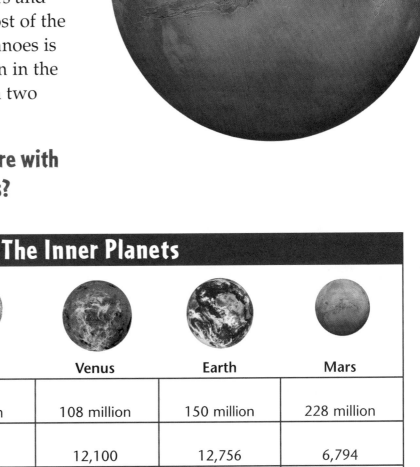

	Mercury	Venus	Earth	Mars
Distance to the Sun (in kilometers)	58 million	108 million	150 million	228 million
Diameter (in kilometers)	4,880	12,100	12,756	6,794
Did you know?	A year on Mercury lasts only 88 days.	Temperatures on Venus can reach 500°C.	Earth's atmosphere protects the surface from space.	Iron oxide, or rust, gives Mars its reddish color.

READING
Diagrams

1. How do the sizes of the planets compare with Earth's size?

2. Which planet is closest to Earth? How far away is it?

What Are the Outer Planets?

The five *outer planets* are far from the Sun. Because of this, they are dark and cold. Jupiter, Saturn, Uranus, and Neptune are giants made up mostly of gas. Each has moons and a ring system. Saturn's rings are quite famous. Pluto, the last of the outer planets, is a bit different from the others. It is solid, rocky, and small.

Jupiter is the largest planet in our solar system. It has 17 moons plus 11 new moons that have just been discovered and a thin ring of dust. Thick, icy clouds of ammonia and water make up much of Jupiter. Another of its features is the Great Red Spot. You can see the spot in many photos of Jupiter. Scientists think that a large storm causes this spot.

Beyond Jupiter is Saturn, the second largest planet and another gas giant. Saturn has 16 moons that we know of. It has thousands of beautiful shiny rings. The rings are made of chunks of ice and rock.

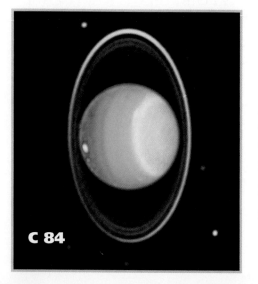

A bluish fog covers Uranus, the seventh planet. This gas giant has faint gray rings and 17 moons. Scientists think the rings might be made of graphite, the material used in pencils. Uranus rotates on such a tilted axis that it looks as if it's lying on its side.

Neptune is the last of the gas giants. It has a Great Dark Spot, similar to the spot on Jupiter. Neptune has rings and eight moons.

Pluto is the ninth and farthest planet from the Sun. It is dark and cold. From distant Pluto the Sun is just a small point of light. Pluto is made up of a mixture of rocky materials and frozen gases. It has a thin atmosphere and one large moon.

▶ **How is Pluto different from the other outer planets?**

READING
Diagrams

1. How do the sizes and orbits of the outer planets compare?

2. Could humans live on the outer planets? Explain your answer.

The Outer Planets

	Jupiter	Saturn	Uranus	Neptune	Pluto
Distance to the Sun (in kilometers)	778 million	1,429 million	2,871 million	4,504 million	5,914 million
Diameter (in kilometers)	143,000	120,536	51,118	49,528	2,300
Did you know?	Jupiter is 1,500 times bigger than Earth.	Winds on Saturn can blow at 500 meters per second.	A day on Uranus lasts only 17 hours.	Neptune takes 165 Earth years to orbit the Sun.	Pluto sometimes moves inside Neptune's orbit.

What Else Is in the Solar System?

The Sun, planets, and their moons are not alone in our solar system. There are also **asteroids** (AS·tuh·roydz), **comets** (KAHM·its), and **meteors** (MEE·tee·uhrz). Asteroids are chunks of rock or metal that orbit the Sun. There are thousands of them. Most are found in the asteroid belt, an area between the inner and outer planets.

Have you ever seen a shooting star? Shooting stars aren't really stars—they're meteors. Meteors are small pieces of ice, rock, or metal that have broken off colliding comets or asteroids. They usually fly through the sky and burn up from friction with Earth's atmosphere.

Very rarely a meteor will hit Earth. Then it is called a *meteorite*. Fortunately, most meteorites are small.

Meteor Crater in the Arizona Desert was made when a huge meteorite crashed into Earth thousands of years ago.

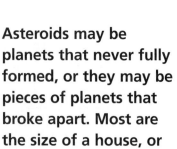

Asteroids may be planets that never fully formed, or they may be pieces of planets that broke apart. Most are the size of a house, or smaller.

Comets move around the Sun in long, narrow orbits. Comets are mostly chunks of ice mixed with bits of rock and dust. They are sometimes called "dirty snowballs." Most comets stay out on the edge of the solar system, but a few get pushed closer to the Sun. These comets develop tails of gas and dust as the Sun melts them. When a comet passes close to Earth, you can see its tail in the sky.

▷ **In addition to the Sun, planets, and moons, what other objects make up our solar system?**

Halley's comet was first reported more than 2,200 years ago. It crosses Earth's orbit and can be seen in the sky once every 76 years. It will next appear in 2061.

QUICK LAB

FOR SCHOOL OR HOME

A Comet's Tail

1. Use a small ball of clay or a small ball to model a comet. Attach a few strips of tissue paper to the model. This will be the tail of the comet.

2. Go outdoors if it is windy, or have your partner wave a notebook or folder to create wind.

3. Hold the comet in the wind in different positions. Try to stretch out the tail.

4. Compare your model to a real comet. How does a comet get its tail?

One of the most familiar constellations is the Big Dipper, seen here over Bonanza Peak Glacier Park in the state of Washington.

How Can You Locate Stars?

Look at all the stars in the sky! How can you make sense of them all? One way is to group stars into **constellations** (kahn·stuh·LAY·shuhnz). A constellation is a pattern or picture outlined by stars. As Earth travels in its orbit, you see different constellations because you are looking into space in different directions.

Long ago, people used constellations for many purposes. Farmers studied them to tell the seasons. Sailors looked at them to tell the direction at night. People included them in myths and stories.

Today scientists still use constellations to group the stars. They have agreed to use 88 constellations, many of them the same as in ancient times.

READING Cause and Effect
Why do we see different constellations at different times of the year?

L·I·N·K·S

Why It Matters

We have learned more about the solar system in the last 50 years than ever before. Humans traveled to the Moon and back. Spacecraft have flown by all of the planets. Powerful telescopes look deep into space. We are discovering new things almost every day.

Would you like to visit another planet? Maybe you will be the first person to set foot on Mars! What you discover there might even help us understand life on Earth.

Think and Write

1. Describe the inner planets.

2. Describe the outer planets.

3. What is a comet made of?

4. How are constellations useful?

5. **Critical Thinking** What if it were possible to begin at the Sun and take a trip through the solar system? Write about all the planets you would see and in what order you would pass by them. What else would you see in addition to the planets?

ART LINK

Make a model. Use art materials to make a model of the solar system. Include the Sun, all nine planets, and some of the other objects in the solar system. Include labels or a key.

WRITING LINK

Send a postcard from space. Pick a planet, moon, asteroid, or other place in our solar system. Imagine that you are on vacation there. Draw a picture, and write a message to a friend back on Earth.

MATH LINK

Solve a problem. A year on Mercury lasts 88 Earth days. How old are you in Mercury years?

TECHNOLOGY LINK

At the Computer Visit **www.mhscience02.com** for more links.

History of Science

VIEWS OF THE UNIVERSE

Long ago, people believed that the Sun, the Moon, and the planets revolved around Earth. As some people watched the sky closely, they found problems with this model. Over time, people from all over the world helped us understand the true model of the solar system. For example, in 613 B.C., Chinese astronomers recorded their observations of comets. Their first records of sunspots date from 28 B.C. About A.D. 900, an Arabian scientist named Al-Battani measured the length of a year and the seasons.

A.D. 400–500
Hypatia (hi·PAY·sha) was a brilliant scientist who lived in Alexandria, Egypt. She built on the work of Ptolemy and others.

1543
Polish astronomer Nicolaus Copernicus (kuh·PUR·ni·kuhs) said the planets revolve around the Sun. He thought the orbits were in the shapes of circles.

1609

The German astronomer Johannes Kepler (KEP·luhr) improved Copernicus's model. Kepler said that the planets move in orbits shaped like ellipses, or ovals.

A.D. 150

Ptolemy (TAHL·uh·mee) of Egypt placed Earth at the center of his model of the universe. He said that the Moon, the Sun, and the other planets circle our planet. Most people accepted Ptolemy's model for 1,400 years.

What Did I Learn?

1. Ptolemy said that the center of the universe was

  A the Sun.
  B Earth.
  C the Moon.
  D the stars.

2. Copernicus's ideas were correct about the

  F shapes of planet orbits.
  G sizes of planet orbits.
  H revolving of planets around the Sun.
  J sizes of the planets.

1609

Galileo (gal·uh·LAY·oh) pointed his telescope to the Moon, planets, and stars. His data proved that Earth orbits the Sun—not the other way around.

AT THE COMPUTER

Visit www.mhscience02.com to learn more about the solar system.

Chapter 7 Review

Vocabulary

Fill each blank with the best word or words from the list.

asteroid, C86   **meteor,** C86

axis, C67   **revolve,** C68

comet, C86   **rotate,** C66

constellation, C88   **solar system,** C81

crater, C71   **star,** C80

1. A planet _____ in an orbit around the Sun.

2. The _____ includes the Sun, planets, and other objects.

3. Between Mars and Jupiter lies the _____ belt.

4. People group stars into _____.

5. A(n) _____ is a "dirty snowball" that orbits the Sun.

6. Earth _____, which is why we have day and night.

7. "Shooting stars" are in fact _____, chunks of rock or metal.

8. A planet rotates about its _____.

9. The Sun is the _____ closest to Earth.

10. An object that strikes the surface of a moon or planet makes a(n) _____.

Test Prep

11. Planets with rings include _____.

    A Saturn only

    B Saturn and Jupiter only

    C Saturn and Mars only

    D all the "gas giant" planets

12. After a waxing gibbous Moon, the next phase is a(n) _____.

    F full Moon

    G first quarter Moon

    H last quarter Moon

    J new Moon

13. We see the Sun rise and set because _____.

    A Earth revolves around the Sun

    B Earth rotates on its axis

    C the Sun revolves around Earth

    D the Moon revolves around Earth.

14. The hottest of the planets is _____.

    F Mercury

    G Venus

    H Earth

    J Jupiter

15. Moonlight is made by _____.

    A the Moon

    B the Sun

    C Earth

    D many stars near the Moon

Concepts and Skills

16. Reading in Science How does distance from the Sun affect a planet?

17. Decision Making Would you want to visit the Moon or another planet? Explain your answer. Discuss the benefits and dangers of the visit.

18. Process Skills: Interpret Data Where on Earth does the Sun never set during the summer and never rise during the winter? Why does this happen?

19. Critical Thinking People have grouped stars into constellations for hundreds of years. If we lived on another planet, would we see the same constellations? Why or why not?

20. Scientific Methods Why might some scientific experiments be best done in space, on the Moon, or someplace else away from Earth? Give an example of a variable that the experiment might test.

Boost *your test scores!*

Be Smart!
Visit **www.mhscience02.com** to learn more.

Dr. Pedro Sanchez
Soil Scientist

Too often farmers around the world use a kind of farming called "slash-and-burn." They cut down a forest and burn the trees. Then they use the ash from the trees to fertilize the land and grow crops. However, the soil quickly loses nutrients. So farmers move on to another area. This is one reason the world's forests are disappearing.

Dr. Pedro Sanchez is a soil scientist. He believes there are much better ways to farm. Dr. Sanchez was born and raised in Cuba. His parents owned a farm and a fertilizer business, so he became interested in soil when he was very young.

For many years Dr. Sanchez lived in the Amazon rain forest and studied the forest soil. The Amazon soil was thought to be very poor for growing crops.

This is why the slash-and-burn method had been used there so often.

Dr. Sanchez found ways to keep farming the same soil over and over. He found that growing local grasses helps the soil become healthier. The grasses produce nutrients for the soil, and their roots help the soil retain water. The grasses also help prevent erosion.

Dr. Sanchez also found local trees that help conserve soil. The trees also produce products such as fruits and nuts.

Dr. Sanchez's research is helping to save the world's forests from destruction. It is also increasing the world's food supply.

AT THE COMPUTER

Visit www.mhscience02.com to learn more about careers.

Write ABOUT IT

1. What is the slash-and-burn farming method?
2. How can farmers in the Amazon rain forest make their soil healthier?

Careers IN SCIENCE

Here is another career related to the study of soil. You can use the Internet or library resources to find out more about this career.

Planetary Geologist

If you're interested in geology, you may want to be a planetary geologist. A planetary geologist studies the rocks, soil, and natural features of planets. It is a new career. Many planetary geologists work for NASA.

Planetary geologists work in a laboratory. They use advanced instruments like computers and spectrometers. These instruments help scientists study the planet's geology.

Planetary geologists usually have graduate degrees in geology or astronomy. They might have a degree in engineering if they want to develop special instruments used in research.

Fossil Footprints

What to Do

1. Dinosaur feet are like birds' claws. They have three toes in front and one in back. Draw an example of a dinosaur footprint.

2. Pretend the dinosaur was traveling in thick mud. Draw its footprints for these actions:

- walking slowly
- running
- fighting another dinosaur

3. Write a short story about a dinosaur. Draw a picture that shows the footprints that the dinosaur in your story would make.

Mini-Earth

What to Do

1. Model one of these topics:

- the layers of Earth
- how glaciers change the land
- how soil forms

2. Include an information sheet for your model.

Mini-Solar System

What to Do

1. Build a model of the Sun, planets, and other objects in the solar system. You may use foam balls, coat hangers, string, construction paper, or other materials.

2. Write a key for your model. The key names each part of the model. Include an interesting fact about each planet.

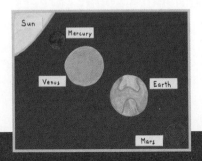

UNIT D
Water and Weather

NATIONAL GEOGRAPHIC

Water and Weather

CHAPTER 8

Earth's Water D2

CHAPTER 9

Earth's Weather. D60

LOOK!

A winter storm covered the riverbanks in ice and snow. How will the land change when spring arrives?

CHAPTER

8

LESSON 1
Water, Water Everywhere, D4

LESSON 2
Follow the Water, D14

LESSON 3
Motions in the Oceans, D26

LESSON 4
Go with the Flow, D36

LESSON 5
Water Please!, D46

Earth's Water

Did You Ever Wonder?

How much water goes over the falls at Niagara Falls? The falls are divided into three sections. The largest section has a volume of water equal to 2.3 million liters or 600,000 gallons spilling over it per second. This amount varies because hydroelectric plants draw water from the falls to generate electricity. How much water is found on Earth's surface?

D 3

Water, Water Everywhere

Vocabulary

atmosphere, D6

water vapor, D6

ice cap, D8

soil water, D10

groundwater, D10

Get Ready

All living beings need water. Even a camel, an animal famous for not needing water, must have water to survive. Fortunately, water can be found in many places on Earth, including the desert.

Where does the water in a desert come from? Where else on Earth is water found?

Process Skill

You infer when you form an idea from facts or observations.

Explore Activity

Where Can Water Be Found?

Materials

6 different-colored markers

white drawing paper

Procedure

1. Form six teams. Place one team at each location. Record your location. What is the state of the water there? Remember, the states of matter are solid, liquid, and gas.

2. Have each team go to the next closest location. Record the location and state of the water. Repeat until every team has visited all six locations.

3. How did the state of water differ from location to location?

4. **Interpret Data** Use your color markers to draw your team's water path.

Drawing Conclusions

1. **Predict** Where might water stay in one place for a short time? A long time? Why?

2. Do you think water that was around at the time of the dinosaurs can still be around today? Why or why not?

3. **Going Further: Infer** What might have caused the change in the state of water from place to place?

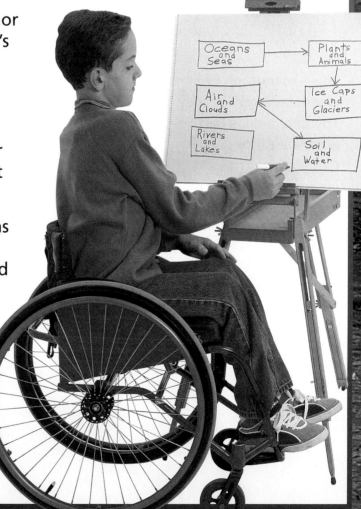

D 5

Main Idea Water can be in different forms in different places.

Where Can Water Be Found?

Do some places have more water than others? Where would you find large amounts of water? Very little water? Water is found in different states in different places.

Look at a globe. It shows that we live in a watery world. Oceans and seas are very large bodies of salt water. They cover about $\frac{70}{100}$ of Earth's surface. Oceans and seas are very deep and hold about $\frac{97}{100}$ of all of Earth's water.

Water is also found in the **atmosphere** (AT·muhs·feer). Gases that surround Earth make up its atmosphere. One of these gases is the oxygen you breathe.

In the atmosphere water is in a gas state and is called **water vapor** (WAW·tuhr VAY·puhr). The atmosphere always contains some water vapor. How much water vapor there is in the atmosphere depends on the location. There is more water vapor in the atmosphere over or near large bodies of water. There is less water vapor in the atmosphere over a desert.

This photograph of Earth was taken from space. The blue area is Earth's oceans and seas. Can you see the landmasses beneath the clouds?

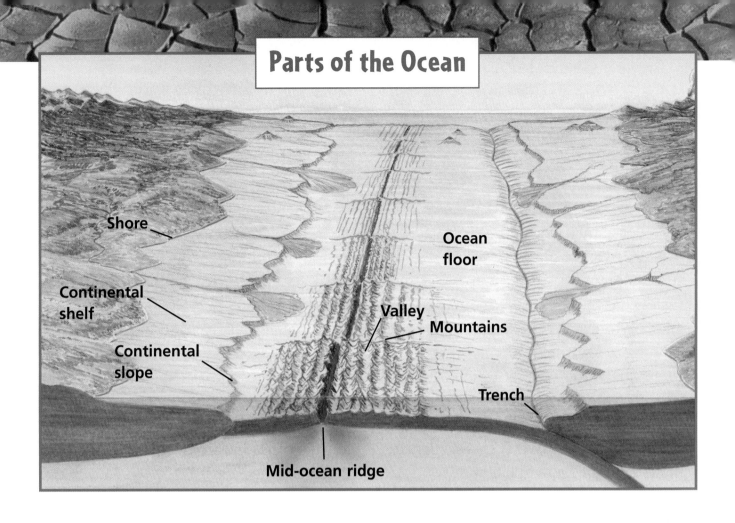

Parts of the Ocean

Shore

Continental shelf

Continental slope

Ocean floor

Valley

Mountains

Trench

Mid-ocean ridge

What do you think the ocean floor is like? Moving out from the shore, you do not immediately find the ocean floor as many people might think. First you find the continental shelf. It is a part of the continent that dips gently downward under the water.

Beyond the continental shelf is the continental slope. This steeper slope of land is part of the continent that is between the continental shelf and the ocean floor.

Although about half of the ocean floor is flat, there also are tall mountains. The mid-ocean ridge is a continuous mountain range that can be found along many parts of the ocean floor. It is found where new sea floor has formed from melted rock being forced up from below the ocean floor. Between mountains are low areas known as valleys, just as on land.

Tall mountains and ridges are not the only features on the ocean floor. Deep, narrow valleys called trenches also exist there. The deepest is the Marianas Trench in the Pacific Ocean. It is more than 11,000 meters (36,000 feet) deep. This trench is about 2,000 meters (6,600 feet) deeper than Earth's tallest mountain, Mount Everest!

READING **Sequence of Events**
How does the mid-ocean ridge form?

Where Else Can Water Be Found?

Fresh Water

Lakes, rivers, and streams make up a very small part of Earth's water. A lake is a large body of water surrounded by land. A river is flowing water that empties into an ocean, a lake, or another river. A stream is flowing water that is smaller than a river. The water in rivers and streams is fresh water, not salty like the ocean. Most lakes are fresh water. However, there are some saltwater lakes, such as the Great Salt Lake in Utah.

Water can also be found in swamps and marshes. Swamps and marshes form when water in the ground rises above the soil. Only plants that can survive with their roots under the water for long periods grow there. Grasses such as cattails and rushes grow in marshes. Trees and shrubs grow in swamps. Marsh and swamp animals include insects, reptiles, and birds. Beavers, raccoons, and ducks are found in many swamps.

About $\frac{2}{3}$ of Earth's fresh water is found in *glaciers* and polar ice caps. Some glaciers form high in the mountains and flow slowly down steep valleys.

Some glaciers flow across land until they reach the sea. There large chunks often break off and float out to sea as icebergs.

Ice caps are very wide, thick sheets of ice that cover large areas of land. Greenland and Antarctica are covered by ice caps.

Icebergs often break off and float away from glaciers that reach the sea.

Saltwater Communities

Saltwater communities make their homes in various saltwater environments. Each community has its own characteristics and organisms.

The types of organisms living in oceans vary depending on depth. You probably are familiar with organisms often seen near the surface, such as whales, sharks, and seaweed. However, in the deepest, darkest parts of the oceans, scientists continue to discover a great variety of interesting organisms.

A beach is the part of the land that meets an ocean. Ocean birds such as gulls and pelicans fly over beaches and shallow water looking for food. They feed on fish, clams, and snails. Tidal pools often form, trapping

This tidal pool is temporary home to many interesting ocean organisms.

organisms and water on a beach when the water level, or tide, is low.

A gulf forms when a large body of water reaches into the land. A gulf in the United States is the Gulf of Mexico. Climate and the amount of salt determine the organisms that can survive in different gulfs.

An estuary is a place where fresh water and salt water meet, such as a river meeting an ocean. The water is brackish, meaning it is more salty than fresh water but not as salty as salt water. The amount of salt in the water changes many times a day, so only a few types of organisms can live in an estuary. These include certain types of mangrove trees, mud snails, soft-shell clams, fiddler crabs, ducks, and a variety of shrimp.

▷ **What are some other places water can be found?**

Although they look like flowers, sea anemones are actually animals. They often attach to a hard surface such as coral.

Where Can Water Be Found Underground?

Oceans and lakes are water you can see on Earth's surface. There is also water in the soil and in the rocks below the ground. How does water get underground? Some water soaks into the soil to become **soil water**. Some soil water is used by plants. The rest moves through the soil into the underground rocks.

Many rocks have tiny spaces and cracks in them. Water passes down through these cracks until it reaches a layer of solid rock that it cannot pass through. Then the water begins to fill the spaces and cracks in the rocks above. Water stored in these cracks and spaces of underground rock is called **groundwater**.

Soil water and groundwater account for a very small amount of Earth's water. Even so, there is almost 20 times more groundwater than all of the water in rivers and lakes.

▶ **Where does groundwater collect?**

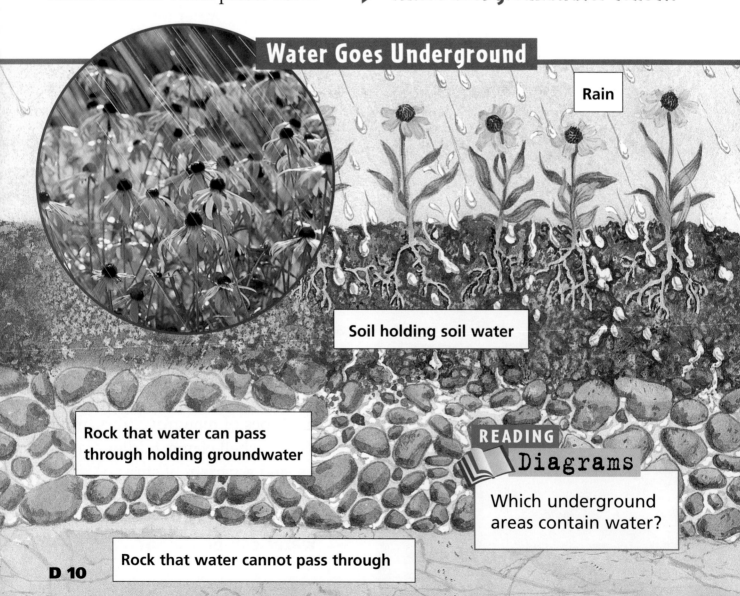

Water Goes Underground

Rain

Soil holding soil water

Rock that water can pass through holding groundwater

Rock that water cannot pass through

READING
Diagrams

Which underground areas contain water?

How Much Water and Where?

What's a good way to show all the information you learned about water? How could you show the different places where water can be found? What about the amount of water that can be found in each place?

A chart is one way to present information. It is especially useful in showing information that you want to compare. The chart at the right gives information about the different places on Earth where water is found. It also tells how much water is found in each place. Each amount given is a fraction of Earth's total amount. Which has more water—Earth's glaciers and ice caps or its soil water, groundwater, and rivers?

▷ **What is one useful way to present information?**

Earth's Water

1 Oceans and seas
About $\frac{97}{100}$ of the total water on Earth

2 Glaciers and ice caps
About $\frac{2}{100}$ of the total water on Earth

3 Soil water and groundwater; lakes, ponds, rivers, and atmosphere; plants and animals
About $\frac{1}{100}$ of the total water on Earth

FOR SCHOOL OR HOME

Water in an Apple

1. **Measure** Measure and record the mass of some apple slices.

2. Lay the apple slices on a tray, and put the tray in a warm place.

3. **Measure** When the slices are completely dried, measure their mass. Record the mass of the dry slices.

4. **Measure** What was the mass of the apple slices before and after drying?

5. Which had a greater mass—the fresh apple slices or the dry apple slices? Why?

6. **Use Numbers** How much of the apple's mass was water? How did you find out?

Is There Water in Living Things?

Have you ever bitten into a juicy apple or other kind of fruit? What do you think the liquid that filled your mouth was made of? It was water.

A small amount of Earth's water can also be found in all living things, large and small. You learned that the jellylike substance inside all cells is made up mostly of water. Water makes up at least half the weight of most plants and animals.

All living things need water. Plants soak up water through their roots. People and other animals drink water. They also get water from the foods they eat.

▶ **Where is the water in living things found?**

This timber wolf, like all animals, needs fresh water to survive.

Why It Matters

Without water there would be no life on Earth. Water is one of our most valuable resources. You use water for drinking and bathing. All the food you eat needs water to grow. If you like to swim or play water sports, you may enjoy spending time near oceans, lakes, and rivers. These places are also homes for different animals and plants.

Think and Write

1. List six kinds of places on Earth where water is found. Name the state of the water in each place.

2. What is the difference between the continental shelf and the continental slope?

3. How are estuaries and marshes similar? Different?

4. How are soil water and groundwater the same? How are they different?

5. **Critical Thinking** What might happen if there was less water in the oceans and seas?

L·I·N·K·S

SOCIAL STUDIES LINK

Use a map. Use a map or globe to locate Earth's major seas and oceans. Which ocean or sea is closest to where you live? Which ocean is the largest? Which sea is the smallest?

WRITING LINK

Write a paragraph. Describe some of your favorite uses of water. What state is the water in when you use it?

LITERATURE LINK

Read *The Water Watchers* to learn how two friends try to give a dog a bath and in the process learn about water. Try the activities at the end of the book.

The Water Watchers

ART LINK

Research water in art. Water is a popular subject in art. French painter Claude Monet spent years painting a lily pond near his home. American Frank Lloyd Wright designed a house that perches over a small waterfall. Find pictures of their work or other examples of such art. Share what you learn about the artist and the architect.

TECHNOLOGY LINK

At the Computer Visit **www.mhscience02.com** for more links.

Follow the Water

Vocabulary

evaporation, D16

condensation, D17

cloud, D17

precipitation, D18

freeze, D19

melt, D19

water cycle, D20

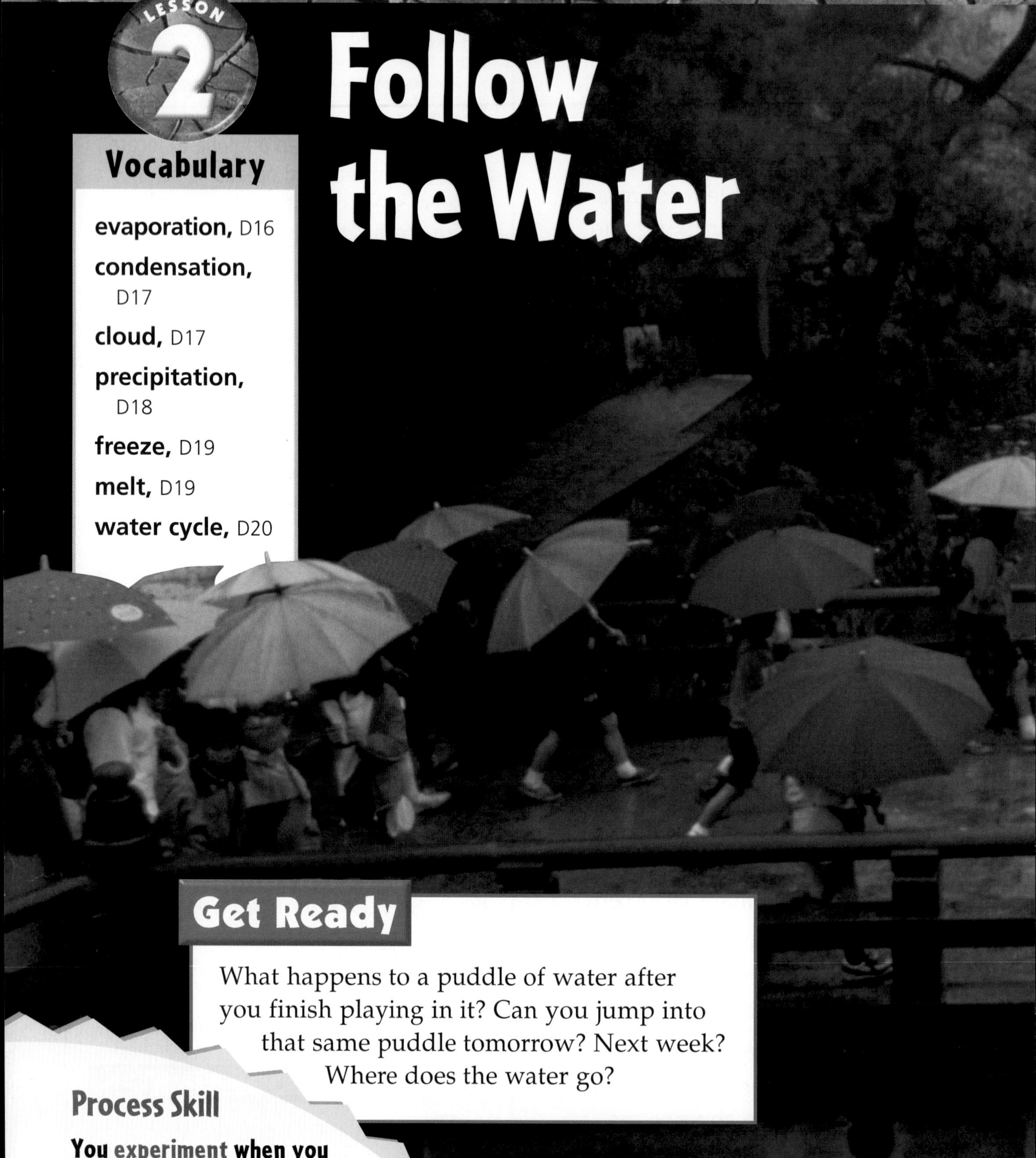

Get Ready

What happens to a puddle of water after you finish playing in it? Can you jump into that same puddle tomorrow? Next week? Where does the water go?

Process Skill

You **experiment** when you perform a test to support or disprove a hypothesis.

Explore Activity

What Makes Water Disappear?

Materials

measuring cup

water

2 index cards

2 lunch trays with sides

Procedure

1 **Measure** Pour a half cup of water into each tray.

2 Place one tray in a sunny area. Place the other in a dark area.

3 Use an index card for each tray. Label one card Sunny and the other card Dark. On each index card, write your name and the date. Then write the time when you placed the tray in its area.

4 **Observe** Check the trays every hour until the water in each is gone. Note on the appropriate index card how long it took the "puddle" to disappear. Record the results.

Drawing Conclusions

1 Which puddle disappeared first? Which took the longest to disappear?

2 What do you think made one puddle disappear faster? The other disappear more slowly?

3 **Going Further: Experiment** Repeat the activity, placing the trays in different places. How were the results similar or different?

Sunny

Dark

Main Idea Water exists in three states—solid, liquid, and gas.

What Makes Water Disappear?

Where does the water on the ground go? How does water get from one place to another? Why does water disappear faster in some places than in others?

You have learned that particles of matter have energy and are always moving. Now you'll find out how heat energy plays a role in how water changes its state. You'll learn how water moves from different Earth surfaces into the atmosphere.

Water in the deepest parts of land and bodies of water is quite cold. Water is warmer on the surface because it is heated by the Sun. Heat energy from the Sun causes the particles of water at the surface to move rapidly. As they absorb heat energy, these moving water particles go through the process of **evaporation** (i·vap·uh·RAY·shuhn). This means that the water particles

Evaporation and Condensation

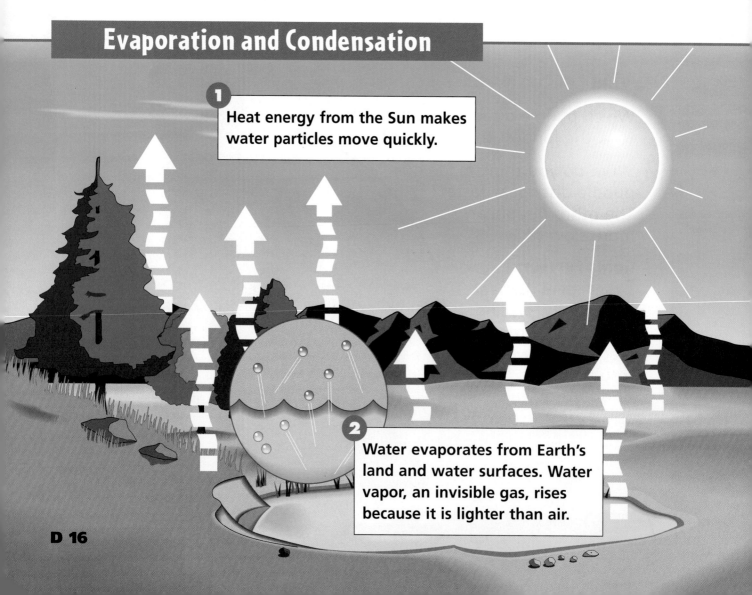

1 Heat energy from the Sun makes water particles move quickly.

2 Water evaporates from Earth's land and water surfaces. Water vapor, an invisible gas, rises because it is lighter than air.

change from a liquid to a gas. The gas, known as water vapor, is invisible and rises into the atmosphere.

High in the atmosphere, particles of water vapor move slowly because it is very cold. These water vapor particles lose heat energy, slow down, and *condense* (kuhn·DENS), or change from a gas to a liquid. This process is known as **condensation** (kahn·den·SAY·shuhn).

Tiny droplets of condensed water in the atmosphere form **clouds**. When droplets of water in clouds come together, they get bigger and heavier. Gravity, the force that pulls things toward Earth, causes the heavy droplets to fall.

▷ **What is the difference between evaporation and condensation?**

READING
Diagrams

Why does water on Earth's land and water surfaces evaporate?

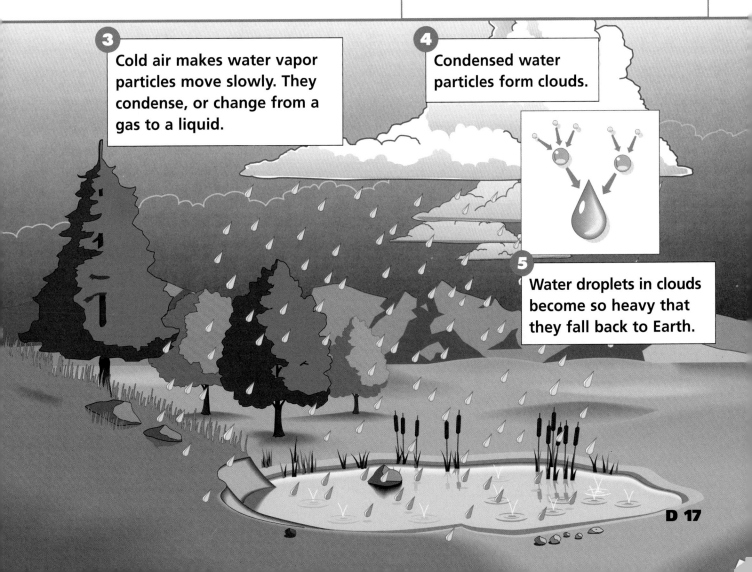

3 Cold air makes water vapor particles move slowly. They condense, or change from a gas to a liquid.

4 Condensed water particles form clouds.

5 Water droplets in clouds become so heavy that they fall back to Earth.

QUICK LAB

Disappearing Water

1. Fill two plastic cups half full with water. Cover one cup with plastic wrap. Use a rubber band to hold it in place. Mark the water level in each cup.

2. Place both cups in a warm, sunny spot.

3. **Predict** What do you think will happen in each cup?

4. **Observe** Check the cups every hour. Record what you see.

5. Where did the water in each cup go?

6. **Infer** Why did this happen?

What Is Precipitation?

Water in the atmosphere falls to Earth as **precipitation** (pri·sip·i·TAY·shuhn)—rain, snow, sleet, or hail. The form in which precipitation falls depends on the temperature. Most precipitation falls into the oceans. The precipitation that falls over land may also fall directly into lakes and rivers. When rainfall is very heavy, water will flow

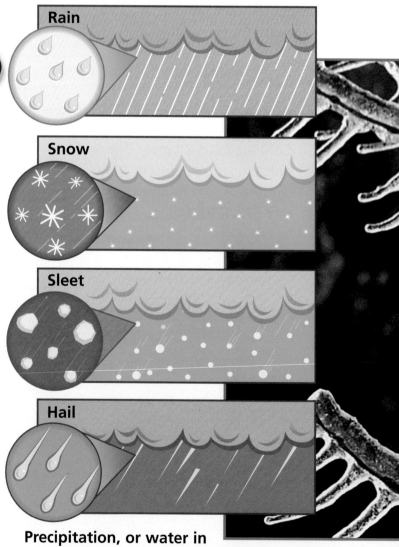

Rain

Snow

Sleet

Hail

Precipitation, or water in the atmosphere that falls to Earth, can be in the form of rain, snow, sleet, or hail.

over land into rivers. Some water also soaks into the ground as soil water or groundwater.

Will the water in the atmosphere fall as rain, snow, sleet, or hail? Are there any clues that you see or feel before it rains or snows?

The type of precipitation depends on the temperature outdoors. It also depends on the amount of heat energy in the particles of water.

Cold temperatures cause water to release heat energy, or lose heat. When this happens, the moving particles in water slow down. The water may **freeze** . This means that the water changes from a liquid to a solid. Ice and snow are solid water.

Warm temperatures allow water particles to absorb heat energy. This causes ice and snow to **melt** , or change from a solid to a liquid.

▷ How do snow and ice form?

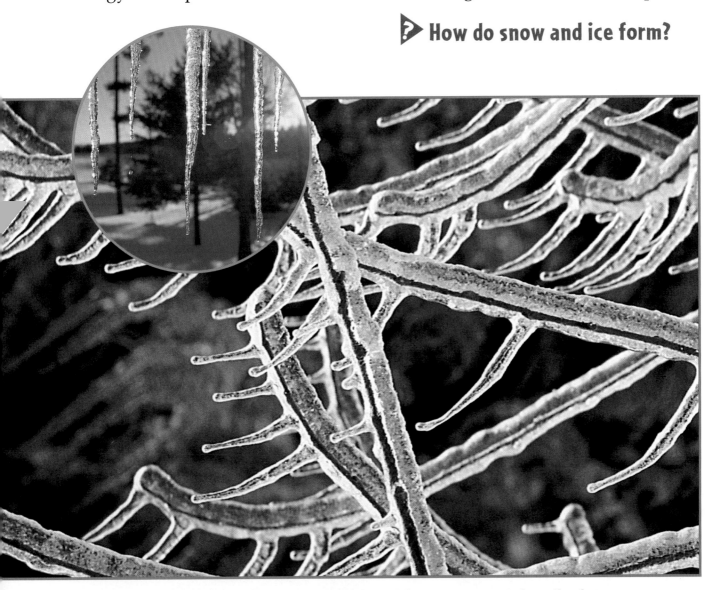

Use the terms *freeze, melt, solid, liquid*, and *heat energy* to describe how temperature is affecting the precipitation in these pictures.

How Does Water Travel?

By now you know a lot about water. You know that water can be found in many different places and in three different states. Water doesn't stay put! It moves continuously from place to place. This never-ending movement of Earth's water through evaporation, condensation, and precipitation is called the **water cycle**.

The Water Cycle

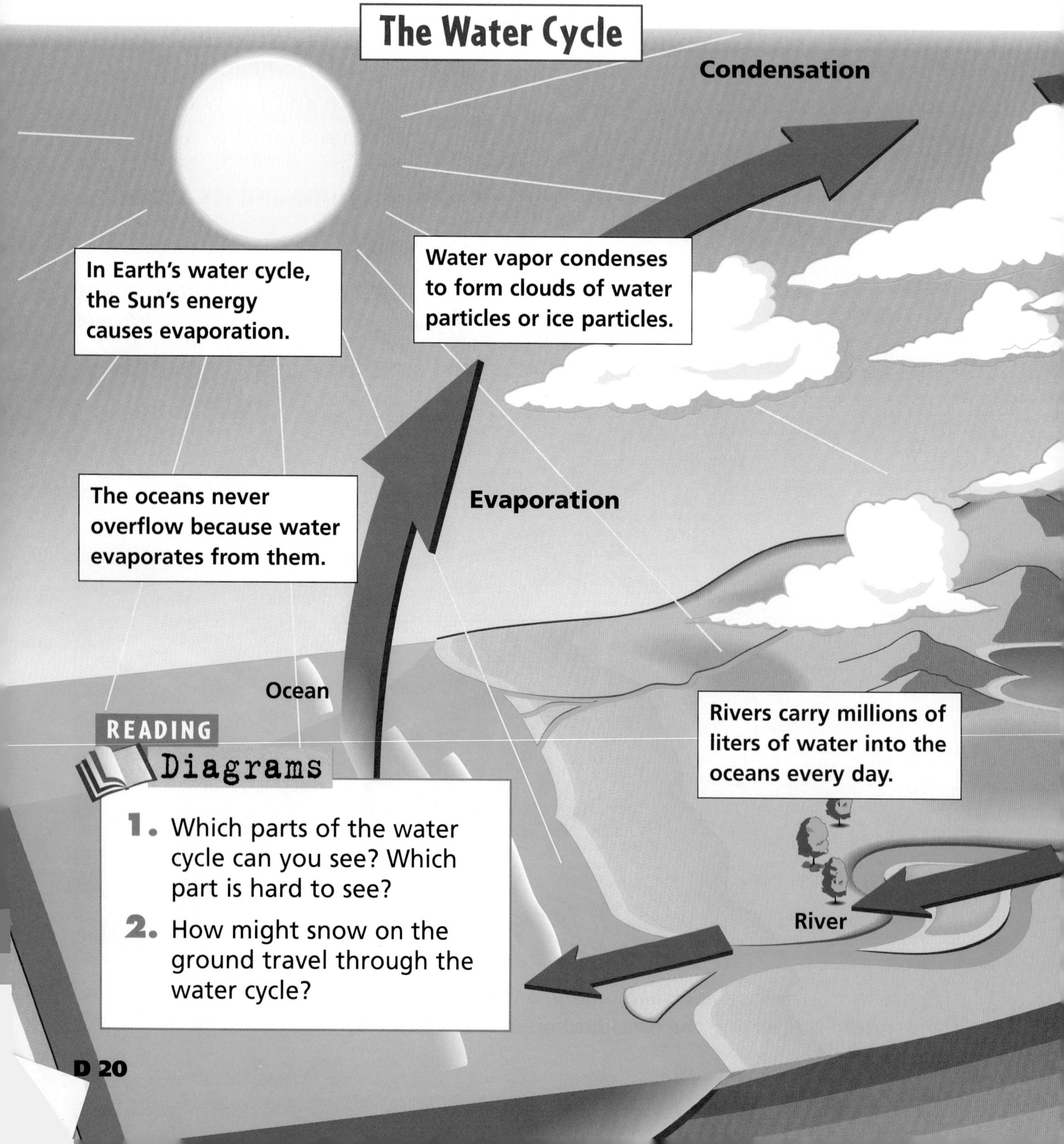

Condensation

In Earth's water cycle, the Sun's energy causes evaporation.

Water vapor condenses to form clouds of water particles or ice particles.

The oceans never overflow because water evaporates from them.

Evaporation

Ocean

Rivers carry millions of liters of water into the oceans every day.

River

READING
Diagrams

1. Which parts of the water cycle can you see? Which part is hard to see?

2. How might snow on the ground travel through the water cycle?

As the diagram shows, water is used over and over again. However, it is never used up. All the water that was present when Earth began is still around today!

The Sun is the energy source for the water cycle. Water changes state when it absorbs or releases heat energy.

READING **Sequence of Events**
Describe the water cycle.

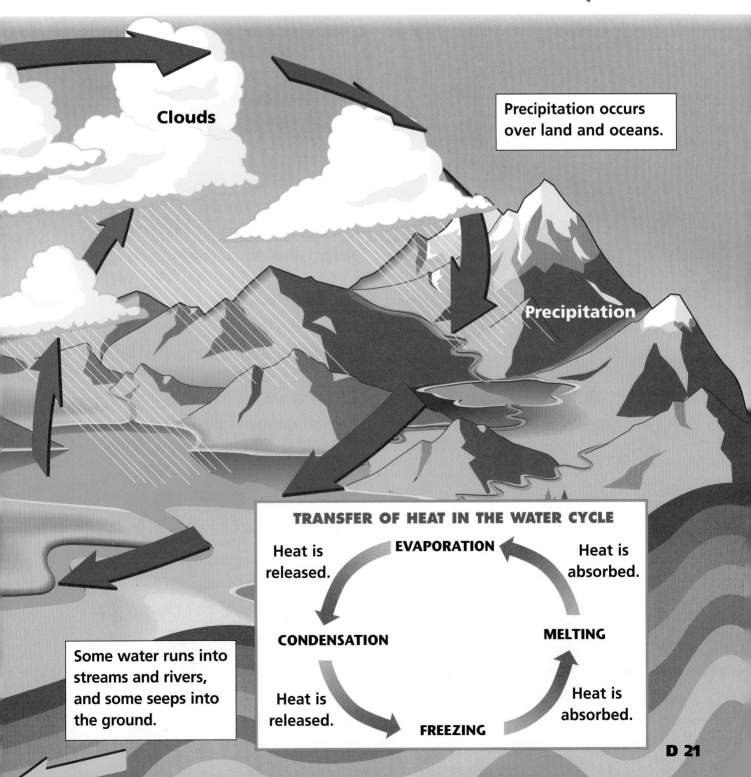

Clouds

Precipitation occurs over land and oceans.

Precipitation

Some water runs into streams and rivers, and some seeps into the ground.

TRANSFER OF HEAT IN THE WATER CYCLE

EVAPORATION

Heat is released.

Heat is absorbed.

CONDENSATION

MELTING

Heat is released.

Heat is absorbed.

FREEZING

What Kinds of Precipitation Do You Get?

How does water in the atmosphere fall where you live? Rain, snow, sleet, and hail are different forms of precipitation. You know that rain falls as a liquid. Snow, sleet, and hail are solids.

Snowflakes are small crystals of ice. Snow forms in air that is well below 0°C (32°F). In very cold air, water vapor changes directly to ice crystals. The crystals grow in size until they are heavy enough to fall as snowflakes.

No two snowflakes have the exact same crystal shape.

Hail forms when frozen drops of rain fall and are blown back up in the air by the wind. The size of a piece of hail increases each time it goes up and down through the layers of air, collecting more water.

Falling pieces of ice that are 5 millimeters ($\frac{1}{5}$ inch) or larger are called hailstones. There have been hailstones as large as 13 centimeters (5 inches) across and weighing more than 450 grams (1 pound)!

When rain falls through layers of cold air, the raindrops freeze to form sleet. The pieces of ice that are called sleet are usually smaller than 5 millimeters ($\frac{1}{5}$ inch) across.

▷ **What types of precipitation fall where you live?**

These hailstones are almost as big as golf balls!

Why It Matters

How water moves in the water cycle affects everyone on Earth. You use water every day to drink and cleanse yourself. By looking at clouds, you can tell if you need to bring an umbrella. Maybe it will snow, and you can test your new sled. Knowing what the precipitation might be is also helpful to farmers when planting crops. The water cycle is nature's way of recycling its resources.

Think and Write

1. What causes a puddle of water to seem to disappear?

2. Does water lose or absorb heat energy when it condenses? Freezes? Evaporates? Melts?

3. Give two examples of how water moves from one place to another in the water cycle. Explain how the water changes state in each example.

4. How is snow different from hail?

5. **Critical Thinking** What do you think might happen if the only precipitation that fell was snow?

L·I·N·K·S

SOCIAL STUDIES LINK

Find water on a map. Do you live near a large body of water? Use a map to help you identify its location. Use directions—such as north, south, east, and west—to describe its location relative to your home.

WRITING LINK

Write a paragraph. Write about where you might see evaporation and condensation occurring in your environment.

ART LINK

Make snowflakes. Create snowflakes by cutting them out of paper. Fold a square piece of white paper in half and then in half again. Cut around the edges of the folded paper to make a circle. Then cut into the folded paper to make a six-sided snowflake.

TECHNOLOGY LINK

Science Newsroom CD-ROM Choose *Soaking It All In* to learn how plants prevent runoff.

At the Computer Visit **www.mhscience02.com** for more links.

Science, Technology,
Let It Rain!

Do you like rain? In some cultures people do dances or hire rainmakers when they want it to rain. Since long droughts end naturally in time, no one has ever proved he or she shortened a drought!

In 1946 researcher Vincent Schaefer was studying the cause of icing on airplane wings. He sprinkled frozen carbon dioxide, or "dry ice," into a box containing an artificial cloud. A tiny snowstorm began in the box!

Schaefer rented a plane and went up to sprinkle dry ice in a real cloud. The result: instant snow!

People thought maybe this new method could be used to end summer droughts. Experiments proved that indeed dry ice could produce rain as well as snow!

Here's how it works: The cold dry ice causes some of a cloud's water vapor to freeze. More water vapor freezes around the first ice to make a snowflake. When the flakes are heavy enough, they fall. In warm weather they melt and become rain.

Another rain-making researcher, Bernard Vonnegut, noted that the chemical silver iodide has particles shaped much like water ice.

Native Americans in the Southwest have complex rituals to make it rain on their crops.

Dry ice is "dry" because it turns into the gas carbon dioxide instead of melting into a liquid.

He proved that particles of silver iodide, that are light enough to float like dust in air, could also start rain!

Now if there's a drought, tiny amounts of silver iodide are floated up into the sky or dropped from planes. If conditions are right, this causes clouds of cool water vapor to turn to rain.

Write ABOUT IT

1. How does the dry-ice method of making rain work?
2. How could the same techniques be used to reduce rainfall when there's too much in a given area?

AT THE COMPUTER

Visit **www.mhscience02.com** to learn more about rain.

Motions in the Oceans

Vocabulary

current, D28

deep ocean current, D28

surface current, D29

tide, D30

wave, D32

Get Ready

Have you ever put a message into a bottle? Did you hope that one day someone on the other side of the ocean might find it?

Long ago, people stranded on islands sent messages in bottles to call for help. What are the chances of a bottle traveling across the ocean?

Process Skill

You experiment when you perform a test to support or disprove a hypothesis.

Explore Activity

What Makes the Ocean Move?

Procedure

BE CAREFUL! Handle the warm water carefully. Wear goggles.

1. Fill the box three-fourths full of room-temperature tap water.

2. Put the rocks in the bag. Fill the bag half full of warm water. Close it with the twist tie.

3. Place the bag in one corner of the box.

4. Float an ice cube in the opposite corner from the bag. If the ice cube melts, replace it.

5. Put food coloring in the dropper. Place four drops of the coloring in the water next to the ice cube.

6. **Observe** Look at the food coloring for several minutes through the sides of the box. Record what you see.

Drawing Conclusions

1. **Observe** Where did the water sink? Where did it rise?

2. Why do you think you added food coloring to the water?

3. **Going Further: Experiment** Repeat the activity without using warm water. Compare your results. What are some strengths and weaknesses of this model?

Materials

clear-plastic shoe box

room-temperature tap water

500 mL of warm tap water

small plastic sandwich bag

twist tie

food coloring

dropper

small rocks

2 or 3 ice cubes

goggles

Read to Learn

Main Idea The ocean moves in ways that affect the weather, the climate, the land, and you!

What Makes the Ocean Move?

One way ocean water moves is in **currents** (KUR·uhnts). Currents are large streams of water that flow in the ocean. One kind of ocean current is known as a **deep ocean current**. These currents flow more than 197 meters (650 feet) deep, where the water is very cold. Cold water is more dense, or heavier, than an equal amount of warm water. This diagram shows how density causes deep ocean currents.

How Deep Ocean Currents Form

1 Deep ocean current begin in polar regions, where the water is very cold and salty.

2 Dense cold water sinks below warm water.

3 Less dense warmer water gets pushed out of the way and rises. This causes a current.

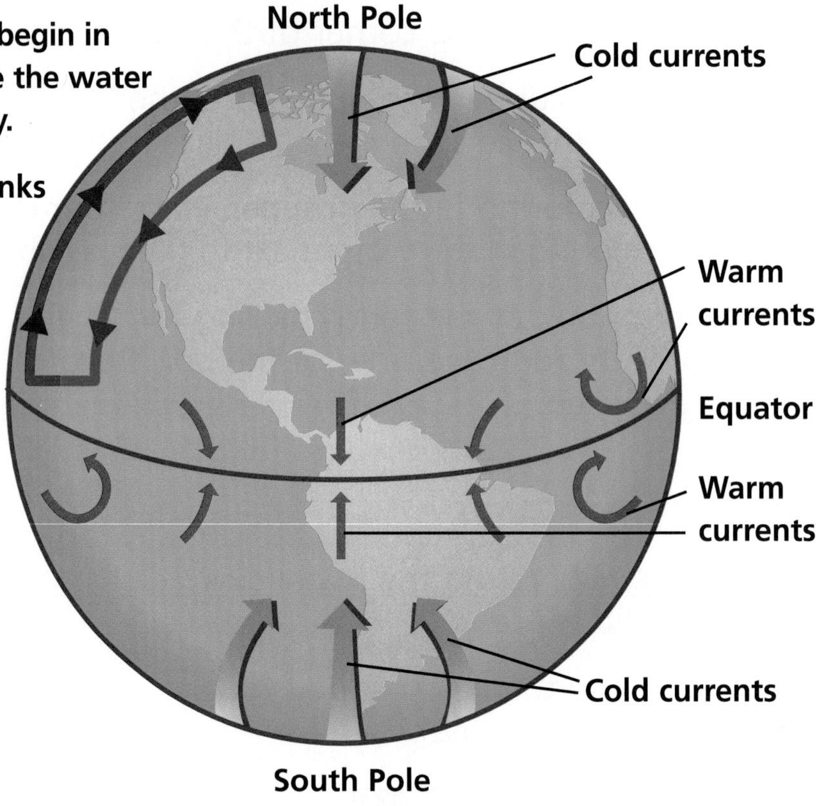

Water

Salt

Cold water

Warm water

North Pole

Cold currents

Warm currents

Equator

Warm currents

Cold currents

South Pole

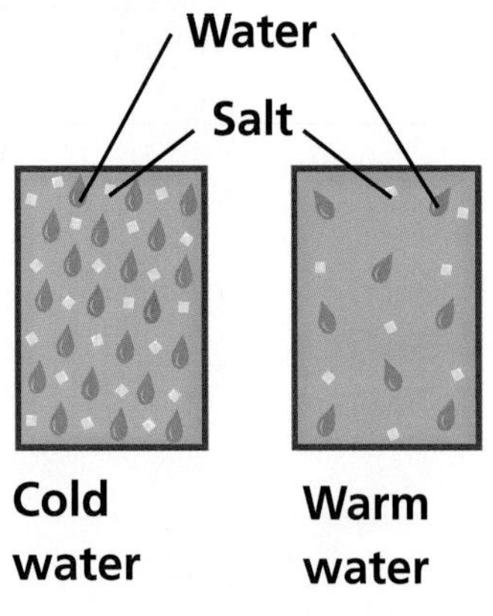

4 Warm, less dense water is pushed up to the surface at the equator.

READING Diagrams

1. Where might the water be warm year round?
2. Where do deep ocean currents begin? Why?

Wind and Surface Currents

Walk along the ocean, and you will see currents moving water at the ocean's surface. When steady winds blow over the ocean, they move the water in currents called **surface currents** .

Some surface currents move warm water from the equator. Other surface currents move cold water from areas near the poles.

The diagram shows you that surface currents move in circular patterns. In the Northern Hemisphere, they move clockwise. In the Southern Hemisphere, they move counterclockwise. This difference in direction is caused by Earth's rotation. It causes winds in the hemispheres to blow in different directions. Large landmasses also cause surface currents to change direction. Surface currents that hit against a continent turn and move along the coast.

▶ **What types of currents move ocean water?**

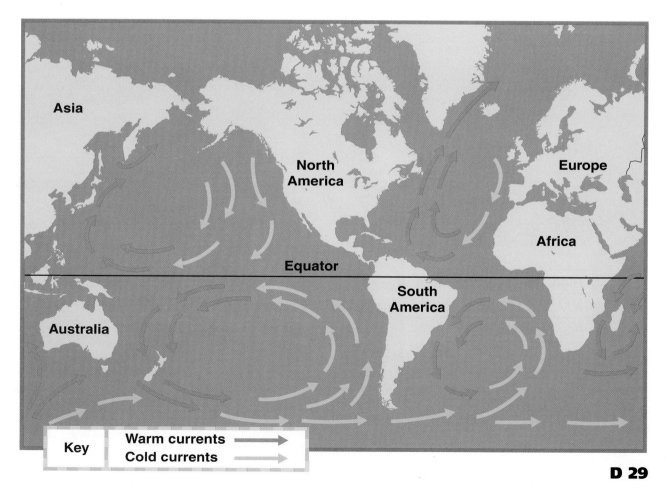

What Ocean Motion Is Caused by Gravity?

The rise and fall of ocean water levels is called a **tide**. Ocean tides are caused by the pull of gravity between Earth and the Moon and the Sun. The Moon affects ocean tides more than the Sun because it is closer to Earth.

The pull of gravity on the side of Earth facing the Moon causes oceans to bulge outward. The bulge moves water higher on the shore, causing a high tide. On the opposite side of Earth, the Moon's pull on solid ground causes oceans to bulge, too.

As Earth rotates, the bulge travels around it. Where the water doesn't bulge, there is a low tide. In a low tide, the ocean water doesn't come up as far onto the shore.

The Moon's orbit around Earth also causes daily tide changes. In most places there are two high tides and two low tides each day. During a full Moon and a new Moon, the pull of gravity is stronger. The tides are higher and lower than usual.

▶ **What causes the tides?**

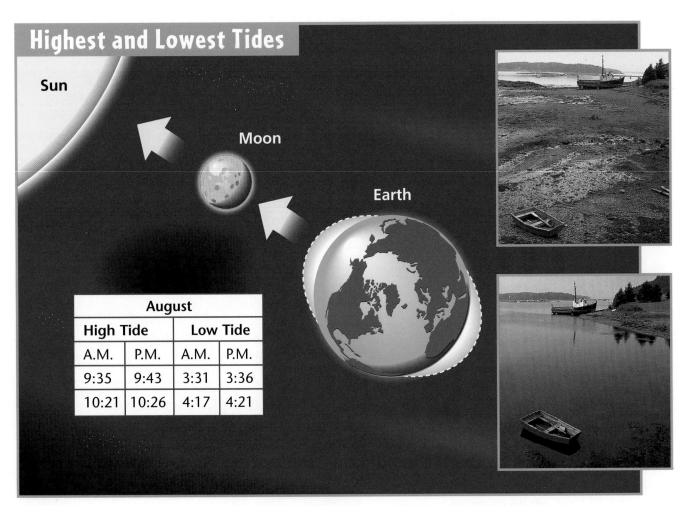

Highest and Lowest Tides

Sun

Moon

Earth

August			
High Tide		Low Tide	
A.M.	P.M.	A.M.	P.M.
9:35	9:43	3:31	3:36
10:21	10:26	4:17	4:21

How Can We Use Tides?

In some places people get energy from the Moon. How? By using the ebbing and flowing tides!

People use rivers and streams to run waterwheels. The water is held behind a wall, or dam. It flows over the dam and turns a wheel that powers machinery.

In some coastal areas, the ocean tides rise several meters twice a day. People make the ocean water flow behind a dam as the tide rises. As the tide goes out, the trapped water is used to turn a wheel. Tidal energy can power machinery and make electricity.

Tidal power isn't as easy to get as river-water power. Places with high tides are usually deep bays, where it's hard to build dams. Waves, currents, and storms can damage the dams. Today only a few places get power from the tides.

Tidal power may become more popular. Some people point out that tidal power plants don't pollute oceans as much as other energy sources. As new energy ideas, techniques, and materials are developed, it may also become easier to build dams in ocean bays.

▷ **What is tidal power used for?**

For years people have used river water to turn waterwheels to power machinery. Today tidal power is doing the same job in places where dams can be easily built.

QUICK LAB

FOR SCHOOL OR HOME

Make Waves!

1. Fill a plastic shoe box halfway with water.

2. Place a cork at one end of the box. Take turns quickly puffing through a straw on the water at the other end. Be sure you each use a fresh straw.

3. **Observe** Record the action of the waves.

4. **Experiment** Puff on the water surface harder and at different distances. How did the cork move?

5. **Communicate** Draw a diagram to show the cork's movements.

What Is a Wave?

Along with currents and tides, ocean waters also move in waves. A **wave** is an up-and-down movement of water.

Water waves have certain characteristics. The highest part of a wave is called the *crest*. The lowest part is the *trough* (TRAWF). A wave's height is measured from the trough to the crest.

A wave can also be described and measured by its *wavelength*. Wavelength is the distance from one crest to another crest.

▷ **What are three characteristics of a wave?**

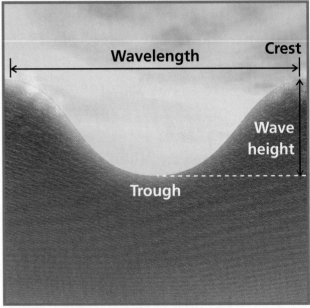

How would you describe a wave in your own words?

How Does Water Move in Waves?

Watching a wave approach the shore, it is easy to think that the water in it moves forward with the wave. However, the water does not move. Only the wave energy moves.

If you could float a cork on a wave, you would see it move forward a little bit as a wave passes by. When the wave moves past, the object moves backward about the same distance it moved forward. However, the object never really moves any distance. It bobs up and down in place.

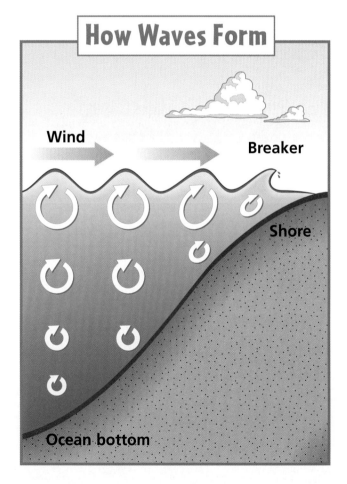

How Waves Form

Wind

Breaker

Shore

Ocean bottom

Why does this happen? Wind blowing across the ocean's surface makes waves move in the direction of the wind. This causes water particles to move up and down in a circular path as shown in the diagram. The size of the circles near the surface equals the wave height. Down in deeper water, the circles get smaller. The deeper the water, the smaller the circle.

As a wave moves toward shore, its trough touches the ocean bottom. This makes the trough slow down. However, the wave's crest keeps moving at the same speed that it was originally. The crest moves ahead of the trough and becomes steeper than the trough. This causes the wave to fall over, or "break," onshore. The steeper the ocean bottom, the quicker the wave height increases. This makes strong waves break onshore. If the ocean bottom is less steep, the waves are smaller and break more gently.

Once a wave breaks onshore, its energy is used up. Gravity then pulls the water back into the ocean, and the process continues.

READING **Sequence of Events**
What happens to water when a wave breaks onshore?

How Do Oceans Change Coastlines?

Powerful ocean waves are always changing coastlines. Waves move against the shore and wear away the land. This is called *erosion*. Soil, sand, gravel, and large rocks are carried out to sea. As a result, the coastline moves inland.

Waves deposit the soil, sand, gravel, and rocks from the shore in other places. This is called *deposition*. Deposition builds up the coastline and moves it out toward the ocean.

Erosion and deposition change coastlines.

Hurricanes

Violent storms with strong winds and heavy rains are called hurricanes. They always begin over the oceans in tropical regions near the equator. Earth's rotation can help start the storm's whirling winds.

Sometimes wind speeds can be more than 240 kilometers (150 miles) per hour. Hurricanes can travel huge distances in a short time. They can cause great damage, destroying trees and houses. Giant waves can cause flooding.

▶ **What is erosion?**

Why It Matters

Oceans are an important part of your life. Ocean currents help warm or cool land temperatures. If you want to keep track of the weather, it helps to know how these currents move. If you live near an ocean, it helps to know when tides will change. This is especially true if you like to go sailing, swimming, or surfing!

Think and Write

1. How does water temperature affect the ocean's movement?

2. How are surface currents different from deep ocean currents?

3. How are gravity and the tides related?

4. Explain how a wave forms.

5. Critical Thinking What if the pull of gravity between Earth and the Moon was much less? How would this affect the oceans?

L·I·N·K·S

WRITING LINK

Write a paragraph. Describe something that you might see happening while spending a day at the beach. Explain what causes each event.

MATH LINK

Pick an ocean to research. Find out math facts about the ocean, and record them. Here are some questions you can find the answers to. How deep is it? How wide is it? What is the ocean's temperature near the surface? What is the temperature near the ocean's floor? What is the ocean's area? What percentage of Earth's surface is covered by the ocean?

LITERATURE LINK

Read *Sylvia Earle: She's in Deep Water* to learn about one of the most famous marine scientists in the world. Try the activities at the end of the book.

TECHNOLOGY LINK

Science Newsroom CD-ROM Choose *A Shore Thing* to learn more about beach erosion and how to stop it.

At the Computer Visit **www.mhscience02.com** for more links.

Go with the Flow

Vocabulary

pore space, D38

water table, D39

runoff, D39

transpiration, D41

Get Ready

Did you ever see water falling from the side of a cliff? How did the water get through the soil and rocks? Where did the water travel from?

Process Skill

You infer when you form an idea from facts or observations.

Explore Activity

How Fast Does Water Flow in Soil and Rocks?

Materials

cup of perlite or soil

cup of marbles

two 12-oz paper cups

pencil

stopwatch

plastic container

1 L of water

measuring cup

Procedure

1. With a pencil tip, make a small hole in the bottom of one paper cup.

2. Place your finger over the hole. Fill the cup with perlite or soil. Hold the cup over a plastic container. Have your partner pour in water to cover the perlite or soil.

3. **Observe** Take away your finger. Time how long it takes the water to drain. Record the results.

4. Repeat using marbles.

Drawing Conclusions

1. Which material let water soak through faster?

2. How does the kind of material affect how fast water flows through it?

3. **Infer** What happens to rainwater falling on soil?

4. **Going Further: Infer** What can you say about the type of soil that probably is found where wells are dug?

Main Idea More than half of Earth's fresh water is groundwater.

How Fast Does Water Flow in Soil and Rocks?

How does the way water flows underground affect the water on Earth's surface?

Soil is the top part of the ground. It is made up of small mineral particles mixed with decaying plant and animal material, water, and air.

There are tiny spaces between the particles, called **pore spaces**. These spaces allow liquids and gases to pass through. Materials with pore spaces are said to be porous. Soil is porous, so water can soak into it because of the pull of gravity. Water in the soil is called soil water.

Water moves quickly through soils that have large pore spaces. Sandy soils have large pore spaces. Water moves more slowly through soils with small particles and small pore spaces, such as clay.

Water passes through the soil and into porous rocks that lie below. River and lake water also soaks into these rocks. Water passes down

How Water Travels Through Soil and Rocks

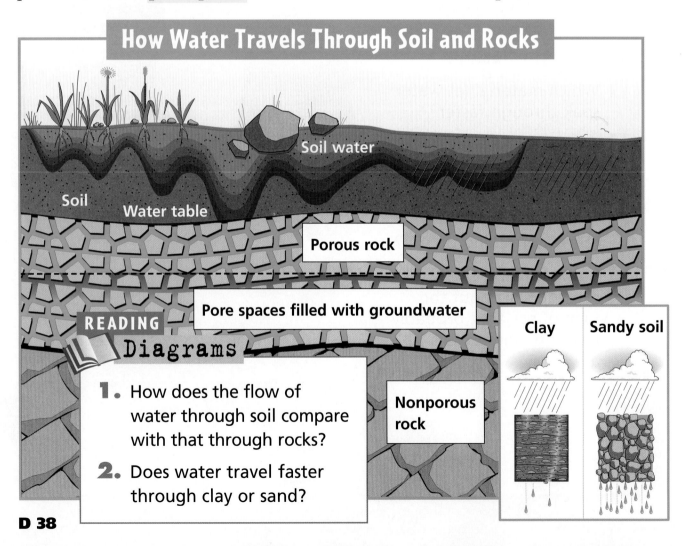

Soil water

Soil

Water table

Porous rock

Pore spaces filled with groundwater

Nonporous rock

Clay

Sandy soil

READING Diagrams

1. How does the flow of water through soil compare with that through rocks?

2. Does water travel faster through clay or sand?

Runoff usually ends up in gutters, ditches, rivers, lakes, and oceans.

through porous rocks until it reaches a layer of nonporous rock. When it can go no deeper, the water begins to fill the spaces in the rocks above. Water in the underground rocks is called groundwater. The upper area of groundwater is known as the **water table**.

Have you ever seen it rain so hard that streams of water rush through the streets? The precipitation that doesn't evaporate or soak into the ground becomes **runoff**. Runoff is the water that flows over Earth's surface.

The amount and size of runoff is greater in some places than in others. It is also greater at some times of the year, such as during seasons of heavy rains. Soil type and *vegetation*, or plant life, affect runoff. So do the amount of rainfall and the slope of the surface.

READING **Sequence of Events**
What happens in your area when there is too much precipitation?

FOR SCHOOL OR HOME

Make Runoffs

BE CAREFUL! Handle scissors carefully.

1. Cut two milk cartons as shown. Label one Soil and the other Sand. Place them on a tray.

2. **Use Variables** Put an equal amount of sand and soil in the cartons.

3. Fill a measuring cup with water. Slowly pour it over the soil until the soil can hold no more water. Record the volume of water used.

4. Repeat step 3 for the sand.

5. **Measure** Which absorbed the most water? Which had the most runoff?

How Do Wells Work?

Groundwater is an important source of fresh water. People use groundwater to meet their many needs, such as household cleaning, farming, and industry. Digging a well is the most common way of getting water from the ground.

For a well to produce water, its bottom must be below the water table. This allows the water to flow through the rock formations into the well. When building a well, it is important to know how deep the water table is from the surface. The water table is closer to the surface in some places and farther away in others. Periods of heavy rain can cause the water table to rise. Lack of rain can cause it to drop.

In some wells, pumps bring well water to the surface. In other wells, water rises on its own because of pressure in the underground rocks.

This diagram puts together what you learned in this lesson with what you learned about the water cycle.

READING Diagrams

1. Why do wells have to be built below the water table?

2. Name the places in the diagram where groundwater might come from.

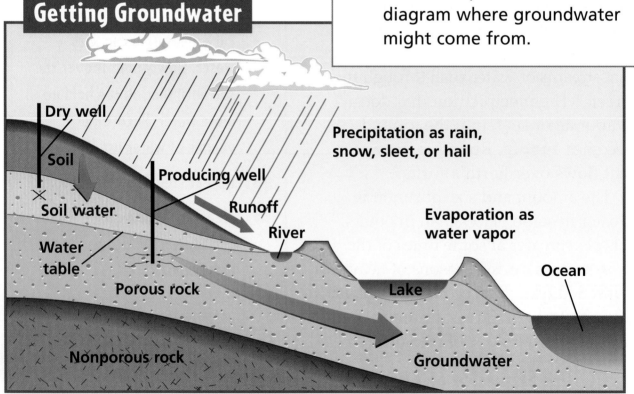

Getting Groundwater

Dry well
Soil
Producing well
Soil water
Runoff
Water table
River
Porous rock
Nonporous rock
Precipitation as rain, snow, sleet, or hail
Evaporation as water vapor
Ocean
Lake
Groundwater

▶ **How does a well work?**

How Do Plants Move Water from the Ground?

Not all of the water that is on or in the ground stays there. It moves through the water cycle. Plants also help move water from the soil and the ground into the atmosphere.

You learned that plant and animal cells are largely made up of water. Both need water to survive.

Plants also contribute to the amount of water vapor in the air. Through its roots a plant soaks up nutrients and water from the soil. The water moves to all the plant's cells. The water combines with carbon dioxide. The green material in the cell's chloroplasts traps energy from the Sun. The energy is used to combine water and carbon dioxide to make the plant's food.

Some of the water that isn't used to make food escapes from the plant's leaves. Plants release water vapor into the air through tiny pores in their leaves. This process is called **transpiration** (tran·spuh·RAY·shuhn).

▷ **Describe how a plant moves water from the ground.**

Plants Move Water from the Ground into the Air

Plants give off water vapor through pores in their leaves.

Plants take up soil water through their roots.

READING Diagrams

What is the function of plant roots? Leaf pores?

What Are Droughts and Floods?

What changes have you observed when it hasn't rained for a while? Water on land surfaces evaporates back into the air. If it hasn't rained in a long time, rivers and lakes may dry up. When there is no precipitation, a *drought* may occur. A drought is a long period of time with little or no precipitation. Droughts often affect crops, vegetation, and water supplies.

Droughts are even more severe when temperatures are high. In hot temperatures, water particles absorb more heat energy. This causes the water particles to move and evaporate quickly.

During a drought, lands that were fertile and green become dry. Wells can go dry as the water table drops. Water for human needs can become scarce if the drought continues. Some plants and animals may die from lack of water.

When it rains again, the water often cannot soak into the dry, hardened ground. As a result, there is a lot of runoff, which creates streams and water holes. Once water collects, it is able to soak into the soil.

A long period of time with little or no precipitation, called a drought, can cause the land surface to crack and vegetation to die.

Sometimes dams cannot hold back rising floodwaters. When floodwaters rise, people must leave their homes and find shelter in a safer area.

Floods are great flows of water over land that is usually dry. When this happens, water accumulates more rapidly than the soil can absorb it. This causes water runoffs over the ground.

Many things can cause floods. Pore spaces in soil and rocks may not be able to take in any more water. This happens because the pore spaces are already full of water or ice. How do pore spaces become so full? It usually happens when there are long periods of heavy rain. It can also happen when snow and ice melt in the spring.

Runoff from heavy rains or from melting ice may become very great in spring. Rivers can't hold all the water pouring into them, and they overflow their banks. In cities, storm drains may not be able to carry away water fast enough. In deserts very dry soil may not be able to soak up water fast enough.

When floods occur, houses can be damaged. Crops can be washed away, and lives can be lost. In an effort to control floods, people build dams and raise riverbanks. Even so, these structures can't always hold back the water. Dams sometimes break or overflow, releasing floodwaters suddenly and without warning.

▶ **What are some possible causes of a flood?**

Process Skill
BUILDER

Surface Area and Evaporation

Variables are things, or factors, in an experiment that can be changed to find answers to questions. In this activity, you'll answer this question: Does size or surface area of a puddle affect how fast it will evaporate? For a fair test, all of the factors in the experiment except the variable must remain the same. The only variable is surface area.

Procedure

BE CAREFUL! Handle scissors carefully.

1 Make a Model Use the sponges to make models of puddles with different surface areas.

2 Measure Place one sponge in each pan of the balance. Add paper clips to the pan with the smaller sponge until both sides of the balance are equal in mass.

3 Infer Find a way to add equal amounts of water to both sponges.

4 Observe Once you have set up your models, turn on the lamp. Check the models every half-hour. Record your observations.

Drawing Conclusions

1 Infer Which model became lighter first? What does this tell you about surface area and evaporation?

2 Identify What variables did you change? Keep the same?

3 Experiment What could you do to make water evaporate faster? Slower? Test your ideas.

Materials

water

measuring cup

spotlight lamp

small box of paper clips

whole kitchen sponge

half kitchen sponge

scissors

pan balance

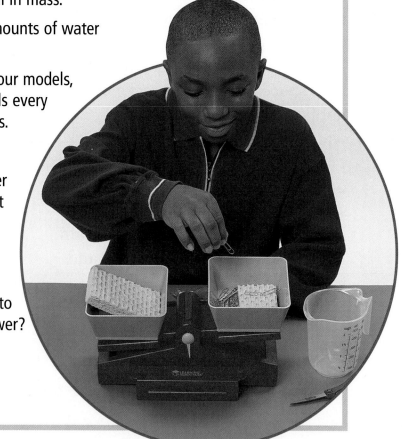

Why It Matters

Water flows through the ground and becomes a source of fresh water for plants, animals, and humans. Understanding how the water flows may help you in some of your everyday activities. You'll also be more aware of areas that flood, and be more prepared! To do a research project on floods, visit **mhscience02.com**.

Think and Write

1. How does soil type affect the movement of water under the ground?

2. What can cause runoff?

3. How do plants move water from the ground into the air?

4. Use Variables How would you set up an experiment to determine how temperature affects the evaporation of water?

5. Critical Thinking How could floods affect people who don't live in a flooded area?

L·I·N·K·S

SOCIAL STUDIES LINK

Research how people got water. For example, how did pioneers in the American West find water? They couldn't always settle near rivers and streams. Many dug wells to reach groundwater, but how did they know where to dig?

HEALTH LINK

Research dried foods. Fruit, fish, and meats can be dried to reduce their volume to 50 percent and their weight to 20 percent. What other benefits do we get from dried foods? What kinds of dried foods can you find in your community?

ART LINK

Draw a picture. Draw a picture of a garden that you'd like to have.

WRITING LINK

Write a paragraph. If your area was in danger of a flood, what could you do to help?

TECHNOLOGY LINK

At the Computer Visit **www.mhscience02.com** for more links.

Water Please!

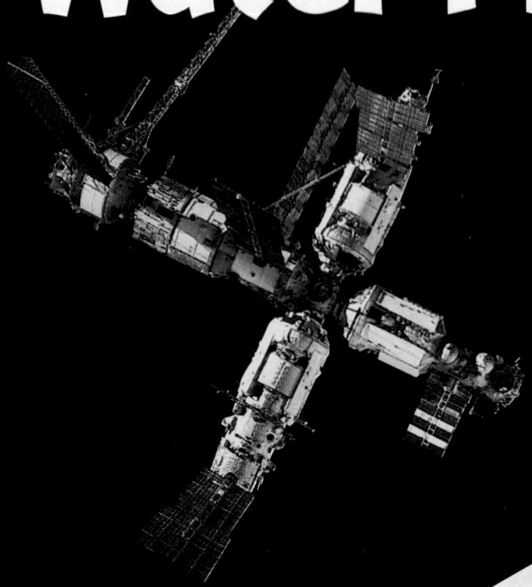

Vocabulary

irrigation, D50

water treatment plant, D52

filtration, D52

sewage, D53

sewer, D53

septic tank, D53

water conservation, D54

Get Ready

Why do you think Earth is known as the blue planet? From a space shuttle, astronauts see Earth as huge brown islands in a sea of blue. Most of Earth's water is salty oceans and seas. There's also a small amount of fresh water. What can we do to make sure there's fresh water in the future?

Process Skill

You communicate when you share information.

Explore Activity

How Much Fresh Water Is Used?

Materials

two 9-oz plastic cups

measuring cup

stopwatch, clock, or watch with second hand

calculator (optional)

Procedure: Design Your Own

1. Determine ways to measure or estimate the amount of water used daily in school.

2. How can you figure out how much water is being used by each student? By each class? Record your results.

3. **Communicate** Design a table to record all the data you gathered from your investigation.

Drawing Conclusions

1. Which activities used the most water each day? Which used the least?

2. **Use Numbers** How can you estimate how much water is used in the whole school in a day?

3. **Infer** From your observations can you think of ways to save water?

4. **Going Further: Communicate** What is another way to record the data you collected? Think about a way to present the information clearly.

Main Idea Only a small part of Earth's water is available for humans.

How Much Fresh Water Is There?

It may seem to you that there is plenty of water around. Actually, only about $\frac{3}{100}$ of Earth's water is fresh. How much do you think is readily available for people to use?

Look at the pie chart. You will see that Earth's fresh water is a slice pulled from the rest of the graph. The slice is then broken into smaller sections. Only $\frac{1}{10}$ of Earth's fresh water supply is easily obtained for human use. This fresh water is found in rivers, lakes, and groundwater.

Fresh water found in frozen ice caps and glaciers isn't readily available. These solid water sources make up about $\frac{7}{10}$ of all the fresh water on Earth.

There is also fresh water under the ground, but the groundwater very deep down is not easy to reach. The very deep groundwater makes up about $\frac{2}{10}$ of Earth's fresh water.

Every day people use water at school, at home, and in office buildings, stores, restaurants, and hotels. Water is also

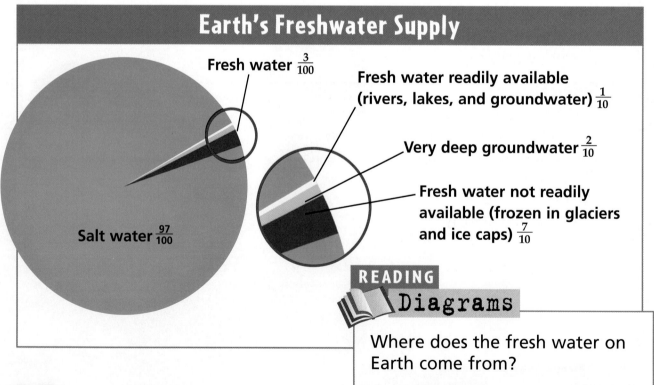

Earth's Freshwater Supply

Fresh water $\frac{3}{100}$

Fresh water readily available (rivers, lakes, and groundwater) $\frac{1}{10}$

Very deep groundwater $\frac{2}{10}$

Fresh water not readily available (frozen in glaciers and ice caps) $\frac{7}{10}$

Salt water $\frac{97}{100}$

READING Diagrams

Where does the fresh water on Earth come from?

used in farming, in industry, and by our communities. Think about the production of goods and the services that are all a part of modern life.

Communities provide many services that require water. These services include street cleaning, firefighting, and watering trees and grass in parks.

A person needs only a few quarts of water a day to stay alive. In the United States, each person may directly use as much as 760 liters (200 gallons) a day. The water is used for personal and household purposes. Some everyday water uses include drinking, cooking, cleaning, flushing toilets, disposing of garbage, and watering gardens.

This pictograph shows how much water is used for some activities.

Firefighting is one community service that needs water.

▷ How much water does each activity use?

Some Household Uses of Water

1 toilet flush	🛢🛢🛢🛢
1 average bath	🛢🛢🛢🛢🛢🛢🛢🛢🛢🛢🛢🛢
1 three-minute shower	🛢🛢🛢🛢🛢🛢🛢🛢
1 dishwasher load	🛢🛢🛢🛢🛢🛢🛢🛢
1 clothes washer load	🛢🛢🛢🛢🛢🛢🛢🛢🛢🛢🛢🛢🛢🛢🛢🛢🛢🛢🛢🛢🛢

🛢 represents 8 liters (about 2 gallons) of water.

Different types of irrigation are used to bring water to farmlands.

How Is Water Used in Farming and Industry?

How much water do you think farms and factories use? In places where rainfall is low or irregular, water for growing crops is supplied by **irrigation** (ir·i·GAY·shuhn). Irrigation is a way to get water into the soil by artificial means. It is used to help increase crop production.

Irrigation water is pumped from rivers, lakes, and under the ground.

It is distributed to fields of growing crops by plowed ditches called furrows, pipes, or sprinklers.

Factories provide us with the products we need and want. Some of the water factories use becomes part of the products they make. However, most of the water is used in washing, cleaning, cooling, and carrying away waste.

Power plants produce electricity that supplies us with the energy for many everyday activities. Hydroelectric power plants produce electricity from the energy of waterfalls and water flowing from dams. Other kinds of power plants use the energy of steam to make electricity. The steam comes from water heated by burning fuel.

▶ **What are some ways water is used in farming and industry?**

The energy of water flowing over dams, such as the one shown here, produces electricity.

How Does Water Get Polluted?

Wastes from industry, farming, and humans are the main sources of water pollution. Rivers and lakes become polluted when untreated wastes are dumped into them. The wastes are full of harmful bacteria and chemicals.

Many farmers use *fertilizers*, which are chemicals or animal waste, to treat soil. *Pesticides*, which are chemicals that kill insects, are also widely used. Sometimes these chemicals are carried along with runoff water that moves into the ground. This polluted water may pass into rivers and lakes, or become part of groundwater. Fish that live in these waters may become sick or die.

Landfills are one way to get rid of waste, but they take up a lot of space.

Even wastes buried in a landfill can pollute groundwater. A landfill is a place where solid wastes are buried between layers of soil. The water table under a landfill must be at least 2 meters (6 feet) deep. A flood in a landfill could cause many problems.

▷ **What things can pollute water?**

Waste emptied into rivers pollutes the water and can harm the organisms that live there.

D 51

How Is Water Cleaned?

Before water can be distributed to homes, it must be made safe for use. This means meeting safe drinking-water rules set by the government.

Some water supplies need little treatment, while others need a great deal more. The place where water is made clean and pure is called a **water treatment plant**.

At the plant water first passes through a screen to remove animals, plants, and trash. Then, various chemicals are mixed with the water in a mixing basin. The chemicals remove impurities and kill harmful bacteria.

From there the water moves to a settling basin, where most other impurities sink. Any impurities that are left are removed by **filtration** (fil·TRAY·shuhn). Filtration is the passing of a liquid through materials that remove impurities.

Finally, the chemical element chlorine is added. The chlorine kills any remaining bacteria. Then, the water is stored and ready to be pumped to where it is needed.

READING **Sequence of Events**
What are the steps in water treatment?

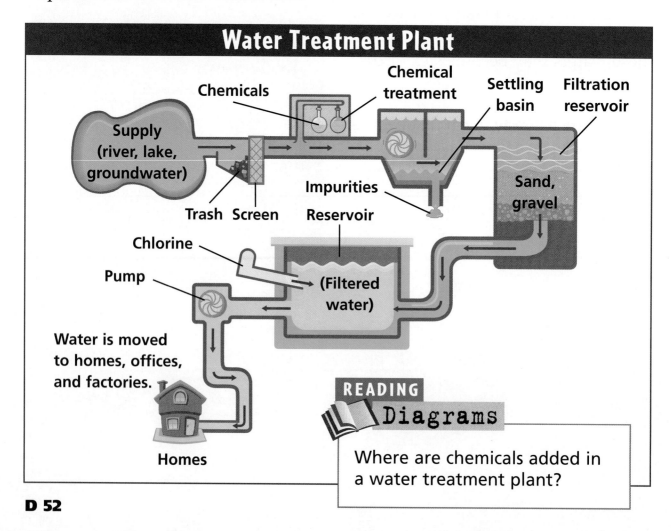

Water Treatment Plant

Chemicals

Chemical treatment

Settling basin

Filtration reservoir

Supply (river, lake, groundwater)

Impurities

Sand, gravel

Trash Screen

Reservoir

Chlorine

Pump

(Filtered water)

Water is moved to homes, offices, and factories.

Homes

READING **Diagrams**

Where are chemicals added in a water treatment plant?

What Happens to Used Water?

Most of the water used in homes and factories is used to carry off waste. Water mixed with waste is **sewage** (SEW·ij). **Sewers** (SEW·uhrz) are large pipes or channels that carry sewage to a sewage treatment plant. This is where sewage is treated before it is returned to rivers and lakes.

At a plant large objects are removed and the *sludge*, or solid material, settles. The waste water is treated to kill germs. Then the clean water flows into rivers and lakes. The sludge is put into tanks, where it is broken down by bacteria. Leftover sludge is used as fertilizer, burned in an incinerator, or dumped out at sea.

Some used water is cleaned at treatment plants such as this.

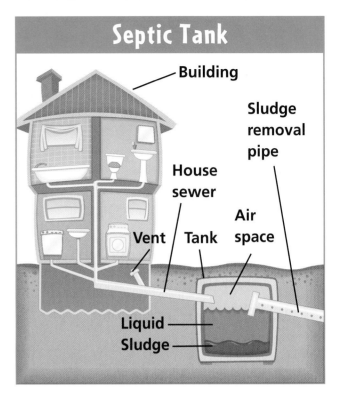

Septic Tank

- Building
- Sludge removal pipe
- House sewer
- Vent
- Tank
- Air space
- Liquid
- Sludge

Areas with no public sewage disposal systems have **septic tanks** (SEP·tik TANGKS). A septic tank is an underground tank in which sewage is broken down by bacteria.

Sewage from a building flows through a pipe into the septic tank. Bacteria in the sewage begin to break it down into liquid, sludge, and gas. The gas escapes through a vent. Leftover sludge is pumped out every so often. The liquid drains into underground pipes that are covered with gravel. The pipes have holes that let the liquid drain out and seep into the ground.

▷ **How is sewage treated?**

QUICK LAB

FOR SCHOOL OR HOME

Wasted Water

1. Turn on a faucet until it drips slowly.

2. Place a pitcher under the faucet for five minutes.

3. **Measure** Measure the collected water. Record the amount.

4. **Observe** How much water was wasted in five minutes?

5. **Use Numbers** If the faucet dripped like this every day, how much water would be wasted in an hour? In a day? In a week? In a year?

How Can We Save Water?

The use of water-saving methods is called **water conservation**. It helps to reduce the amount of water needed for homes, farms, industries, and businesses. Here are some ways you and your family can conserve water:

- Fix leaky faucets.
- Run only full loads in clothes washers and dishwashers.
- Take short showers instead of baths.
- Use shower heads that conserve water.
- Place a brick in the toilet tank.
- Use water only when you need it.
- Don't run water while you are brushing your teeth!
- Don't run water to get cold water. Put drinking water in the refrigerator to keep it cold.

A front-loading washing machine uses less water than a top-loading machine of the same size. This is a water-conserving feature.

▷ **How can you save water at home?**

Why It Matters

Only a small part of Earth's water is fresh. Because we all need fresh water, it is important that we know how to use it wisely. Think about how you use water every day. Do you keep the water running when you wash dishes? How much water could you save by using tubs of water? Try it! Just think about the amount of water that could be saved if everyone on the planet conserved.

Think and Write

1. How much water do you use at school compared with at home?

2. What are the three main sources of fresh water?

3. How does groundwater become polluted? How can it be cleaned?

4. Make a table to show how water can be wasted at home. Then show how this wasted water could be conserved.

5. **Critical Thinking** Since all water is reused and can be cleaned, why is it important to conserve water?

L·I·N·K·S

SOCIAL STUDIES LINK

Research the Dead Sea. The Dead Sea is the saltiest body of water on Earth. It is nine times saltier than the oceans. Find the Dead Sea on a globe or map. What kinds of living things can survive there?

HEALTH LINK

Find out why you need water. Do research to learn how much water you need to drink every day. Make a list of reasons why drinking enough water is important to your health.

MATH LINK

Solve a problem. If you save $7\frac{1}{2}$ gallons of water a week, how much water will you save in a month? How much water will you save in a year?

WRITING LINK

Write an ad. Write a public service ad to persuade people in your community to conserve water.

TECHNOLOGY LINK

At the Computer Visit **www.mhscience02.com** for more links.

DESALINATION

"Water, water everywhere.
Nor any drop to drink."

This is a line from an old poem about sailors and the sea. People cannot drink seawater because it is too salty. Water picks up salt from the ground as it flows from land to sea.

Earth has lots of water, but not much fresh water, the kind we can drink. Fresh water comes from rivers, lakes, and streams. We also dig wells to get fresh water from the ground. However, we sometimes use fresh water faster than it is restored. We also pollute it.

Can seawater be turned into fresh water? Yes, it can! Removing salt from seawater is called desalination. Sometimes, special filters remove the salt. In another process, seawater is heated to boiling. Fresh water evaporates and collects in containers, leaving the salt behind. Both processes are very expensive because they use a lot of energy.

Scientists are working on ways to make desalination cheaper. One way is to use ocean waves as a source of energy. The motion of the waves powers the pumps. The pumps bring seawater into a desalination plant.

One day, we might turn a lot of seawater into fresh water. How do you think this might change life on Earth?

NATIONAL GEOGRAPHIC

What Did I Learn?

1. Desalination procedures change seawater into

  A polluted water.
  B fresh water.
  C groundwater.
  D salty water.

2. Desalination can be expensive because it uses a lot of

  F seawater.
  G salt.
  H time.
  J energy.

AT THE COMPUTER

Visit www.mhscience02.com to learn more about desalination.

The largest desalination plant in the world at Al-Jubayl in Saudi Arabia

Chapter 8 Review

Vocabulary

Fill each blank with the best word or words from the list.

condensation, D17 **septic tank,** D53

evaporation, D16 **sewage,** D53

filtration, D52 **water table,** D39

irrigation, D50 **water vapor,** D6

precipitation, D18 **wave,** D32

1. Water in the atmosphere is a gas called _____.

2. A liquid is passed through materials that remove impurities. This is called _____.

3. A(n) _____ is a place where bacteria break down sewage.

4. The upper area of groundwater is known as the _____.

5. Water mixed with waste is _____.

6. An up-and-down movement of water is a(n) _____.

7. Moving water to farms in dry places is called _____.

   The three steps of the water cycle:

8. _____

9. _____

10. _____

11. Plants lose water through their leaves in a process called _____.

    A condensation
    B evaporation
    C transpiration
    D irrigation

12. When you look at a cloud, you see _____.

    F water vapor
    G water droplets or ice
    H electricity
    J many different gases

13. Winds cause oceans to have _____.

    A tides
    B pollution
    C waves
    D runoff

14. At a water treatment plant, water is _____.

    A cleaned with filters
    B used to make electricity
    C converted to steam
    D used for irrigation

Concepts and Skills

15. Reading in Science After you clean the dishes, what happens to the water you just used? Write a paragraph that describes where the water goes and how it changes.

16. Process Skills: Use Variables Does salt water or fresh water evaporate faster? Form a hypothesis, then describe an experiment to test it. Identify the variable that you are testing.

17. Critical Thinking When digging a well, why is it important to find out where the water table is?

18. Product Ads Drinking water is sold in grocery stores. Read the labels for these products, or find ads. How do these products claim to be better than water from the faucet?

19. Decision Making Write a paragraph describing some of the ways you use water every day. Do you think you are using water wisely or unwisely? How might you change the way you use water to conserve it in your community?

Boost *your test scores!*

Be Smart!
Visit **www.mhscience02.com**
to learn more.

Earth's Weather

LESSON 6

Air, Wind, and the Atmosphere, D62

LESSON 7

Weather and Climate, D76

Did You Ever Wonder?

How hot can the desert get? During the day some deserts have an average temperature of about 49°C, (120°F). Deserts are not always this hot, however. At night a desert can get as cold as 0°C (32°F). This happens because the air is dry and the skies are cloudless, so the heat escapes easily. Why do different locations have different weather conditions?

Air, Wind, and the Atmosphere

Vocabulary

humidity, D66

air pressure, D67

stratus cloud, D71

cumulus cloud, D71

cirrus cloud, D71

Get Ready

Splash! Jump into a pool, and you can feel the water surrounding you. Water is a fluid. On land you are surrounded by a fluid, too. That fluid is air. You may not notice air until you inflate a balloon, fly a kite, or blow bubbles. What is air? How can you observe it?

Process Skill

You use variables when you identify and separate things in an experiment that can be changed or controlled.

Explore Activity

What Can Air Do?

Materials

large plastic sandwich bag

string

scissors

two washers

Procedure: Design Your Own

BE CAREFUL! Handle scissors carefully.

1. **Make a Model** Use the plastic bag and string to make a parachute for a washer. Cut the sides of the bag, but leave the bag in one piece. Tie four pieces of string to the washer. Tie the other ends of the strings to the corners of the bag.

2. **Observe** Drop the parachute. Observe how the plastic bag changes as it falls.

3. **Experiment** Hold the parachute in one hand and the second washer in the other hand. Let them go at the same time. Observe both as they fall to the floor.

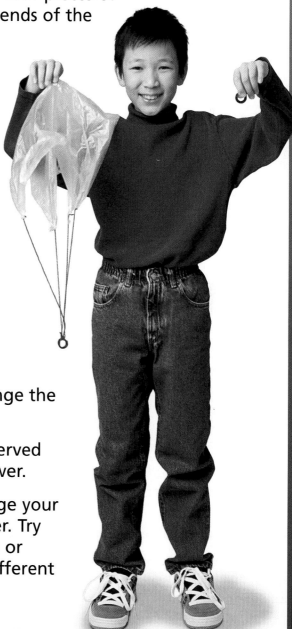

Drawing Conclusions

1. How did the plastic bag change when you dropped the parachute?

2. How does adding a parachute change the way a washer falls?

3. **Infer** Is air real? Use what you observed in this activity to support your answer.

4. **Going Further: Use Variables** Change your parachute. Try to make it fall slower. Try changing the lengths of the strings or where you tie the strings, or use different plastic bags.

Main Idea The conditions of the atmosphere create our weather.

What Is the Atmosphere?

Air is all around you. What do you think air is made of? Air is a mixture of gases. Look at the graph. It shows that air is mostly nitrogen and oxygen. Air also contains small amounts of other gases, such as carbon dioxide and water vapor. All gases are made up of tiny particles in constant motion.

Living things depend on the gases in air. Animals breathe oxygen, which they use to release energy from food. Without oxygen most animals would die in a few minutes. Animals and plants need nitrogen, too.

Only small amounts of carbon dioxide and water vapor are present in the air. They play many roles, however. Plants use carbon dioxide to make food. Water vapor forms clouds that can make rain and snow.

Layers of Earth's Atmosphere

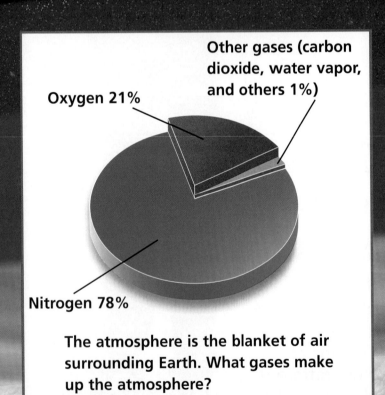

Other gases (carbon dioxide, water vapor, and others 1%)

Oxygen 21%

Nitrogen 78%

The atmosphere is the blanket of air surrounding Earth. What gases make up the atmosphere?

Air wraps around Earth like a giant blanket. The blanket of air surrounding Earth is called the atmosphere. The atmosphere covers both land and sea. Earth's gravity holds it in place.

Earth's atmosphere has four different layers. The layer closest to Earth is between 8 and 11 kilometers (5 and 7 miles) thick. This layer contains most of the air particles in the atmosphere. All life exists here. Above this layer, air gradually thins out. Fewer and fewer air particles can be found as you move toward space, which is nearly empty.

▷ What are the four layers of the atmosphere?

READING Diagrams

1. Make a table showing the thickness of each layer.

2. How does the temperature change in the different layers of the atmosphere?

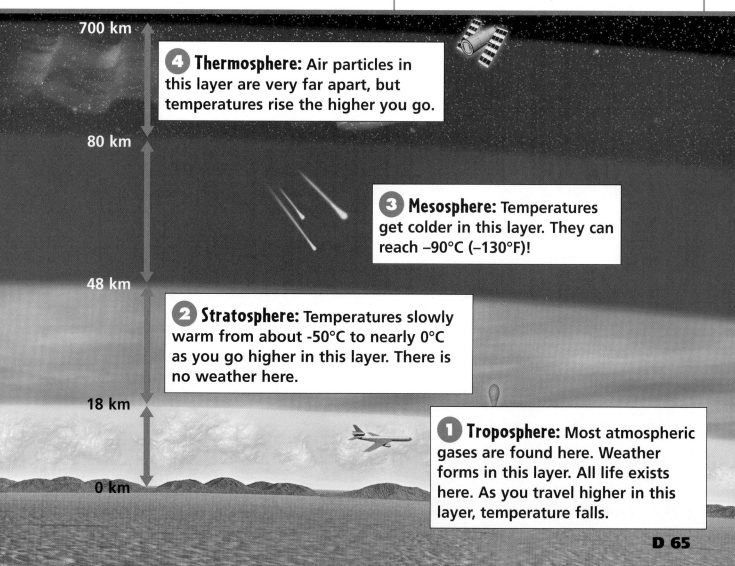

700 km

4 Thermosphere: Air particles in this layer are very far apart, but temperatures rise the higher you go.

80 km

3 Mesosphere: Temperatures get colder in this layer. They can reach −90°C (−130°F)!

48 km

2 Stratosphere: Temperatures slowly warm from about -50°C to nearly 0°C as you go higher in this layer. There is no weather here.

18 km

1 Troposphere: Most atmospheric gases are found here. Weather forms in this layer. All life exists here. As you travel higher in this layer, temperature falls.

0 km

What Makes Weather?

To describe weather, scientists measure four properties of the air. These things are air temperature, humidity, air pressure, and wind.

Air Temperature

The Sun's energy heats Earth's surface. When the surface heats up, it warms the air above it. The air particles move farther apart.

Humidity

If air feels damp and sticky, we say the weather is humid. **Humidity** (hyew·MID·i·tee) is a measurement of how much water vapor is in air.

When the weather is humid, the air feels hot and sticky. On cold autumn days, the air is cool and crisp. There is less humidity.

Air always contains some water vapor. Most of it comes from ocean water that evaporated, or changed from liquid to gas.

Why is some air very humid and other air very dry? Air over oceans and lakes is usually humid. Air over deserts is usually dry. Air moves from place to place carrying water vapor.

The air pressure of cool air is greater than the air pressure of warm air.

Air Pressure

A submarine sits at the bottom of the ocean. The weight of the water pushes against it. The force of the water pushing against it is water pressure. You live at the bottom of an "ocean" of air. The force of air pushing on an area is **air pressure**.

Particles of cool air are closer together than particles of warm air. This means that cool air weighs more than warm air weighs in the same space. Air that weighs more has greater air pressure. Cool air usually has higher air pressure than warm air.

Wind

Air in motion is called *wind*. Wind speed varies. On a calm day, you may feel no wind at all. During a hurricane the wind may blow at speeds of more than 180 km (120 miles) per hour!

▶ **What four things describe the air?**

Weather can be calm or windy.

What Makes the Wind Blow?

You can't see it, but you can feel it. You can see what it does. It blows off your hat. It lifts up your kite. It rattles the leaves from the trees. What is it? It's the wind!

Wind is caused by uneven heating of Earth. In places where Earth's surface absorbs a lot of the Sun's energy, the air above it warms up. Dark surfaces such as soil and city streets absorb heat well, so air above them tends to be warm. Light-colored surfaces such as snow and water do not absorb much energy from the Sun. They stay cool, so the air above them is cool, too.

Compare how these surfaces absorb the Sun's energy. Where is the air above the surface warmer? Where is it cooler?

You learned that cool air particles are closer together than warm air particles. This means that cool air weighs more than warm air, so cool air has higher air pressure.

Air moves from a place of high pressure to one of low pressure. This movement of air is the wind.

Have you ever noticed the wind changing direction from one day to the next, or from day to night? This happens when air pressures change over a region. The diagram below shows how winds can change at the ocean's shore.

Although you may not be able to see air, you can see it in motion. You can feel it, too! Wind is air in motion.

▷ **How do Earth's different temperatures cause winds?**

During the day water heats up more slowly than the land. The water is cooler than the land. The air above the water is also cooler. Air pressure is higher above the water, and winds blow from ocean to shore.

At night land loses heat more quickly than water. The land is now cooler than the water, and the air above the land is cooler, too. The air pressure is higher above the land, and winds blow from shore to ocean.

Process Skill BUILDER

SKILL Infer

Homemade Barometer

What happens to the air inside a container if the container's size changes? In this activity you will make a *barometer* (buh·RAHM·i·tuhr), a device for measuring air pressure. You will infer how a barometer measures changing air pressure. When you infer, you use observations to form an idea.

Procedure

BE CAREFUL! Handle scissors carefully.

1 **Make a Model** Use the scissors to cut the neck off one of the balloons. Stretch the bottom of the balloon over the mouth of the small jar. Hold it in place with a rubber band.

2 Glue the large end of the toothpick to the stretched balloon. Let the glue dry. Put the small jar inside the wide-mouthed jar.

3 Cut the neck from the second balloon. Stretch the bottom of the balloon over the mouth of the large jar. Hold it in place with a rubber band.

4 **Observe** Pull up and push down on the balloon stretched over the large jar. What happens to the toothpick on the small jar?

Drawing Conclusions

1 **Infer** How did the air pressure inside the large jar change when you pushed down on the balloon? What evidence helped you determine this?

2 **Infer** How did the air pressure inside the large jar change when you pulled up on the balloon? What evidence helped you determine this?

Materials

small jar, such as a baby food jar

1-qt or 1-L wide-mouthed jar

two 9-in. balloons

glue

scissors

flat toothpick

2 rubber bands

Why Do Clouds Form?

Clouds come in many different shapes, sizes, and even colors. What do you think clouds are made of?

The air is filled with water vapor. When the water vapor cools enough, it condenses. This means that the water vapor particles clump together on bits of dust or other material in the air. They change into tiny droplets of water. Millions of tiny water droplets join to form clouds. Cold-air clouds are made of ice crystals rather than water droplets.

You can often tell whether a cloud is made of water droplets or ice crystals by looking at it. Water-droplet clouds tend to have sharp, distinct edges. If the clouds are thick, they may be gray or black. Ice-crystal clouds are whiter. They tend to have fuzzy, less defined edges.

These pictures show the three main types of clouds. **Stratus** (STRAY·tuhs) **clouds** form in layers. Fog is really a stratus cloud that develops near Earth's surface. **Cumulus** (KYEW·myuh·luhs) **clouds** are puffy clouds that appear to rise from a flat bottom. **Cirrus** (SIR·uhs) **clouds** are made of ice crystals and have wispy shapes, like feathers. Combinations of these clouds also happen.

The amount of the sky covered by clouds is called cloud cover. The terms *clear, scattered clouds, partly cloudy, mostly cloudy,* and *overcast* describe cloud cover. Symbols used to describe cloud cover are shown here.

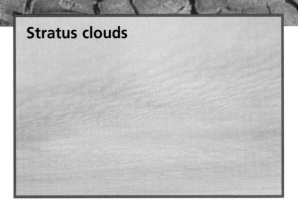
Stratus clouds

Cumulus clouds

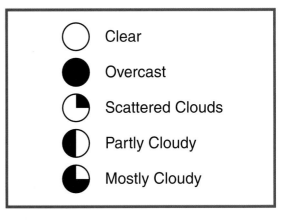
Cirrus clouds

○ Clear

● Overcast

◔ Scattered Clouds

◑ Partly Cloudy

◕ Mostly Cloudy

READING **Compare and Contrast**
How would you describe the three main types of clouds?

D 71

How Can You Describe Weather?

Weather is described by measuring four properties of the air. The tools for measuring temperature, humidity, air pressure, and wind, as well as precipitation are shown here.

A *hygrometer* (hi·GRAHM·i·tuhr) measures humidity by determining how quickly water evaporates from a wet surface.

A *thermometer* measures air temperature. When air temperature rises, the mercury expands and moves higher in the tube.

A *weather vane* measures wind direction. It tells you where the wind is blowing from.

An *anemometer* (an·uh·MAHM·i·tuhr) measures wind speed.

A *barometer* measures air pressure.

The height of the water collected in a *rain gauge* tells how much rain has fallen.

▷ **What are six tools used to describe weather?**

L·I·N·K·S

Why It Matters

Farmers, airplane pilots, sailors, people going on picnics—everyone wants to know what the weather will be like! Knowing what the weather will be like helps people plan their days. To do a research project on weather, visit **www.mhscience02.com**.

Think and Write

1. What gases make up air? Which gas is most abundant?

2. In what way is Earth's atmosphere like an orange peel? How is it different?

3. Name four properties of air that describe the weather. What tools measure these properties?

4. Infer Your eardrum is a thin layer between your inner ear and the outside. Why might your eardrum hurt when you travel in an airplane?

5. Critical Thinking Why do airlines supply oxygen to their passengers in flight?

ART LINK

Make a poster. Use art materials to make a poster of the different kinds of clouds. Label each cloud, and include facts about it.

MUSIC LINK

Do research. How do people use the wind to make music? Find out about wind-operated musical instruments.

WRITING LINK

Write a story. How do people depend on the weather? How can weather change people's lives?

MATH LINK

Graph the weather. Use weather instruments or values reported in the newspaper to track the weather for one week. Make a graph or chart to show your observations. When one reading changed, did others?

Air Pressure						
Sun	Mon	Tues	Wed	Thurs	Fri	Sat
1						
2						
3						

TECHNOLOGY LINK

At the Computer Visit **www.mhscience02.com** for more links.

Endangered: Earth's Ozone Layer

To avoid a sunburn, you put on sunscreen lotion before heading outdoors. It may be hard to believe, but Earth has a sunscreen, too. Earth's sunscreen is the ozone layer, a thin layer of ozone particles in the atmosphere. The ozone layer blocks much of the Sun's ultraviolet radiation—harmful rays of energy.

Ozone is a type of oxygen. It forms in the upper atmosphere when sunlight alters oxygen gas. Ozone also forms near the ground when car exhaust and factory smoke mix in sunlight. Ozone is toxic, or harmful, to the lungs. Near the ground it is a pollutant. High in the atmosphere, however, ozone protects our health.

In the 1970s scientists became concerned that the ozone layer was disappearing. Evidence showed that gases called CFCs could destroy ozone. CFCs have been used in air conditioners, aerosol spray cans, and refrigerators. All scientists did not agree, however. Some thought the ozone layer was safe.

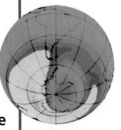

1979

These illustrations show an ozone change over many years.

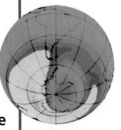

1982

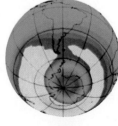

1983

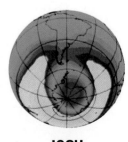

1984

Then in 1985 British scientists made an alarming discovery. A huge hole in the ozone layer, the size of the United States, had developed over Antarctica. The hole grows and shrinks over time.

Destruction of the ozone layer poses a risk to human health and the health of crops. It can also change the climate in ways no one can predict. Substitutes for CFCs are now being developed. What can you do to help save the ozone layer?

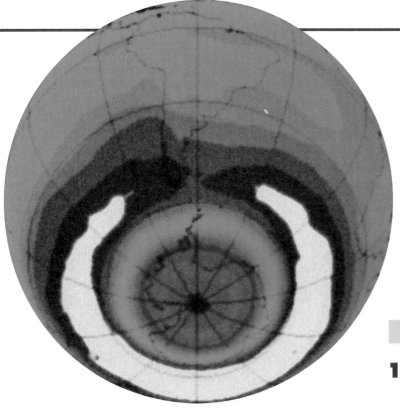

1990

Did you know many older refrigerators have chemicals that destroy the ozone layer?

Many aerosal cans contain harmful products that are not safe for our environment.

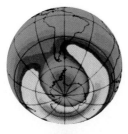 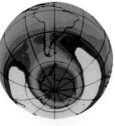 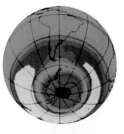

1987   1988   1989

Write ABOUT IT

1. What can you do to help save the ozone layer?

2. Why is the ozone layer so imporant?

 **AT THE COMPUTER**

Visit www.mhscience02.com to learn more about Earth's ozone layer.

D 75

Weather and Climate

Vocabulary

air mass, D79

front, D80

warm front, D80

cold front, D81

stationary front, D81

Get Ready

Did you know that the driest place on the planet is a desert in Chile, South America? It hasn't rained there for over 400 years! The rainiest place on Earth is the island of Kauai in Hawaii. It rains there about 350 days each year! Why is it so dry in some places and so rainy in others? What makes rain?

Process Skill

You experiment when you perform a test to support or disprove a hypothesis.

Explore Activity

How Do Raindrops Form?

Materials

1-qt or
1-L jar with lid

ice cubes

water

Procedure

1. **Make a Model** Pour water into the jar so that the bottom of the jar is covered.

2. Turn the jar lid upside down, and rest it on the mouth of the jar. Put three or four ice cubes inside the lid.

3. **Observe** Watch the underside of the lid for ten minutes.

4. **Communicate** Record your observations.

Drawing Conclusions

1. **Infer** Where did the moisture on the underside of the lid come from?

2. **Infer** Why was it necessary to cool the lid with ice to make "raindrops"?

3. What evaporated in this experiment? What condensed?

4. **Going Further: Experiment** What other types of setups can you find that will also create a model of "rain"?

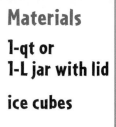

Main Idea Many things affect our weather and climate.

What Are Air Masses?

In Lesson 6 you learned that air is made up of oxygen, nitrogen, carbon dioxide, water vapor, and other gases. Where do you think the water vapor in air comes from?

Evaporation from the oceans produces most of the water vapor in the atmosphere. Not every place on Earth has the same amount of water vapor. For example, the air near an ocean is generally moist.

The properties of the air in different places on Earth vary. The air in one place will be warmer or colder, drier or more moist than air in other places. Large areas of air

Satellite photos such as this one help scientists to study weather patterns. Here you can see clouds covering areas of North America.

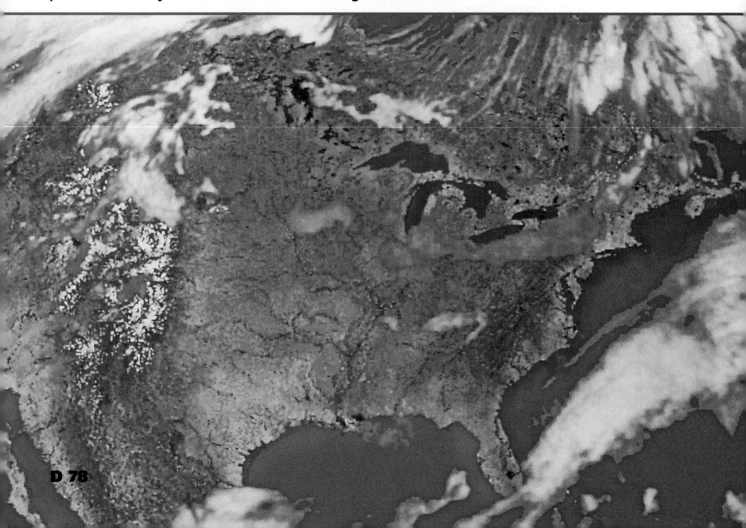

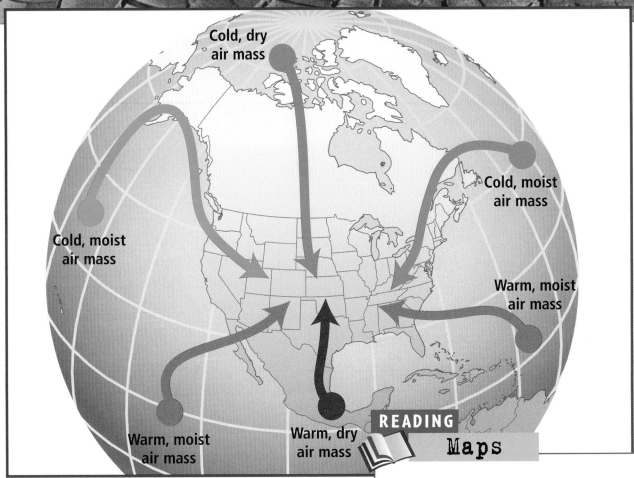

Cold, dry
air mass

Cold, moist
air mass

Cold, moist
air mass

Warm, moist
air mass

Warm, moist
air mass

Warm, dry
air mass

READING

Maps

**Air masses form over land or water,
usually over the tropics or polar regions.
Four words are used to describe an air
mass—*warm*, *cold*, *moist*, or *dry*.**

1. What can you tell
about the air mass that
develops over the land
portion of northern
Canada? Over land in
the tropics?

2. Where do the air masses
that affect the United
States come from?

with nearly the same temperature and
moisture are called **air masses** . Air masses
are very large regions of air with the same
weather. Some air masses are so big they
can cover much of an ocean or continent!

Air masses are always forming. Mostly
they form in the tropics and the polar regions. An air mass
gets its properties from the region where it develops. For
example, an air mass that forms over land near the North
Pole will be cold and dry. An air mass that forms over the
warm water of the Gulf of Mexico will be warm and moist.

Air masses are always on the move. As they move, they
bring the weather with them. There are six major air masses
that affect the United States.

▷ **What are
air masses?**

What Happens When Air Masses Meet?

Imagine one huge air mass of cold, dry air from the North Pole traveling south. Now think of a warm and wet air mass from the Gulf of Mexico traveling north. What happens when these air masses meet? Crash! Like two cars in a crash, the air masses smash into each other. The area where they meet is called a **front** . A front is a boundary between air masses that have different temperatures.

Fronts form along the boundary of warm air masses and cold air masses. Fronts usually bring changing weather. They may even cause strong storms. How do you think fronts change the weather?

When a warm air mass pushes into a cold air mass, a **warm front** results. A warm front is a boundary between air masses where the warm air mass slides up and over the cold air mass. The cold air mass moves back as the warm air mass advances.

As the diagram shows, warm air rises slowly along a warm front. Layers of clouds form. Usually there is light rain. A steady drizzle may last a few hours or longer. When the warm front passes, the temperature in the area rises as advancing warm air replaces cooler air.

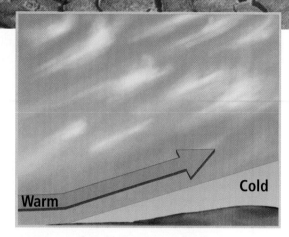

Warm

Cold

A warm front forms when a mass of light, warm air slides over a cold air mass. Light rain may fall over a large area. High cirrus clouds may also form.

A storm is developing over this area of farmland. What type of front may be approaching?

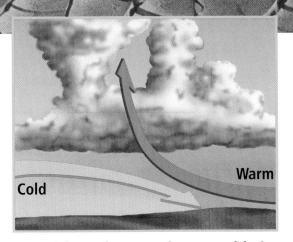

A cold front forms as heavy, cold air pushes under a warm air mass. The warm air is pushed upward along a steep front. Dark storm clouds can bring violent weather.

A stationary front is a boundary between air masses that does not move. Rainy weather may persist for several days.

When cold air pushes into an area of warm air, a **cold front** forms. A cold front is a boundary where cold air pushes under warm air. As a cold front advances, warm air is forced upward very quickly along the boundary. The upward movement of warm air creates a steep, sloping front. Thick clouds form as the warm air rises and cools.

Air in a cold front moves quickly and rises rapidly. Therefore, a cold front often brings violent weather,

perhaps a thunderstorm. However, cold fronts move faster than warm fronts, and their storms pass quickly.

Sometimes rainy weather lasts for a few days. There may be a **stationary front** at work. A stationary front is a boundary between air masses that doesn't move. Either a warm front or a cold front can become a stationary front.

What happens when air masses meet?

How Do Weather Maps Help Predict the Weather?

Weather maps show weather conditions at a certain time and place. The locations of fronts, wind direction, and temperature and air pressure measurements are all important clues about what the weather will be like. All of this information—and more—can be shown on a weather map.

Look at the weather map below. Information on weather maps is often shown by using symbols and numbers. Read the map key to understand the symbols. You can see an area

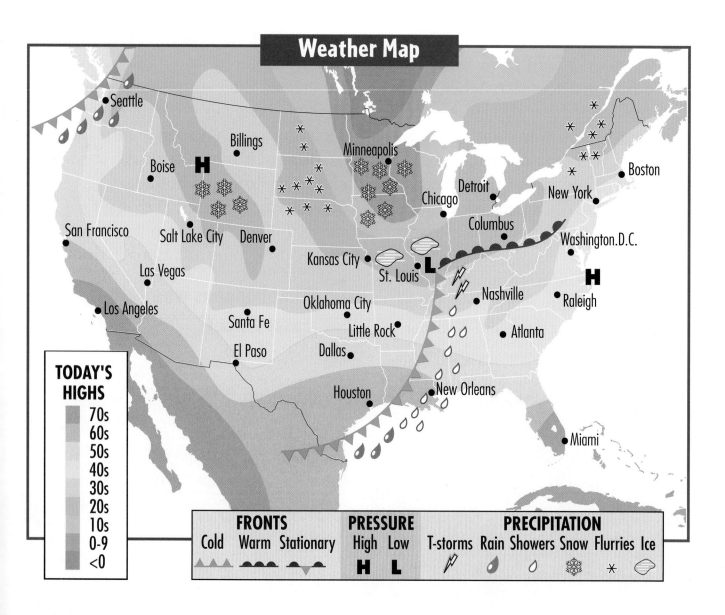

Weather Map

TODAY'S HIGHS
- 70s
- 60s
- 50s
- 40s
- 30s
- 20s
- 10s
- 0-9
- <0

FRONTS			PRESSURE		PRECIPITATION				
Cold	Warm	Stationary	High	Low	T-storms	Rain	Showers	Snow	Flurries	Ice
			H	L						

of high pressure in the northwest. The area around St. Louis is an area of low pressure. How might this help you predict the weather? You learned that air moves from areas of high pressure to areas of low pressure. Therefore, windy weather is likely near areas of pressure highs and pressure lows.

Also look at the locations of the warm and cold fronts and the directions they are moving. You can predict that a light, steady rain may fall where the warm front passes through. Stormy weather is likely where the cold front is going.

How hot or cold is it going to be in a certain place? Current temperatures and weather fronts help answer this question. For example, look at the Great Lakes region along the northern border of the midwestern United States. As the weather map for Day 1 shows, a cold front is moving through. Watch for temperatures to drop. Now look at the weather map for Day 2. See how temperatures did indeed drop. The weather map for Day 3 shows how the cold air followed the direction of the cold front.

▷ How do weather maps help predict the weather?

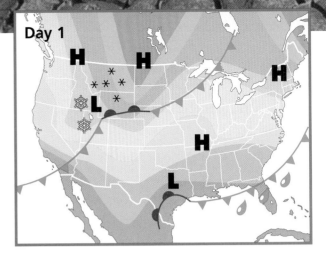

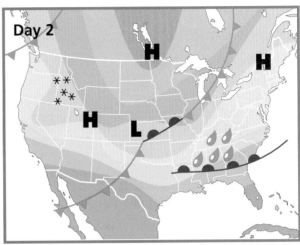

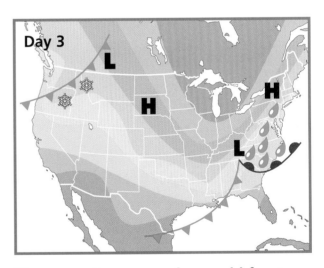

These weather maps show cold fronts moving from the northwest to the southeast. Warm fronts move from southwest to northeast. Notice that temperature changes and storms often occur along fronts. Air pressure changes as one air mass replaces another.

What Is Climate?

Weather is the daily condition of the atmosphere. Climate is the average weather in a certain place for a long period of time. Important features of climate are average temperature, prevailing winds, humidity, and patterns and types of precipitation.

The continental United States can be divided into seven climate zones. A climate zone is a large area with a similar climate. Look at the map. It shows the seven climate zones in the United States. What region has the warmest climate? The coldest?

READING Compare and Contrast How is climate different from weather?

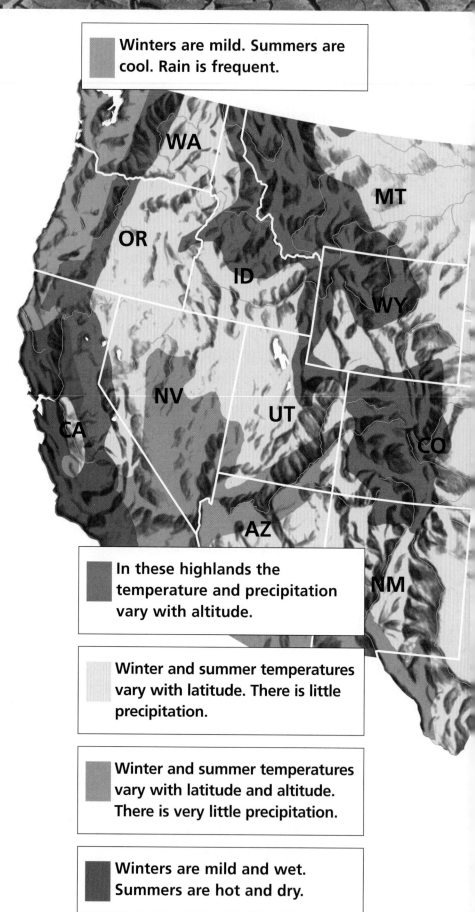

Winters are mild. Summers are cool. Rain is frequent.

WA

MT

OR

ID

WY

NV

UT

CA

CO

AZ

NM

In these highlands the temperature and precipitation vary with altitude.

Winter and summer temperatures vary with latitude. There is little precipitation.

Winter and summer temperatures vary with latitude and altitude. There is very little precipitation.

Winters are mild and wet. Summers are hot and dry.

U.S. CLIMATE ZONES

Winters are cold. Summers are hot or warm. Precipitation is plentiful.

Winters are mild or warm. Summers are hot. Precipitation is plentiful.

ND
MN
SD
WI
MI
NE
IA
IL
IN
OH
KS
MO
KY
TN
OK
AR
MS
AL
GA
TX
LA
FL
ME
VT
NH
NY
MA
CT
RI
PA
NJ
MD
DE
WV
VA
NC
SC

READING Maps

1. Find your climate zone on the map. Do you think the description is accurate?

2. How would you describe the climate in Oregon? In Virginia?

What Affects Climate?

Why do different places have different climates? Several factors affect temperature and precipitation over a long period of time.

Latitude *Latitude* is a measure of how far north or south of the equator a place is. Latitude is an important factor affecting climate.

Near the equator the Sun's rays strike Earth directly. Temperatures are high all year. It is often rainy. Midway between the equator and the poles, climate is moderate. Summers are warm, and winters are cool or cold. Some locations are rainy. Near the poles the Sun's rays strike Earth at a slant. Winters are long and cold, and summers are short but warm. Precipitation is low.

Large Bodies of Water Places near oceans or large lakes have climates that are cloudier and rainier than places farther inland. Summers are cooler and winters are warmer.

Large bodies of water affect air temperature because land and water heat up and cool down at different rates. Land heats up faster than water but also cools down faster. Nearness to water reduces temperature extremes. Nearness to water also increases moisture in the air.

Mountains Warm, moist air from the Pacific Ocean blows up the sides of the Sierra Nevada and Cascade mountain ranges. As the air moves up, clouds form and rain falls. Then the dry air moves down the other side of the mountain.

Mountain ranges also affect climate.

Cold moist air

Hot dry air

Leeward side

Warm moist air

Windward side

Sea Level

Altitude *Altitude* is a measure of how high above sea level a place is. The higher the altitude, the cooler its climate. At the base of a mountain, you may find tropical plants growing. Halfway up, the climate is much different. You may find pine trees growing. On the peak you may find ice and snow.

Winds Some winds affect local areas and start and stop quickly. Other winds tend to blow continuously in the same general direction. Such winds circle the globe. They are called *global winds*. Differences in air pressure cause global circulation of air. Remember, wind blows from areas with high pressure to areas with low pressure.

Warm air near the equator has low air pressure. This warm air rises and moves toward the poles. Cold air near the poles has high air pressure. This cold air sinks and moves toward the equator.

Because Earth spins on its axis, these winds curve, or bend, as they travel. Winds are named for the direction from which they come. In the middle latitudes, winds called "westerlies" continuously blow from west to east. They bring warm, moist air to the west coast. They push air masses and weather fronts across the country. Winds blowing from east to west at the poles and in the tropical zone are called "easterlies."

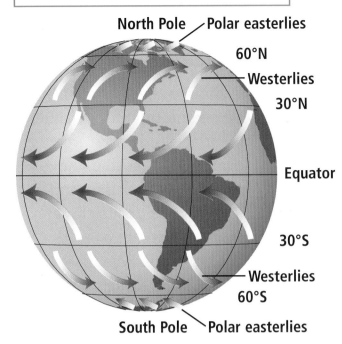

North Pole — Polar easterlies
60°N
Westerlies
30°N
Equator
30°S
Westerlies
60°S
South Pole — Polar easterlies

Global wind patterns are caused by the unequal heating of Earth's surface. This creates differences in air pressure. Winds blow from areas of high pressure to areds of low pressure.

El Niño About every three to seven years, ocean water along the coast of Peru becomes warmer than usual. This changes the air circulation in the atmosphere. This changes weather patterns around the world. The El Niño that happened from 1997 to 1998 brought very heavy rain and flooding in the eastern United States and California. However, El Niño also brought drought to other parts of the United States and Asia. Scientists aren't sure why the ocean warms up in this repeated pattern. They continue to study it and the way it affects the weather.

▶ **What affects climate the most?**

How Do People Change Climate?

Earth's climate changes over time. There have been long periods called ice ages when ice and snow covered much of Earth. Long periods have also been much warmer than today's climates. However, Earth's climate now may be warming at a faster rate than usual. Scientists are concerned that people's actions are causing this. If global warming continues, there could be serious problems. These include bad storms, droughts, and floods. Forests and food production could be harmed.

Why is Earth's temperature rising? Carbon dioxide and other gases in the atmosphere trap solar energy and warm Earth's surface. This helps keep Earth warm and comfortable, not cold like outer space. This is known as the *greenhouse effect*.

Certain actions of people may be increasing the amount of carbon dioxide in the atmosphere. By cutting down forests and burning coal, oil, and natural gases, people are adding carbon dioxide to the atmosphere. This may be causing our environment to become warmer.

▶ **Why is Earth's temperature rising?**

Global Warming

READING Diagrams

What steps lead to the greenhouse effect?

Sunlight comes through the atmosphere and heats the Earth's surface.

Heat from Earth rises. Some of it escapes into space.

Water vapor, carbon dioxide, and other gases trap some of the heat. The air temperature rises.

People are producing more greenhouse gases. The gases stay in the atmosphere and trap more heat. Earth's climate gets warmer.

Why It Matters

Preparing for the weather is important to everyone. That is why people often listen to the weather report. Farmers listen to know when to plant or harvest crops or to protect them from freezing. Pilots need to know whether flying conditions are safe. Skiers need to know whether there will be enough snow to ski, or if a storm is coming. Sometimes being prepared for the weather is not just a matter of comfort. It can be a matter of your own safety!

Think and Write

1. What is the difference between weather and climate?

2. How would you describe an air mass that forms over the Sahara?

3. How do warm fronts differ from cold fronts?

4. A cold front is moving southeast. What kind of weather is likely along the front?

5. Critical Thinking What are two forms of precipitation? In what climate zone would you find each form?

L·I·N·K·S

SOCIAL STUDIES LINK

Find out about floods. Research the dates and locations of some great floods in the past. Try to find the cause or causes of the floods.

LITERATURE LINK

Read *Everyone Always Complains About the Weather* to learn how two friends tried to control the weather. Try the activities at the end of the book.

WRITING LINK

Write a paragraph. Choose a climate zone that is different from your own. Describe how people in that climate zone live differently from you.

ART LINK

Make a poster. Find out about the many symbols used on weather maps to represent different kinds of weather. Make a labeled poster of the symbols.

TECHNOLOGY LINK

At the Computer Visit **www.mhscience02.com** for more links.

WATCH OUT FOR WILD WEATHER!

Cumulonimbus clouds, also called "thunderheads," are taller and darker than cumulus clouds. These clouds bring thunderstorms.

Many storms bring rain that we need. However, some storms are violent.

Storms form when air masses with big differences in temperature, humidity, and air pressure meet. If the air pressure drops suddenly, expect a storm.

Thunderstorms happen when warm air rises and cools rapidly, often along a cold front. The water vapor in the rising air condenses to form huge, dark clouds called cumulonimbus clouds. They create lightning and pouring rain.

Lightning heats the air. This makes the air expand. When the warm air crashes into the cool air surrounding it—CRACK!—you hear thunder.

Hurricanes are another kind of powerful storm. They bring high winds and heavy rain. The average hurricane is about 600 kilometers (373 miles) across. Hurricanes form in warm, moist air masses, above warm ocean waters. They begin as ordinary storms but grow bigger as they absorb heat and moisture. Differences in air pressure start winds blowing in a spiral pattern.

Hurricane winds blow from 119 to over 300 kilometers (74 to over 186 miles) an hour! As much as 25 centimeters (10 inches) of rain can fall in one day.

Tornadoes are sometimes called "twisters." They are columns of dark, spinning, twisting air. They begin when air masses with big temperature differences meet. The warm air is pushed upward very rapidly by the colder air. Tornadoes can travel 800 kilometers (497 miles) per hour! They usually pass in just a few minutes, but they can destroy everything in their path.

Tornadoes are most common in the United States. They occur most often in spring and early summer.

AT THE COMPUTER

Visit www.mhscience02.com to learn more about weather.

What Did I Learn?

1. Hurricanes form in

A warm, moist air masses.
B on cold ocean waters.
C high winds and heavy rains.
D blowing winds.

2. How do tornadoes begin?

F in dark, spinning clouds
G when winds get stronger
H when air masses with big temperature differences meet
J in winter time weather

D 91

Chapter 9 Review

Vocabulary

Fill each blank with the best word or words from the list.

air mass, D79

air pressure, D67

cirrus cloud, D71

cold front, D81

cumulus cloud, D71

front, D80

humidity, D66

stationary front, D81

stratus cloud, D71

warm front, D80

1. A(n) _____ cloud forms in layers, like a pile of blankets in the sky.

2. The water vapor in the air is the _____.

3. A(n) _____ forms high in the sky, is made of ice crystals, and has a featherlike shape.

4. A(n) _____ is a large patch of the atmosphere that has the same weather conditions throughout.

5. Cold air has higher _____ than warm air because it is heavier.

6. A(n) _____ is a puffy cloud that appears to rise from a flat bottom.

7. Air masses meet at a(n) _____.

8. At a(n) _____ warm air rises slowly and light rain may fall for several hours.

9. At a(n) _____ air moves quickly and rises rapidly, which may cause storms.

10. A(n) _____ is a boundary between air masses that don't move.

Test Prep

11. Many scientists argue that global warming comes from a rise in _____.

   A carbon dioxide in the air

   B water pollution

   C land pollution

   D forest fires

12. A weather map can tell _____.

   F locations of fronts

   G cloud cover

   H temperature

   J all of the above

13. A barometer measures _____.

   A temperature

   B wind speed

   C humidity

   D air pressure

14. An area's climate can be best predicted by its _____.

   F population

   G soil conditions

   H latitude

   J size

15. Humidity can be measured using a _____.

   A weather vane

   B hygrometer

   C thermometer

   D all of the above

Concepts and Skills

16. **Reading Skill in Science** Air masses that form in the tropics are warmer than air masses that form in other places. Why is this so?

17. **Process Skills: Infer** What type of front probably caused the weather in this picture?

18. **Critical Thinking** Why can you see your breath outside on a cold winter day but not on a warm summer day?

19. **Safety** What can you do to protect yourself on a hot, humid day?

20. **Scientific Methods** Find a weather forecast for the next five days. Then record the weather each day. Compare the weather with the forecast. How accurate was the forecast? Why isn't a forecast always completely accurate?

Boost *your test scores!*

Be Smart!
Visit **www.mhscience02.com** to learn more.

Dr. Sylvia Earle

OCEANOGRAPHER

Did you know that some U.S. national parks are underwater? They are called marine sanctuaries. Dr. Sylvia Earle studies the living things in these parks.

Dr. Earle has loved the sea since she was 3 years old. When she was 12, her family moved to Florida, and her backyard became the Gulf of Mexico. Instead of squirrels and birds, she saw sea stars and sea urchins.

Today, Dr. Earle is an oceanographer, a scientist who studies oceans. She has led over 50 trips and has found many new species of ocean life. She has also designed boats that can dive deep into the ocean.

Dr. Earle is currently working on the Sustainable Seas Expeditions. She is trying to better understand the oceans so they can be enjoyed for years to come.

Write ABOUT IT

1. Describe Dr. Earle's work.
2. Why does Dr. Earle study oceans?

Careers IN SCIENCE

Meteorologist

A meteorologist studies the atmosphere and changes in the weather. Some work for radio and TV stations. Others work for the U.S. government or teach in colleges and universities.

Meteorologists get information from radar and weather satellites. They also work with computers. They need to know patterns in the weather to predict how the weather will change.

A meteorologist needs to go to college. If you want to be a meteorologist, study math and science. Read the weather report in the newspaper or visit weather sites on the Internet.

AT THE COMPUTER

Visit **www.mhscience02.com** to learn more about careers.

The Story of WATER

What to Do

1. Write a story, play, or poem about water. You may write from the point of view of a water droplet or someone who uses water.

2. Your writing should answer at least one of these questions:

- What are the steps of the water cycle?
- Where can water be found?
- How do we use water?
- How can water become polluted, and how can people stop pollution?

3. If you wrote a story or poem, read it to the class. If you wrote a play, ask classmates to help you present it.

Be a Weather Reporter

Your goal is to do the job of a TV weather reporter. Prepare a weather report for a newscast.

What to Do

1. Carefully read the weather section of the daily newspaper.

2. Write a script for a weather report to present to the class. Tell about the weather in your area or around the country. Discuss any large storms that are forming.

3. Make a chart or diagram to show with your report. The chart may show the weather for the upcoming week, or it may be a weather map.

4. Practice presenting your weather report. The report should last about three minutes.

5. Present the weather report to your class.

Monday
Sunny and warm.
High: 25°c
Low: 18°c

UNIT

E Matter

NATIONAL GEOGRAPHIC

Matter

CHAPTER 10

Properties of Matter E2

CHAPTER 11

Changes in Matter E28

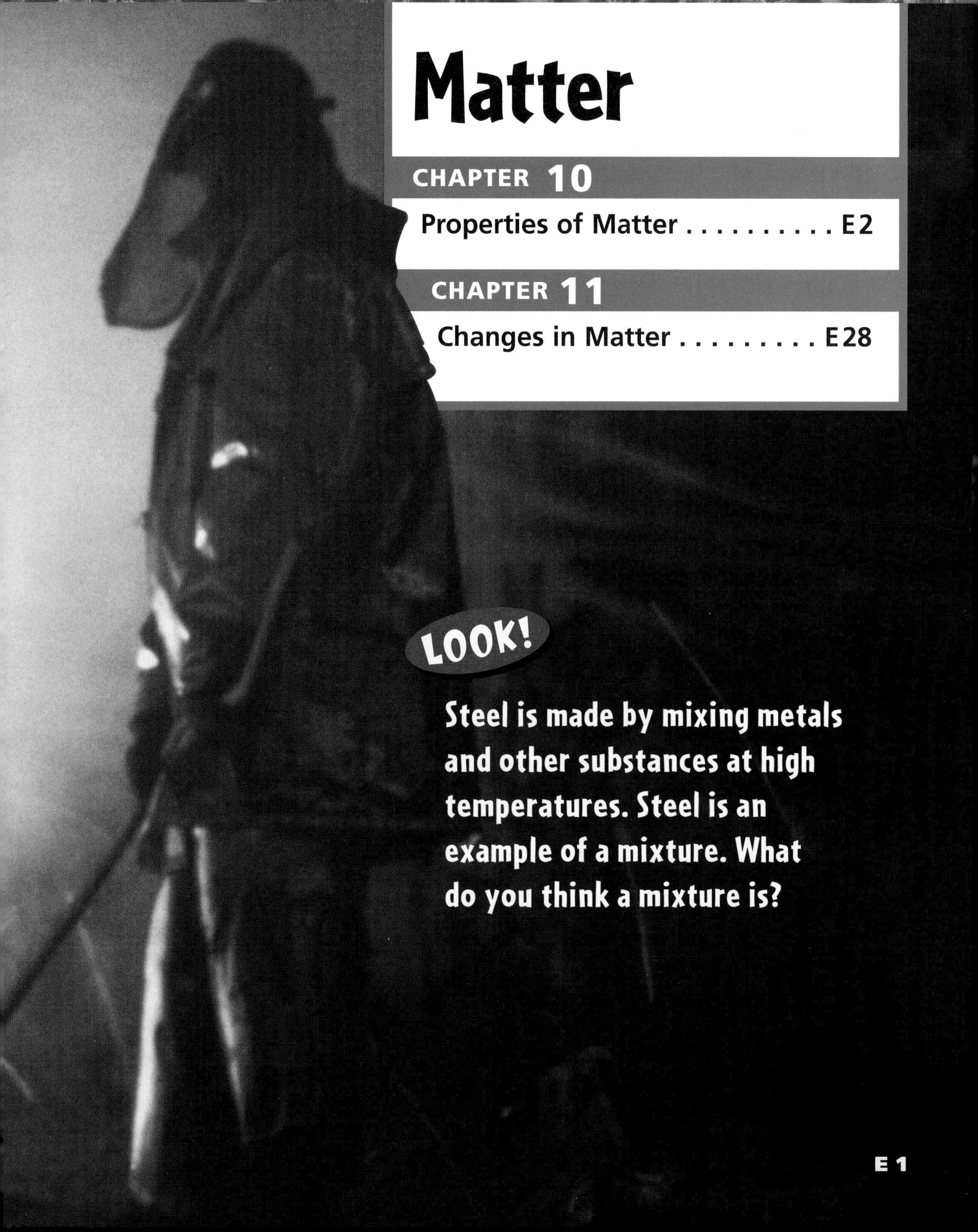

LOOK!

Steel is made by mixing metals and other substances at high temperatures. Steel is an example of a mixture. What do you think a mixture is?

Properties of Matter

LESSON 1

Matter, E4

LESSON 2

Measuring Matter, E14

Did You Ever Wonder?

How many geysers are there in the world? There are approximately 700. Four hundred of those are in Yellowstone National Park in northwestern Wyoming. When a geyser erupts, steam and water droplets rise hundreds of feet into the air. How can water exist as both a liquid and a gas?

Matter

Vocabulary

matter, E6

buoyancy, E7

mass, E8

solid, E8

liquid, E9

gas, E9

Get Ready

Everything that takes up space, has mass, and that you can see, touch, or feel is matter. Matter is all around you. Do you think air is matter? How could you find out?

Process Skill

You infer when you form ideas from facts or observations.

Explore Activity

How Can You Identify Matter?

Materials

2 identical balloons

meterstick

string

scissors

tape

Procedure: Design Your Own

BE CAREFUL! Handle scissors carefully.

1 Experiment Using the materials, design an experiment to determine whether air is matter.

2 Use Variables Do the experiment. Record each step, all your observations, and your results.

Drawing Conclusions

1 Is air matter? What evidence do you have to support your conclusion?

2 Infer Dan blew up a balloon until it burst. Does the broken balloon support the idea that air is matter? Explain.

3 Going Further: Infer Think of another object that is filled with air. Does it also provide evidence that air is matter? Explain.

Main Idea All substances can be described and classified by their properties.

What Is Matter?

Do you think air is matter? Remember, everything that takes up space and has mass is matter.

The photograph shows one way you can find out if air is matter. What observations can you make?

- The inflated balloon takes up more space than the deflated balloon.
- The inflated balloon tips the meterstick. This means that it is heavier than the deflated balloon.
- You can feel that there is something inside the inflated balloon by gently squeezing it.
- You can also feel air rushing out of an inflated balloon when you release the top.

Like other things, air is **matter** (MAT·uhr). Matter is anything that takes up space and has mass. Matter also has *properties* (PRAHP·uhr·teez). A property is a characteristic of something that you can observe. Examples of the properties of matter include color, texture, shape, size, and hardness.

Matter is the "stuff" that makes up the things around you. However, not all things are matter. Think about the color yellow, the month of October, and the number 46. They are not matter but ideas. They do not take up space. They do not have mass. They cannot be described by properties. For example, the color yellow is used to describe matter. Yellow can't be hard, small, or cold. It has no texture or shape.

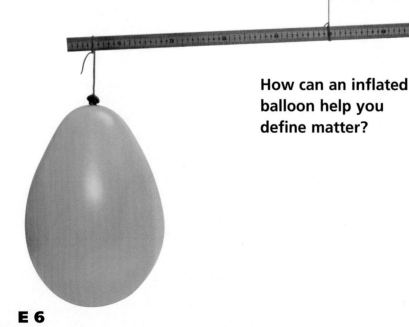

How can an inflated balloon help you define matter?

You just learned that some of the properties used to describe matter are color, texture, shape, size, and hardness. Some other properties include smell, temperature, magnetic attraction, and **buoyancy** (BOY·uhn·see).

You are probably familiar with most of these properties, but what is buoyancy? Buoyancy is the upward force of water, another liquid, or air that keeps things afloat. What examples of buoyancy can you find in this drawing?

Is there some way you can use properties? Properties help people choose the right types of matter for different jobs. What properties does glass have that make it good for classroom windows but bad for gym windows? Based on their properties, where might you use iron instead of wood? Where might you use wood instead of iron?

There are several examples of buoyancy in this drawing. Which ones can you identify?

 **What are some properties of matter?**

This table shows some useless items. Note the properties that make the first item useless. Copy and complete the table. Make up some useless items of your own.

Useless Items	
Useless Item	**Properties That Make It Useless**
Glass baseball bat	too brittle, not strong enough
Rubber mirror	
Wooden bicycle tires	
Aluminum foil tissues	

Is It Matter?

As you learned on page E6, all matter has **mass**. Mass is the amount of matter making up an object. Mass is measured in units called *kilograms* (KIL·uh·gramz). Objects with small masses are measured in units called *grams* (g). There are 1,000 grams in 1 kilogram (kg).

An instrument called a *balance* (BAL·uhns) is used to measure mass. As you can see, it looks a little like a seesaw. To use this pan balance, the object you want to measure is placed in one pan. Known masses are placed in the other pan until the balance is even. The mass of the object is equal to the sum of all the known masses.

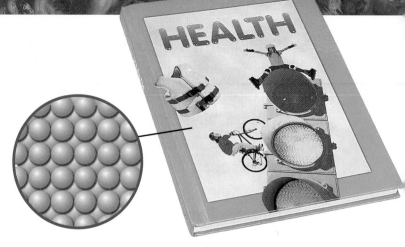

The particles making up a solid are packed together tightly.

Matter is found in different forms. This textbook, water, and helium filling a balloon are three examples of *states*, or forms, of matter.

A textbook is an example of a **solid**. A solid has a definite shape. It takes up a definite amount of space. The particles of matter making up a solid are packed together tightly.

The mass of the object is equal to the sum of all the masses needed to balance the instrument.

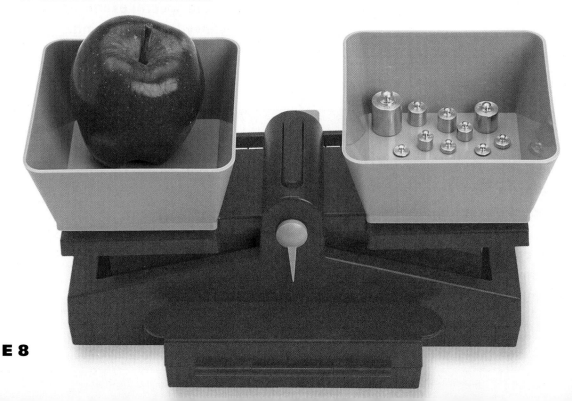

How would you describe the water you drink? Water is an example of a **liquid**. In a liquid the particles of matter move more than they do in a solid. They can change position and move past one another.

A liquid does not have a definite shape. It takes the shape of its container. However, it does take up a definite amount of space. For example, one cup of milk is one cup of milk. It doesn't matter whether it is in a measuring cup or spilled on a table.

The helium in a balloon is an example of a **gas**. In a gas the particles of matter can move freely. They can move farther apart from one another than in a solid or liquid.

A gas does not have a definite shape. It does not take up a definite amount of space. The helium in a balloon takes the shape of the balloon. If the balloon bursts, the particles of helium spread out into the air.

The particles making up a gas can move about freely. They are far apart.

▷ **Choose an object. How can you tell if it is matter?**

States of Matter

	Definite Shape?	Size
Solid	yes	fixed size
Liquid	takes shape of container	fixed size
Gas	takes shape of container	no fixed size

The particles making up a liquid are not as tightly packed as those in a solid. They can move past one another.

READING

Charts

What are the properties of solids, liquids, and gases?

E 9

QUICK LAB

FOR SCHOOL OR HOME

Is Bigger Always More?

1. **Predict** Which has more mass, an inflated balloon or a quarter?

2. **Experiment** Inflate a balloon. Attach it to one end of a meterstick. Attach a quarter to the other end.

3. **Observe** What happens to the meterstick?

4. Which object has more mass?

5. **Infer** Do small objects ever have more mass than larger objects?

6. Can you name some examples of matter that are smaller than a balloon but have more mass than a balloon?

What Are Matter's Characteristics?

These four points will help you review the characteristics of matter.

- **Matter has mass.** Mass is a measure of how much matter an object contains. Mass can be measured using a balance. The standard unit of mass is the kilogram.

- **Matter takes up space.** A balloon expands as it is filled with air. Air is matter.

- **Matter has properties.** Different types of matter have different properties. Diamonds are hard and shiny. Cotton is soft and fluffy. Glass is hard and can shatter.

- **Matter can exist as a solid, a liquid, or a gas.** Some types of matter, such as water, can exist in all three states.

▷ **What are four characteristics of matter?**

Can you identify the three states of matter?

What Happens to the Matter We Use?

What do you think we do with all the trash we create? Too often, we bury garbage in a landfill, burn it, or dump it in the ocean. Each of these actions causes problems. We can run out of places to bury garbage. Burning it pollutes the air. Dumping it in the ocean pollutes the water. What are some other solutions? Try the "three Rs."

Reduce

Reduce the number of things you use that become garbage. The package is much larger than the toy. Try to buy things that don't have a lot of extra packaging.

Reuse

Try to use something again instead of throwing it away. Can you think of another use for a plastic milk container?

Recycle

Many things can be made into something else. These boxes were made from recycled paper. The bottle was made from recycled glass. Check if your community has a recycling program. Find out what materials are accepted.

READING Sequence of Events
How can you use the "three Rs" to reduce pollution?

Can Plastics Be Recycled into Clothing?

Did you ever think you could wear recycled plastics? This shirt, and others like it, are made in part from recycled plastics. Up to 150 pieces of clothing can be made from 3,700 two-liter bottles!

Some of the fibers in this shirt were made from recycled plastics.

Fabric from Plastic

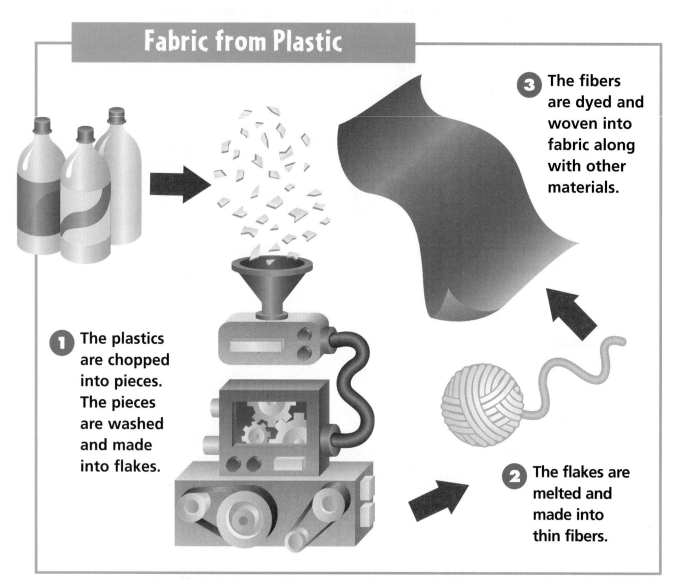

1 The plastics are chopped into pieces. The pieces are washed and made into flakes.

2 The flakes are melted and made into thin fibers.

3 The fibers are dyed and woven into fabric along with other materials.

▶ How are plastics turned into a shirt?

Why It Matters

Colors, numbers, and ideas are not matter. You and everything you touch are matter. The more you know about what something is made of and its properties, the better choices you can make about how to use it. For example, knowing about the properties of certain types of plastics allows people to recycle them into other useful things. This helps reduce pollution and gives new life to old things!

Think and Write

1. Choose two items that are examples of matter. List all the properties you can to describe each one.

2. What is mass?

3. How can the "three Rs" help you reduce pollution?

4. What are the three states of matter? How are they different from one another?

5. **Critical Thinking** Why is the number 12 not matter, but 12 marbles are matter?

L·I·N·K·S

MATH LINK

Make a chart. Look around your home for examples of the three states of matter. Make a chart to list the items you find in each category. Bring your list to school and compare it with those of your classmates.

SOCIAL STUDIES LINK

Do research. Find out what your community is doing to recycle. What products are being recycled? How is each being collected? Are people helping the process? What can you do to help?

WRITING LINK

Write an ad. If you could invent a way to reuse a material or recycle it into something else, what would it be? Write an ad for your new product. What is your product made of? How can it be used?

ART LINK

Draw pictures. Make some drawings of your new product to illustrate your ad.

TECHNOLOGY LINK

At the Computer Visit **www.mhscience02.com** for more links.

Measuring Matter

Vocabulary

metric system, E16

length, E16

area, E17

volume, E17

weight, E19

density, E20

Get Ready

The winner of this race runs the distance in the shortest amount of time. To describe the distance, the track was measured. The track is matter. Measuring matter is important in daily life. How is matter measured?

Process Skill

You experiment when you perform a test to support or disprove a hypothesis.

Explore Activity

How Can You Measure Matter?

Materials

3 different paper shapes labeled A, B, and C

ruler

pencil

Procedure

1. **Observe** Carefully look at shapes A and B.

2. **Predict** Predict which shape you think is bigger. Record your prediction.

3. **Measure** Use the ruler to draw one-inch squares on each shape. How can you use the squares to determine which shape is bigger?

4. Follow steps 2 and 3 to compare shapes A and B with shape C. Put all three in order from smallest to largest.

Drawing Conclusions

1. **Communicate** How did you compare the shapes in step 2? In step 3?

2. **Infer** Which method is more accurate? Why?

3. **Classify** Which paper was the largest? Smallest?

4. **Going Further: Experiment** Make two different shapes of your own. Challenge a classmate to determine which is larger.

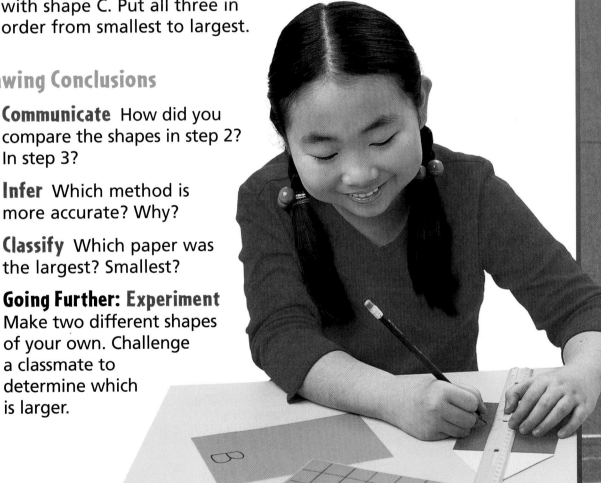

How Can You Measure Matter?

Measuring and counting squares is an accurate way to compare size. To measure matter, systems of *standard units* have been developed. A standard unit is a unit of measure that people agree to use, such as the inch, pound, yard, and gallon. These are units in the English system, which is used mostly in the United States.

Most other countries and all scientists use standard units in the **metric system** (MET·rik SIS·tuhm). The metric system is based on units of 10. For example, 1 meter (m) is divided into 100 centimeters (cm). A meter is a bit longer than a yard. One centimeter is about the width of your little finger's nail. The table below shows you how different units in the metric system relate to one another.

Matter can be described by certain measurements. They include length, area, and volume.

Length tells you the number of units that fit along one edge of an object. In the metric system, units of length are based on the meter. Lengths in the English system are based on the yard. One yard equals 36 inches, or 3 feet.

Which units you use depends on what you are measuring. You wouldn't measure the length of a butterfly wing in meters. You wouldn't measure the floor of your room in inches.

Comparing Metric Units

Metric Unit	Equal To
1 centimeter	$\frac{1}{100}$ meter
1 decimeter	10 centimeters
1 meter	10 decimeters or 100 centimeters
1 decameter	10 meters
1 hectometer	100 meters
1 kilometer	1,000 meters

Some Examples of Lengths

Matter	Length
Fourth grader	54 inches
Python snake	31 feet
Football field	100 yards
Butterfly wing	$21\frac{1}{2}$ centimeters
Giant squid	17 meters
Blue whale	30 meters
The highway from Cleveland to Miami	1,710 kilometers

READING Charts

1. How many centimeters are in one meter? One decimeter?

2. How long is a giant squid?

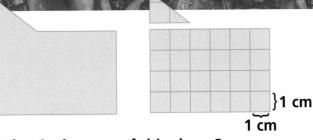

}1 cm

1 cm

What is the area of this shape?

Area (AYR·ee·uh) is a measurement that describes the number of unit squares that cover a surface. Area is measured in units such as square centimeters or square inches. An easy way to find the area of a rectangular object is to multiply its length by its width.

How can you find the area of an irregular shape? First, divide it into smaller shapes. Then, find the area of each shape. You might need to estimate parts of shapes. Add the area of each shape to find the total area.

Volume (VAHL·yewm) describes how much space an object takes up. It measures the number of cubes that can fit in an object. Solids are measured in units such as cubic centimeters or cubic inches. To find the volume of a solid rectangle, multiply its length by its width and its height.

You can also measure the volume of a liquid. In the metric system, it is measured in units called *liters* (L). One liter is made up of 1,000 milliliters (mL). One mL of a liquid takes up the same amount of space as a 1-cm cube.

You can use water to measure the volume of a solid. First, measure some water. Then, completely submerge the object. Subtract the original water level from the new water level. The water level rises by the exact volume of the object.

▷ **What are three measurements of matter you can make?**

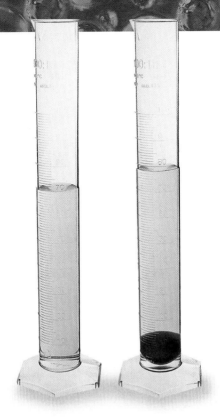

How can you use a graduated cylinder and water to measure the volume of a rock?

Volume: 3 cm x 2 cm x 2 cm = 12 cm³, or 12 cubic cm

Length: 3 cm

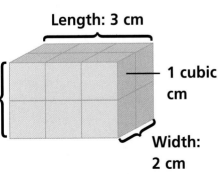

Height: 2 cm

1 cubic cm

Width: 2 cm

E 17

Process Skill
BUILDER

Examine If Shape Affects Volume

Does the volume of an object change if its shape changes? In this activity you will use water to help you find the volume of clay molded into different shapes. You will use your observations and measurements to infer the answer to the question. When you infer, you use observations to figure something out.

Materials

clay

graduated cylinder

water

string

paper towels

Procedure

1 Fill the graduated cylinder with 50 mL of water.

2 Make a solid figure out of the clay. Press the string into it.

3 **Observe** Hold the string. Lower the clay into the water until it is completely covered. Carefully observe and record the new water level.

4 Remove the figure. Rearrange it to make a different shape. Do not add or take away any clay.

5 Repeat step 3.

Drawing Conclusions

1 **Measure** What was the volume of each figure? How did you find out?

2 **Infer** Does an object's volume change when you change its shape? How do you know?

3 Repeat the procedure with a third shape of clay to verify your results.

4 **Infer** Toy A raised the water level in a tank 1 cm. Toy B raised the water level 2 cm. What can you infer about their volumes?

How Can Weight Be Measured?

Another way matter can be measured is by **weight** (WAYT). Mass and weight may seem similar, but they are not the same. Weight is the measure of the pull of gravity between an object and Earth. Gravity is an attracting force between objects. This force depends on the mass of the objects and the distance between them.

Weight can be measured using an instrument called a scale. The metric unit for weight is the *newton* (NEW·tuhn).

An object has the same mass anywhere, on Earth or on the Moon. However, the keys would weigh less on the Moon than on Earth. Why? The pull of gravity on the Moon is less than on Earth. As a result, the weight of an object on the Moon is only about $\frac{1}{6}$ of its weight on Earth.

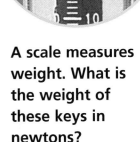

A scale measures weight. What is the weight of these keys in newtons?

▶ **What is a newton?**

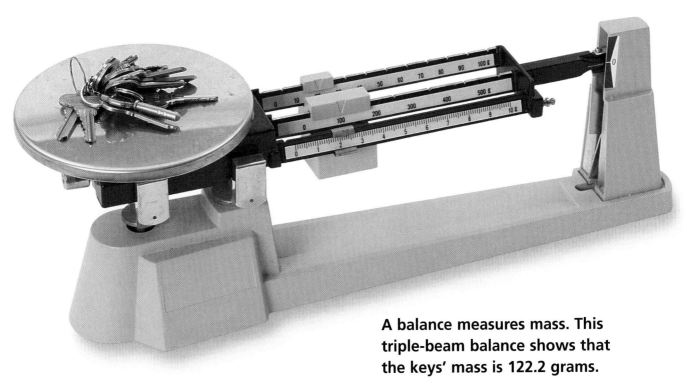

A balance measures mass. This triple-beam balance shows that the keys' mass is 122.2 grams.

FOR SCHOOL OR HOME

Comparing Densities

1. **Obtain** samples from your teacher. Does each sample have the same volume?

2. **Predict** Which sample do you think has the greatest density? The least?

3. **Measure** Use the balance to compare the masses of the samples. Record the data in a table.

4. **Rank** the items from greatest to least density.

5. **Infer** Why would you need information about both mass and volume to compare density?

What Is Density?

Do a kilogram of foam and a kilogram of rocks have the same size? They both have the same mass, yet they are very different in volume. One kilogram of foam takes up more space than 1 kilogram of rocks. That is because the **density** (DEN·si·tee) of foam is less than the density of rocks.

Density is the amount of matter in a given space. It describes how tightly packed matter is. It is the mass in a given unit of volume.

The density of an object is given in grams per cubic centimeter. One cubic centimeter is written as 1 cm^3. Density is a property of matter. A large piece and a small piece of the same matter have the same density.

How can you find an object's density? First, use a balance to find the object's mass in grams (g). Then, find its volume in cubic centimeters. Write the fraction as $\frac{\text{g}}{\text{cm}^3}$.

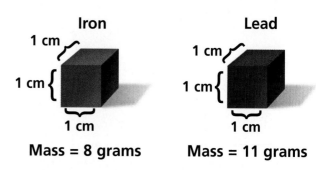

These samples have the same volume. The denser sample is the one with more mass—lead.

Real-World Density

Why does a hot-air balloon float? Adding heat energy causes the air particles inside the balloon to move about more quickly. This makes them spread out. They are less dense than the cooler air particles outside the balloon. The force of gravity pulls down the cooler, more dense air. This forces up the warmer, less dense air.

In space there are stars known as red supergiants. When a red supergiant becomes very massive, it can lose its outer layers in a huge explosion. After the star blows itself apart, it is known as a supernova. All the matter making up a supernova becomes tightly pressed together by the force of gravity. It occupies a very small volume. This very dense star is called a *neutron* (NEW·trahn) *star*.

How dense is a neutron star? One cubic centimeter of matter from a neutron star would have a mass of 1,000,000,000,000,000 kilograms! Now that's dense!

▶ **How would you define density?**

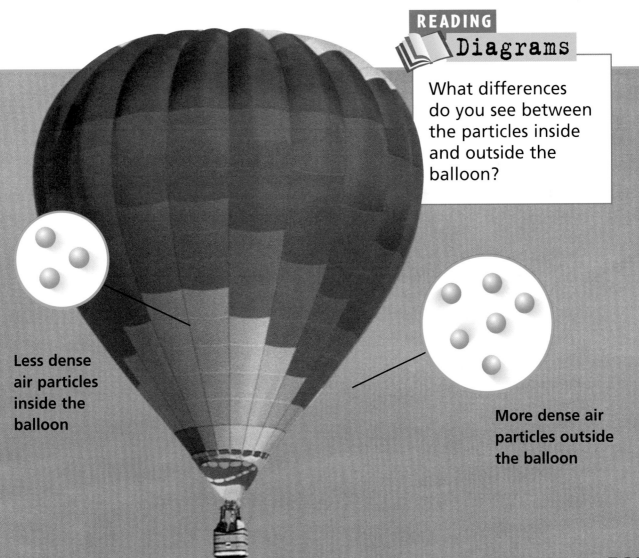

READING
Diagrams

What differences do you see between the particles inside and outside the balloon?

Less dense air particles inside the balloon

More dense air particles outside the balloon

Why Set Standards?

About 5,000 years ago, people began using standard weights. The earliest weights, the *shekel* (SHEK·uhl) and the *mina* (MIGH·nuh), were developed in what is now Iraq.

The shekel was about 8 grams. The mina was equal to 60 shekels. It was about $\frac{1}{2}$ kilogram. A common weight about the size of a mina was used in Europe. It was the pound. *Pound* means "weight" in Latin.

The metric system was developed in the 1790s. The original standard mass was the gram—the mass of a cubic centimeter of pure water at 4°C. This was later replaced by a simpler standard—a metal mass of 1 kilogram. Today the standard kilogram is still a piece of metal. It's kept in a safe place in Sèvres, France, which is near Paris.

The platinum-iridium standard kilogram in Sèvres, France

ENGLAND
BELGIUM
GERMANY
Sèvres •✪ Paris
SWITZERLAND
FRANCE
ITALY
SPAIN

READING **Sequence of Events**
How was a standard for mass developed?

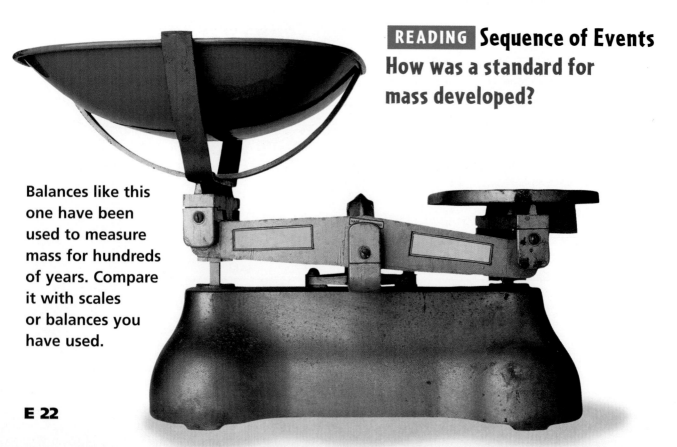

Balances like this one have been used to measure mass for hundreds of years. Compare it with scales or balances you have used.

Why It Matters

Imagine trying to buy clothes, take medicine, bake cookies, or read a map without standard units of measure. To do a research project about measurement, visit **www.mhscience02.com**.

Think and Write

1. Why is it important to make measurements using standard units?

2. What is the difference between mass and weight?

3. Explain how you would find the area of this shape.

} 1 cm

4. Infer What should a hot-air balloonist do to go higher? What should she do to make her balloon come down?

5. Critical Thinking Two cubes have the same mass. Cube A has twice the length, width, and depth of cube B. What can you conclude about their densities?

LITERATURE LINK

Read *Big and Small* to learn about the largest and smallest objects that make up our universe. What are they and where can they be found? Try the activities at the end of the book.

Big & Small

written by Christopher Erickson
Illustrated by John Carazza

WRITING LINK

Write a story or essay. Describe at least three ways in which matter is measured. Explain why measuring matter is important. Include a diagram that helps to show the three measurements.

MATH LINK

Solve a problem. A playing field is 110 meters long and 50 meters wide. What is the area of the playing field?

TECHNOLOGY LINK

Science Newsroom CD-ROM Choose *Sink or Swim* to learn more about density, mass, and volume and the ability to sink or float.

At the Computer Visit **www.mhscience02.com** for more links.

HELP FOR LANDFILLS

This family is recycling trash.

Garbage piles up at a landfill.

In the United States, most people produce about 2 kilograms (4 pounds) of trash every day. Only a small fraction of the trash is recycled. Most ends up in landfills. A landfill is ground in which trash is buried.

There are problems with landfills. They create pollution. Rotting trash gives off gases that pollute the air. Some trash contains harmful chemicals. The chemicals seep through layers of trash and pollute the soil and groundwater. Also, we fill landfills quickly. Sites for new landfills are getting hard to find.

Fortunately, scientists who study landfills have found ways to improve them. Chopping trash into small pieces before it is buried helps it rot faster. Landfills can use special plastic liners to protect the ground below. We also can trap harmful gases that trash gives off. One of these gases is methane, a useful fuel. Methane can be collected and burned for energy.

How can you help? Practice the three Rs: reduce, reuse, and recycle. Using resources wisely saves money, saves space in landfills, and helps make Earth a better place for everyone.

Write ABOUT IT

1. What problems can landfills cause? How can landfills be improved?
2. How can you help to save space in landfills?

AT THE COMPUTER Visit www.mhscience02.com to learn more about landfills.

Chapter 10 Review

Vocabulary

Fill each blank with the best word or words from the list.

area, E17

buoyancy, E7

density, E20

gas, E9

length, E16

liquid, E9

mass, E8

matter, E6

metric system, E16

solid, E8

volume, E17

weight, E19

1. In a(n) _____ particles move about freely, take up a definite amount of space, but do not have a definite shape.

2. Scientists use the _____ to measure matter.

3. The upward force of water or air on an object is _____.

4. In a _____ particles move about freely, without a definite shape or volume.

5. How much space an object takes up is its _____.

6. The "stuff" that makes up things is called _____.

7. The force of gravity affects the _____ of an object.

8. The amount of matter making up an object is its _____.

9. To find the _____ of a rectangle, measure its length and width.

10. The amount of matter in a given space is _____.

Test Prep

11. Matter that changes size to fill its container is a _____.

   A gas

   B liquid

   C mass

   D solid

12. Which of the following is a metric unit of measurement?

   F cubic centimeter

   G mass

   H element

   J buoyancy force

13. Which of the following is an element?

   A water

   B heat

   C volume

   D gold

14. A wooden boat floats better than a lead boat because it has the greater _____.

   F mass

   G density

   H buoyancy

   J volume

15. How many centimeters are in one decimeter?

   A 100

   B 10

   C 1,000

   D none of the above

Concepts and Skills

16. **Reading in Science** Which has the greater area—the square or the rectangle? Explain.

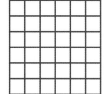 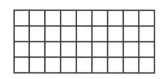

17. **Process Skills: Infer** Why is it important to use standard units of measure? Write a short paragraph to explain.

18. **Critical Thinking** Some boats are made of steel, which is very heavy. Why do you think steel boats can float?

19. **Product Ads** What if you had to choose between a house made of wood and a house made of aluminum. Which would you buy? Explain your reasons.

20. **Decision Making** Do you recycle paper, metal, and plastic? Do you think it is worth the time it takes to recycle? Write a paragraph to explain your opinions about recycling.

Boost *your test scores!*

Be Smart!
Visit www.mhscience02.com to learn more.

CHAPTER

11

LESSON 3

What Matter Is Made Of, E30

LESSON 4

Physical Changes, E42

LESSON 5

Chemical Changes, E50

Changes in Matter

Did You Ever Wonder?

How much ash and debris come from a volcanic explosion? Mount St. Helens in southwestern Washington has been an active volcano for 50,000 years. Its eruptions have produced enough lava, pumice, and ash to build the entire mountain that we see today. How do the materials within Earth change to form these products?

What Matter Is Made Of

Vocabulary

element, E32

atom, E32

mixture, E34

filter, E35

evaporation, E35

compound, E36

Get Ready

How do you classify things? You sort them into groups according to characteristics that vary from case to case. Look at the objects in the photo. How have they been classified?

Process Skill

You classify when you place things that share properties together in groups.

Explore Activity

How Can You Classify Matter?

Procedure: Design Your Own

1 Write the name of each item on an index card.

2 **Classify** Sort the items into groups based on properties you can observe. Record the properties. Use a system like the one shown here. Then try another system.

Drawing Conclusions

1 What properties did you use to classify the items?

2 **Communicate** Were you able to place all the items into the groups? Why or why not? Write a paragraph explaining your answer.

3 **Going Further: Classify** Find more items to classify.

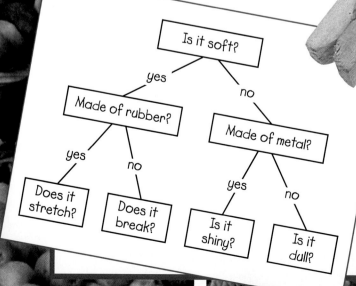

Main Idea Matter is made of tiny particles that can be classified, mixed, and combined.

How Is Matter Classified?

People once thought that all matter was made up of combinations of water, air, earth, and fire. We now know that all matter is made up of **elements** (EL·uh·muhnts). An element is a substance made up of only one type of matter. Gold, silver, and oxygen are elements. Elements are the building blocks of matter.

Each element is made up of **atoms** (AT·uhmz). Atoms are the smallest particles of an element. The atoms of one element are all alike. They are different from the atoms of another element.

An element cannot be broken down into other simpler materials with different properties. The properties of the pieces of an element are the same because its atoms are all alike.

A Table of Elements

All known elements are classified according to their properties. They are classified in a table called the periodic table of the elements. Here you see a part of this table. The name of each element is in a box. The boxes are arranged according to the elements' properties. In this table the symbols for the elements that are gases are colored red. Liquids are colored purple. Solids are colored black.

This is part of the periodic table.

Metallic Properties
- Li Metal
- B Metalloid
- C Nonmetal

			13	14	15	16	17	18
								2 He Helium
			5 B Boron	6 C Carbon	7 N Nitrogen	8 O Oxygen	9 F Fluorine	10 Ne Neon
10	11	12	13 Al Aluminum	14 Si Silicon	15 P Phosphorus	16 S Sulfur	17 Cl Chlorine	18 Ar Argon
28 Ni Nickel	29 Cu Copper	30 Zn Zinc	31 Ga Gallium	32 Ge Germanium	33 As Arsenic	34 Se Selenium	35 Br Bromine	36 Kr Krypton
46 Pd Palladium	47 Ag Silver	48 Cd Cadmium	49 In Indium	50 Sn Tin	51 Sb Antimony	52 Te Tellurium	53 I Iodine	54 Xe Xenon
78 Pt Platinum	79 Au Gold	80 Hg Mercury	81 Ti Thallium	82 Pb Lead	83 Bi Bismuth	84 Po Polonium	85 At Astatine	86 Rn Radon
110	111	112		114		116		118

63 Eu Europium	64 Gd Gadolinium	65 Tb Terbium	66 Dy Dysprosium	67 Ho Holmium	68 Er Erbium	69 Tm Thulium	70 Yb Ytterbium
95 Am Americium	96 Cm Curium	97 Bk Berkelium	98 Cf Californium	99 Es Einsteinium	100 Fm Fermium	101 Md Mendelevium	102 No Nobelium

Periodic means "repeating in a pattern." The elements in the periodic table are arranged in columns called groups. The elements in a group have similar properties.

As you study the elements, you might notice that many have interesting or unusual names. The Latin name for silver is *argentum*. The names *oxygen* and *nitrogen* come from Greek words.

Some elements are named to honor scientists. The element mendelevium is named after the Russian scientist Dmitry Mendeleyev (duh·MEE·tree men·duh·LAY·uhf). He developed the first periodic table.

Other elements are named after the place in which they were discovered. Where do you think californium was discovered?

Each element has a standard shorthand symbol for its name. Some elements use just the first letter of their name, such as C for carbon. Calcium also starts with a C. To avoid confusing it with carbon, its

chemical symbol uses the first two letters of its name, Ca. Some elements' symbols come from their Latin name, such as Ag for silver.

When writing chemical symbols, remember that the first letter is always uppercase. The second letter, if there is one, is always lowercase.

▷ What are elements?

C	Ca
Carbon	Calcium

Ag
Silver

Dmitry Mendeleyev (1834–1907). His first periodic table listed the elements in order of increasing mass.

E 33

What Happens If You Mix Elements?

Have you ever heard the story of King Midas? Everything he touched turned to gold, a valuable metal. In the Middle Ages, people tried to make gold out of other substances. They tried everything—boiling, burning, mixing, and melting matter from one form to another. They learned a lot about the properties of matter, but they never got close to making gold.

Gold is an element. An element can't easily be changed into another element. However, elements can be combined to form a **mixture** . In a

Why couldn't you turn a copper teakettle into gold?

mixture two or more types of matter are combined. Each type keeps its original chemical properties.

Have you ever eaten a mixture of peas and carrots? The peas are still peas, and the carrots are still carrots. The ingredients of a mixture do not change their chemical properties.

▷ **What is a mixture?**

Peas + carrots = a mixture of peas and carrots

How Can Mixtures Be Separated?

The parts of a mixture can be separated using their physical properties. These properties include size, shape, color, volume, density, and state. One way to separate a mixture is simply to pick out each different type of matter. In a mixture of peas and carrots, you can easily pick out the carrots or the peas based on physical properties such as size, shape, and color.

You can also separate some mixtures by using a **filter** (FIL·tuhr). A filter separates things by size. Items smaller than the holes in the filter pass through it. Larger pieces are left behind.

Filters come in a variety of sizes. The type of filter you use depends on the size of the particles you want to separate. For example, a colander separates water from cooked pasta. The water passes through the holes, and the noodles stay behind.

How might you separate a mixture of salt and water? The salt particles dissolved in the water are very small. They would pass through most filters.

One way to separate this mixture is by **evaporation** (i·vap·uh·RAY·shuhn). Evaporation is the change of a liquid to a gas. When liquid water evaporates, it becomes a gas. It goes into the air. The salt is left behind. Another example of evaporation is the solids left behind as a ring after bathwater evaporates.

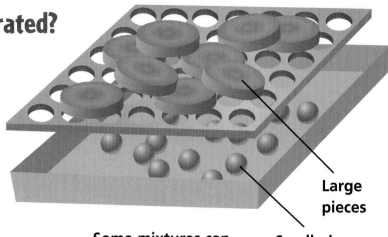

Large pieces

Small pieces

Some mixtures can be separated by using a filter.

READING Cause and Effect
What are two methods of separating mixtures?

Water evaporates.   Water is gone.

A solid mixed in water can be separated by evaporation. As the water evaporates, the solid is left behind.

QUICK LAB

FOR SCHOOL OR HOME

Mix and Unmix

BE CAREFUL! Wear goggles.

1. **Observe** Design an experiment to separate a mixture. You may use more than one method. Record your observations and the results.

2. **Observe** Were you able to completely separate the mixture? How do you know?

3. **Form a Hypothesis** How could you separate a mixture of white sand and salt? Test your ideas.

What Is a Compound?

Do you think all combinations of elements can be separated physically into their parts? No, they cannot. For example, no amount of crushing, grinding, or bending can separate sugar into its components. That is because sugar is a **compound** (KAHM·pownd). A compound forms when two or more elements are combined chemically.

The properties of a compound are different from the properties of the elements it is made of. Each element loses its properties when elements are combined chemically. A compound can be separated only by chemical means, not by physical properties.

Sodium and chlorine make up table salt. Hydrogen and oxygen make up water. Use the chart below to help you determine if each is a mixture or a compound.

Comparing Mixtures and Compounds

	Mixture	Compound
How are the parts combined?	Two or more components or elements are mixed together.	Two or more elements are combined chemically.
Do the parts keep their own properties?	Yes	No
How can it be separated?	By physical properties	By chemical means

Water, table salt, sugar, and rust are examples of common compounds. Your body is made up of many different compounds. Each compound is made up of a combination of elements.

▶ **What are some compounds? What are they made of?**

READING
Diagrams

1. What do all compounds have in common?

2. How do the properties of the compound compare with those of the elements that form it?

Common Compounds

1 Oxygen and hydrogen are gases. If you simply mix them, they keep their properties. Under certain conditions they can combine to form the compound water.

Oxygen   Hydrogen   Water

2 Sodium is a shiny metal. Chlorine is a poisonous, yellow-green gas. Together they combine to form the compound sodium chloride—common table salt.

Sodium   Chlorine   Salt

3 Sugar is a compound. It is formed when carbon, a black solid, and two gases, oxygen and hydrogen, are combined and changed chemically.

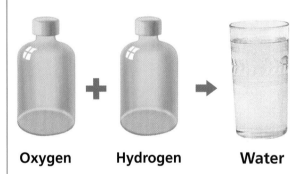

Carbon   Oxygen   Hydrogen   Sugar

4 Rust is a compound that results when iron is exposed to oxygen. The properties of rust are unlike those of both elements it is made of.

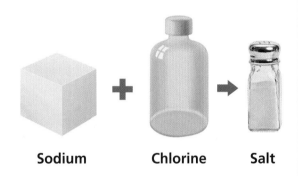

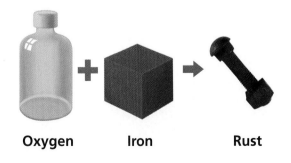

Oxygen   Iron   Rust

What Are Some Real-Life Uses of Mixtures?

Some elements can't be put to good use in their pure form. Pure gold is too soft for jewelry. Pure aluminum is too light and weak for pots and pans. Pure iron is too brittle and rusts too easily for use in cars. How then do people make gold jewelry, aluminum pans, and cars made of iron?

The answer is in *alloys* (AL·oyz). An alloy is a mixture of two or more elements, at least one of which is a metal. A mixture of gold and a little copper is stronger than pure gold. A mixture of aluminum and carbon is stronger than pure aluminum. A mixture of iron, chromium, nickel, and carbon is called steel.

Making alloys is a little like cooking. Different recipes give alloys different properties. For example, low-carbon steel is strong but flexible. High-carbon steel is strong but brittle. Medium-carbon steel is somewhat strong and somewhat flexible.

▷ **What common items do you use that are made of alloys?**

Many common items are made of alloys.

Lesson Review

Why It Matters

Knowing the properties of elements and compounds is a major goal of scientists working in the field of chemistry. Chemistry affects just about everything in your world. Scientists use chemical knowledge to change, improve, or invent such things as foods, medicines, and materials of all kinds. They also use chemistry to understand the world of living things around us and how the universe itself functions. Visit **mhscience02.com** to do a research project on medicines.

Think and Write

1. What is an element?

2. How are elements named?

3. How does a compound differ from a mixture?

4. Why are alloys used to make certain products?

5. **Critical Thinking** You can breathe oxygen when it is mixed with other gases. You can't breathe oxygen when it is combined with iron in the form of rust. Why not?

L·I·N·K·S

SOCIAL STUDIES LINK

Do research. Learn about an ancient culture's jewelry. For example, you could research ancient Egyptians, Greeks, or Romans or pre-Colombian people such as the Mayans. Draw some examples.

MATH LINK

Solve a problem. The amount of gold in jewelry is described by carats. A 24-carat ring would be pure gold. A 12-carat ring would be half gold. How much gold is in a 6-carat ring?

WRITING LINK

Write a paragraph. Describe the types of things you would like to learn about elements if you were a chemist.

LITERATURE LINK

Read *The Angel Food Cake Disaster* to learn how a mixture really gets mixed up. Try the activities at the end of the book.

TECHNOLOGY LINK

At the Computer Visit **www.mhscience02.com** for more links.

A Chemist Who MATTER-ed

Jöns Jacob Berzelius

Jöns Jacob Berzelius (1779–1848) was born in Sweden. He was a doctor, but had many ideas about the nature of matter. Therefore, he became a chemist. He tested his ideas by doing experiments and keeping careful records.

Berzelius helped to organize the field of chemistry. He wasn't always right. Some of his ideas later proved to be wrong, but his work led to many discoveries. He coined new words to name his discoveries. Berzelius was the first to use rubber tubing, filter paper, and other equipment that's now used in most labs.

Berzelius's work led to many achievements in science. Here are just a few.

- Berzelius set up a quick way to write the names of the elements. Each element is written as one or two letters. For example, oxygen is O, gold is Au, silver is Ag, and carbon is C.

- He discovered three elements—cerium, selenium, and thorium.

- He figured out the weight of each element.

- He studied many compounds and discovered which elements were in them.

- He was the first to isolate the elements calcium and silicon.

- He suggested the name for protein.

- He made valuable contributions about what an atom looks like.

Write
ABOUT IT

1. How do we know Jöns Jacob Berzelius did many experiments?

2. What were some of Berzelius's contributions to science?

Jöns Jacob Berzelius kept careful records of his experiments.

AT THE COMPUTER

Visit www.mhscience02.com to learn more about chemistry.

Physical Changes

Get Ready

Changes take place around you all the time. You cut a square piece of paper into an interesting shape for an art project. An ice cube melts in your glass of water. A half-eaten sandwich waits for you on the lunch table. Each object has changed in some way.

Think about the objects that you encounter every day that change. What observations can you make? How has each object changed?

Process Skill

You **communicate** when you share information.

Explore Activity

How Can Things Change?

Procedure

BE CAREFUL! Handle scissors and a knife carefully.

1. Make a table like the one shown below. Record each object in the first column.

2. **Observe** Carefully observe each object. What properties does each have? Record the properties in the second column.

3. **Experiment** How many different ways can you change each object? Record each change in the third column.

4. **Observe** Carefully observe each object after the change. What properties does each have now? Record the properties in the last column.

Drawing Conclusions

1. How are the properties of each object similar and different before and after the changes?

2. **Infer** Do you think the changes you made actually changed the matter making up each object? Why or why not?

3. **Going Further: Communicate** Make more changes to different types of matter. Keep a list of those changes.

Materials

flat sheet of paper

modeling clay

scissors

ice cube

plastic plate with rim

whole fruit, such as an orange, lemon, or apple

plastic knife

Object	Properties	Changes	Properties After Changes

Main Idea Physical changes are responsible for many of the things we encounter in everyday life.

What Are Physical Changes?

You have just seen one way matter can change—through **physical changes** (FIZ·i·kuhl CHAYNJ·uhz). A physical change begins and ends with the same type of matter. For example, an ice cube is solid water. If the ice cube was crushed into smaller pieces, the type of matter would not change. The smaller pieces would still be frozen water. If the ice cube melted, the type of matter would not change. It would still be water, just in its liquid state.

How can you tell if a physical change has taken place? Sometimes a physical change may not be as easy to identify as a melting ice cube. A change in state may look like the type of matter has changed, although it has not.

Change in size or shape
The original properties of the matter do not change even if it is cut, folded, or stretched.

Change in position or texture
The original properties of the matter do not change even if it is moved, rearranged, or crumpled.

The following guidelines will help you to identify a physical change easily. They describe a few different kinds of physical changes, such as:
• a change in size or shape
• a change in position or texture
• a change in state

▶ **What are three ways matter can change physically?**

READING
Diagrams

Why is a change in state a physical change?

Change in state
The original properties of the matter do not change even if it is melted, frozen, or heated.

What Makes Matter Change State?

In Lesson 1 you learned that matter can exist in three states. It can exist as a solid, a liquid, or a gas. Your science textbook is a solid. It will remain a solid no matter what you do to it. Heating it will not make it melt into a liquid nor change into a gas.

However, some types of matter can exist in more than one state. For example, water can exist as a solid, a liquid, and a gas. If a solid ice cube was left outside the freezer long enough or if it was heated, it would melt into a liquid. If the liquid water was left outside or heated, it would evaporate into a gas.

Solids The particles of a solid are fixed. They move only a little. They vibrate more rapidly when heat energy is added to them. If enough heat energy is added, a solid may melt and form a liquid.

Liquids Particles of a liquid move past one another. Adding more heat energy causes the particles to move fast enough so that they break away from one another. Some particles may escape as a gas.

What happens to this snow house when summer comes?

What makes matter change from solid to liquid to gas? The answer is heat energy. Heat energy makes the particles of matter move faster. The more heat energy matter has, the faster its particles move. Taking away heat energy slows particles down.

READING **Cause and Effect**
Why do you think warm water boils faster than cold water?

Gas Particles of a gas are very far apart. They move very fast. Adding more heat energy causes the particles to move even faster and farther apart from one another.

Process Skill
B U I L D E R

How Heat Energy Affects Evaporation

When you perform an experiment, you first form a hypothesis. Then you test your hypothesis. Follow the steps to test how heat energy affects evaporation.

Materials

3 paper towels

3 rubber bands

three 10-oz clear-plastic glasses

thermometer

clock or watch

desk lamp

container of water

Procedure

1 Place a wet paper towel across the top of each plastic glass. Secure each with a rubber band.

2 **Hypothesize** Place one glass where you think the paper towel will dry fastest. Place another where you think it will dry slower. Place the third where you think it will dry slowest.

3 **Measure** Use the thermometer to measure the temperature near each glass. Record the temperatures.

4 Record the time you start timing. Then touch each paper towel every two minutes. Record the time the first paper towel is dry.

5 Repeat step 4 until the other towels are dry.

Drawing Conclusions

1 **Interpret** In which place did a paper towel dry the fastest? What was the temperature?

2 **Interpret** In which place did a paper towel dry the slowest? What was the temperature?

3 **Experiment** Would water evaporate from a paper towel as fast if you put an inverted glass over it? Try it.

Why It Matters

People have learned a lot about matter in our world. They have learned how matter can be changed to make our lives better. For example, physical changes to water help to make our lives more comfortable every day. We enjoy water that has been changed to its solid form when we use ice cubes to cool our drinks off. Water vapor helps heat our homes.

Think and Write

1. A sculptor chisels a square piece of marble into a face. Is this a physical change? How do you know?

2. What causes a solid to change into a liquid? A liquid to change into a gas? Explain what happens.

3. Describe and explain some types of physical changes you can see every day.

4. Experiment Is salt dissolving in water a physical change? Design an experiment to test your answer.

5. Critical Thinking Would pond water evaporate faster in winter or summer? Answer in complete sentences.

L·I·N·K·S

WRITING LINK

Write a paragraph. What if the ice at Earth's poles changes from ice to water? What would that mean for Earth and the people and animals on it?

SOCIAL STUDIES LINK

Do research. The Japanese art of origami involves folding paper into shapes such as flowers and animals. Research origami. Use a reference book, and work with classmates to make some simple figures.

MATH LINK

Solve a problem. Bob boils a cup of water that's at room temperature. Joe boils a cup of cold water. It takes Bob one minute and a half to boil the water. It takes Joe two and three-fourths minutes to boil the water. How many minutes less does it take Bob?

ART LINK

Draw pictures. Draw pictures showing ways you have observed water in its three states.

TECHNOLOGY LINK

At the Computer Visit **www.mhscience02.com** for more links.

Chemical Changes

Vocabulary

chemical
change, E52

Get Ready

Have you ever visited the Statue of Liberty? The Statue of Liberty is perhaps the best-known symbol of freedom in all the world. It was a gift to the United States from France. The shiny copper statue was erected in New York Harbor and unveiled at a festive ceremony on October 28, 1886. However, after years of being outdoors, the copper statue turned green. Why do you think this happened?

Process Skill

You experiment when you perform a test to support or disprove a hypothesis.

Explore Activity

What Causes the Change?

Materials

goggles

petri dish or 10-oz clear-plastic glass

modeling clay

shiny penny

vinegar

10-oz clear-plastic glass or plastic wrap

Procedure

BE CAREFUL! Wear goggles.

1. Put a small wad of modeling clay on the bottom of the petri dish or plastic glass.

2. Wedge the penny in the clay so that it is vertical.

3. Add vinegar to cover the bottom of the petri dish or glass. Cover the petri dish with the plastic glass. If you put the penny in the glass, cover the glass tightly with plastic wrap.

4. **Predict** What do you think will happen to the penny? Record your prediction.

Drawing Conclusions

1. **Observe** What happens to the penny after one hour? After three hours? Overnight? Record your observations.

2. How is this penny different from the penny that your teacher soaked in vinegar overnight?

3. **Form a Hypothesis** What do you think caused the changes to your penny but not the soaked penny?

4. **Going Further: Experiment** Do you think other materials would change also? Repeat the activity using a paper clip.

Main Idea Chemical changes are responsible for many of the things we encounter in everyday life.

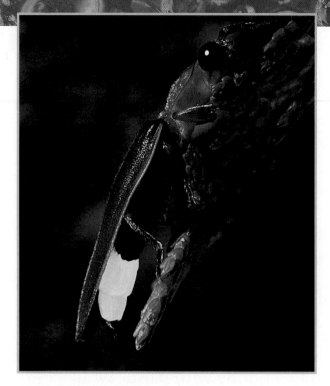

A firefly's light results from a chemical reaction.

What Are Chemical Changes?

In order for a penny to turn green, it must undergo a **chemical change** (KEM·i·kuhl CHAYNJ). Chemical changes are changes in matter itself. In a chemical change, you start with one kind of matter and end with another. The new matter has properties different from the matter you started with. A chemical change is also called a chemical reaction.

Chemical changes have another characteristic. They involve energy. All chemical changes either take in or give off energy. The energy may be in the form of electricity, heat, or light. Sometimes a change takes place so slowly, you cannot notice that light or heat is released. Sometimes the amount released is so small, it can hardly be noticed.

For example, if you expose a penny to vinegar vapors, you can cause a chemical reaction. The copper in the penny will react with the vinegar vapors to create a compound called copper acetate. Copper acetate has properties different from copper and vinegar. It is not hard and shiny like copper. It is not a liquid like vinegar.

Copper

+

Vinegar vapors

=

Copper acetate

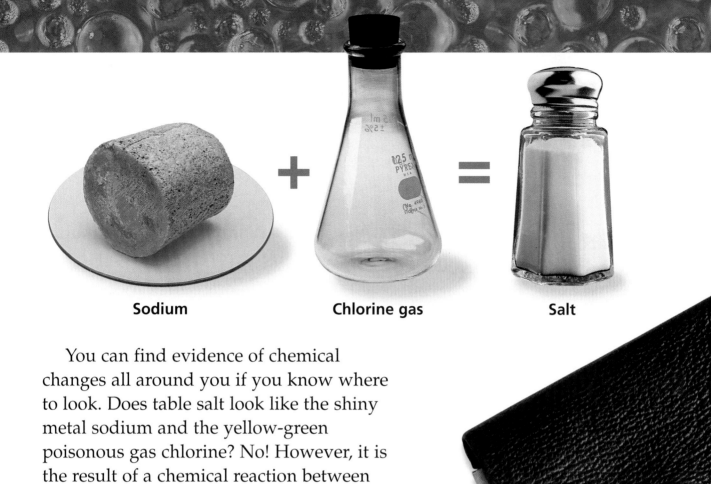

Sodium + Chlorine gas = Salt

You can find evidence of chemical changes all around you if you know where to look. Does table salt look like the shiny metal sodium and the yellow-green poisonous gas chlorine? No! However, it is the result of a chemical reaction between those elements.

Does sugar look like the black element carbon? No! However, it is the result of a chemical reaction between carbon and the gases oxygen and hydrogen.

Tarnish is a compound that forms on some metals when they are exposed to air. Although tarnish is not harmful, it can be annoying. It coats shiny silver with a dull black finish.

Tarnish is a compound that forms from a chemical reaction, or change. A compound has properties that are different from the elements it is made of.

READING **Cause and Effect**
What are some chemical changes?

What Are the Products of Chemical Changes?

In a chemical change, the product has properties different from the matter you started with. Sometimes the product is a compound. Sometimes the product is the elements making up a compound.

These diagrams show how a compound forms and how it can be broken down.

READING Diagrams

1. What elements make up the compound sugar?

2. What are the products of the chemical change in step 2?

Making and Breaking Down Sugar

Carbon   Oxygen   Hydrogen   Sugar

1 A chemical change makes a new substance. When carbon, oxygen, and hydrogen are combined in the right amounts, they form sugar. New substances can be compounds, such as sugar. A compound does not look like the elements that make it up and has different properties.

2 A chemical change can break compounds apart. What is left behind are the elements and simpler compounds they were made of. For example, the compound sugar can be broken down into water and carbon. This type of chemical change needs energy to take place. Energy is always involved in a chemical change. Some changes need energy. Others give off energy.

As you learned, some chemical changes can form compounds. Some compounds, such as sugar, are beneficial. Some, such as tarnish, are only annoying. Others, such as rust, can be harmful. Rust can weaken a bridge so cars and people cannot cross it safely.

What can people do to prevent, or at least slow down, some chemical changes? Some silver polishes add a protective layer to the silver as it is being cleaned. Some bridges are built so that a small amount of electricity can be run through the metal supporting structure. This helps slow the formation of rust.

▷ **Is this chemical change beneficial or harmful?**

QUICK LAB

FOR SCHOOL OR HOME

Preventing Chemical Change

BE CAREFUL! Wear goggles.

1. **Hypothesize** Follow the procedure in the Explore Activity. Think about something you can do to keep the penny from turning green. Record your ideas.

2. **Experiment** Test your ideas. Record your results.

3. **Compare** Make a class table of the results for each test. What kept the pennies from turning green?

4. **Infer** What do you think prevents the pennies you use every day from turning green?

What Are Some Real-World Changes?

What kinds of chemical and physical changes take place in the real world? Here are some examples.

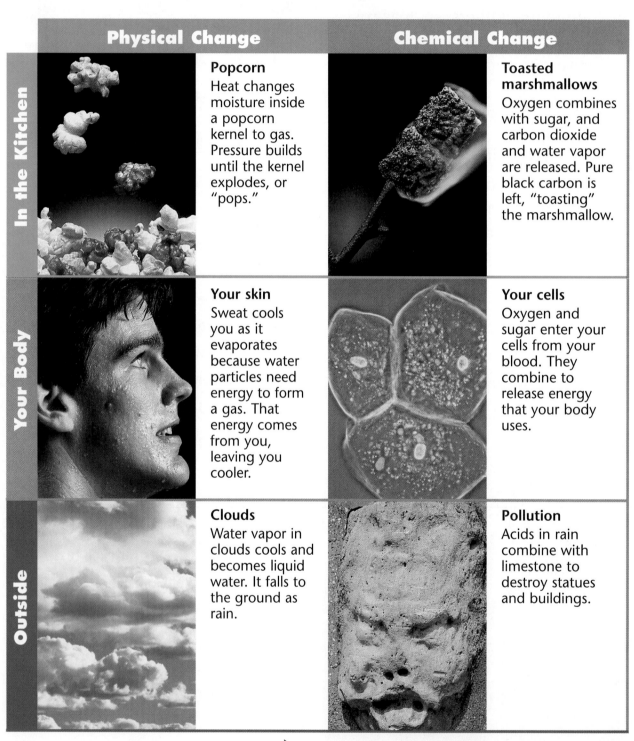

	Physical Change	Chemical Change
In the Kitchen	**Popcorn** Heat changes moisture inside a popcorn kernel to gas. Pressure builds until the kernel explodes, or "pops."	**Toasted marshmallows** Oxygen combines with sugar, and carbon dioxide and water vapor are released. Pure black carbon is left, "toasting" the marshmallow.
Your Body	**Your skin** Sweat cools you as it evaporates because water particles need energy to form a gas. That energy comes from you, leaving you cooler.	**Your cells** Oxygen and sugar enter your cells from your blood. They combine to release energy that your body uses.
Outside	**Clouds** Water vapor in clouds cools and becomes liquid water. It falls to the ground as rain.	**Pollution** Acids in rain combine with limestone to destroy statues and buildings.

▶ **Can you think of any other physical and chemical changes?**

Answers will vary.

Why It Matters

Chemical changes take place all around you every day. Did you know that baking is a chemical change? Food scientists study how combining ingredients and cooking them results in tasty combinations. To be able to do so, they need to know all about chemical changes.

Think and Write

1. What is the difference between a physical change and a chemical change?

2. What are the two things that tell you a chemical change has taken place?

3. What products can result from a chemical change?

4. Make a table of three physical changes and three chemical changes. How did you identify each?

5. **Critical Thinking** The flesh of a cut apple turns brown after a little while. Is this a chemical change or a physical change? Why?

L·I·N·K·S

WRITING LINK

Make a list. Tour your house with an adult family member. Find examples of chemical changes. Look for metals that have rusted or tarnished. List the examples.

SOCIAL STUDIES LINK

Do research. Acid rain is the result of a chemical change. Acid rain is harmful to the environment. Find out about how it forms, how it harms the environment, and what can be done to reduce it.

LITERATURE LINK

Read *A Chemist in the Kitchen* to learn how you practice chemistry every day. You'll find a tempting menu of experiments that you can do at home. Try the activities at the end of the book.

A CHEMIST IN THE KITCHEN:
EXPERIMENTS YOU CAN DO AT HOME
by Howard Gutner
illustrated by Craig Brown

TECHNOLOGY LINK

Science Newsroom CD-ROM Choose *What's the Matter?* to learn more about how heat transfer makes salt act in two seemingly opposite ways.

At the Computer Visit **www.mhscience02.com** for more links.

EVERYTHING CHANGES

Look around you. You already know a lot of physical and chemical changes that take place. Weathering and erosion are two more.

Weathering causes both physical and chemical changes. Did you ever trip over a crack in a sidewalk? It was probably caused by a physical change.

First, rainwater filled a tiny crack in the sidewalk. Then, it froze and expanded. The ice pushed the crack farther open. In time the crack was big enough to trip you!

Erosion is a physical change. It can be caused by water, wind, or gravity.

Moving water can carry away tiny bits of soil and rock. During storms water moves faster and carries away more soil. As the water slows down, it drops the soil in a new place.

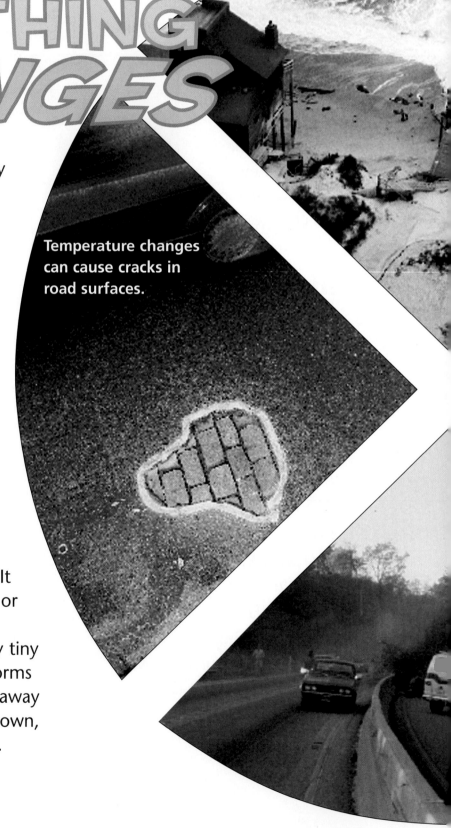

Temperature changes can cause cracks in road surfaces.

Weathering erodes the Earth.

Strong winds blow soil and dust across the land.

Strong winds can pick up bits of soil and drop them somewhere else. Plant roots help hold soil in place. The roots slow down both water and wind erosion.

Gravity can also cause a sudden physical change. If freezing rain cracks rocks on a hillside, gravity can pull the hill down in a landslide!

What Did I Learn?

1. The sequence of forming a crack is

A rain, freezing, expansion
B moving water, erosion, freezing
C gravity, rain, weathering
D expansion, rain, freezing

2. Erosion can be caused by

F freezing
G gravity
H cracks
J soil

AT THE COMPUTER

Visit www.mhscience02.com to learn more about physical and chemical changes to Earth.

Chapter 11 Review

Vocabulary

Fill each blank with the best word or words from the list.

atom, E32

chemical change, E52

compound, E36

element, E32

evaporation, E35

filter, E35

mixture, E34

physical change, E44

1. In a(n) _____ two or more types of matter are combined, and each type keeps its chemical properties.

2. A change that begins and ends with the same type of matter is a(n) _____.

3. The change of a liquid to a gas is _____.

4. A substance made up of only one type of matter is a(n) _____.

5. A(n) _____ traps large pieces from a mixture.

6. Water, rust, and salt are examples of _____.

7. The building blocks of elements are _____.

Fill in each blank to identify the change as chemical or physical.

water + salt → salt water	**8.** _____
iron + oxygen → rust	**9.** _____
milk + cornflakes + fruit → breakfast	**10.** _____

Test Prep

11. Freezing salt water is _____.

   A a compound

   B evaporation

   C a chemical change

   D a physical change

12. Rice and noodles could be separated by _____.

   F heating in an oven

   G boiling in a pan

   H filtering

   J freezing

13. Which is an element?

   A rust

   B water

   C oxygen

   D salt water

14. Which is a chemical change to a piece of paper?

    F folding

    G cutting

    H coloring

    J burning

15. Steel is made by mixing iron and other metals. Steel is an example of a(n) _____.

    A compound

    B alloy

    C element

    D gas

Concepts and Skills

16. **Reading in Science** Explain what happens when heat is added to ice. Discuss what happens to the particles in the ice.

17. **Critical Thinking** Observe your home, neighborhood, or classroom for five minutes. Write down all the changes that you observe or infer. Classify the changes as physical changes or chemical changes. Did you observe any changes that you could not classify?

18. **Process Skills: Experiment** What makes steel wool rust faster? Form a hypothesis. Write down a procedure to test the hypothesis. Ask your teacher's permission if you want to run the procedure.

19. **Product Ads** Some ads claim that products are made of "rust-proof" metals. How might a metal object be made to resist rust? Research your ideas.

20. **Scientific Methods** Imagine that you had a mixture of marbles. Some of the marbles are 1 inch wide. All the others are 3 inches wide. You have four filters with hole widths of 0.5 inches, 1.5 inches, 2.5 inches, and 3.5 inches. Which filters could you use to separate the mixture?

Boost *your test scores!*

Be Smart!
Visit **www.mhscience02.com**
to learn more.

People in Science

Dionne Jackson
Research Chemist

Chemicals are part of everything around us. Chemists combine these chemicals to create new things and make our lives better. Their research helps save energy and reduce pollution.

Dionne Jackson is a research chemist for the Materials Science Laboratory (MSL) at the Kennedy Space Center. Dionne knew when she graduated from high school that she wanted to be a chemist. She won a NASA scholarship for her education at Spelman College. She was able to work at MSL as part of her studies. After she graduated, the laboratory hired her full time. One of Dionne's jobs at MSL is to find out which materials are best for aircraft such as the space shuttle. Dionne is also working on the next probe to Mars. She and her teammates are trying to re-create the Martian environment to test new materials for NASA.

Write ABOUT IT

1. What ways are chemists trying to make our lives better?
2. Why is Dionne Jackson's work so important?

Careers IN SCIENCE

Pharmacist

If you're interested in medicine, you may want to be a pharmacist. A pharmacist provides medicines that doctors order for their patients. When the pharmacist gives out the medicine, she tells the patient how to use it correctly.

To become a pharmacist, you need five years of education in a college of pharmacy. After that, you still need many hours of on-the-job training with a pharmacist. Pharmacists also must have a license from the state in which they work.

Pharmacists usually work in drugstores or hospitals. You can use the Internet or library resources to find out more about this career.

AT THE COMPUTER

Visit **www.mhscience02.com** to learn more about careers.

Twenty Questions

Play a game of 20 questions with your classmates.

What to Do

1. Play the game in small groups or as a class.

2. Think of an object. Give the group a hint about the object.

3. Your classmates' goal is to guess the object after asking 20 questions or fewer.

You may answer each question with only a yes or no.

4. Play as many rounds as time allows.

Make Your Own Table

Your goal is to make an illustrated periodic table of the elements.

What to Do

1. Choose an element from the periodic table. Work with your teacher so that everyone in the class chooses a different element.

2. Research facts about the element. Find its atomic number, its atomic symbol, and any interesting facts about it.

3. Write the number, symbol, and name of the element on an index card. Add one or more facts about the element that you learned. Draw a picture of something that the element is a part of. Print your name on the back of the index card.

4. With your classmates, arrange the index cards on the wall to form part of the periodic table.

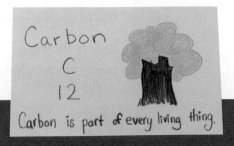

Carbon
C
12
Carbon is part of every living thing.

UNIT F

Energy

NATIONAL GEOGRAPHIC

LOOK!

**Bolts of lightning strike
the ground. The sound of
thunder will follow soon.
Why do you see lightning
before you hear thunder?**

Energy

CHAPTER 12

Forms of Energy F2

CHAPTER 13

Electricity and
Magnetism F66

CHAPTER

12

LESSON 1
Forces, Motion, and Energy F4

LESSON 2
Energy and Tools, F18

LESSON 3
Heat, E32

LESSON 4
Light, F40

LESSON 5
Sound, F52

Forms of Energy

Did You Ever Wonder?

How fast do wild horses run? Some horses have been known to gallop as fast as 61 kilometers/hour (38 miles/hour). Where do they get the power and energy to run this fast? A car moves through town with this speed. Where does it get its energy?

Motion, Forces, and Energy

Vocabulary

speed, F8
force, F10
friction, F11
inertia, F11
work, F13
energy, F14

Get Ready

Have you ever gone ice skating? If so, did you skate as fast as this Olympic speed skater? Probably not! Speed skaters move very fast and with lots of energy.

What is motion? How can you tell if an object is moving? How are speed and motion related?

Process Skill

You use variables when you identify and separate things in an experiment that can be changed or controlled.

Explore Activity

Materials

paper

marking pens

watch or clock

How Can You Tell Something Is Moving?

Procedure

1 Make a map of your classroom. Mark where the main objects are placed. For example, show the location of doors, windows, chalkboards, and desks.

2 For five minutes, slowly follow a path around the room. Stop once every minute, and mark an X on the map to show your location. Mark the time. Rest at some places for a short time. Next to those Xs, write the time that you got there and the time you left.

3 **Communicate** Trade maps with your partner. Determine at which positions he or she was moving.

Drawing Conclusions

1 **Interpret Data** How could you tell when your partner was moving? Standing still?

2 **Infer** Who is moving faster—a student whose Xs are far apart or one whose Xs are close together? Give the reason for your answer.

3 **Going Further: Use Variables** Repeat the activity by making a map of your home. Is your motion visible?

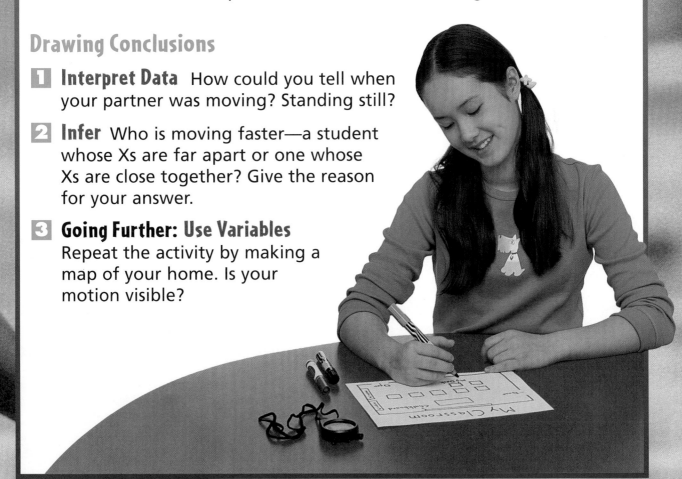

F 5

Main Idea Objects move when they change their position.

How Do Things Move?

How can you tell if something is moving? Look at the baseball player in the pictures. Can you tell if he has moved? You can tell he has moved because his position has changed. Position is the location of an object. The player's final position is at first base. All objects have a position. You know something has moved when its position has changed.

Words such as *above* and *below*, *left* and *right*, *ahead* and *behind*, and *north* and *south* give clues about position. For example, you could say the girl is behind the tree, or the storm is south of Atlanta. When we describe the position of something, we compare it with surrounding objects that seem not to be moving. The objects used for comparing are called a *frame of reference*.

Bases can be used as a frame of reference in a game of baseball. They can be used to describe a runner's position.

Your frame of reference is Earth, so the Sun appears to move in the sky. Sunrises, such as this, and sunsets are actually caused by the movement of Earth on its axis.

What if you're in a bus riding to school? What do you see when you look out the window? Houses, trees, apartment buildings, stores? These objects, which don't move, are your frame of reference.

Earth is usually our frame of reference. A car, boat, and bicycle all appear to move because they change their position compared with Earth's surface. We assume Earth is not moving.

However, when viewed from space, Earth is moving. It's traveling around the Sun. If outer space is our frame of reference, then Earth and all the objects on it are moving.

▷ How do you know that something has moved?

The winner of this race will be the girl with the fastest speed. She will cover the same distance as the other runners but will finish in the shortest time.

What Is Speed?

All the runners in the one-kilometer race will start at exactly the same time. They will all go exactly the same distance. One runner will reach the finish line before the others. The winning runner has the fastest **speed**. All moving objects have speed. Speed is the distance an object moves in a certain amount of time.

You can measure the speed of an object if you know two things about its motion: first, how far the object traveled; second, how long it took to go that distance. With these two measurements, you can figure out an object's speed. To calculate speed, divide the distance traveled by the time spent moving.

If a car goes 50 miles in 1 hour, its speed is 50 miles per hour. If you walk 10 kilometers in 2 hours, your speed is 5 kilometers per hour.

Objects in motion often change their speed. They can speed up or slow down. They can also change their direction. Any change in the speed or direction of a moving object is called *acceleration* (ak·sel·uh·RAY·shuhn).

 **How do you calculate speed?**

Process Skill
BUILDER

Marble Motion

How fast can a marble move? You could answer this question by saying "fast" or "slow." However, if you make measurements, you can determine speed more exactly.

Procedure

1 **Measure** Work with two partners. Measure the length of the tube with a ruler. Record your measurement.

2 Stack three books to make a tower. Place one end of the tube on the books. Let the other end of the tube touch the fourth book, which is standing straight up. Tape the tube in place.

3 **Measure** Time the marble as it rolls down the tube. One partner should release the marble, while another partner starts the stopwatch. The third partner should hold the standing book in place. When you hear the marble hit the book, record the time.

4 **Measure** Repeat step 3 ten times.

5 Calculate the speed for each trial.

Drawing Conclusions

1 What two measurements did you need to calculate speed?

2 **Use numbers** What is the equation you used to calculate speed?

3 What was the marble's fastest speed? Its slowest speed?

> **Materials**
>
> **long cardboard tube or several shorter tubes taped together**
>
> **marble**
>
> **4 books**
>
> **ruler**
>
> **tape**
>
> **stopwatch**

How Do Forces Affect Motion?

How many times each day do you push or pull something to make it move? Each push or pull is a **force**. Forces can be big or small. The force a crane uses to lift a truck is huge. The force of a feather landing on the ground is tiny.

Forces are important! Forces make objects start moving, stop moving, speed up, slow down, or change direction. A large force can cause a large change in speed or direction. A small force may produce a smaller change. If you tap a basketball with your finger, the ball hardly moves.

You use about one newton of force to lift a piece of corn to your mouth.

This boy applies a force to the ball when he hits it with his racket. As a result, the ball changes its direction.

If you kick the ball, it rolls away quickly. The tap is a small force that produces a small change in motion. The kick is a larger force that produces a larger change.

Forces are measured in units called *newtons*. This unit is named after the British scientist Sir Isaac Newton (1652–1727). Newton explained how force and motion are related. To lift a mass of one kilogram on Earth requires 9.8 newtons of force.

Think again about the basketball you kicked to make it roll. Does it roll forever? No, a force brings it to a stop. That force is **friction** (FRIK·shuhn). Friction works against motion. Friction acts between surfaces of objects that touch. The surfaces rub against each other, slowing the object or stopping it from moving. There is friction between a car's tires and the road, and between your feet and the ground.

How much friction there is depends on the objects. There may be a lot of friction between two rough surfaces, for example. If you push a cardboard box along a sidewalk, there is a lot of friction. The box is hard to move along the sidewalk's rough surface. You can skate easily across an icy surface because there is little friction between the smooth ice and the sharp blades of your skates.

If there was no friction, would a moving object stop moving? You may be surprised to learn that the answer is no! A moving object will continue to move until a force is applied to it. In a similar way, an object at rest will not start to move unless a force acts on it. This property of matter is called **inertia** (i·NUR·shuh). If a skateboard is resting on the floor, it won't move unless you push it. If the skateboard is moving forward, it won't turn, speed up, or slow down unless a force acts on it. In both cases, the skateboard has inertia.

Friction can be a helpful force. Gymnast Amy Chow uses chalk on her hands to increase friction and prevent her hands from slipping off the uneven bars.

READING **Compare and Contrast**
What are friction and inertia?

What Is Gravity?

One force acting on you right now is *gravity*. It is pulling you toward Earth's surface. Gravity pulls two objects together. The force of gravity between objects depends on two things. One is how much matter is in the objects. The other is how close together the objects are.

When things go up, the force of gravity pulls them down. Jump up, and you will fall back to Earth because of gravity. Earth has a huge amount of matter. The pull between it and other objects is very strong.

You are probably familiar with the word *weight*. What is weight? Weight is a measure of force.

The force of gravity on the Moon is less than that on Earth because the Moon is less massive.

It tells the amount of gravity acting on an object. When you weigh yourself at home, you measure the force of gravity between you and Earth.

More massive objects exert a greater force of gravity than less massive objects do. The Moon is less massive than Earth. It has less gravity. If you weighed yourself on the Moon, you would weigh one-sixth your Earth weight.

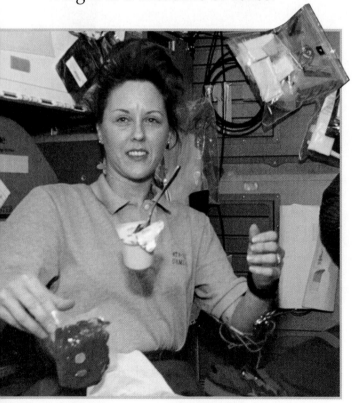

Eating could be difficult without the force of gravity.

▶ How is weight related to gravity?

What Is Work?

Do you know what **work** is? You may say, "Of course! I do homework every night!" In science the word *work* has a special meaning. Work is done when a force is used to move an object a certain distance.

When you are sitting at your desk reading, you are not doing any work! A weightlifter holding a barbell above her head isn't doing any work either. Why not? She is using a force, but she is not moving an object through a distance. To do work, a force needs to push or pull on an object and the object needs to move. What could the weightlifter do so that she is doing work?

What types of things are work? Pushing a lawn mower is work. Pulling a door open is work. Picking up a cup and kicking a soccer ball are work. Even pushing the buttons on a telephone is an example of work.

This weightlifter is applying a large force, but she is doing no work. Does the weightlifter do work while she is picking up the barbell?

▷ **How is force related to work?**

What kind of work do you like to do best?

What Is Energy?

Have you ever described yourself as having lots of **energy**, or perhaps being tired and having little energy? In science energy is the ability to do work. That means energy is needed to apply a force to an object to make it move. Energy is also needed to make matter change.

The wind blows. Sunshine warms Earth. A leaf falls. You cannot always see it happen, but in each situation, matter is moving or changing. Energy is what makes the motion and change possible.

This wrecking ball has kinetic energy. The force it applies causes the bricks to collapse. Work is done on the building.

Sometimes an object has energy because it is moving. A rolling bowling ball, a swinging hammer, and a moving bulldozer all have energy because they are moving. This energy is called *kinetic energy*.

An object can also have energy because of its position. This kind of energy is called *potential energy*. Potential energy is stored, or is waiting to be used. It gives an object the potential, or future ability, to do work. A rock on the top of a hill has potential energy. The rock can do work on any object it touches as it rolls down the hill.

The stretched bow has potential energy, or energy of position. When the archer releases the bow, its potential energy will become kinetic energy.

There are many forms of energy. The table lists some of them. What do all these kinds of energy have in common?

Forms of Energy

Chemical
The energy your body uses to walk, run, and lift things is chemical energy. It comes from the food you eat. Chemical energy is stored in the particles that make up food, fuel, and other kinds of matter.

Electrical
Electrical energy is related to the movement of charged particles. Some electrical energy comes from batteries. However, most of it comes from power plants that burn fuels to make electricity. The electrical energy is then sent through wires to homes and businesses.

Light
The Sun is a major source of light energy. Plants use light energy to make food. Scientists have found another use for light energy—lasers. Lasers are light beams that can cut through steel and other materials.

Mechanical
Matter that is in motion has energy. This energy of motion is mechanical energy. Wind, water in a waterfall, and a jet plane speeding through the air have mechanical energy. Sound is a type of mechanical energy, too.

Thermal
A stove, a heater, and a match give off thermal energy. Thermal energy comes from the motion of the tiny particles in matter. The faster the particles in a substance move, the warmer the substance and the more thermal energy it has.

Nuclear
Nuclear energy comes from the tiniest particles of matter. When these particles split apart or join together, huge amounts of nuclear energy are released. The Sun's energy is produced from such nuclear reactions.

▷ **What are some different forms of energy?**

Can Energy Change Form?

Energy does not always stay in one form. Energy can change its form. Energy changes are all around you. These pictures show some examples.

Before a rocket lifts off, its fuel contains a lot of chemical energy. Some of this chemical energy changes to mechanical energy as the engine gives a loud roar. Some changes to thermal and light energy as flames shoot forth during the launch. The rocket blasts off. Remaining chemical energy changes to kinetic energy as the rocket climbs through the sky.

Energy not only changes form, it can be passed from one object to another. When you kick a ball, you transfer energy from your body to the ball.

The energy of moving water can be changed to electrical energy.

▷ **What are some ways that energy changes form?**

When a rocket blasts off, chemical energy changes form.

Why It Matters

The universe is always in motion. Understanding motion helps you explain how the Sun rises and why we have seasons. It also helps you choose the fastest bicycle or in-line skates.

Energy in its many forms is all around you. Energy allows you and other objects to do work. Knowing about energy can help you use it wisely!

Think and Write

1. What if you are riding on a bus with some of your friends? Are they a good frame of reference for your motion? Why?

2. How can a force change the motion of an object?

3. Is it usually easier to move a smooth object across a smooth surface or a rough object across a rough surface? Why?

4. **Measure** Choose an object that moves. Describe how to calculate its speed.

5. **Critical Thinking** Name five ways you observe energy changing form in your everyday life.

L·I·N·K·S

SOCIAL STUDIES LINK

Do research. In many Native American stories, coyotes can change form as they wish. They can become snakes, birds, or other animals. How is energy like the coyote character of Native American stories? Find stories like these, and share them with your classmates.

MATH LINK

Solve problems. What is the speed of a ship that travels 25 kilometers in 5 hours? If a plane is traveling 600 miles per hour, how far does it go in 3 hours? If a car goes 10 miles per hour, how long does it take the car to travel 50 miles?

WRITING LINK

Write a paragraph. There is lots of motion and change all around you. Choose an active scene such as your school bus or classroom. Name the motion and change you observe. Predict which type of energy causes each. Report your observations and predictions in a paragraph.

TECHNOLOGY LINK

At the Computer Visit **www.mhscience02.com** for more links.

Energy and Tools

Vocabulary

simple machine, F20

load, F22

effort force, F22

efficiency, F30

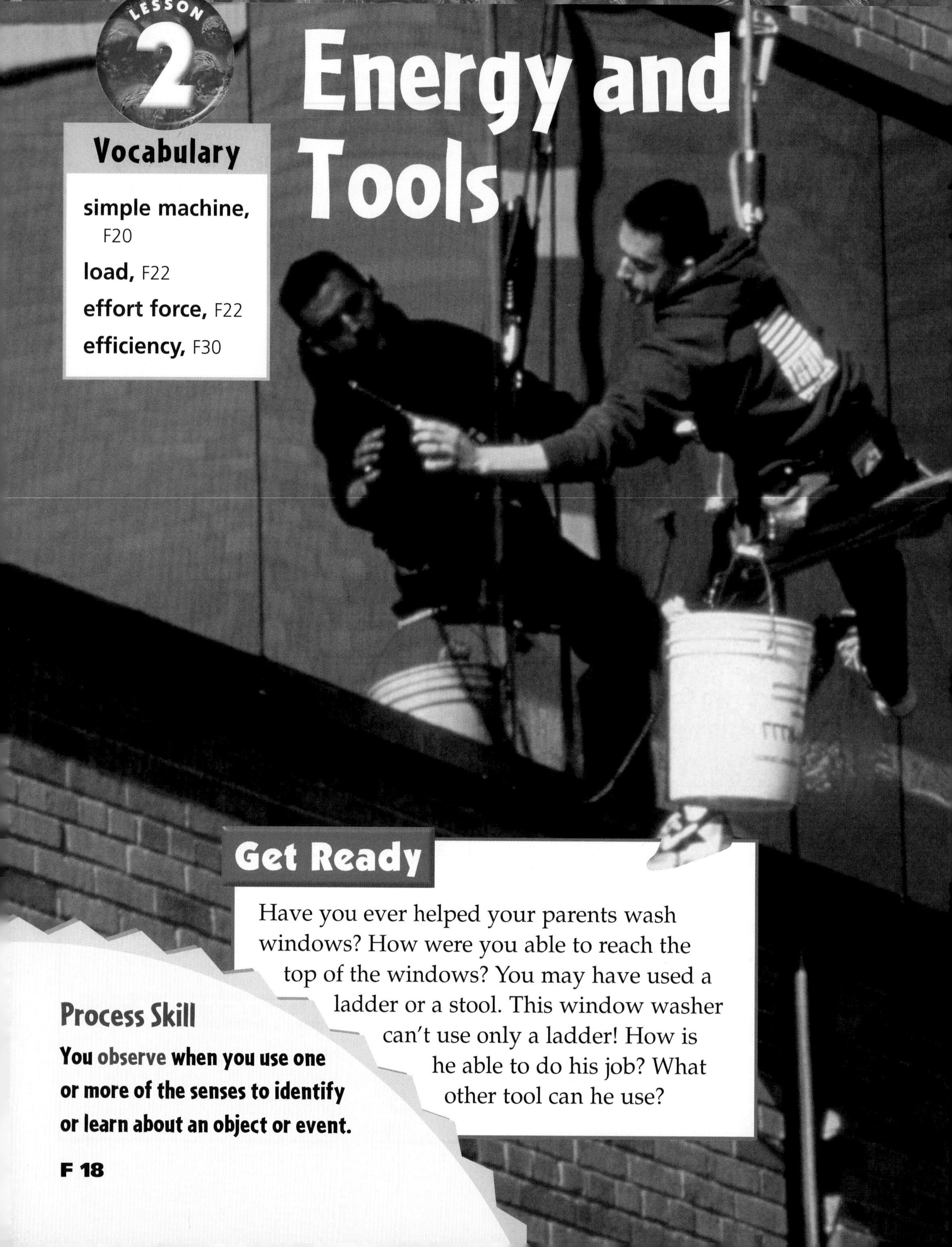

Get Ready

Have you ever helped your parents wash windows? How were you able to reach the top of the windows? You may have used a ladder or a stool. This window washer can't use only a ladder! How is he able to do his job? What other tool can he use?

Process Skill

You observe when you use one or more of the senses to identify or learn about an object or event.

Explore Activity

How Does a Pulley Work?

Materials

pulley

2 pieces of cord (thick string)

book

spring scale

Procedure

1. Tie the longer piece of cord around the book. Have a partner hold the pulley. Thread the cord through the pulley's groove.

2. **Observe** Pull down on the cord. What happens? Draw the pulley, cord, and book system. Use arrows to show the direction you pull and the direction the book moves.

3. **Observe** Attach one end of the second cord to something that won't move. Thread the free end through the pulley's groove so that you can pull up on it. Attach the book to the hook on the pulley. Pull up on the free end of the cord. What happens to the pulley? What happens to the book? Draw the system. Use arrows to show the direction you pull and the direction the book and pulley move.

Drawing Conclusions

1. Was it easier to lift the book in step 2 or 3? Why do you think so?

2. **Infer** In which step did you pull one way and the book moved the opposite way?

3. **Going Further: Experiment** Repeat the procedures but attach a spring scale to the end of the cord you pull on. Record the readings on the scale for each trial. What do you notice?

Main Idea Simple machines make work easier in different ways.

What Are Simple Machines?

How would you describe a *machine*? It is anything that helps you do work or makes work easier. What machines do you use?

Many machines, such as cars, cranes, and clocks, have lots of parts. Some machines have few parts, such as a pulley or a screwdriver. These are **simple machines**. There are six types of simple machines. They are the lever, the pulley, the wheel and axle, the inclined plane, the wedge, and the screw.

Have you ever used any of these simple machines? What were you doing? You might be surprised to learn that you use many simple machines every day.

Some simple machines are called tools. Think about the tools people use every day. Builders, cooks, doctors, and gardeners all need tools to do their work.

The first tools were made by hitting one stone with another until sharp-edged pieces broke off. With these sharp-edged pieces, a hunter could easily cut the skin from a dead animal or shape spears.

People invented tools to help them hunt, gather plants, make clothes, build shelters, and protect themselves. Everything had to be invented—axes, hammers, scrapers, saws—even the wheel. No one knows who invented the wheel. Most likely it was invented between 5,000 and 6,000 years ago. Among the first people to use the wheel were the Sumerians. They lived where the country of Iraq is today.

Ax

Clovis point

These tools are thousands of years old. The Clovis point was the end of an object that was tossed or thrown. The ax was used as we use it today.

What made ancient people start inventing tools? Maybe they got their ideas by watching animals. Lions, for instance, use their sharp teeth to slice the meat off the bones of animals they kill. Some otters use stones to help them crack the thick shells of clams.

Some types of birds, called finches, use sticks to loosen bark from trees. Under the bark there may be insects the birds eat.

A beaver can cut down a tree by gnawing around the trunk with its front teeth. It cuts the fallen tree into the pieces it needs to build a dam. A mole digs underground tunnels by scooping soil with its big front paws.

Many of the tools people invented work just like the body parts of these animals. A chisel chips through wood like a beaver's front teeth. A shovel scoops out soil like a mole's paws.

▷ What are the six simple machines?

What simple machines are the mole, otter, and woodpecker illustrating?

How Do Levers Work?

How are a wheelbarrow, a seesaw, and a shovel alike? They are all examples of *levers* (LEV·uhrz).

A lever consists of two parts—a bar or plank and a fixed point, called a *fulcrum*. The fulcrum supports the bar and allows it to turn, or pivot.

Levers can make it easier for people to lift heavy objects or open things. The object being moved by a simple machine such as a lever is called a **load**.

How could you move a rock too heavy to lift? You could make a lever. You would put one end of a pole under the rock. Then you would place a small stone under the pole close to the rock. This is the fulcrum. When you pushed down on the other end of the pole, the rock would rise.

A lever doesn't make you stronger. It changes how much force you use to move something. This force is called the **effort force**. You would need a small effort force to push down on the long end of the pole. The short end of the pole would push up against the rock with a force greater than the effort force. You would use less energy using a lever than if you simply tried to lift the rock.

Types of Levers

READING

Diagrams

What class of lever has the load in between the fulcrum and the effort force?

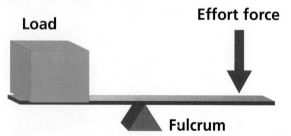

A first-class lever has the fulcrum between the load and the effort force.

Load   **Effort force**

Fulcrum

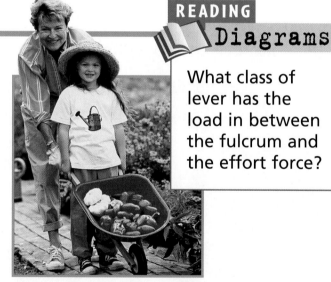

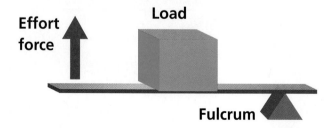

A second-class lever has the fulcrum at the end and the load in the middle.

Effort force   **Load**

Fulcrum

F 22

There is one catch. Which moves more, the short or the long end of the pole? The long end does. You have to push the long end down a greater distance than the rock moves up.

There are three kinds of levers. The difference between kinds is where the fulcrum is located. The diagrams below show the three kinds of levers.

▷ **How does a lever help you do work?**

A third-class lever has the fulcrum at the end and the effort force in the middle.

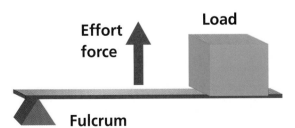

Effort force

Load

Fulcrum

QUICK LAB

FOR SCHOOL OR HOME

Make Levers

1. **Make a Model** Place about an inch of a ruler under the edge of a book. Place a pencil under the ruler close to the book.

2. Push down on the other end of the ruler. Record what happens.

3. Place as much of the ruler under the book as fits. Remove the pencil.

4. Lift up on the end of the ruler sticking out from under the book. Record what happens.

5. When you pushed down in step 2, which way did the lever push?

6. **Draw Conclusions** Can a lever change the direction of the force? Explain.

7. **Draw Conclusions** What kind of lever did you make? Explain.

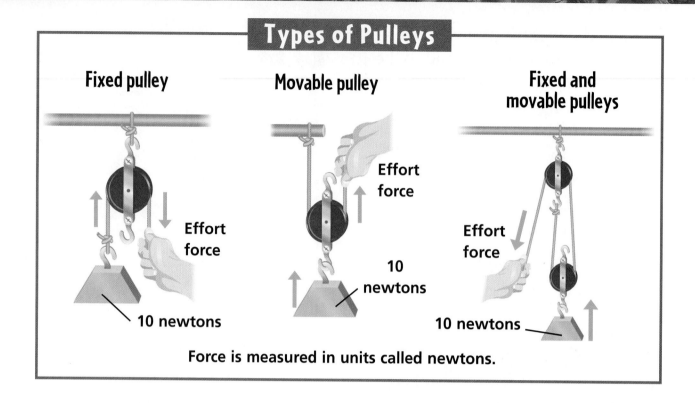

Types of Pulleys

Fixed pulley

Effort force

10 newtons

Movable pulley

Effort force

10 newtons

Fixed and movable pulleys

Effort force

10 newtons

Force is measured in units called newtons.

How Do Pulleys Work?

As you learned on page F19, the *pulley* made it easier to move an object. There are two types of pulleys. In a *fixed pulley,* the wheel is attached to something so that it cannot change position. One end of the rope is passed around the wheel. The other end is tied to an object—the load. Pulling the rope lifts the load.

A single fixed pulley makes work easier by changing the direction of the effort force. You pull down, and the load moves up. However, a fixed pulley can't change how much effort force you need to move a load. A force equal to the weight of the load is needed.

A *movable pulley* is not attached to some fixed object. It moves with the load. It can be used to decrease the effort force you need to apply to move the load.

Look at the drawing of a fixed and a movable pulley hooked up together. In this system the rope runs around both pulleys. The load is attached to the movable pulley.

When pulleys are used, they can decrease the effort force needed to lift a load. The more pulleys, the less force is needed. However, the rope needs to be pulled a great distance to lift the object a small distance.

**READING Compare and Contrast
How does a fixed pulley differ
from a movable pulley?**

How Do Wheels and Axles Work?

When you turn a doorknob, you are using a *wheel and axle* (AK·suhl). It has two parts. One part is a wheel. The other part is a bar that passes through the center of the wheel.

Why don't you have to use a lot of force to open a door with a doorknob? A small effort force applied to the doorknob, or wheel, turns into a larger force from the axle. The larger force can lift the latch, which is the load. The wheel has a larger diameter than the axle. You have to turn the wheel a long way around for the axle to turn a short distance.

A Ferris wheel is a wheel and axle. However, in a Ferris wheel, the effort force is applied to the axle, not the wheel. The large Ferris

wheel moves farther and faster than the axle. To make the wheel move faster and farther takes a lot of effort force from an engine.

A screwdriver is a wheel and axle. The thick handle is the wheel. The shaft is the axle. Try turning a screw into a piece of wood using the shaft. Try it using the handle. Which required less effort force?

▷ **What are some examples of a wheel and axle?**

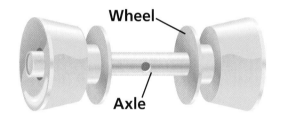

Wheel

Axle

A Ferris wheel is a wheel and axle, as is a doorknob. Where is the effort force applied in each?

How Do Inclined Planes Work?

There is a simple machine that has only one part. It is an *inclined plane* (in·KLIGHND PLAYN), or a flat, slanted surface.

A ramp is an inclined plane. So is a long board that slants from the back of a truck to the ground. Movers use inclined planes to slide heavy objects in and out of their trucks.

Inclined planes make work easier by reducing the effort force needed to move an object. Imagine if you had to move a very heavy barrel onto a truck 120 centimeters (4 feet) off the ground. You could not lift it, but you could push or pull it up the inclined plane. It helps you do the work by holding up, or supporting, most of the barrel's weight. Your muscles have to give only a small

push or pull to move the barrel. However, you have to push or pull the barrel up the entire length of the board instead of lifting it only 120 centimeters.

Inclined planes are also used to make it easier for handicapped people to get around. You will find inclined planes in many buildings for this reason.

▷ **Why do you use less force to move something with an inclined plane?**

An inclined plane makes moving a heavy object easier. The worker uses less effort force but must push the object a greater distance.

How Do Wedges and Screws Work?

What do you get if you put two inclined planes back to back? You get one machine called a *wedge* (WEJ). A wedge changes a downward or forward force into a sideways force. Can you think of any wedges?

Many common items are wedges. A needle pushes apart threads of fabric. A zipper changes effort force to unhook the teeth or push them together. The blade of an ax is a wedge with a sharp edge. So are razor blades, saw teeth, snippers, knives, and just about all cutting tools.

How does a knife work? As you push and pull the sharp end of a wedge into food, the sides of the wedge push the food apart with a greater force than you use.

Believe it or not, a *screw* is an inclined plane twisted into a spiral. To see how, cut a piece of paper into a right triangle. Wrap the triangle

An ax is an example of a wedge. The downward effort force splits the wood.

around a pencil. Watch how the slanted edge of the triangle goes up and around the pencil.

When a screw is turned, it moves forward. It also presses on whatever is around it, such as wood. You have to keep turning a screw for it to move a short distance. You need only a small effort force to turn the screw. The screw increases the force to move deeper into the wood.

▷ **How are a wedge and a screw similar to an inclined plane?**

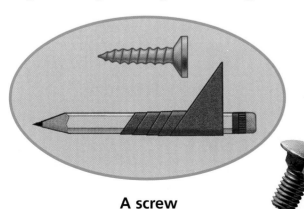

A screw

How Do Gears Work?

Have you ever looked closely at a bicycle? There are wheels with teeth that make the chain and tires turn as the pedals are pushed. These wheels with teeth are *gears* (GEERZ).

One gear cannot work on its own. The teeth on one gear have to fit into, or be connected to, the spaces between the teeth on another gear. When a gear is attached to the axle of a wheel-and-axle system, it will turn as the axle turns. When one gear turns, the other gear turns, too.

Look at the picture. One gear is larger than the other. Count the teeth on each. The large wheel has more teeth. When you turn the large wheel once, the small wheel turns more than once in the same amount of time. It also turns in the opposite direction. It is usually easier to turn a larger gear than a smaller gear. Gears can change the direction and amount of the applied force.

Turning the large gear clockwise causes the smaller gear to turn a greater distance counterclockwise.

Think about the bicycle again. Bicycle gears are connected by a chain. When you push the pedals, gears make the wheels turn faster than the pedals are turning. When you switch gears, you change to a different-sized gear. That way you can make your bike move faster or slower.

▶ **How can gears be used?**

How Can Simple Machines Be Combined?

Not all machines are simple machines. A *compound machine* is a machine that is made up of two or more simple machines. Most machines are compound machines.

Scissors are made up of two wedges that are arranged as two first-class levers. The point where the blades are connected is the fulcrum.

When the handles are pushed together, the blades cut through material.

A bicycle is also an example of a compound machine. It is made up of many different simple machines. Look at the photograph below. Notice that the pedals and tires are wheels and axles. The pedals are attached to gears. As the pedals turn, they turn the gears. The turning gears then make a chain move, which turns the bicycle tires. The turning gear and moving chain act like a pulley system. Levers are found at the handle brakes and gearshift controls. Also, many different-sized screws are used to hold the bicycle parts together.

Fulcrum

Scissors are an example of a compound machine.

Wedge

Lever

▷ **What is a compound machine?**

A bicycle is an example of a compound machine because it is made up of several simple machines.

How Much Work Can a Machine Do?

When people purchase a machine, such as a snowplow, they want a machine that can do a lot of work in a short amount of time. You can remove a lot more snow in less time using a snowplow than using a shovel.

Although a machine can save you time, no machine ever works perfectly to change the energy used for an effort force into an output force. In other words, not all the energy you put into the machine comes out of the machine. The measure of how much useful work a machine puts out compared to the amount of work put into it is called its **efficiency** (i·FISH·uhn·see).

However tiny the amount, there is always friction in a machine. Gears that rub against each other are an example of friction in some machines. A certain amount of input energy is always lost due to friction.

The more gears and moving parts a machine has, the more energy is lost to friction. Simple machines tend to be more efficient than compound machines.

You can improve the efficiency of a machine by limiting friction. This can be done by keeping machines clean, well oiled, and rust free. Rust and dirt increase friction. If you have ever tried to open a rusty door or ride a rusty bike, you know a lot of force was needed to overcome the extra friction caused by rust.

▷ **Why don't you get the same amount of energy out of a machine as you put into it?**

Rusty gears such as these increase the amount of friction. Increased friction decreases a machine's efficiency.

L·I·N·K·S

Why It Matters

Did you know that your lower arm is an example of a third-class lever? When you lift a ball in your hand, your arm muscles supply the effort force. Your hand lifts the ball. Where is the fulcrum? It is in your elbow joint.

How different the world would be without machines. It took people thousands of years to understand how simple machines make work easier. Once they did, they also understood more about the human body and the animal world. With time people invent newer and better machines that save time and energy.

Think and Write

1. How does a wheel and axle make work easier?

2. What is the difference between a first-class and a second-class lever?

3. What is effort force?

4. What is the difference between an inclined plane and a wedge?

5. **Critical Thinking** How is a compound machine related to a simple machine?

ART LINK

Invent a machine. Using at least two of the simple machines you have learned about, design a new tool. What can your tool do? How does it make work easier to do?

SOCIAL STUDIES LINK

Do research. The Sumerians were among the first people to use the wheel. Where and in what period did the Sumerians live? What was their culture like? Use the Internet or an encyclopedia for your research. Write a short report to tell what you have learned.

WRITING LINK

Write a paragraph. What simple machines do you use every day? Choose one, and tell how it has made life easier.

LITERATURE LINK

Read *How the Lever Changed the World* to learn about one of the important simple machines. Try the activities at the end of the book.

TECHNOLOGY LINK

At the Computer Visit **www.mhscience02.com** for more links.

Heat

Vocabulary

heat, F34

insulator, F34

convection, F36

radiation, F36

fossil fuel, F38

Get Ready

How can walruses survive in freezing-cold places? Both people and walruses are mammals. They live in very different places, however. Walruses spend much of their time near the North Pole. People can survive only a short time in freezing areas without protection. What helps walruses live in such cold places?

Process Skill

You **infer** when you form an idea from facts or observations.

Explore Activity

How Does Fat Keep Mammals Warm?

Materials

plastic bag containing lard or solid vegetable shortening

2 vinyl surgical gloves

bucket or pan of ice water

stopwatch or clock with second hand

paper towels

Procedure

1. **Measure** Put on one glove. Ask your partner to time how long you can comfortably keep your hand in the ice water. Record the results.

2. **Use Variables** Move your gloved hand around in the bag of lard to coat it well. Be sure to spread the lard over your entire hand and between your fingers.

3. **Measure** Ask your partner to time how long you can keep your lard-coated hand in the ice water. Record the results.

4. Trade places, and let your partner repeat the procedure.

5. **Use Numbers** Take an average of both of your results.

Drawing Conclusions

1. **Communicate** How long on average were you able to keep your hand in the ice water in step 1? In step 3?

2. **Infer** What role do you think the lard played in keeping your hand warm?

3. **Going Further: Infer** If the lard represents a walrus's blubber, how might blubber help the walrus survive?

Main Idea Heat travels and affects matter in different ways.

What Is Heat?

You know that matter is made of particles. These particles have energy and are always moving. **Heat** is the flow of this energy from one material to another. Heat moves from warmer objects to cooler objects.

When warm and cool objects touch, energy is transferred from the warmer object to the cooler object. Remember, the more energy an object has, the faster its particles move. The particles of a warm object cause the particles of a cool object touching it to move faster. The particles of the warm object slow down as they transfer their energy. Eventually the particles making up both objects move at the same speed.

Bundling up on a cold day provides insulation to keep the body warm.

When you are cold, you wrap yourself in a blanket to get warm. Walruses have a built-in "blanket" of fat, or blubber. Why does a blanket keep you warm?

A blanket and a walrus's blubber are examples of *insulators* (IN·suh·lay·tuhrz). An insulator is a material that does not transfer heat very well. A glove is an insulator. The glove does not transfer the heat from your hand to the air very well. The heat builds up inside the glove. Your hand stays warm.

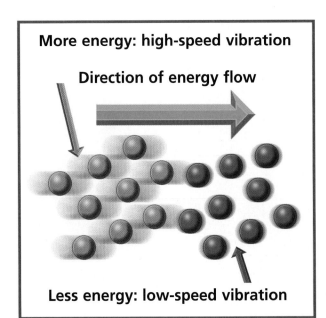

More energy: high-speed vibration

Direction of energy flow

Less energy: low-speed vibration

Heat always flows from the object with more energy to the object with less energy.

The opposite of an insulator is a *conductor* (kuhn·DUK·tuhr). A metal frying pan is an example of a conductor. It transfers heat quickly from a burner to the food.

Temperature

Heat is not the same as *temperature* (TEM·puhr·uh·chuhr). Temperature is a measure of how hot or cold something is.

Temperature is measured with an instrument called a *thermometer* (thuhr·MAHM·i·tuhr). A thermometer is filled with a liquid—usually mercury or alcohol. When the temperature increases, the particles of the liquid begin to move faster and farther apart. The liquid expands. The expanding liquid rises in the glass thermometer tube. When the temperature decreases, the particles of the liquid slow down. The liquid contracts and falls back down the tube.

Two commonly used scales for measuring temperature are the Fahrenheit scale and the Celsius scale. How are these two scales different? Water freezes on the Fahrenheit scale at 32° (32 degrees) and boils at 212°. On the Celsius scale, water freezes at 0° and boils at 100°.

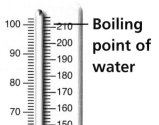
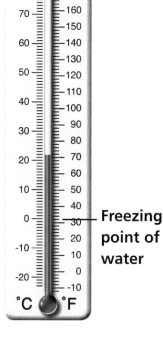

100 Boiling point of water

Freezing point of water

This thermometer shows both the Celsius and Fahrenheit scales. Can you read the temperature in Fahrenheit? In Celsius?

READING **Compare and Contrast**
How are heat and temperature related?

Wood is a good insulator. Why do you think it is often used to make handles for pots and pans?

How Is Heat Transferred?

Heat can be transferred in three different ways. One of these is by **conduction** (kuhn·DUK·shuhn). Conduction can occur between two objects that are touching. It can also occur within an object, such as a pot.

Heat can also be transferred by the flow of a liquid or gas. This is called **convection** (kuhn·VEK·shuhn). One example of convection is heating a liquid in a pot.

The third way heat is transferred is by **radiation** (ray·dee·AY·shuhn). Radiation is the transfer of heat

Energy from the Sun travels to Earth by radiation.

through space. Matter does not need to be present in order for radiation to occur. Heat from the Sun reaches Earth by radiation.

▷ **How are conduction, convection, and radiation related?**

READING
Diagrams

By what method does heat travel through liquids or gases? Through matter that is touching?

Heat is transferred through water by the flow of particles.

Heat from the coil is transferred through the pot by conduction.

How Does Heat Affect Size?

Most matter *expands* (ek·SPANDZ), or gets larger, when heated. When cooled, most matter *contracts* (kuhn·TRAKTS), or shrinks.

The particles making up matter are constantly colliding and bouncing off one another. Adding energy makes the particles move faster and farther apart. They take up more space. This makes matter expand. The opposite happens when energy is taken away.

Examples of matter expanding and contracting are all around you. The way a thermometer works is based on this idea. Can you think of another example?

▷ **What happens to matter when it is heated?**

Expansion joints are built between sections of a road to keep the concrete from cracking or buckling when it expands.

QUICK LAB

FOR SCHOOL OR HOME

Matter and Heat

BE CAREFUL! Wear goggles.

1. **Measure** Use a string and ruler to measure a balloon. Mark the spot where you measured it. Record the data.

2. **Measure** Heat the balloon with a blow dryer for one minute. Measure the distance around the balloon at the marked spot. Record the data.

3. How did heat affect the size of the balloon?

4. **Communicate** What happens to the air particles in the balloon when the balloon is heated?

Huge amounts of heat, called geothermal energy, are produced within Earth. At a geothermal plant, the energy is gathered and can be used.

What Are Some Sources of Heat?

One of the major sources of heat is the Sun. The Sun is a hot ball of gases that has a temperature of about 15 million °C (27 million °F) at its center. The Sun gets its energy from nuclear reactions. These reactions take place within the ball of gases.

Although the Sun is about 150 million kilometers (93 million miles) from Earth, enough of its light and heat reaches Earth to support life.

Another source of heat on Earth is **fossil fuels** . Fossil fuels formed millions of years ago from the remains of ancient plants and animals. Fossil fuels provide energy when they are burned. Coal, oil, and natural gas are examples of fossil fuels.

Fossil fuels are *nonrenewable resources*. That means once they are used up, they are gone forever. Fossil fuels also cause pollution when they are burned. That is why scientists are looking for other ways to produce heat, using products that are renewable and do not cause much pollution. Some of these ways include using wind power, water power, the power of tides, and energy from within Earth.

▶ **What are two sources of heat on Earth?**

Why It Matters

In the past scientists thought that heat was a mysterious substance that flowed from object to object. Heat does flow between objects, but it isn't a substance. We now understand heat to be a form of energy.

That understanding has allowed us to create products to keep us warm or cool and to construct buildings to prevent as much heat loss as possible.

Think and Write

1. What is heat?

2. How is heat transferred?

3. What is the difference between a conductor and an insulator?

4. Bob at Bob's Bike Shop says it isn't wise to fill tires full of air on a cold day. What is Bob worried about?

5. Critical Thinking A room's temperature is 70°F. In the room object A touches object B. Object A has a temperature of 70°F, and it doesn't change. What is the temperature of object B?

L·I·N·K·S

SOCIAL STUDIES LINK

Do research. What kind of material is a foam cup? Is it an insulator or a conductor? When was it discovered? Use the Internet or an encyclopedia for your research. Tell in a paragraph what you've learned.

WRITING LINK

Write a story. How is heat transferred from a mug of hot chocolate to your hand? Explain in a story how energy is transferred.

HEALTH LINK

Make a chart. What are some ways you keep warm in the winter? What are some ways you stay cool in the summer? How do animals such as pigs stay warm and cool? Make a list of winter and summer tips, and organize them in a chart.

MATH LINK

Use numbers. The morning temperature is 42°F. By afternoon it is 60°F. How much has it increased? If it drops to 30°F at night, how much has it decreased from the afternoon?

TECHNOLOGY LINK

At the Computer Visit **www.mhscience02.com** for more links.

Light

Vocabulary

wavelength, F42

spectrum, F42

reflection, F45

refraction, F46

Get Ready

Look around you. What do you see? You live in a world full of color—the leaves on trees, the clothes you wear, a rainbow in the sky. Do you know where color comes from? The colors you see are part of light. What is light, and how does it behave?

Process Skill:

You experiment when you perform a test to support or disprove a hypothesis.

Explore Activity

What Do You See When You Mix Colors of Light?

Materials

cardboard

compass

scissors

markers or colored crayons

pencil

goggles

Procedure

BE CAREFUL! Wear goggles.

1. **Measure** Use a compass to draw a circle on the cardboard. The circle should be about 13 cm (5 in.) across. Divide the circle into 12 equal sections. Color each section a different color.

2. Cut out the circle. Put on your goggles. Carefully push a pencil into the center of the circle. Spin your spinner away from your body.

3. **Observe** What color do you see while the spinner is spinning?

4. **Experiment** Repeat steps 1–3 to make another spinner. This time choose colors that you think will make the disk appear white when you spin it. Make as many spinners as you need to find the color combinations that work best.

Drawing Conclusions

1. What color did you see in step 3?

2. What colors did you mix together to make the best white?

3. **Going Further: Experiment** Repeat steps 1–3 to make another spinner. This time color the spinner only three colors, and see if you can make the spinner still look white. Make as many spinners as you need to find the color combinations that work best.

Main Idea Light is a form of energy that travels in waves.

What Is Light?

Everything around you seems to have color. What is color? Why do you see color? To answer these questions, you need to learn about light.

Light is a form of energy. Light travels to Earth from the Sun. Two other sources of light on Earth include fire and light bulbs. Often sources of light also give off heat.

Usually a source of light gives off white light. White light is actually made up of all colors. These colors range from red to violet.

You can see the seven colors of light when white light from the Sun passes through tiny raindrops. The raindrops act like *prisms*. A prism is an object that separates white light into the colors that make it up. When raindrops separate light from the Sun, you observe a rainbow.

All light is made of waves. Light can be described using **wavelengths** (WAYV·lengkths). A wavelength is the distance from the top of one wave to the top of the next wave. Red light has the longest wavelength. Violet light has the shortest.

Scientists call the seven colors of light that make up white light the *visible spectrum*. A **spectrum** (SPEK·truhm) is a range of light

Electromagnetic Spectrum

The electromagnetic spectrum contains a range of electromagnetic waves. These waves vary by their amount of energy.

Radio waves are used to transmit radio and TV signals.

Microwaves can cook your food.

Infrared waves are felt as heat. Photos showing the heat given off by objects can be taken.

| Radio waves | Micro waves | Infrared waves | Visible waves |

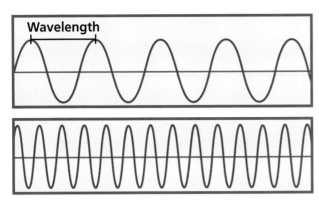

Wavelength

Low-energy waves have long wavelengths. As the energy of a wave increases, the wavelength decreases.

waves with different wavelengths and energies. The seven colors that make up white light are called the visible spectrum because they are light waves we can see.

As you read this book, light waves are traveling all around you.

The light waves you can see are in the visible spectrum. However, there are many waves you cannot see. The visible spectrum is only a small part of the *electromagnetic spectrum*.

The electromagnetic spectrum contains waves of many different wavelengths. Electromagnetic waves with the longest wavelengths are radio waves. They have the lowest energy. The electromagnetic waves with the shortest wavelengths are gamma waves. They have the highest energy. Look at the chart to see all of the waves that make up the electromagnetic spectrum.

▷ **What is the electromagnetic spectrum?**

Visible light allows you to see colors.

X rays have many uses in medicine.

High-energy gamma waves are found in radioactive materials used in nuclear power plants.

Ultraviolet light tans your skin but can also give you a sunburn.

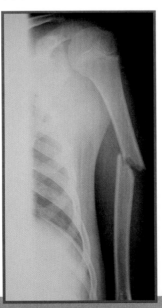

CAUTION

RADIOACTIVE MATERIAL IS STORED INSIDE THIS REFRIGERATOR

Ultraviolet waves

X-ray waves

Gamma waves

How Does Light Travel?

Have you ever made a shadow puppet? Shadows are places where light does not fall. A shadow forms when light is blocked. The light strikes an object but cannot pass through it. A shadow has the shape of whatever is blocking the light.

Shadows show that light travels in straight lines, or *rays*. Light spreads out from a source in all directions. However, light cannot bend and go around things. It cannot curve and "fill in" a shadow.

The size of a shadow depends on where the light source is. The closer an object is to a light source, the bigger the shadow. Light coming from above an object creates a shorter shadow. Light coming from the side of an object creates a longer shadow. A sundial tells time in this way.

A sundial tells time by using the position of the dial's shadow. As Earth rotates on its axis, the Sun moves across the sky. It casts its shortest shadow when it is directly overhead, at noon. It casts its longest shadow when it first appears and before it disappears.

▷ **Why do shadows form?**

If you read the shadow on this sundial, it tells you the time is 1:00.

The shadow of a street lamp was formed when sunlight was blocked by the object.

Light travels away from a source in straight lines and in all directions.

What Is Reflection?

Most of the light that reaches your eyes is reflected light. **Reflection** (ri·FLEK·shuhn) occurs when light strikes a surface and bounces off. When you throw a ball against a wall, it bounces off it. In a similar way, light bounces off, or is reflected, when it strikes a surface.

Most surfaces reflect at least some light. Smooth, shiny surfaces reflect almost all of the light falling on them. Very smooth, shiny objects reflect the most light and are used as mirrors.

What happens to light when it is reflected? Light changes direction when it is reflected off a surface. You can easily see this with a small mirror. Hold the mirror so it catches light rays coming from a flashlight. Move the mirror around, and see the spot of reflected light jump and jiggle. The rays bounce off the mirror and travel in a new direction.

Incoming angle

Outgoing angle

The law of reflection says that the incoming angle is equal to the outgoing angle.

The light rays from the flashlight are called the incoming rays. The reflected light rays are called the outgoing rays. Incoming rays strike the mirror at an angle called the *incoming angle*. Outgoing rays are reflected from the mirror at an angle called the *outgoing angle*.

Look at the diagram. What do you notice about the incoming angle and the outgoing angle? They are equal. With reflection the incoming angle is equal to the outgoing angle. This is called the *law of reflection*.

▷ What happens to light when it strikes a surface?

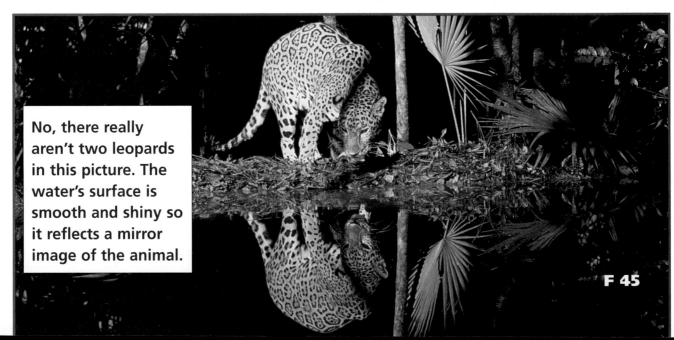

No, there really aren't two leopards in this picture. The water's surface is smooth and shiny so it reflects a mirror image of the animal.

What Is Refraction?

Look at the pencil in the picture. Is the pencil really cut in two pieces? No! It just appears to be. What do you think is happening?

The picture shows one example of **refraction** (ri·FRAK·shuhn). Refraction is the bending of light as it passes from one material into another.

Most materials reflect the light falling on them. However, some materials allow light to pass through. Refraction happens when light passes through glass, water, light plastic, and other transparent materials.

What do you think causes refraction? Light travels at different speeds in different materials. The more dense the material, the slower light travels through it. As light travels more slowly, it bends more. For example, water is more dense than air. It's harder for you to walk through water than air. It is also harder for light to move through water. Light slows and bends at the point where it passes from air to water.

Earlier in the lesson, you learned that light travels in straight lines. This is still true during refraction. It is important to remember that a ray of light doesn't curve. During refraction the ray simply changes

Refraction makes this pencil appear to be in two pieces!

direction as it passes from one material to another.

Lenses are tools that refract light. They are used to gather light rays or spread them apart. When you wear glasses or use a camera, magnifying glass, or binoculars, you use one or more lenses.

There are two kinds of lenses. One type, the *convex lens*, bulges in the middle. A convex lens brings

A telescope uses convex lenses to make distant objects appear larger and closer. Astronomers use telescopes to observe the stars and other planets.

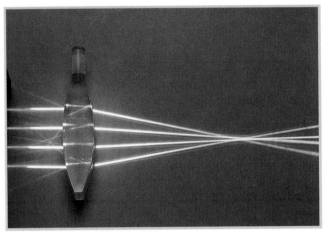

The convex lens gathers light rays together.   **The concave lens spreads them apart.**

rays of light together. Another type of lens, the *concave lens*, curves inward. A concave lens spreads light rays apart.

A magnifying glass is a convex lens. When you hold a magnifying glass near an object, light rays are reflected from the object to the lens of the magnifying glass. The lens then refracts the rays in such a way that the object looks bigger to you. Microscopes, telescopes, and cameras also use convex lenses.

Binoculars

▶ When does refraction occur?

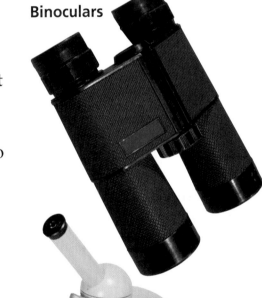

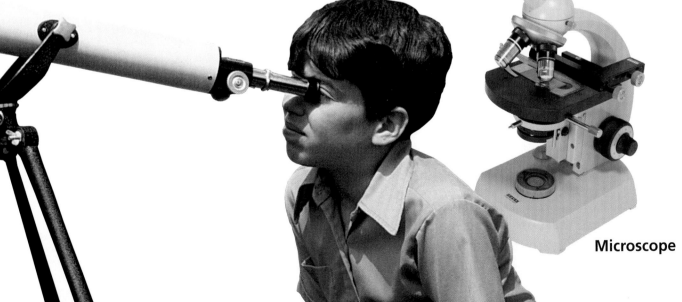

Microscope

How Do You See?

What happens to light when it reaches your eyes? First, it passes through a thin, clear tissue covering each eye called the *cornea* (KAWR·nee·uh). Then, light passes through an opening called the *pupil*. The pupil is the black spot in the center of each eye. After light passes through your pupils, it travels through your lenses. Each lens focuses light onto the back of your eye. A tissue called the *retina* (RET·uh·nuh) covers the back of your eyes.

Did you know that the images focused on your retinas are actually upside down? Your retinas change the images into signals that travel along your optic nerves to your brain. Your brain sees the picture right-side up.

Why do you see green grass, red apples, and purple grapes? The answer has to do with the way that matter reflects and absorbs light.

What if white light is shining on a green leaf? The leaf absorbs the entire visible spectrum of light energy except for light that has wavelengths for green light. These light waves are reflected off the leaf and into your eyes. The leaf appears green. The color of an object depends on the color of the visible spectrum it reflects.

This photo shows you how an image is formed upside down on the retina. After it travels to the brain, you see the image right side up.

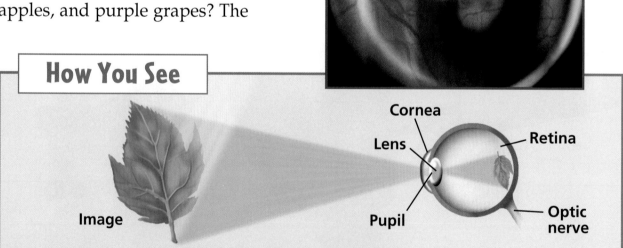

How You See

Image

Cornea

Lens

Retina

Pupil

Optic nerve

You see objects because light reflected by them enters your eyes. A lens in the front of each eye bends the light and makes an image. Nerves bring this image to your brain.

White and black are not true colors. White things appear white because they reflect all wavelengths of light. White objects do not absorb any light energy. They tend to be cooler when placed in sunlight because of this. Black objects do just the opposite. Things appear black because they absorb all the wavelengths of the visible spectrum. Black objects tend to be warmer when placed in sunlight.

When light strikes different objects, it can be blocked or it can pass through. Many materials block light rather than let it pass through. Such materials are described as *opaque*. Wood, metal, and people are opaque objects.

Some materials are *transparent*. They let light pass through. Glass and water are transparent. You can see through them.

Translucent materials reflect some light and let the rest pass through. Cloudy looking plastics are translucent.

▷ **Why do objects appear to be a certain color?**

FOR SCHOOL OR HOME

Absorbing Light

1. Predict Wrap a thermometer in black paper. Wrap a second thermometer in white paper. Put the two thermometers on a sunny windowsill or under a desk lamp. Predict which thermometer will heat up faster.

2. Measure Read and record each temperature after ten minutes.

3. Which thermometer warmed up faster?

4. Infer Why do you think this happened?

5. Hypothesize What do you think would happen if you tried different colors of paper? Test your hypothesis.

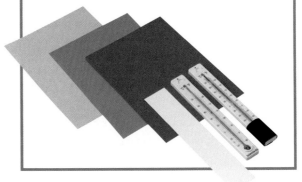

What New Technology Uses Light?

Have you ever seen a laser? Lasers read the bar codes at supermarket checkout counters. Lasers are used in many other ways, too.

Lasers are tubes of gas. They use electricity to produce thin beams that have one wavelength of light. All the rays of a laser travel in the same direction. This creates a very intense, high-energy beam. Lasers are so powerful that they can cut through steel! Doctors use lasers to do surgery because the beams are so narrow. Lasers are also used to make and interpret compact discs.

Another important technology that uses light is optical fibers. They are tubes made of glass or plastic.

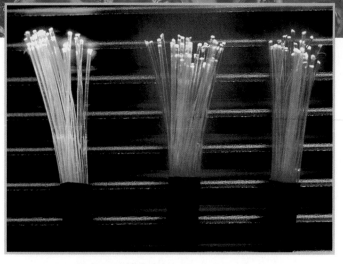

Today most long-distance phone calls are carried along optical fibers.

Optical fibers keep the light energy inside the entire length of their fiber. They are also called *light pipes* because they carry light from place to place.

Scientists have found ways to code information in light. Optical fibers can carry large amounts of coded information from place to place. This information includes voices, images, and other data. The information can travel at nearly the speed of light. That's the fastest anything can possibly go! This means that optical fibers can bring you e-mail, colorful websites, music, and more over the Internet. Optical fibers deliver the Internet fast! What other light-based technologies might be next?

READING **Compare and Contrast How are lasers and optical fibers alike? Different?**

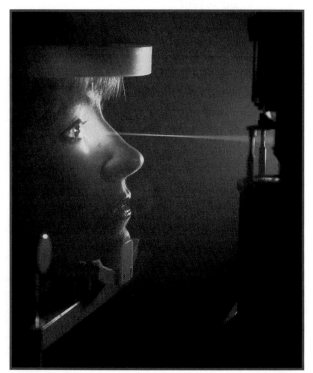

Lasers are used to do delicate surgery.

L·I·N·K·S

Why It Matters

Visible light, in all its colors, allows you to see. If you understand light's properties, you can explain shadows, color, refraction, and your reflection in a mirror. You can also understand the tools and technologies that use light.

Many new technologies that use light are still being developed. Visit **www.mhscience02.com** to do a research project on light technology.

Think and Write

1. Which has more energy—radio waves or X rays? Which waves have a longer wavelength?

2. How do we know that light travels in straight lines?

3. Why can you see your reflection when you look at a mirror and not at a book?

4. Does the light that passes through binoculars get refracted? Explain.

5. **Critical Thinking** Why does it feel cooler in the shadow of a big tree on a sunny day?

WRITING LINK

Write a paragraph. Traffic lights make transportation by foot, bicycle, and car safer. How is light used to make other forms of transportation safer?

SOCIAL STUDIES LINK

Do research. Who were the first people to use lenses? Who were the first people to use telescopes? How were telescopes invented? Use the Internet or an encyclopedia to learn more about lenses and how they have developed. Write a report to tell what you have learned.

HEALTH LINK

Make a chart. Some light rays can be dangerous. Too much sunlight, for example, can be harmful to your skin. Make a list of radiation sources. Tell ways you can protect yourself from too much radiation. Organize your safety tips in a chart.

MATH LINK

Solve a problem. If the incoming angle of light is 45 degrees, how big is the outgoing angle? How do you know?

TECHNOLOGY LINK

At the Computer Visit **www.mhscience02.com** for more links.

Sound

Vocabulary

vibration, F54

sound wave, F55

frequency, F58

pitch, F59

amplitude, F59

Get Ready

Have you ever sung in a chorus? Was there more than one part? What makes these parts different? Instruments can make different sounds, too. How can the sound of an instrument changed?

Process Skill

You use variables when you identify and separate things in an experiment that can be changed or controlled.

Explore Activity

Materials

milk carton

fishing line or string

scissors

How Do Vibrations Produce Sound?

Procedure

BE CAREFUL! Handle scissors carefully.

1. Cut off the top and one of the sides of the milk carton as shown in the picture. Make a hole in the bottom of the carton.

2. Thread the string through the hole. Tie a knot at one end to keep it from slipping through the hole.

3. **Observe** Hold the box at the end near the hole. Ask your partner to hold the free end of the string and pluck it. Record what you hear. What happens to the string?

4. **Experiment** How can you make different sounds?

Drawing Conclusions

1. **Communicate** How did you make sound?

2. **Communicate** How did you make different sounds?

3. **Going Further: Use Variables** Try changing the length of the string. What happens now?

Main Idea Sound is produced when energy causes particles to vibrate.

What Causes Sound?

When you pluck the string on a guitar, it moves quickly back and forth. This back-and-forth motion is called a **vibration** (vigh·BRAY·shuhn). Vibrations make the sounds you hear coming from a guitar.

Think about all the different sounds you hear. Some sounds are musical, like the notes from a guitar or flute. Other sounds are loud, like an air hammer, or quiet, like a whisper. All these sounds begin when something vibrates.

Energy is needed to start an object vibrating to make sound. You can clap, pluck, blow, hit, or move something in many ways to make vibrations.

An air hammer drills through the street. You can feel the vibrations in the sidewalk if you are standing nearby. As this photo shows, the vibrations cause the driller's body to move. Sound transfers energy.

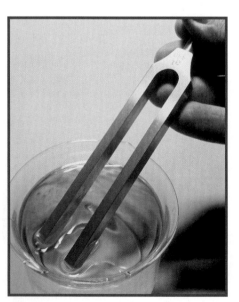

Have you ever seen a singer shatter glass? The voice carries energy. Energy makes the vocal cords inside the throat vibrate. You sing and talk by vibrating your vocal cords. The energy in booming thunder can shake your house! That is because the energy that starts something vibrating is carried by the sound produced. Sound carries energy.

A tuning fork produces vibrations when it is struck. You can see these vibrations as waves in the water.

Imagine you could see the vibrations from a guitar string moving toward your ear. The diagram below shows how they might appear.

As the string moves outward, it pushes against nearby air particles. This makes the particles bunch together. Then the string moves back. This creates an area with fewer air particles that are more spread out.

Like ripples in a pond, areas of bunched-up and spread-out air particles move away from the string. As the string vibrates, more of these areas are produced. An area of crowded particles followed by widely spaced particles is called a **sound wave** . Sound waves move in all directions away from a vibrating object. You hear something when the vibrations strike your ear.

▷ **What is a sound wave?**

The zone of crowded particles followed by widely spaced particles is a sound wave. A vibrating object makes many sound waves that move away from it in all directions. On a guitar it is the strings that vibrate.

How Does Sound Travel Through Different Materials?

Listen carefully as you tap your pencil on your desk. What do you hear? Now put your ear against your desk. Tap your pencil again. What do you hear now? Does sound travel through the wood or metal material of your desk?

Sound travels through air, of course. If it didn't, everyday sounds couldn't reach our ears! Sound travels through other substances, too. You observed this when you heard your pencil through your solid desk. When you're swimming underwater, can you hear sounds? Yes, sound travels in water, too. Sound travels through solids, liquids, and gases.

Sound does not travel at the same speed through all materials, however. Sound travels slowest in a gas. It travels faster in a liquid. It travels the fastest through a solid. Sound travels farther before dying out when it travels through a solid. It is also louder.

▷ **Which material does sound travel through the fastest?**

Speed of Sound in Different Substances

Substance	Speed (in meters/second)
Air	330
Water	1,500
Copper	3,550
Wood	4,000
Steel	5,000
Iron	5,000
Glass	5,500
Granite rock	6,000

Sound travels at different speeds in different substances.

Sound travels through gases, such as air. It also travels through liquids, such as water. The whale pup hears its mother calling.

How Do We Hear Sound?

When something vibrates, it creates sound waves. What happens to these sound waves when they reach your ears? How do they result in sound?

▷ **How do your ears help you hear sound?**

1 **Outer Ear** The outer ear collects sound waves. It acts like a funnel to direct sound waves into the ear.

2 **Eardrum** Sound waves make the eardrum vibrate like the head of a drum.

3 **Middle Ear** The vibrating eardrum makes three tiny bones in the middle ear vibrate. They are the hammer, anvil, and stirrup.

4 **Inner Ear** The little vibrating bones pass sound vibrations along to a tube that is filled with fluid in the inner ear. The fluid then vibrates. The vibrating fluid makes tiny hair cells vibrate, too.

5 **Nerve to Brain** The vibrations of the hair cells are passed along to a nerve that carries sound messages to the brain. The brain processes the messages, and you hear sound.

READING Diagrams

What is the function of the eardrum? The fluid in the ear?

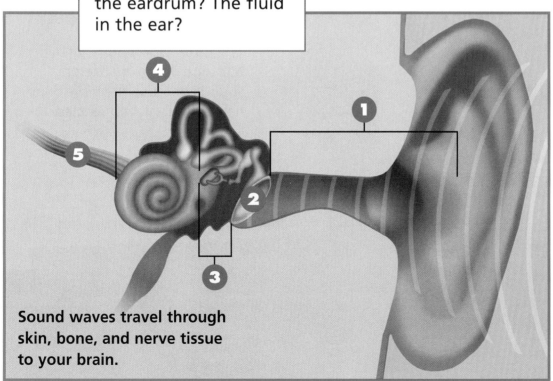

Sound waves travel through skin, bone, and nerve tissue to your brain.

Why Aren't All Sounds the Same?

Close your eyes and listen. What sounds do you hear around you? Do you hear the sharp chirp of a bird, the dull whir of a fan, voices of people you know? If all those sounds result from vibrations, why don't they sound the same?

Every sound wave has three features that make it special. First, a sound wave has a certain wavelength. One wavelength is the distance from one area of squeezed particles to the next area of squeezed particles.

Second, a sound wave has a **frequency** (FREE·kwuhn·see). Frequency is the number of times a sound source vibrates in one second. Tightening and loosening guitar strings changes their frequency.

The flute, vibraphone, and baritone produce different sounds because the vibrations have different frequencies.

Airplanes take off with a lot of energy. This energy results in high-amplitude sound waves.

Frequency determines **pitch** . Pitch is the highness or lowness of sound. A mosquito beats its wings 600 times each second! This rapid vibration makes high-frequency sound waves with a high pitch. A frog's vocal cords vibrate slowly. The frog's croaks make low-frequency sound waves with a low pitch.

The third feature of a sound wave is the amount of energy it carries. The energy in a sound wave is called **amplitude** (AM·pli·tewd). Sounds with high amplitude are made by objects that vibrate with a lot of energy.

Amplitude is related to the loudness of sound. As a rocket blasts off, high-amplitude sound waves fill the air. When you whisper, your vocal cords vibrate lightly to make sound waves of very low amplitude.

READING **Compare and Contrast**
How do sound waves differ from one another?

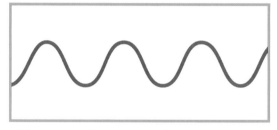

This wave has a low frequency. How would you describe its pitch?

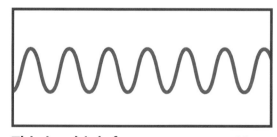

This is a high-frequency wave. How would its pitch compare with that of the wave above?

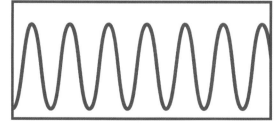

This wave has both high frequency and high amplitude. What might have produced this sound?

What Tools Help Us Hear Sound?

Do you use a hearing aid to help you hear? Hearing aids have a *receiver* to collect sound waves and an *amplifier* to give them more energy. Many hearing aids send the sound waves to the bony part of the skull, which then vibrates. These vibrations go to the auditory nerve and brain.

Your heart and lungs make sounds that help a doctor tell how healthy they are. To hear them, your doctor uses a *stethoscope.* The bell on the end gathers sound waves from your chest. The waves travel along the rubber tube into the doctor's ears. They are loud enough for the doctor to hear.

Do you have a CD player? Sound systems use *speakers* to change electrical energy into sound. A CD player makes electrical signals that are a code for a song or other sounds. The signals go to an amplifier, which increases their energy. Then they go to a speaker. The speaker has a thin, flexible sheet that vibrates when it receives the electrical signals. The vibrating sheet sends sound waves through the air to your ears, so you hear the music!

▷ **What tools in your home help you hear?**

The stethoscope is actually an old medical device, invented nearly 200 years ago!

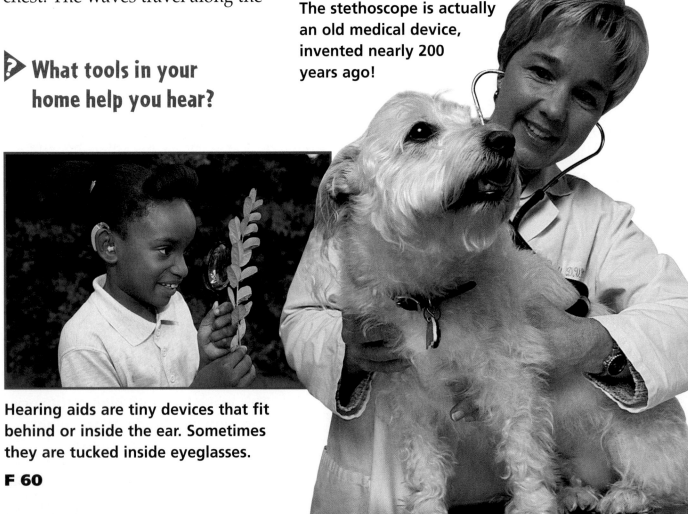

Hearing aids are tiny devices that fit behind or inside the ear. Sometimes they are tucked inside eyeglasses.

Why It Matters

Sound is everywhere. Along with sight, hearing is our most important sense. Sound is a means of communication. Sound brings us information and entertainment. You can use your knowledge of sound to play a musical instrument. Because hearing sound is so important, you should protect your ears from damage.

Think and Write

1. What is sound? What makes sound? How does sound travel?

2. Why do different musical instruments make different sounds?

3. Which sound waves have more amplitude—sound waves from exploding dynamite or sound waves made by a bird singing?

4. Legend says Native American buffalo hunters put their ear to the ground to listen for buffalo. How would this help them hunt?

5. **Critical Thinking** Why can't sound travel through space?

WRITING LINK

Write a paragraph. What is noise pollution? What are some sources of noise pollution? In which areas would you want little noise? In which areas would you expect a lot of noise?

HEALTH LINK

Do research. Too much noise can harm your ears. It is important to protect your ears from loud noises. How might you protect your ears? What are some places where you would need to protect your ears?

MUSIC LINK

Make an instrument. Construct a drum by stretching a rubber or canvas sheet across a coffee can or other round container. Use rubber bands to attach the rubber or canvas to the container. Experiment with your drum. How can you make a loud sound? A soft sound? What vibrates when a drum makes sound?

TECHNOLOGY LINK

At the Computer Visit **www.mhscience02.com** for more links.

Circling the Globe in a Hot-Air Balloon

Could a hot-air balloon be flown nonstop all the way around the world? In 1999, pilots Bertrand Piccard and Brian Jones did just that! The trip was not easy. They traveled 46,000 kilometers (29,000 miles) in almost three weeks. They flew about 7 kilometers (4 miles) above the surface of Earth.

Why did Piccard and Jones fly so high, where the air is very cold and thin? The reason is the jet stream. The jet stream is a band of high-speed winds high in the atmosphere. The winds can blow as fast as 500 kilometers (310 miles) per hour. Piccard and Jones needed the fast winds to blow their balloon along.

How does a hot-air balloon work? A burner under the balloon heats the air inside the balloon. The hot air is lighter than the cooler air around it. The hot air rises, and so does the balloon. When the burner is turned down, the air inside the balloon cools. This makes the balloon come down.

In 1784, this hot-air balloon flew over the English Channel.

Write ABOUT IT

1. Why did Piccard and Jones fly 7 kilometers above Earth's surface?
2. Would you like to fly in a hot-air balloon? Why or why not?

In 1999, Bertrand Piccard and Brian Jones flew around the world in this hot-air balloon.

AT THE COMPUTER

Visit www.mhscience02.com to learn more about hot-air balloons.

Chapter 12 Review

Vocabulary

Fill each blank with the best word from the list.

amplitude, F59   inertia, F11

conduction, F36   refraction, F46

convection, F36   spectrum, F42

effort force, F22   vibration, F54

energy, F14   work, F13

1. Sound is produced by the _____ of moving particles.

2. A range of light waves with different wavelengths and energies is called a(n) _____.

3. _____ is performed when a force is applied through a distance.

4. The amount of energy in a sound wave is described by its _____.

Two ways in which heat may be transferred are:

5. _____.

6. _____.

7. _____ is the ability to do work.

8. When light passes from one material to another, you may observe _____.

9. The force you use to move something is called _____.

10. _____ describes the tendency of an object to stay in motion or at rest until acted upon by a force.

Test Prep

11. Energy from the Sun reaches Earth by _____.

  A friction

  B convection

  c reflection

  D radiation

12. All of the following are examples of a simple machine EXCEPT _____.

  F screw

  G pulley

  H fulcrum

  J inclined plane

13. Sound waves may travel through _____.

  A solids

  B liquids

  c gases

  D all of the above

14. The distance an object travels in a given time describes its _____.

   F position

   G speed

   H frame of reference

   J energy

15. When matter is heated it tends to _____.

   A expand

   B contract

   C conduct

   D insulate

Concepts and Skills

16. Process Skills: Measure What two scales are used to measure temperature?

17. Reading in Science How do the waves in the electromagnetic spectrum differ?

18. Making Decisions Is it better to use fossil fuels, such as oil and gas, or alternative energy sources, such as geothermal and solar energy? Explain why.

19. Scientific Methods Explain how a lever can be used to make work easier.

20. Critical Thinking If you pushed a toy car across the floor and did not stop it or push it again, would it continue moving on its own? Why or why not?

Boost your test scores!

Be Smart! Visit www.mhscience02.com to learn more.

CHAPTER

LESSON 6

Static Electricity, F68

LESSON 7

Current Electricity, F76

LESSON 8

Electricity and
Magnets, F88

Electricity and Magnetism

Did You Ever Wonder?

What are the "windmills" you often see on
the side of a road? What are they used for?
These windmills are called wind turbines.
They can be used to capture the energy in
wind. What is this energy used for?

Static Electricity

Vocabulary

static electricity, F71

discharge, F72

conductor, F72

insulator, F72

Get Ready

Have you ever been "zapped"? You walk across a carpeted floor and then touch a doorknob. Zap!—you feel a shock. To understand what's going on, scientists study electricity. With a machine such as this, they make electrical charges. What they learn is often hair-raising!

Process Skill

You communicate when you share information.

Explore Activity

What Happens to Rubbed Balloons?

Materials

two 9-in.-round balloons, inflated

2 pieces of string, 50 cm each

tape

wool cloth

Procedure

1. Tie a piece of string to each inflated balloon. Hang the balloons from a table as shown here. Tape the loose end of the string to the table.

2. Observe any action of the balloons.

3. **Predict** What do you think will happen if you rub one balloon with a piece of wool cloth? Both balloons? Record your predictions.

4. **Experiment** Test your predictions.

5. **Predict** What do you think will happen if you hold the wool cloth between the balloons? Test your prediction.

6. **Predict** What do you think will happen if you put your hand between the two balloons? Test your prediction.

Drawing Conclusions

1. **Communicate** What happened when you rubbed one balloon with the wool cloth? Both balloons?

2. **Communicate** What happened when you put the wool cloth between the balloons? Your hand?

3. **Going Further: Experiment** Untie one balloon. Rub it with the wool. Try to stick it to the wall. What happens? Why?

Main Idea A buildup of electrical charge causes static electricity.

What Is Electrical Charge?

Electrical charge is not something you can see, smell, or weigh. We know about charge because we can see its effects on matter.

You know that all matter is made up of tiny particles, called atoms. Inside atoms are even tinier particles. Some have a negative electrical charge. Others have a positive electrical charge. A negative electrical charge is shown as a minus sign (–). A positive electrical charge is shown as a plus sign (+).

Electrical Charge

Some particles have a negative electrical charge. Others have a positive electrical charge.

Opposite charges attract each other. Like charges repel each other.

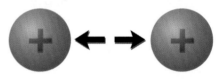

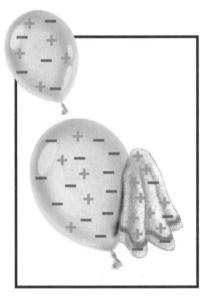

A balloon has no overall charge. There are as many negative charges as there are positive charges. Rubbing the balloon knocks negative charges off the cloth and onto the balloon, making it negative.

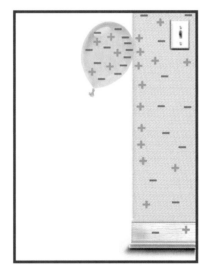

The balloon's negative charges repel negative charges in the wall. This leaves a row of positive charges on the outside edge of the wall. The negatively charged balloon is attracted to the wall's positive charges and sticks to it.

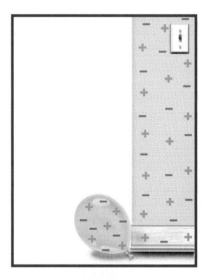

After a while the negative charges on the balloon "leak" away. The balloon is no longer attracted to the wall. It falls away.

Atoms usually have no overall charge. This is because the number of positive charges equals the number of negative charges. However, atoms can become charged. They can pick up electrical charges from other atoms. This can happen when you rub two different materials together—such as balloons and wool.

Rubbing two different materials together knocks negative charges off one material. This makes the material positive. The negative charges collect on the other material, making it negative.

The two materials are now attracted to each other because they have opposite charges. Opposite charges attract. Positives attract negatives. Negatives attract positives. Charges that are similar repel, or push each other away. Two positive charges repel each other. Two negative charges do, too.

The buildup of electrical charge on a material is called static electricity. The electrical charges build up because negative charges have moved from one material to another.

▷ **What are the two types of electrical charges in atoms?**

QUICK LAB

FOR SCHOOL OR HOME

Making Static Electricity

1. Comb your hair several times with a plastic comb. Bring the comb near your hair without touching it. Move it around.

2. **Experiment** Comb your hair again. Place the comb near a faucet with running water.

3. **Communicate** Explain your observations in steps 1 and 2.

4. Rub an inflated balloon against your hair. Place the balloon against a wall. What happens? Why?

Insulators	Conductors
Wood	Metal
Air	Water
Rubber	

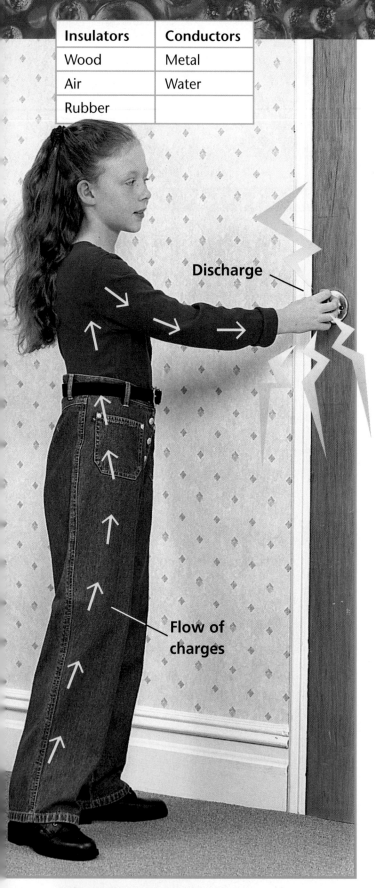

Discharge

Flow of charges

Not all materials are good conductors. Metals allow electricity to flow through them, but wood and rubber do not.

What Is an Electrical Discharge?

You learned that static electricity is the buildup of electrical charges on a material. Do the charges stay there, or do they move onto another material? Your experience may help you answer this question. When you walk on a rug, static electricity builds up on your shoes. The charge keeps building until you touch something. Then—zap! It suddenly moves onto the object. This movement of charge is called a **discharge** (DIS·charj). You might feel this discharge as a small shock.

Static electricity doesn't discharge into all types of materials because electricity flows only where it can. It flows easily through materials called **conductors** (kuhn·DUK·tuhrz). An **insulator** (IN·suh·lay·tuhr) is a material through which electricity does not flow.

What types of materials do you think are good conductors? Metals are very good conductors. That is why you might feel a shock when you touch a doorknob. The static electricity on your shoes travels through your body, to your hand, and then into the doorknob.

▷ **What types of materials can electricity easily discharge into?**

How Does Lightning Form?

How big can a static electricity buildup get? It can form a lightning bolt! *Lightning* is a discharge of static electricity from a huge cloud called a thundercloud. It is no different from the shock you get from touching a doorknob—just bigger. A single lightning bolt has enough power to light 100 million light bulbs!

▸ **What is lightning?**

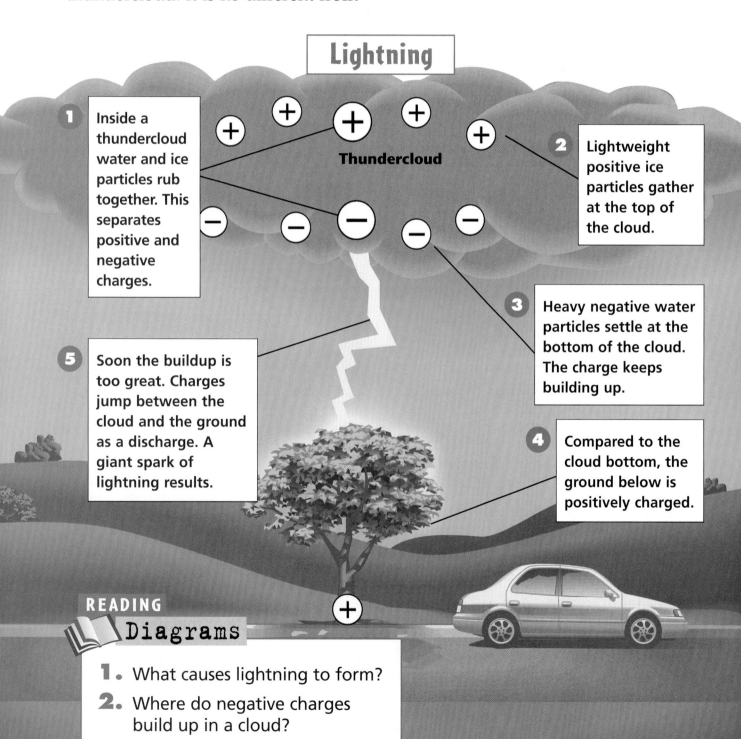

Lightning

Thundercloud

1. Inside a thundercloud water and ice particles rub together. This separates positive and negative charges.

2. Lightweight positive ice particles gather at the top of the cloud.

3. Heavy negative water particles settle at the bottom of the cloud. The charge keeps building up.

4. Compared to the cloud bottom, the ground below is positively charged.

5. Soon the buildup is too great. Charges jump between the cloud and the ground as a discharge. A giant spark of lightning results.

READING
Diagrams

1. What causes lightning to form?
2. Where do negative charges build up in a cloud?

How Do You Keep Safe from Lightning?

Lightning gives off energy in several forms—light, heat, and sound. You hear the sound as thunder. Some electrical energy can also travel through an object that has been struck. This energy moves into the ground, or is grounded.

Lightning takes the clearest, shortest path to the ground. Lightning also targets the best conductor.

That is why people often use lightning rods. A lightning rod safely discharges lightning into the ground. It is usually placed at the very top of a building. A wire connects the lightning rod to the ground. When lightning strikes the rod, the electrical energy flows through the wire and into the ground.

Lightning can be very dangerous. To be safe, you should follow these simple rules if you hear thunder or see lightning.

1. Stay away from high places, such as hilltops.
2. Stay away from trees and other tall objects.
3. Crouch down if you feel your hair stand on end.
4. Get out of the water.
5. Don't use the telephone.

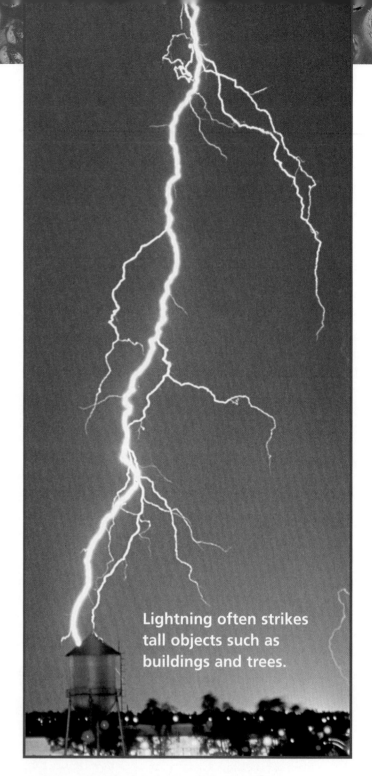

Lightning often strikes tall objects such as buildings and trees.

6. If you are in a car, stay inside. Close the windows and doors.
7. Don't touch electrical devices or anything made of metals.

READING **Cause and Effect**
Why can a lightning rod protect you from lightning?

Why It Matters

About 2,600 years ago, the ancient Greeks noticed the effects of static electricity when they rubbed fur on amber, which is hardened tree sap. They named the force they felt elektron, their word for amber. Today our understanding of static electricity explains what causes shocks and lightning.

Think and Write

1. Why does a rubbed balloon stick to the wall?

2. What is an insulator? A conductor?

3. How is lightning formed? What can you do to keep safe from lightning?

4. Balloon A was rubbed with a wool cloth, balloon B with plastic wrap. The balloons attracted each other. Was balloon B positive or negative? Explain.

5. Critical Thinking Would a wooden lightning rod work? Why or why not?

L·I·N·K·S

SOCIAL STUDIES LINK

Do research. The ancient Greeks were the first people to investigate static electricity. Learn more about their culture by doing research. Use the Internet or an encyclopedia.

ART LINK

Make an advertisement. Draw a picture of an outdoor scene—a city or a beach perhaps. Use your picture to advertise safety tips for a lightning storm.

TECHNOLOGY LINK

 Science Newsroom CD-ROM Choose *In a Flash* to learn more about lightning and electrical discharge.

 At the Computer Visit **www.mhscience02.com** for more links.

Current Electricity

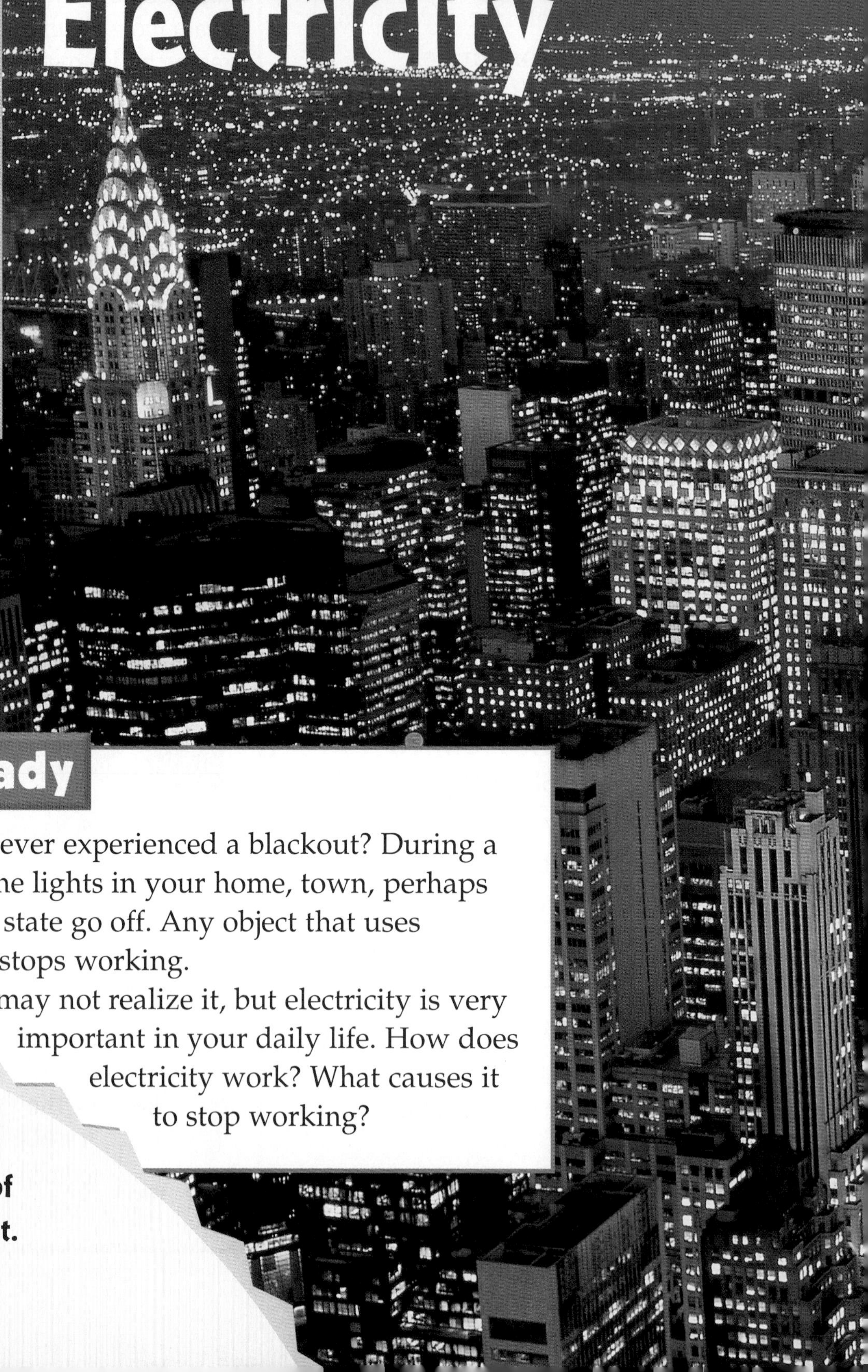

Vocabulary

circuit, F78

current electricity, F78

series circuit, F82

parallel circuit, F82

fuse, F84

circuit breaker, F84

Get Ready

Have you ever experienced a blackout? During a blackout the lights in your home, town, perhaps even your state go off. Any object that uses electricity stops working.

You may not realize it, but electricity is very important in your daily life. How does electricity work? What causes it to stop working?

Process Skill

You predict when you state possible results of an event or experiment.

Explore Activity

What Makes a Bulb Light?

Materials

flashlight bulb

20 cm of wire with stripped ends

2 D-cells

cell holder

Procedure

1. **Experiment** Work with your group to try to light the bulb using the materials. Draw each setup. Record your results.

2. **Predict** Study the drawings on this page. Predict in which setups the bulb will light and in which it will not light. Record your predictions.

3. **Experiment** Work with another group of students to test each setup. Can you see a pattern?

Drawing Conclusions

1. **Observe** How many ways could you arrange the materials to make the bulb light in step 1?

2. How were the ways to light the bulb using only one wire similar?

3. How were the ways that did not light the bulb using only one wire similar?

4. In which drawings did the bulb light? How are the setups similar?

5. **Going Further: Predict** Draw another setup. Challenge a classmate to determine if the bulb will light.

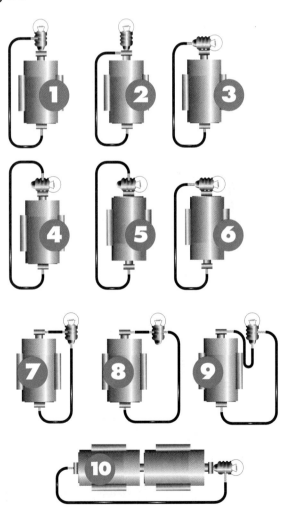

Main Idea Electricity needs a complete path along which to travel.

How Does Electricity Flow?

In order for electricity to flow, it must follow a complete path. The path that electricity can move through is called a **circuit** (SUR·kit). A circuit is made up of parts that work together to allow electricity to flow.

The electricity that flows through a circuit is called **current electricity**.

Current electricity is moving electrical charge. Current electricity is different from static electricity. Static electricity is a buildup of electrical charge. Static electricity does not flow.

Current electricity will flow through a *closed circuit*. In a closed circuit, there are no gaps or breaks in the path. The path is complete. An incomplete path is called an *open circuit*. No current will flow through an open circuit. There are gaps or breaks in an open circuit.

This circuit consists of a source of electrical current, a wire through which the current flows, a switch to control the flow of current, and an object to be lighted. This circuit is closed because there are no gaps in the path.

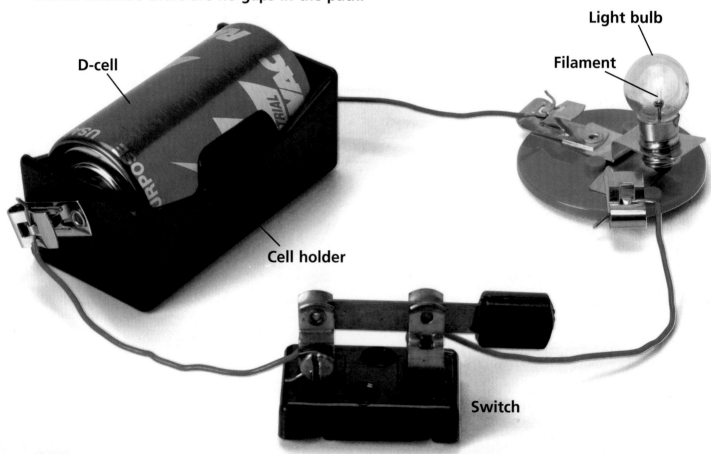

Light bulb

Filament

D-cell

Cell holder

Switch

The current that flows through a circuit can be turned on or off. A device known as a *switch* (SWICH) controls the current in a circuit. When the switch is in the closed position, the circuit is closed. The path is complete, and current flows. When the switch is in the open position, the circuit is open. The path is incomplete, and no current flows.

How much current is flowing in a circuit can be measured in units called *amperes* (AM·peerz). The ampere is named after the French physicist André Ampère, who lived from 1775 to 1836. Amperes are measured with an instrument called an *ammeter*.

▶ **What is a circuit?**

This model train is like current electricity. The complete track is like a complete circuit. This real train runs on electricity. Electrical energy is an important form of energy.

QUICK LAB

FOR SCHOOL OR HOME

Conductor Test-Off

1. **Experiment** Make a circuit as shown, using a test object. Record your observations.

2. Test other objects. Record your observations.

3. **Observe** Which objects were good conductors? Which were not? How could you tell?

4. **Infer** Examine a length of wire. Which part of the wire is a conductor? Which part is an insulator? Why do you think the wire is made this way?

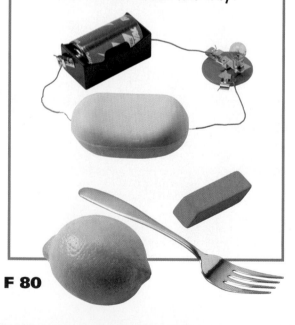

What Affects the Flow of Electricity?

As you know, some materials are good conductors. Electricity flows best through conductors. The base and the wires of a light bulb are good conductors. The filament in a light bulb, however, is a poor conductor. It is a *resistor*. Current does not flow easily through resistors. Resistors allow electrical energy to be changed into other forms of energy. A light bulb produces light and heat due to resistance in the filament.

Current always flows through the path that offers the least resistance. Sometimes this path is a side circuit of very low resistance that occurs by accident. This is called a *short circuit*. A short circuit is dangerous. When too much current is flowing, the wires can heat up. Hot wires can cause a fire.

In your home a short circuit can also occur if frayed or broken wires touch. This may heat wires as well.

READING **Cause and Effect**
What can happen when too much electricity flows through a circuit?

Where Does Current Come From?

One way to make current is to use a cell. A cell changes chemical energy into electrical energy. A battery is made up of several connected cells.

One type of cell is a *dry cell*. In the center of a dry cell is a carbon rod. Around the rod is a moist chemical paste. Around the paste is a zinc container. Never open a cell. The paste is harmful.

Wires can be attached to the two *terminals* (TUR·muh·nuhls) on the outside of the cell. The positive terminal is attached to the carbon rod. The negative terminal is attached to the zinc container.

A chemical change in the cell makes the container more negatively charged. The carbon rod becomes more positively charged. Current flows when a conductor is attached between the cell's positive and negative terminals. The negative charges travel from the negative terminal to the positive terminal through the conductor.

Another type of cell is called a *wet cell*. In its simplest form, a wet cell contains two different metal bars placed in a liquid. The liquid contains certain chemicals and is an acid. A car battery is made up of many connected wet cells. The negative and positive terminals of a wet cell are called *electrodes* (i·LEK·trohdz). The positive electrode in some wet cells is made of copper. The acid strips away negative charges from the copper, leaving it positive.

The negative charges that leave the copper bar move to the negative electrode. It is often made of zinc. The zinc bar gets a negative charge. If a wire is connected between the electrodes, a current will flow.

▷ How do dry cells and wet cells produce current?

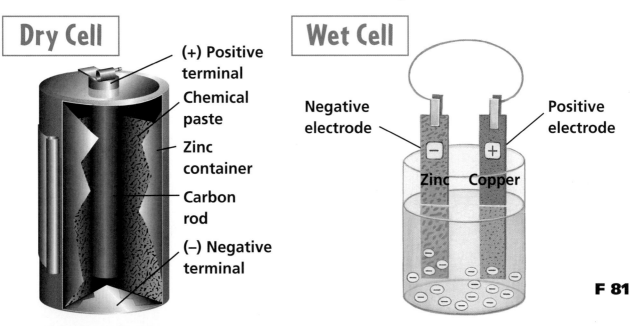

Dry Cell

(+) Positive terminal
Chemical paste
Zinc container
Carbon rod
(–) Negative terminal

Wet Cell

Negative electrode
Positive electrode
Zinc   Copper

What Kinds of Circuits Are There?

Many circuits have two or more objects in the circuit. How can these paths be set up?

One type of circuit has the two objects connected in a single path. This arrangement is called a **series circuit**. In a series circuit, electricity can flow in only one way.

The arrows in the diagram below show how the current flows.

When both bulbs are in place in a series circuit, it is a closed circuit. When one bulb is removed, an open circuit is created. In an open circuit, current can't complete its path. The remaining bulb does not light without current flowing through it. A series circuit does not work when a part is removed.

Another type of circuit has the two objects connected in a **parallel circuit**. A parallel circuit connects each object to the cell

Kinds of Circuits

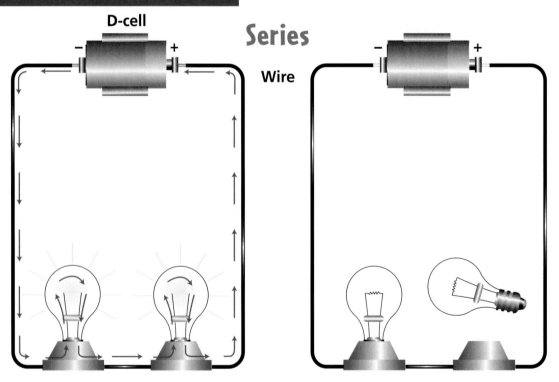

D-cell

Series

Wire

	Series	Parallel
Connection	Both bulbs are on the same circuit.	Each bulb is on a separate circuit.
Removing one bulb	Both bulbs go off.	Only the removed bulb goes off.
Brightness	Dim	Bright

separately. There are two paths through which current can flow.

When one bulb is removed from a parallel circuit, the other bulb is still a part of a complete circuit. That is why it remains lit. A parallel circuit still works when a part is removed because there is still a complete circuit.

The chart on page F82 compares series and parallel circuits that contain two bulbs.

Electrical devices in homes and other places are connected in parallel circuits. If they were series circuits, all the lights and appliances would come on every time you turned on the switch. Likewise, everything would turn off if one bulb burned out. Circuits in homes and other places are controlled by switches.

▷ **What are two ways that a circuit can be arranged?**

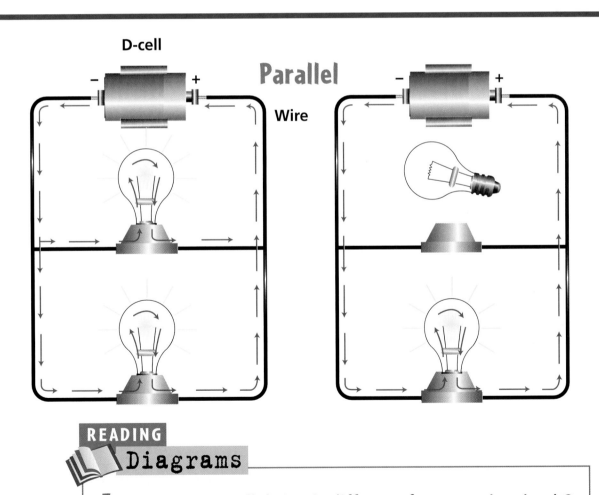

Parallel

D-cell

Wire

READING
Diagrams

1. How is a parallel circuit different from a series circuit?

2. How are the circuits similar?

How Can Circuits in Homes Be Protected?

As you have learned, a short circuit is dangerous. Too much current flowing in a short circuit can cause wires to heat up. Hot wires can start a fire. Too much current can also damage electrical devices.

Fuses keep too much electrical current from flowing through wires. They do this by melting and creating an open circuit.

One device that keeps too much electrical current from flowing through wires is called a **fuse** (FYEWZ). A fuse has a thin strip of metal in it. The strip is a resistor, like the filament in a light bulb. If a dangerously high current flows through the fuse, the metal strip heats up. At a certain temperature, it melts. This creates an open circuit. The current stops flowing. Once a fuse melts, it cannot be reused. It must be replaced with a new fuse.

Most new homes do not have fuses. They are built with **circuit breakers**. A circuit breaker is a switch that protects circuits. When a dangerously high current flows through the switch, the metal becomes heated. The overheated metal in the switch expands. This pushes the switch open. A spring holds the switch open, creating an open circuit.

If some electrical devices stop working, an adult should check the circuit breakers. One or more of the switches will be in the *off* position if there was a short circuit. The switch needs to be pushed back to the *on* position. This should be done only after the problem is fixed, or another short circuit will occur.

▷ **How does a fuse work to protect circuits in homes?**

Fuses in a fuse box

Switches in a circuit breaker

Why It Matters

Electricity has become an important part of our lives. As a matter of fact, almost every part of our lives depends on electricity. We use it to communicate. Electricity powers machines large and small. We use it to keep our food cold and our homes warm.

Think and Write

1. How does a dry cell work to provide electricity?

2. What are two ways that a circuit can be connected using two light bulbs and one cell?

3. How is an open circuit different from a short circuit?

4. Why does a radio go off when you unplug it? Explain in terms of closed and open circuits.

5. **Critical Thinking** Should a fuse be in a series or a parallel circuit with the main power coming into a house? Explain.

L·I·N·K·S

WRITING LINK

Write a story. What was used to heat and light homes, run trains, and run factories before electricity was discovered? Imagine living in a time before electricity. Use the Internet or an encyclopedia to do research. Then write a fictional story about your life before electricity.

SOCIAL STUDIES LINK

Do research. Who invented the battery? In what year was it invented? Use the Internet or an encyclopedia for your research.

LITERATURE LINK

Read *The Future Is Now* to learn about the uses of electricity and computers. Try the activities at the end of the book.

THE FUTURE IS NOW

by Susan Meyers

TECHNOLOGY LINK

Science Newsroom CD-ROM Choose *Are You Positive?* to learn more about electricity and electrical charge.

At the Computer Visit **www.mhscience02.com** for more links.

Critical Circuits

Any electrical tool must have a complete circuit or current can't flow to make the tool work! Most circuits, like those in flashlights and video games, can fit into the palm of your hand.

Other circuits are gigantic! Electric power plants are linked in a giant circuit called a grid. Power demands from one plant can interrupt the whole circuit. On November 9, 1965,

one switch failed at a power station in Ontario, Canada. The power overload spread throughout eastern North America, causing a blackout for hours over the entire region!

Other circuits are tiny. The heart of a computer is a small silicon chip. It's

Enlarged picture
of a chip

about the size of a fingernail but may contain hundreds of thousands of tiny regions. Together they do the computer's "thinking." Each region must be connected to the others by a tiny circuit that's on the chip.

There can be millions of circuits on a single computer chip. That's why the computer-chip circuits are so tiny. If they were made of regular electrical parts with wires and switches, they'd cover a large area.

It's important to fit as many circuits as possible on a computer chip. Why? The farther apart they are, the farther the electrical signal has to travel and the slower the computer! The more circuits, the faster and more powerful the computer.

Creating the tiny circuits on computer chips is a difficult process. Workers wear protective suits to prevent dust and dirt from getting into the circuits.

This worker is assembling circuits on a computer chip.

Write ABOUT IT

1. What is the advantage of making smaller and smaller circuits for computer chips?
2. How small or large do you think circuits can get? Why?

AT THE COMPUTER Visit www.mhscience02.com to learn more about circuits.

Electricity and Magnetism

Vocabulary

pole, F90

magnetic field, F91

electromagnet, F92

electric motor, F93

generator, F94

Get Ready

Have you ever gone walking in the woods? How did you know which way to go? Perhaps you followed a marked trail. Did you use a compass?

A compass needle always points north. That is how it helps you find your way. Which way does a hanging bar magnet point? Are a magnet and a compass related in some way?

Process Skill

You infer when you form an idea from facts or observations.

Explore Activity

How Is a Bar Magnet Like a Compass?

Materials

2 bar magnets

1 m of string

compass

ruler

tape

heavy book

Procedure

1. **Observe** How do the bar magnets interact when you place them next to each other in different positions?

2. **Predict** Which way will the bar magnet point if you hang it as shown? Record your prediction.

3. **Observe** Test your prediction. Record the result.

4. Place the compass on a flat surface away from the magnets. Compare the directions in which the compass and magnet point.

5. **Observe** Hold the compass near the hanging magnet. What happens?

Drawing Conclusions

1. **Communicate** How do the two magnets interact with each other?

2. How did your hanging magnet compare with other students' magnets?

3. **Communicate** What happened when you brought the compass near the hanging magnet?

4. **Going Further: Infer** Of what must a compass be made?

Main Idea **Electricity and magnetism can be used together in many ways.**

North pole

South pole

A magnet has two poles—a north pole and a south pole.

What Is a Magnet?

About 2,000 years ago, people from an area called Magnesia (mag·NEE·shuh) found rocks that would attract small pieces of iron. The rocks are called magnetite (MAG·ni·tight). They contain magnetized iron.

A magnet is a material or device that attracts items containing the elements iron, nickel, or cobalt (KOH·bawlt).

Magnets have some important properties. Every magnet has two ends, or **poles**. One pole is the "north-seeking magnetic pole," or "north pole" for short. The opposite end is the "south-seeking magnetic pole," or "south pole" for short. The pull of a magnet is strongest at its poles.

Unlike poles of magnets attract. Like poles repel. A south pole and a north pole attract each other. Two south poles repel, or push away, each other. Two north poles do, too. The hanging bar magnets shown below illustrate this idea.

When free to move, magnets will line up in a north-south direction. Thus a hanging magnet acts as a compass.

A compass is a magnet. The needle of a compass is a small magnet. It is attached to the base by a small pin. The pin does not move but allows the needle to turn toward Earth's North Pole.

What makes a hanging magnet line up in a north-south direction?

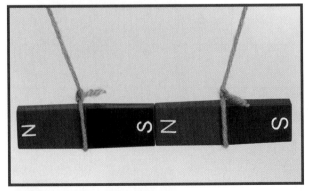

Unlike poles attract.

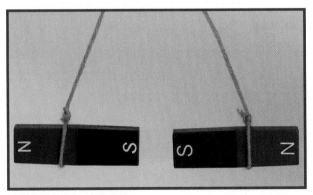

Like poles repel.

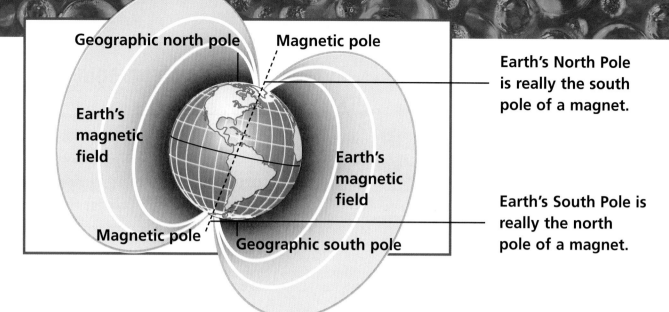

Geographic north pole

Magnetic pole

Earth's North Pole is really the south pole of a magnet.

Earth's magnetic field

Earth's magnetic field

Earth's South Pole is really the north pole of a magnet.

Magnetic pole

Geographic south pole

The answer may surprise you. Earth itself is a magnet.

Imagine a huge bar magnet running through Earth from the North Pole to the South Pole. This magnet would create a region of magnetic force called a **magnetic field**. What we call Earth's North Pole is actually the south pole of a magnet. What we call Earth's South Pole is actually the north pole of a magnet.

Because opposites attract, the north pole of a magnet or a compass lines up with Earth's North Pole. Likewise, the south pole of a magnet or a compass lines up with Earth's South

Pole. A magnet or a compass needle lines up with Earth's magnetic field.

What gives a magnet its properties? A piece of magnetized iron, like all matter, is made up of particles. Each particle of iron has its own magnetic field. When the particles are all lined up in the same direction, their magnetic fields act together. This makes the piece of iron have a strong magnetic field. The piece of iron is now magnetized. Magnetized iron can make the particles of another material line up in one direction. That material gets magnetized.

When the particles of a material line up pole to pole, the material is magnetic.

READING **Cause and Effect** **What causes a metal to be magnetic?**

N   S

Magnetized

Unmagnetized

QUICK LAB

FOR SCHOOL OR HOME

Electromagnets

1. **Wind a wire 20 times around a nail near its head. Attach each end of the wire to a D-cell.**

2. **Predict** Predict how many paper clips your electromagnet can hold. Test your prediction.

3. **Experiment** Repeat using two D-cells in series. Record how many paper clips the nail held.

4. **Experiment** Wind the wire 20 more times. Repeat steps 2-3.

5. **Interpret Data** How did increasing current affect the strength of the electromagnet? Increasing the number of coils?

What Is an Electromagnet?

Magnets can also be created using electric current. Current running in a wire creates a weak magnetic field. When current flows, a magnetic field forms around the wire. When the current is turned off, the magnetic field goes away.

A stronger magnetic field can be made by winding the wire in loops around an iron bar. When current flows, this creates a temporary magnet called an **electromagnet** (i·lek·troh·MAG·nit).

Electromagnets can be powerful. They can attract all items made of iron, steel, nickel, and cobalt in a junkyard. Doctors use electromagnets to take iron splinters out of a patient's skin. Recyclers use them to separate scrap metals. Electromagnets are also used in machines such as tape players, bells, motors, buzzers, loudspeakers, and televisions.

▷ **How are magnets related to current?**

How Can You Put Electromagnets to Work?

Have you ever used an **electric motor**? Electric motors work on the idea that electricity produces magnetism. Electric motors are clean and quiet power sources. They transform electrical energy into movement, or mechanical energy. This energy can power video recorders, some appliances, and other devices.

One of the first electric motors was built in 1829 by an American scientist, Joseph Henry. In his electric motor, electromagnets made a beam that was balanced on a pivot move up and down.

Some toys, such as this robot dog, are powered by electric motors.

A simple electric motor

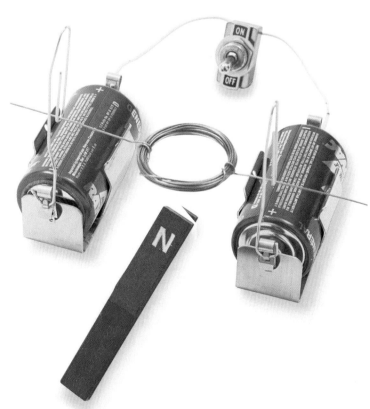

How does an electric motor work? Here you see a simple electric motor made of D-cells, paper clips, a coil of wire, and a bar magnet. You learned that magnetic fields can interact with each other. You also learned that current passing through a conductor creates a magnetic field.

When the switch of an electric motor is closed, current passes through the coiled wire. This creates an electromagnet. When the bar magnet is brought near it, their magnetic fields interact. As the two magnets attract and repel each other, they make the coil spin.

▷ **How are electromagnets used in motors?**

How Is Electricity Made?

What if you make a coil of wire and attach it to a compass? Then you insert a bar magnet into the coil. The compass needle will move in one direction. When you pull the magnet out, the needle will move in the other direction. You have produced an electrical current. You can also create current by holding the magnet steady and moving the coil.

The current created using the bar magnet is like the current that flows in your home. This two-way current is called *alternating current*, or AC for short. The current first flows in one direction. Then it flows in the opposite direction. This happens

many times every second. It is so quick that lights don't flicker.

Alternating current is produced by a device called a **generator** (JEN·uh·ray·tuhr). A generator changes mechanical energy into electrical energy. How does this compare with a motor?

Alternating current is different from the current produced by dry cells. That current is called *direct current*. It flows in only one direction.

How Generators Work

Outside power

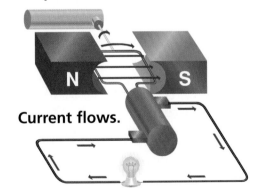

An outside force spins the coil between the poles of a powerful magnet. Current flows as one side of the coil passes up through the magnetic field.

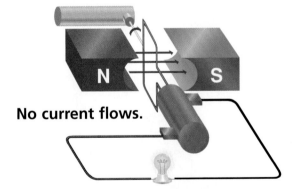

When no part of the coil is actually passing through the magnetic field, no current flows.

The wind turbines provide the power to generate electricity.

For a generator to work, an outside force must spin the coil. The coil is turned by a *turbine* (TUR·bin). A turbine must also be powered by an outside force.

Most turbines are turned by steam. The steam comes from heating water by burning fossil fuels such as coal, oil, and natural gas. The rising steam is caught by the blades of the turbine, making it turn.

In certain places wind is the power that turns turbines. Wind turbines work best in areas that have strong and steady winds.

Another source of power is moving water. Many power plants are found near rivers. A dam controls the flow of water. When the water is released, its kinetic energy turns the turbine.

▷ **What is a generator?**

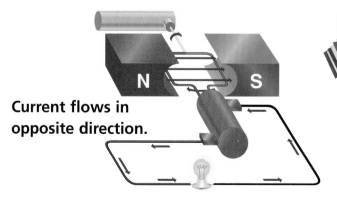

Current flows in opposite direction.

As the coil continues to spin, the side now passes down through the field. Current once again flows, but in the opposite direction.

READING
Diagrams

How is current produced in a generator?

Power plant

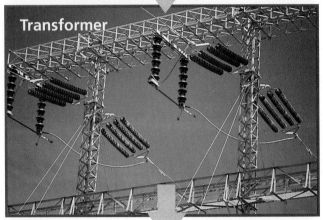

Transformer

Transmission wires

Home use

How Does Current Get to Your Home?

The alternating current that enters your home comes from power plants that have huge generators. The generators are run by energy from wind, water, fossil fuels, or nuclear power.

The current produced by a power plant travels to a transformer, which increases the voltage. This is done because high-voltage current is best for traveling long distances. It loses less energy along the way. *Voltage* is a measure of the force with which negative charges flow. The unit of voltage is the *volt*.

Current with high voltage cannot be used in your home. It is dangerous. That is why it travels on wires often placed high above the ground. After it travels to a specific place where it is needed, it reaches another transformer. This transformer decreases the voltage. Then an even smaller transformer decreases the voltage again. The current finally enters your home.

▶ **What are the steps by which current travels from a power plant to your home?**

Reading an Electric Meter

An electric meter measures the amount of electrical power used, in units called kilowatt-hours.

Procedure

1 **Observe** Observe the dials. There are 10 numbers on each. They appear clockwise from 0 to 9. An arrow points to a number on each dial. Read the number on each dial.

2 **Record** Draw a place-value chart. Record the number on the first dial to the right in the "ones" space.

3 **Record** Repeat step 2 for each dial, correctly filling in the place-value chart.

4 **Record** Repeat steps 2 and 3 for the second set of dials.

Drawing Conclusions

1 How many kilowatt-hours were used as of June 1? June 3?

2 **Use Numbers** How many kilowatt-hours were used between June 1 and June 3?

3 **Infer** Why are the meter readings different every day?

4 **Predict** At what time of the year would you use the most electrical power where you live? Why?

Two readings from an electric meter as shown:

June 1

June 3

How Can You Use Electricity Safely?

Plug in a toaster. Turn on the television. Turn on a light. You use electrical energy every day.

Electric devices can be dangerous if they are not used properly. Knowing a few safety rules is important. They can help you make sure electricity doesn't pose a danger to you.

▷ **Why is it important to use electricity safely?**

Safety Rule		Reason
• Never touch a wall socket with anything but a plug.		Current could flow from the socket to the item to you.
• Never touch the metal part of a plug when you plug it in.		Your finger could create a short-circuit path for the current.
• Never use a cord that is torn or has a hole in it.		You could create a short circuit.
• Don't pull the cord to remove a plug.		You could damage the plug or create a hole in the cord.
• Don't overload a plug or extension cord with too many devices.		Overloaded plugs draw too much current. They could get hot and cause a fire.
• Stay away from high-voltage cables and train rails.	WARNING HIGH VOLTAGE	You could accidentally touch them and be electrocuted.
• Never use electric devices when you are wet or standing in water.		You are a better conductor when wet. You could get a shock or be electrocuted.

L·I·N·K·S

Why It Matters

Knowing how to make and use electricity safely is important. We depend on electricity every day to help us perform a variety of tasks. Huge generators produce current that travels across the continent.

Generators can get their power in many ways. Wind, water, and the Sun can power generators.

Visit **www.mhscience02.com** to learn more about power sources.

Think and Write

1. How are a magnet and a compass alike?

2. What is an electrical motor? What does it do?

3. Use a model to explain how a generator produces alternating current.

4. Use Numbers How is electrical power use measured?

5. Critical Thinking A friend is about to plug a fourth appliance into an extension cord. What would you tell her?

SOCIAL STUDIES LINK

Do research. Lewis Latimer made an important contribution to the development of electricity and circuits. What did he discover? Use the Internet or an encyclopedia for your research.

LITERATURE LINK

Read *Magnets Everywhere!* to learn about the many uses of magnets. Try the activities at the end of the book.

ART LINK

Make a collage. Cut pictures of energy sources from magazines. Organize your pictures and paste them onto a poster.

TECHNOLOGY LINK

At the Computer Visit **www.mhscience02.com** for more links.

Chapter 13 Review

Vocabulary

Fill each blank with the best word or words from the list.

conductor, F72

current electricity, F78

electromagnet, F92

fuse, F84

generator, F94

insulator, F72

magnetic field, F91

parallel circuit, F82

series circuit, F82

static electricity, F71

1. Winding a wire in loops around an iron bar creates a(n) _____.

2. A(n) _____ has more than one device in the same circuit.

3. A buildup of electric charge that causes lightning is called _____.

4. A device that creates alternating current is called a(n) _____.

5. _____ is a moving electrical charge.

6. A(n) _____ is a material that does not allow electricity to flow through it easily.

7. When two light bulbs are connected to a cell through separate paths, the circuit is a(n) _____.

8. Copper is an example of a good _____.

9. A(n) _____ helps to keep too much current from flowing through a circuit.

10. A region of magnetic force is called a(n) _____.

Test Prep

11. Electrical charge builds up when _____.

    A negative charges move from one object to another

    B positive charges move from one object to another

    C lightning is discharged

    D too much current flows through a wire

12. A circuit is a closed circuit when _____.

    F it contains a switch

    G there is a gap in its path

    H there are no gaps in its path

    J it has two or more batteries

13. The two ends of a magnet are called _____.

    A charges

    B poles

    C magnetic fields

    D none of the above

14. Electric motors transform electrical energy into _____.

    F chemical energy

    G nuclear energy

    H magnetic energy

    J mechanical energy

15. Electricity in most homes flows through _____.

    A series circuits

    B parallel circuits

    C open circuits

    D fuses

Concepts and Skills

16. **Reading in Science** What happens when opposite poles of a magnet are brought together? When the same poles are brought together? What causes this to happen?

17. **Product Ads** A company makes a lightning rod out of plastic. It is advertised as being lighter and cheaper than a metal lightning rod. Is this rod a better product? Will it work? Explain why or why not.

18. **Process Skills: Use Numbers** What if a transformer changes an electrical force from 100 volts to 50 volts? How would the same transformer change an electrical force of 20 volts?

19. **Making Decisions** If you were caught in a thunderstorm would you be safer inside a car or under a tree? Where would you wait while the storm blew over?

20. **Critical Thinking** What energy sources can be used to power a generator?

Boost *your test scores!*

Be Smart!
Visit www.mhscience02.com
to learn more.

Dr. Ellen Ochoa
ENGINEER AND ASTRONAUT

It will be the size of two football fields. It will contain six laboratories powered by huge solar panels. It will house crews from around the world conducting important scientific research. What is it? It is the International Space Station due to be finished by 2006.

As an astronaut and engineer, Dr. Ellen Ochoa has helped in the development of the International Space Station. Dr. Ochoa is also one of NASA's astronauts and has already been on three space flights. Dr. Ochoa received a doctorate in electrical engineering from Stanford University in 1985. She was selected by NASA in 1990.

Dr. Ochoa studies robotics—the use of machines to perform human tasks. She is leading much of the robotics research for the space station. On her missions into space, Dr. Ochoa used robotic arms to retrieve satellites and transfer equipment to the International Space Station. The equipment is for crews who will live on the space station in the future.

Write ABOUT IT

1. What will be the source of power for the International Space Station?
2. How did Dr. Ochoa use robotics on her NASA space missions?

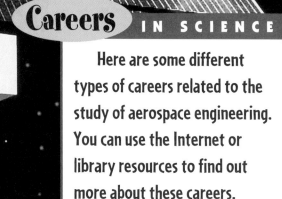

Careers IN SCIENCE

Here are some different types of careers related to the study of aerospace engineering. You can use the Internet or library resources to find out more about these careers.

- aircraft mechanic
- robotics technician
- astronaut
- astronomer
- physicist

AT THE COMPUTER

Visit www.mhscience02.com to learn more about careers.

Energy Scrapbook

Motion, forces, and energy are all around you. Create a scrapbook in which you can record drawings, pictures, and observations of all the different ways you use and see motion, forces, and energy. Think about the ways you move and move things around you.

What types of forces are being used? What types of tools are being used, and how do they help you do work? In what ways do you depend on and use heat, light, and sound? In what ways is energy changing from one form to another all around you?

The "EAT" Mystery

Write a Hypothesis

The EAT restaurant sign is made of 17 light bulbs. The sign works when all the bulbs are on. If one bulb burns out, the whole sign goes dark. Finding the burned-out bulb takes a long time. Write a hypothesis that will help you solve the problem. What can you do to change the system so one burned-out bulb doesn't make the whole sign go dark?

Experiment

How can you test the hypothesis? What materials would you need? What variables do you need to control? What variable changes? Write down a plan. Have your teacher approve it. Follow your plan. Record your observations.

Analyze the Results

Write a report that summarizes your observations.

For Your Reference

Science Handbook

Units of Measurement R2
Use a Hand Lens R4
Use a Microscope R5
Measure Time R6
Measure Length R7
Measure Mass R8
Measure Volume R9
Measure Weight/Force R10
Measure Temperature R11
Use Calculators R12
Use Computers R14
Make Graphs to Organize Data R16
Make Maps, Tables, Charts .R18

Health Handbook

The Skeletal System R20
The Muscular System R23
The Circulatory System R24
The Respiratory System R26
Activity Pyramid/Food Guide Pyramid R27
The Digestive System R28
The Excretory System R29
The Nervous System R30
The Endocrine System R31
The Senses R32
The Immune System R34

Glossary

Glossary R35

Index

Index R53

Units of Measurement

Temperature

1. The temperature is 77 degrees Fahrenheit.

2. That is the same as 25 degrees Celsius.

3. Water boils at 212 degrees Fahrenheit.

4. Water freezes at 0 degrees Celsius.

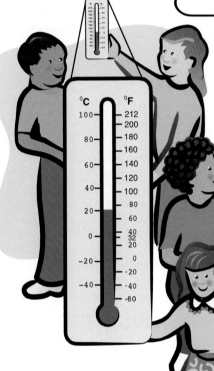

Length and Area

1. This classroom is 10 meters wide and 20 meters long.

2. That means the area is 200 square meters.

Mass and Weight

1. That baseball bat weighs 32 ounces.

2. 32 ounces is the same as 2 pounds.

3. The mass of the bat is 907 grams.

Measurement

Volume of Fluids

Weight/ Force

Rate

1. This bottle of juice has a volume of 1 liter.

2. That is a little more than 1 quart.

3. I weigh 85 pounds. That is a force of 380.8 newtons.

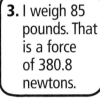

1. She can walk 20 meters in 5 seconds.

2. That means her speed is 4 meters per second.

Table of Measurements

SI (International System) of Units	English System of Units
Temperature Water freezes at 0 degrees Celsius (°C) and boils at 100°C.	**Temperature** Water freezes at 32 degrees Fahrenheit (°F) and boils at 212°F.
Length and Distance 10 millimeters (mm) = 1 centimeter (cm) 100 centimeters = 1 meter (m) 1,000 meters = 1 kilometer (km)	**Length and Distance** 12 inches (in.) = 1 foot (ft) 3 feet = 1 yard (yd) 5,280 feet = 1 mile (mi)
Volume 1 cubic centimeter (cm^3) = 1 milliliter (mL) 1,000 milliliters = 1 liter (L)	**Volume of Fluids** 8 fluid ounces (fl oz) = 1 cup (c) 2 cups = 1 pint (pt) 2 pints = 1 quart (qt) 4 quarts = 1 gallon (gal)
Mass 1,000 milligrams (mg) = 1 gram (g) 1,000 grams = 1 kilogram (kg)	**Weight** 16 ounces (oz) = 1 pound (lb) 2,000 pounds = 1 ton (T)
Area 1 square kilometer (km^2) = l km x l km 1 hectare = 10,000 square meters (m^2)	**Rate** mph = miles per hour
Rate m/s = meters per second km/h = kilometers per hour	
Force 1 newton (N) = 1 kg x 1m/s^2	

Use a Hand Lens

You use a hand lens to magnify an object, or make the object look larger. With a hand lens, you can see details that would be hard to see without the hand lens.

Magnify a Piece of Cereal

1. Place a piece of your favorite cereal on a flat surface. Look at the cereal carefully. Draw a picture of it.

2. Hold the hand lens so that it is just above the cereal. Look through the lens, and slowly move it away from the cereal. The cereal will look larger.

3. Keep moving the hand lens until the cereal begins to look blurry. Then move the lens a little closer to the cereal until you can see it clearly.

4. Draw a picture of the cereal as you see it through the hand lens. Fill in details that you did not see before.

5. Repeat this activity using objects you are studying in science. It might be a rock, some soil, a seed, or something else.

Use a Microscope

Hand lenses make objects look several times larger. A microscope, however, can magnify an object to look hundreds of times larger.

Examine Salt Grains

1. Place the microscope on a flat surface. Always carry a microscope with both hands. Hold the arm with one hand, and put your other hand beneath the base.
2. Look at the drawing to learn the different parts of the microscope.
3. Move the mirror so that it reflects light up toward the stage. Never point the mirror directly at the Sun or a bright light. Bright light can cause permanent eye damage.
4. Place a few grains of salt on the slide. Put the slide under the stage clips on the stage. Be sure that the salt grains are over the hole in the stage.
5. Look through the eyepiece. Turn the focusing knob slowly until the salt grains come into focus.
6. Draw what the grains look like through the microscope.
7. Look at other objects through the microscope. Try a piece of leaf, a strand of human hair, or a pencil mark.
8. Draw what each object looks like through the microscope. Do any of the objects look alike? If so, how? Are any of the objects alive? How do you know?

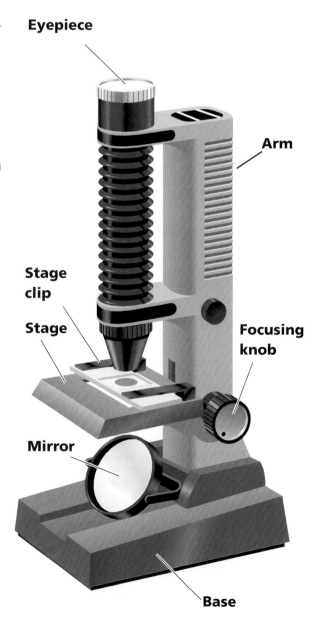

Eyepiece

Arm

Stage clip

Stage

Focusing knob

Mirror

Base

Measure Time

You use timing devices to measure how long something takes to happen. Some timing devices you use in science are a clock with a second hand and a stopwatch. Which one is more accurate?

Comparing a Clock and a Stopwatch

1. Look at a clock with a second hand. The second hand is the hand that you can see moving. It measures seconds.

2. Get an egg timer with falling sand. When the second hand of the clock points to 12, tell your partner to start the egg timer. Watch the clock while the sand in the egg timer is falling.

3. When the sand stops falling, count how many seconds it took. Record this measurement. Repeat the activity, and compare the two measurements.

4. Look at a stopwatch. Click the button on the top right. This starts the time. Click the button again. This stops the time. Click the button on the top left. This sets the stopwatch back to zero. Notice that the stopwatch tells time in hours, minutes, seconds, and hundredths of a second.

5. Repeat the activity in steps 1–3, but use the stopwatch instead of a clock. Make sure the stopwatch is set to zero. Click the top right button to start timing. Click the

button again when the sand stops falling. Make sure you and your partner time the sand twice.

0 minutes **25 seconds 72 hundredths of a second**

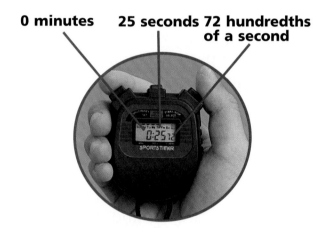

More About Time

1. Use the stopwatch to time how long it takes an ice cube to melt under cold running water. How long does an ice cube take to melt under warm running water?

2. Match each of these times with the action you think took that amount of time.

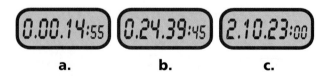

a.   b.   c.

1. A Little League baseball game
2. Saying the Pledge of Allegiance
3. Recess

Measure Length

Find Length with a Ruler

1. Look at this section of a ruler. Each centimeter is divided into 10 millimeters. How long is the paper clip?
2. The length of the paper clip is 3 centimeters plus 2 millimeters. You can write this length as 3.2 centimeters.
3. Place a ruler on your desk. Lay a pencil against the ruler so that one end of the pencil lines up with the left edge of the ruler. Record the length of the pencil.
4. Trade pencils with a classmate. Measure and record the length of each other's pencils. Compare your answers.

Measuring Area

Area is the amount of surface something covers. To find the area of a rectangle, multiply the rectangle's length by its width. For example, the rectangle here is 3 centimeters long and 2 centimeters wide. Its area is 3 cm x 2 cm = 6 square centimeters. You write the area as 6 cm^2.

1. Find the area of your science book. Measure the book's length to the nearest centimeter. Measure its width.
2. Multiply the book's length by its width. Remember to put the answer in cm^2.

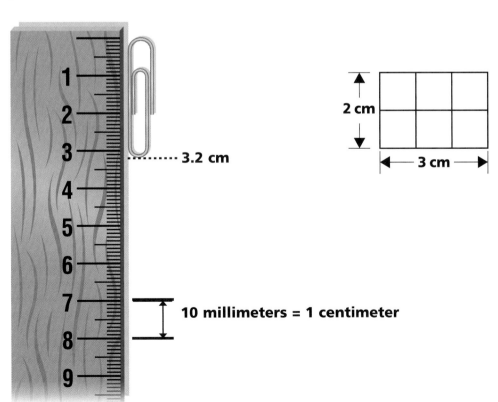

3.2 cm

10 millimeters = 1 centimeter

2 cm

3 cm

Measure Mass

Mass is the amount of matter an object has. You use a balance to measure mass. To find the mass of an object, you balance it with objects whose masses you know. Let's find the mass of a box of crayons.

Measure the Mass of a Box of Crayons

1. Place the balance on a flat, level surface.
2. Make sure the empty pans are balanced with each other. The pointer should point to the middle mark. If it does not, move the slider a little to the right or left to balance the pans.
3. Gently place a box of crayons on the left pan.
4. Add masses to the right pan until the pans are balanced.

5. Count the numbers on the masses that are in the right pan. The total is the mass of the box of crayons, in grams. Record this number. After the number, write a *g* for "grams."

More About Mass

What would happen if you replaced the crayons with a pineapple? You may not have enough masses to balance the pineapple. It has a mass of about 1,000 grams. That's the same as 1 kilogram, because *kilo* means "1,000."

Measure Volume

Have you ever used a measuring cup? Measuring cups measure the volume of liquids. Volume is the amount of space something takes up. In science you use special measuring cups called beakers and graduated cylinders. These containers are marked in milliliters (mL).

Measure the Volume of a Liquid

1. Look at the beaker and at the graduated cylinder. The beaker has marks for each 25 mL up to 200 mL. The graduated cylinder has marks for each 1 mL up to 100 mL.

2. The surface of the water in the graduated cylinder curves up at the sides. You measure the volume by reading the height of the water at the flat part. What is the volume of water in the graduated cylinder? How much water is in the beaker?

3. Pour 50 mL of water from a pitcher into a graduated cylinder. The water should be at the 50-mL mark on the graduated cylinder. If you go over the mark, pour a little water back into the pitcher.

4. Pour the 50 mL of water into a beaker.

5. Repeat steps 3 and 4 using 30 mL, 45 mL, and 25 mL of water.

6. Measure the volume of water you have in the beaker. Do you have about the same amount of water as your classmates?

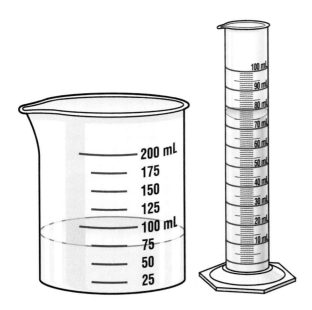

Measure Weight/Force

You use a spring scale to measure weight. An object has weight because the force of gravity pulls down on the object. Therefore, weight is a force. Like all forces, weight is measured in newtons (N).

Measure the Weight of an Object

1. Look at your spring scale to see how many newtons it measures. See how the measurements are divided. The spring scale shown here measures up to 10 N. It has a mark for every 1 N.

2. Hold the spring scale by the top loop. Put the object to be measured on the bottom hook. If the object will not stay on the hook, place it in a net bag. Then hang the bag from the hook.

3. Let go of the object slowly. It will pull down on a spring inside the scale. The spring is connected to a pointer. The pointer on the spring scale shown here is a small arrow.

4. Wait for the pointer to stop moving. Read the number of newtons next to the pointer. This is the object's weight. The mug in the picture weighs 3 N.

More About Spring Scales

You probably weigh yourself by standing on a bathroom scale. This is a spring scale. The force of your body stretches a spring inside the scale. The dial on the scale is probably marked in pounds—the English unit of weight. One pound is equal to about 4.5 newtons.

Here are some spring scales you may have seen.

Measure Temperature

Temperature is how hot or cold something is. You use a thermometer to measure temperature. A thermometer is made of a thin tube with colored liquid inside. When the liquid gets warmer, it expands and moves up the tube. When the liquid gets cooler, it contracts and moves down the tube. You may have seen most temperatures measured in degrees Fahrenheit (°F). Scientists measure temperature in degrees Celsius (°C).

Read a Thermometer

1. Look at the thermometer shown here. It has two scales—a Fahrenheit scale and a Celsius scale. Every 20 degrees on each scale has a number.
2. What is the temperature shown on the thermometer? At what temperature does water freeze? Give your answers in °F and in °C.

How Is Temperature Measured?

1. Fill a large beaker about one-half full of cool water. Find the temperature of the water by holding a thermometer in the water. Do not let the bulb at the bottom of the thermometer touch the sides or bottom of the beaker.
2. Keep the thermometer in the water until the liquid in the tube stops moving— about a minute. Read and record the temperature on the Celsius scale.

3. Fill another large beaker one-half full of warm water from a faucet. Be careful not to burn yourself by using hot water.
4. Find and record the temperature of the warm water just as you did in steps 1 and 2.

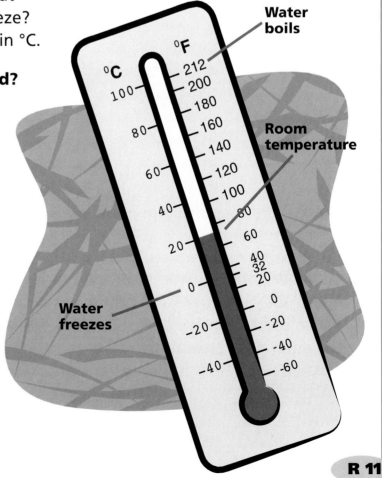

Water boils

Room temperature

Water freezes

Use Calculators: Add and Subtract

Sometimes after you make measurements, you have to add or subtract your numbers. A calculator helps you do this.

Add and Subtract Rainfall Amounts

The table shows the amount of rain that fell in a town each week during the summer.

Week	Rain (cm)
1	3
2	5
3	2
4	0
5	1
6	6
7	4
8	0
9	2
10	2
11	6
12	5

1. Make sure the calculator is on. Press the **ON** key.
2. To add the numbers, enter a number and press **+**. Repeat until you enter the last number. Then press **=**. You do not have to enter the zeros. Your total should be 36.

3. What if you found out that you made a mistake in your measurement? Week 1 should be 2 cm less, week 6 should be 3 cm less, week 11 should be 1 cm less, and week 12 should be 2 cm less. Subtract these numbers from your total. You should have 36 displayed on the calculator. Press **−**, and enter the first number you want to subtract. Repeat until you enter the last number. Then press **=**.

Use Technology

Use Calculators: Multiply and Divide

Sometimes after you make measurements, you have to multiply or divide your measurements to get other information. A calculator helps you multiply and divide, especially if the numbers have decimal points.

Multiply Decimals

What if you are measuring the width of your classroom? You discover that the floor is covered with tiles and the room is exactly 32 tiles wide. You measure a tile, and it is 22.7 centimeters wide. To find the width of the room, you can multiply 32 by 22.7.

1. Make sure the calculator is on. Press the **ON** key.
2. Press **3** and **2**.
3. Press **×**.
4. Press **2**, **2**, **.**, and **7**.
5. Press **=**. Your total should be 726.4. That is how wide the room is in centimeters.

Divide Decimals

Now what if you wanted to find out how many desks placed side by side would be needed to reach across the room? You measure one desk, and it is 60 centimeters wide. To find the number of desks needed, divide 726.4 by 60.

1. Turn the calculator on.
2. Press **7**, **2**, **6**, **.**, and **4**.
3. Press **÷**.
4. Press **6** and **0**.
5. Press **=**. Your total should be about 12.1. This means you can fit 12 desks across the room with a little space left over.

What if the room was 35 tiles wide? How wide would the room be? How many desks would fit across it?

Use Computers

A computer has many uses. The Internet connects your computer to many other computers around the world, so you can collect all kinds of information. You can use a computer to show this information and write reports. Best of all, you can use a computer to explore, discover, and learn.

You can also get information from CD-ROMs. They are computer disks that can hold large amounts of information. You can fit a whole encyclopedia on one CD-ROM.

Use Computers for a Project

Here is how one group of students uses computers as they work on a weather project.

1. The students use instruments to measure temperature, wind speed, wind direction, and other parts of the weather. They input this information, or data, into the computer. The students keep the data in a table. This helps them compare the data from one day to the next.

2. The teacher finds out that another group of students in a town 200 kilometers to the west is also doing a weather project. The two groups use the Internet to talk to each other and share data. When a storm happens in the town to the west, that group tells the other group that it's coming its way.

Use Technology

email: It's going to storm here. The sky is turning dark gray. The winds are sometimes 65 km per hour from the northwest.

3. The students want to find out more. They decide to stay on the Internet and send questions to a local TV weather forecaster. She has a website and answers questions from students every day.

4. Meanwhile some students go to the library to gather more information from a CD-ROM disk. The CD-ROM has an encyclopedia that includes movie clips with sound. The clips give examples of different kinds of storms.

5. The students have kept all their information in a folder called Weather Project. Now they use that information to write a report about the weather. On the computer they can move paragraphs, add words, take out words, put in diagrams, and draw their own weather maps. Then they print the report in color.

6. Use the information on these two pages to plan your own investigation. Use a computer, the Internet, a CD-ROM, or any other technological device.

Make Graphs to Organize Data

When you do an experiment in science, you collect information. To find out what your information means, you can organize it into graphs. There are many kinds of graphs.

Bar Graphs

A bar graph uses bars to show information. For example, what if you are growing a plant? Every week you measure how high the plant has grown. Here is what you find.

Week	Height (cm)
1	1
2	3
3	6
4	10
5	17
6	20
7	22
8	23

The bar graph at right organizes the measurements you collected so that you can easily compare them.

1. Look at the bar for week 2. Put your finger at the top of the bar. Move your finger straight over to the left to find how many centimeters the plant grew by the end of week 2.

2. Between which two weeks did the plant grow most?

3. When did plant growth begin to level off?

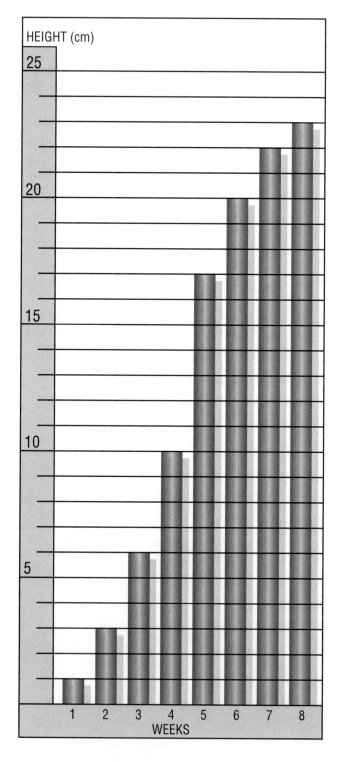

Represent Data

Pictographs

A pictograph uses symbols, or pictures, to show information. What if you collect information about how much water your family uses each day? Here is what you find.

Activity	Water Used Each Day (L)
Drinking	10
Showering	100
Bathing	120
Brushing teeth	40
Washing dishes	80
Washing hands	30
Washing clothes	160
Flushing toilet	50

You can organize this information into the pictograph shown here. In this pictograph each bottle means 20 liters of water. A half bottle means half of 20, or 10 liters of water.

1. Which activity uses the most water?
2. Which activity uses the least water?

A Family's Daily Use of Water

Drinking	🍶
Showering	🍶🍶🍶🍶🍶
Bathing	🍶🍶🍶🍶🍶🍶
Brushing teeth	🍶🍶
Washing dishes	🍶🍶🍶🍶
Washing hands	🍶🍶
Washing clothes	🍶🍶🍶🍶🍶🍶🍶🍶
Flushing toilet	🍶🍶🍶

🍶 = 20 liters of water

Line Graphs

A line graph shows information by connecting dots plotted on the graph. It shows change over time. What if you measure the temperature outdoors every hour starting at 6 A.M.? Here is what you find.

Time	Temperature (°C)
6 A.M.	10
7 A.M.	12
8 A.M.	14
9 A.M.	16
10 A.M.	18
11 A.M.	20

You can organize this information into a line graph. Follow these steps.

1. Make a scale along the bottom and side of the graph. The scales should include all the numbers in the chart. Label the scales.
2. Plot points on the graph.
3. Connect the points with a line.

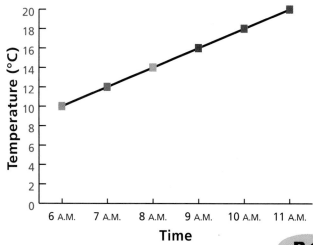

Represent Data

Make Maps, Tables, Charts

Locate Places

A map is a drawing that shows an area from above. Most maps have numbers and letters along the top and side. What if you wanted to find the library on the map below? It is located at D7. Place a finger on the letter D along the side of the map and another finger on the number 7 at the top. Then move your fingers straight across and down the map until they meet. The library is located where D and 7 meet.

1. What building is located at G3?
2. The hospital is located three blocks south and three blocks east of the library. What is its number and letter?
3. Make a map of an area in your community. It might be a park or the area between your home and school. Include numbers and letters along the top and side. Use a compass to find north, and mark north on your map. Exchange maps with classmates.

Idea Maps

The map below left shows how places are connected to each other. Idea maps, on the other hand, show how ideas are connected to each other. Idea maps help you organize information about a topic.

Look at the idea map below. It connects ideas about water. This map shows that Earth's water is either fresh water or salt water. The map also shows four sources of fresh water. You can see that there is no connection between "rivers" and "salt water" on the map. This reminds you that salt water does not flow in rivers.

Make an idea map about a topic you are learning in science. Your map can include words, phrases, or even sentences. Arrange your map in a way that makes sense to you and helps you understand the ideas.

North

	1	2	3	4	5	6	7	8	9	10
A										
B										
C						Library				
D										
E										
F		Store						Hospital		
G										

West   **East**

South

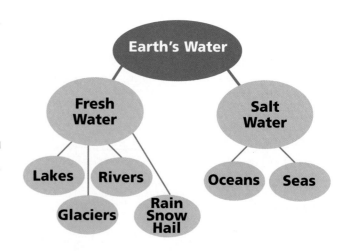

Earth's Water — Fresh Water, Salt Water; Fresh Water — Lakes, Rivers, Glaciers, Rain Snow Hail; Salt Water — Oceans, Seas

Make Tables and Charts to Organize Data

Tables help to organize data during experiments. Most tables have columns that run up and down, and rows that run across. The columns and rows have headings that tell you what kind of data goes in each part of the table.

A Sample Table

What if you are going to do an experiment to find out how long different kinds of seeds take to sprout? Before you begin the experiment, you should set up your table. Follow these steps.

1. In this experiment you will plant 20 radish seeds, 20 bean seeds, and 20 corn seeds. Your table must show how many of each kind of seed sprouted on days 1, 2, 3, 4, and 5.

2. Make your table with columns, rows, and headings. You might use a computer. Some computer programs let you build a table with just the click of a mouse. You can delete or add columns and rows if you need to.

3. Give your table a title. Your table could look like the one here.

Make a Table

Plant 20 bean seeds in each of two trays. Keep each tray at a different temperature, as shown above, and observe the trays for seven days. Make a table that you can use for this experiment. You can use the table to record, examine, and evaluate the information of this experiment.

Make a Chart

A chart is simply a table with pictures, as well as words to label the rows or columns. Make a chart that shows the information of the above experiment.

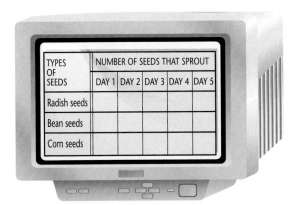

TYPES OF SEEDS	NUMBER OF SEEDS THAT SPROUT				
	DAY 1	DAY 2	DAY 3	DAY 4	DAY 5
Radish seeds					
Bean seeds					
Corn seeds					

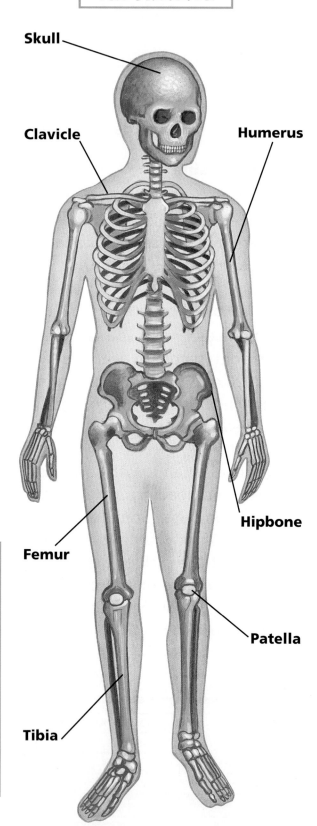

HEALTH Handbook

The Skeletal System

The body has a supporting frame, called a skeleton, which is made up of bones. The skeleton has several jobs.

- It gives the body its shape.
- It protects organs in the body.
- It works with muscles to move the body.

Each of the 206 bones of the skeleton is the size and shape best fitted to do its job. For example, long and strong leg bones support the body's weight.

The Skeleton

Skull

Clavicle

Humerus

Femur

Hipbone

Patella

Tibia

CARE!

- Exercise to keep your skeletal system in good shape.
- Don't overextend your joints.
- Eat foods rich in vitamins and minerals. Your bones need the minerals calcium and phosphorus to grow strong.

Bones

1 A bone is covered with a tough but thin membrane that has many small blood vessels. The blood vessels bring nutrients and oxygen to the living parts of the bone and remove wastes.

2 Inside some bones is a soft tissue known as marrow. Yellow marrow is made mostly of fat cells and is one of the body's energy reserves. It is usually found in the long, hollow spaces of long bones.

3 Part of the bone is compact, or solid. It is made up of living bone cells and non-living materials. The nonliving part is made up of layers of hardened minerals such as calcium and phosphorus. In between the mineral layers are living bone cells.

4 Red marrow fills the spaces in spongy bone. Red marrow makes new red blood cells, germ-fighting white blood cells, and cell fragments that stop a cut from bleeding.

5 Part of the bone is made of bone tissue that looks like a dry sponge. It is made of strong, hard tubes. It is also found in the middle of short, flat bones.

CARE!

- Eat foods rich in vitamins and minerals. Your bones need the minerals calcium and phosphorus to grow strong.

- Be careful! Avoid sprains and fractures.

- Get help in case of injury.

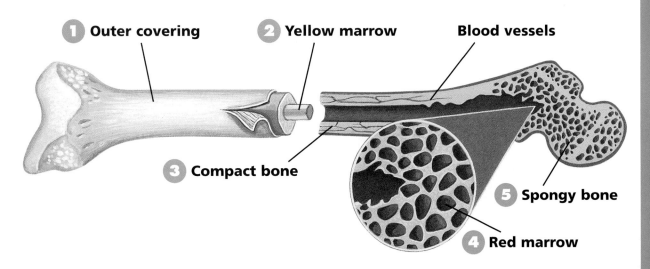

1 Outer covering   **2** Yellow marrow   Blood vessels

3 Compact bone

5 Spongy bone

4 Red marrow

Joints

The skeleton has different types of joints. A joint is a place where two or more bones meet. Joints can be classified into three major groups—immovable joints, partly movable joints, and movable joints.

Types of Joints

IMMOVABLE JOINTS

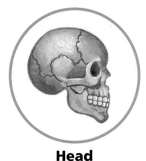

Head

Immovable joints are places where bones fit together too tightly to move. Nearly all the 29 bones in the skull meet at immovable joints. Only the lower jaw can move.

PARTLY MOVABLE JOINTS

Partly movable joints are places where bones can move only a little. Ribs are connected to the breastbone with these joints.

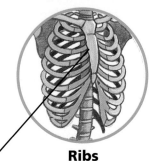

Ribs

Breastbone

MOVABLE JOINTS

Movable joints are places where bones can move easily.

Gliding joint

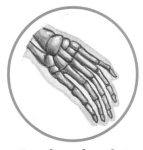

Hand and wrist

Small bones in the wrists and ankles meet at gliding joints. The bones can slide against one another. These joints allow some movement in all directions.

The hips are examples of ball-and-socket joints. The ball of one bone fits into the socket, or cup, of another bone. These joints allow bones to move back and forth, in a circle, and side to side.

Ball-and-socket joint

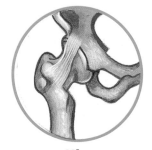

Hip

Hinge joint

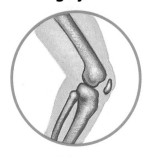

Knee

The knees are hinge joints. A hinge joint is similar to a door hinge. It allows bones to move back and forth in one direction.

The joint between the skull and neck is a pivot joint. It allows the head to move up and down, and side to side.

Pivot joint

Neck

The Muscular System

1 A message from your brain causes this muscle, called the biceps, to contract. When a muscle contracts, it becomes shorter and thicker. As the biceps contracts, it pulls on the arm bone it is attached to.

2 Most muscles work in pairs to move bones. This muscle, called the triceps, relaxes when the biceps contracts. When a muscle relaxes, it becomes longer and thinner.

3 To straighten your arm, a message from your brain causes the triceps to contract. When the triceps contracts, it pulls on the bone it is attached to.

4 As the triceps contracts, the biceps relaxes. Your arm straightens.

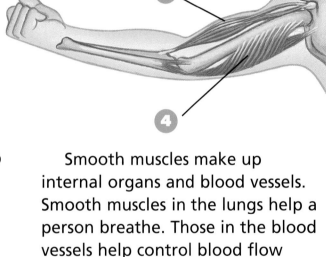

Three types of muscles make up the body—skeletal muscle, cardiac muscle, and smooth muscle.

The muscles that are attached to and move bones are called skeletal muscles. These muscles are attached to bones by a tough cord called a tendon. Skeletal muscles pull bones to move them. Muscles do not push bones.

Cardiac muscles are found in only one place in the body—the heart. The walls of the heart are made of strong cardiac muscles. When cardiac muscles contract, they squeeze blood out of the heart. When cardiac muscles relax, the heart fills with more blood.

Smooth muscles make up internal organs and blood vessels. Smooth muscles in the lungs help a person breathe. Those in the blood vessels help control blood flow around the body.

CARE!

- **Exercise to strengthen your muscles.**
- **Eat the right foods.**
- **Get plenty of rest.**

The Circulatory System

The circulatory system consists of the heart, blood vessels, and blood. Circulation is the flow of blood through the body. Blood is a liquid that contains red blood cells, white blood cells, and platelets. Red blood cells carry oxygen and nutrients to cells. White blood cells work to fight germs that enter the body. Platelets are cell fragments that make the blood clot.

The heart is a muscular organ about the size of a fist. It beats about 70 to 90 times a minute, pumping blood through the blood vessels. Arteries carry blood away from the heart. Some arteries carry blood to the lungs, where the cells pick up oxygen. Other arteries carry oxygen-rich blood from the lungs to all other parts of the body. Veins carry blood from other parts of the body back to the heart. Blood in most veins carries the wastes released by cells and has little oxygen. Blood flows from arteries to veins through narrow vessels called capillaries.

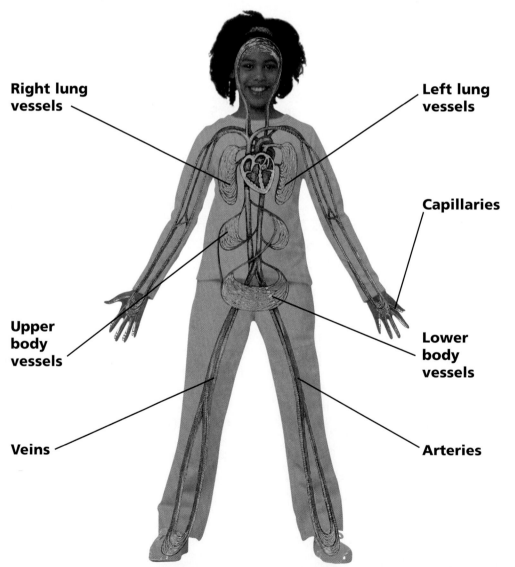

Right lung vessels

Left lung vessels

Capillaries

Upper body vessels

Lower body vessels

Veins

Arteries

The Heart

The heart has two sides, right and left, separated by a thick muscular wall. Each side has two chambers for blood. The upper chamber is the atrium. The lower chamber is the ventricle. Blood enters the heart through the vena cava. It leaves the heart through the aorta.

The pulmonary artery carries blood from the body into the lungs. Here carbon dioxide leaves the blood to be exhaled by the lungs. Fresh oxygen enters the blood to be carried to every cell in the body. Blood returns from the lungs to the heart through the pulmonary veins.

CARE!

- **Don't smoke. The nicotine in tobacco makes the heart beat faster and work harder to pump blood.**

- **Never take illegal drugs, such as cocaine or heroin. They can damage the heart and cause heart failure.**

To the Lungs

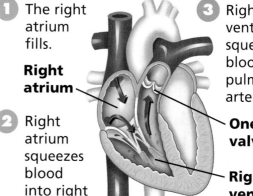

1. The right atrium fills.

Right atrium

2. Right atrium squeezes blood into right ventricle.

3. Right ventricle squeezes blood into pulmonary artery.

One-way valve

Right ventricle

How the Heart Works

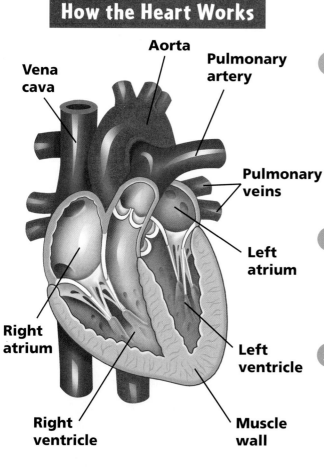

Aorta

Pulmonary artery

Vena cava

Pulmonary veins

Left atrium

Right atrium

Left ventricle

Right ventricle

Muscle wall

From the Lungs

1. The left atrium fills.

2. Left atrium squeezes blood into left ventricle.

3. Left ventricle squeezes blood into aorta.

Left atrium

One-way valve

Left ventricle

The Respiratory System

The process of getting and using oxygen in the body is called respiration. When a person inhales, air is pulled into the nose or mouth. The air travels down into the trachea. In the chest the trachea divides into two bronchial tubes. One bronchial tube enters each lung. Each bronchial tube branches into smaller tubes called bronchioles.

At the end of each bronchiole are tiny air sacs called alveoli. The alveoli exchange carbon dioxide for oxygen.

Oxygen comes from the air we breathe. Two muscles control breathing, the lungs and a dome-shaped sheet of muscle called the diaphragm.

To inhale, the diaphragm contracts and pulls down. To exhale, the diaphragm relaxes and returns to its dome shape.

CARE!

- **Don't smoke. Smoking damages your respiratory system.**
- **Exercise to strengthen your breathing muscles.**
- **If you ever have trouble breathing, tell an adult at once.**

Air Flow

Carbon dioxide | Oxygen

Carbon dioxide diffuses into the alveoli. From there it is exhaled.

Capillary net

Alveoli

Fresh oxygen diffuses from the alveoli to the blood.

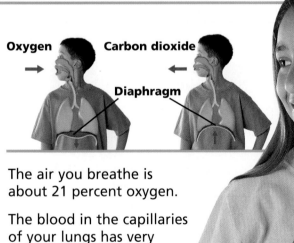

Oxygen →   Carbon dioxide ←

Diaphragm

The air you breathe is about 21 percent oxygen.

The blood in the capillaries of your lungs has very little oxygen.

The blood has a higher concentration of carbon dioxide than air.

Throat

Trachea

Lungs

Activity Pyramid

Physical fitness is the condition in which the body is healthy and works the best it can. It involves working the skeletal muscles, bones, joints, heart, and respiratory system.

Occasionally
Inactive pastimes such as watching TV, playing board games, talking on the phone

2–3 times a week
Leisure activities such as gardening, golf, softball

3–5 times a week
Aerobic activities such as swimming, biking, climbing; sports activities such as basketball, handball

The activity pyramid shows you the kinds of exercises and other activities you should be doing to make your body more physically fit.

Daily Substitute activity for inactivity—take the stairs, walk instead of riding, bike instead of taking the bus

Food Guide Pyramid

To make sure the body stays fit and healthy, a person needs to eat a balanced diet. The Food Guide Pyramid shows how many servings of each group a person should eat every day.

CARE!
- **Stay active every day.**
- **Eat a balanced diet.**
- **Drink plenty of water—6 to 8 large glasses a day.**

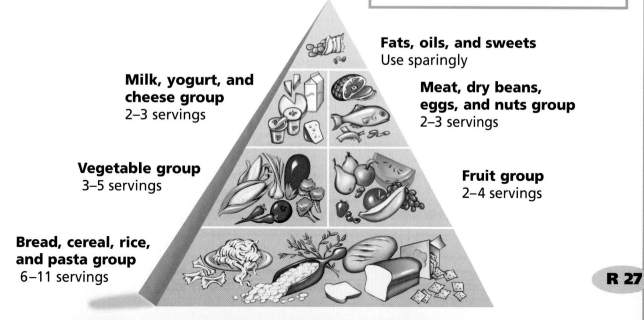

Milk, yogurt, and cheese group
2–3 servings

Fats, oils, and sweets
Use sparingly

Meat, dry beans, eggs, and nuts group
2–3 servings

Vegetable group
3–5 servings

Fruit group
2–4 servings

Bread, cereal, rice, and pasta group
6–11 servings

R 27

The Digestive System

Digestion is the process of breaking down food into simple substances the body can use. Digestion begins when a person chews food. Chewing breaks the food down into smaller pieces and moistens it with saliva. Saliva is produced by the salivary glands.

Digested food is absorbed in the small intestine. The walls of the small intestine are lined with villi. Villi are tiny fingerlike projections that absorb digested food. From the villi the blood transports nutrients to every part of the body.

CARE!

- Chew your food well.
- Drink plenty of water to help move food through your digestive system.

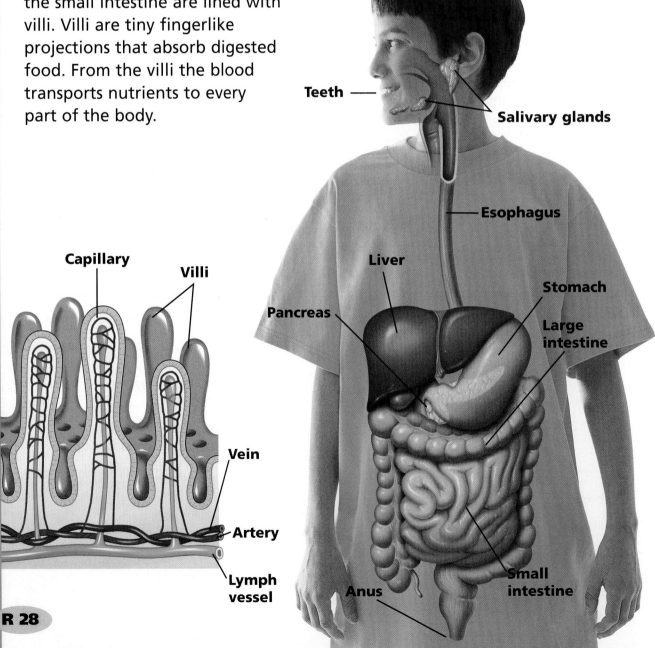

Capillary

Villi

Vein

Artery

Lymph vessel

Teeth

Salivary glands

Esophagus

Liver

Pancreas

Stomach

Large intestine

Small intestine

Anus

The Excretory System

Excretion is the process of removing waste products from the body. The liver filters wastes from the blood and converts them into urea. Urea is then carried to the kidneys for excretion.

The skin takes part in excretion when a person sweats. Glands in the inner layer of the skin produce sweat. Sweat is mostly water. Sweat tastes salty because it contains mineral salts the body doesn't need. There is also a tiny amount of urea in sweat.

Sweat is excreted onto the outer layer of the skin. Evaporation into the air takes place in part because of body heat. When sweat evaporates, a person feels cooler.

How You Sweat

Glands under your skin push sweat up to the surface, where it collects.

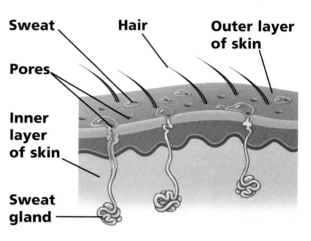

Sweat Hair Outer layer of skin
Pores
Inner layer of skin
Sweat gland

CARE!

● **Wash regularly to avoid body odor, clogged pores, and skin irritation.**

How Your Kidneys Work

1 Blood enters the kidney through an artery and flows into capillaries.

2 Sugars, salts, water, urea, and other wastes move from the capillaries to tiny nephrons.

3 Nutrients return to the blood and flow back out through veins.

4 Urea and other wastes become urine, which flows down the ureters.

5 Urine is stored in the bladder and excreted through the urethra.

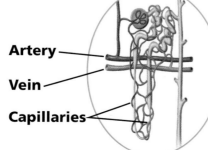

Artery
Vein
Capillaries

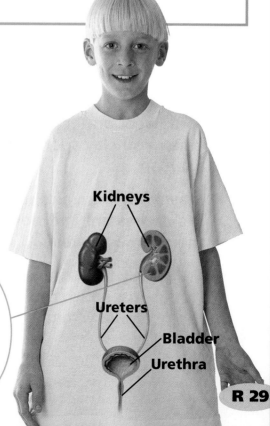

Kidneys
Ureters
Bladder
Urethra

The Nervous System

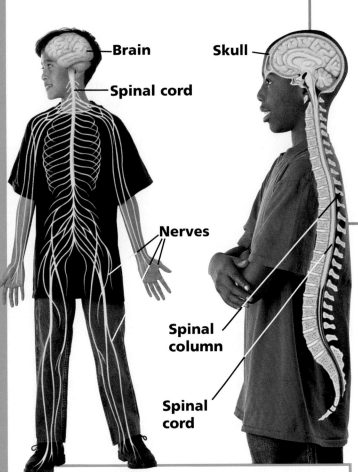

Brain

Spinal cord

Skull

Nerves

Spinal column

Spinal cord

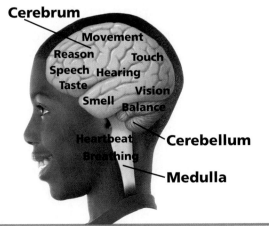

Cerebrum

Movement
Reason   Touch
Speech   Hearing
Taste
          Vision
Smell   Balance

Heartbeat   Cerebellum
Breathing

Medulla

The nervous system has two parts. The brain and the spinal cord are the central nervous system. All other nerves are the outer nervous system.

The largest part of the brain is the cerebrum. A deep groove separates the right half, or hemisphere, of the cerebrum from the left half. Both sides of the cerebrum contain control centers for the senses.

The cerebellum lies below the cerebrum. It coordinates the skeletal muscles. It also helps in keeping balance.

The brain stem connects to the spinal cord. The lowest part of the brain stem is the medulla. It controls heartbeat, breathing, blood pressure, and the muscles in the digestive system.

CARE!

- To protect the brain and spinal cord, wear protective headgear when you play sports or exercise.

- Stay away from alcohol, which is a depressant and slows down the nervous system.

- Stay away from drugs, such as stimulants, which can speed up the nervous system.

The Endocrine System

Hormones are chemicals that control body functions. A gland that produces hormones is called an endocrine gland. Sweat from sweat glands flows out of tubes called ducts. Endocrine glands have no ducts.

The endocrine glands are scattered around the body. Each gland makes one or more hormones. Every hormone seeks out a target organ. This is the place in the body where the hormone acts.

Some Glands in the Endocrine System

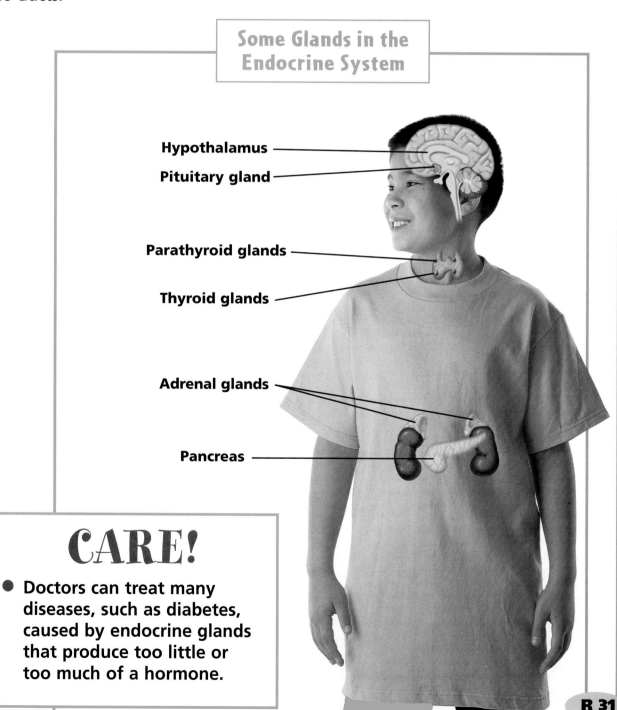

Hypothalamus

Pituitary gland

Parathyroid glands

Thyroid glands

Adrenal glands

Pancreas

CARE!

- Doctors can treat many diseases, such as diabetes, caused by endocrine glands that produce too little or too much of a hormone.

The Senses

Seeing

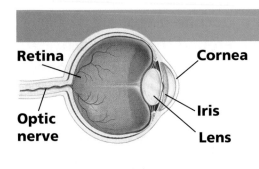

Retina
Optic nerve
Cornea
Iris
Lens

Light reflected from an object enters the eye and falls on the retina. Receptor cells change the light into electrical signals, or impulses. These impulses travel along the optic nerve to the vision center of the brain.

1 Light reflects off the tree and into your eyes.

2 The light passes through your cornea and the pupil in your iris.

3 Your eye bends the light so it hits your retina.

4 Receptor cells on your retina change the light into electrical signals.

5 The impulses travel along neurons in your optic nerve to the seeing center of your brain.

Hearing

Hearing center
Hammer
Auditory nerve
Eardrum
Anvil
Stirrup
Cochlea

1 Your outer ear collects sound waves.

2 They are funneled down your ear canal.

3 The eardrum vibrates.

4 Three tiny ear bones vibrate.

5 The cochlea vibrates.

6 Receptor cells inside your cochlea change.

7 The impulses travel along your auditory nerve to the brain's hearing center.

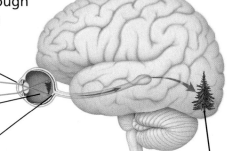

Sound waves enter the ear and cause the eardrum to vibrate. Receptor cells in the ear change the sound waves into impulses that travel along the auditory nerve to the hearing center of the brain.

CARE!

- Avoid loud music.
- Don't sit too close to the TV screen.

The Senses

Smelling

The sense of smell is really the ability to detect chemicals in the air. When a person breathes, chemicals dissolve in mucus in the upper part of the nose. When the chemicals come in contact with receptor cells, the cells send impulses along the olfactory nerve to the smelling center of the brain.

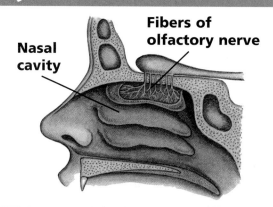

Nasal cavity

Fibers of olfactory nerve

Tasting

When a person eats, chemicals in food dissolve in saliva. Inside each taste bud are receptors that can sense the four main tastes—sweet, sour, salty, and bitter. The receptors send impulses along a nerve to the taste center of the brain. The brain identifies the taste of the food.

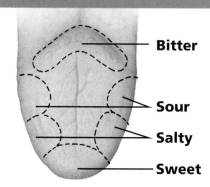

Bitter

Sour

Salty

Sweet

Touching

Receptor cells in the skin help a person tell hot from cold, wet from dry, and the light touch of a feather from the pressure of stepping on a stone. Each receptor cell sends impulses along sensory nerves to the spinal cord. The spinal cord then sends the impulses to the touch center of the brain.

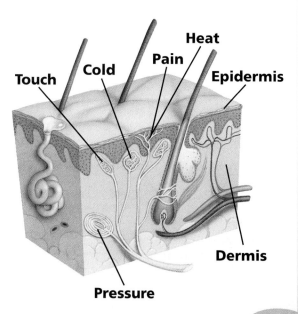

Touch **Cold** **Pain** **Heat** **Epidermis**

Dermis

Pressure

CARE!

- To prevent the spread of germs, always cover your mouth and nose when you cough or sneeze.

The Immune System

The immune system helps the body fight disease. When a person has a cut, germ-fighting white blood cells rush to the wound. There are white blood cells in the blood vessels and in the lymph vessels. Lymph vessels are similar to blood vessels. Instead of blood, they carry lymph. Lymph is a straw-colored fluid surrounding body cells.

Lymph nodes filter out harmful materials in the body. They also produce white blood cells to fight infections. Swollen lymph nodes in the neck are a clue that the body is fighting germs.

Lymph vessels run through your body to collect fluid and return it to the bloodstream.

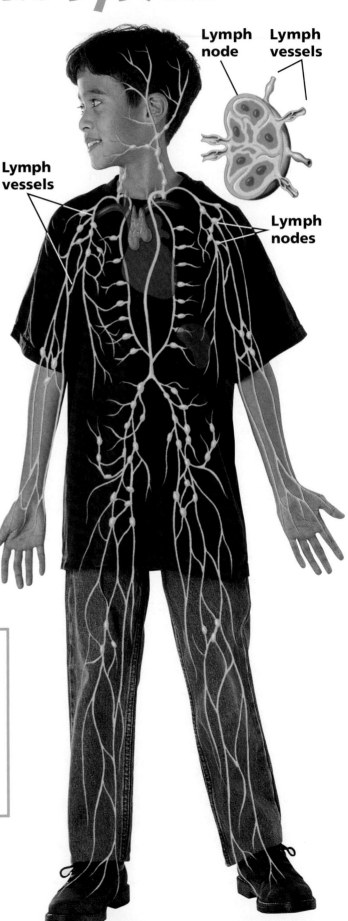

Lymph node

Lymph vessels

Lymph vessels

Lymph nodes

CARE!

● **Be sure to get immunized against common diseases.**

● **Keep cuts clean to prevent infection.**

Glossary

This Glossary will help you to pronounce and understand the meanings of the Science Words introduced in this book. The page number at the end of the definition tells where the word appears.

A

acceleration (ak sel′ə rā′shən) Any change in the speed or direction of a moving object. (p. F8)

acid rain (as′id rān) Harmful moisture that falls to Earth after being mixed with wastes from burned fossil fuels. (p. A59)

adaptation (a′dap′tā′shən) A special trait that helps an organism survive. (p. B66)

air mass (âr mas) A large region of the atmosphere where the air has similar properties throughout. (p. D79)

air pressure (âr presh′ər) The force put on a given area by the weight of the air above it. (p. D67)

alloy (al′oi) A mixture of two or more elements, very often of metals. (p. E38)

alternating current (ôl′tər nā ting kûr′ənt) Current that flows in a circuit, first in one direction, then in the opposite direction. (p. F94)

amber (am′bər) Hardened tree sap, yellow to brown in color, often a source of insect fossils. (p. C20)

ampere (am′pîr) The unit used to measure the number of electrical charges that flow past a certain point in one second. (p. F79)

amphibian (am fib′ē ən) A cold-blooded vertebrate that spends part of its life in water and part of its life on land. (p. B31)

amplitude (am′pli tüd′) The energy in a sound wave. (p. F59)

anther (an′thər) The part of the plant that produces the pollen. (p. A84)

area (âr′ē ə) The number of unit squares that fit inside a surface. (p. E17)

PRONUNCIATION KEY

The following symbols are used throughout the McGraw-Hill Science 2002 Glossaries.

a	at	e	end	o	hot	u	up	hw	white	ə	about
ā	ape	ē	me	ō	old	ū	use	ng	song		taken
ä	far	i	it	ôr	fork	ü	rule	th	thin		pencil
âr	care	ī	ice	oi	oil	u̇	pull	th	this		lemon
ô	law	îr	pierce	ou	out	ûr	turn	zh	measure		circus

′ = primary accent; shows which syllable takes the main stress, such as **kil** in **kilogram** (kil′ə gram′).

′ = secondary accent; shows which syllables take lighter stresses, such as **gram** in **kilogram**.

arthropod (är'thrə pod') An invertebrate with jointed legs and a body that is divided into sections. (p. B21)

asteroid (as'tə roid') An undeveloped planet that orbits the Sun. (p. C86)

atmosphere (at'məs fîr') The blanket of gases that surrounds Earth. (pp. D6, D64)

atom (at'əm) The smallest particle of an element. Atoms of one element are all alike but are different from those of any other element. (p. E32)

axis (ak'sis) A real or imaginary line that a spinning object turns around. (p. C67)

B

bacteria (bak tîr'ē ə) *pl. n., sing.* **bacterium** (-ē əm) One-celled organisms that have cell walls but no nuclei. (p. A13)

balance (bal'əns) An instrument used to measure mass. (p. E8)

basalt (bə sôlt') A fine-grained volcanic rock. (p. C9)

budding (bud'ing) A form of asexual reproduction in simple invertebrates where a bud forms on the adult's body and slowly develops into a new organism before breaking off. (p. B60)

buoyancy (boi'ən sē) The upward force of water, another liquid, or air that keeps things afloat. (p. E7)

C

camouflage (kam'ə fläzh') An adaptation by which an animal can hide by blending in with its surroundings. (p. B66)

carnivore (kär'nə vôr') A consumer that eats only animals. (p. A48)

cast (kast) A fossil formed or shaped within a mold. (p. C19)

cell (sel) The smallest unit of living matter. (p. A7)

cell membrane (sel mem'brān) A thin envelope surrounding the nucleus of a cell. (p. A9)

chemical change (kəm'i kəl chānj) A change that produces new matter with different properties from the original matter. *See* **physical change**. (p. E52)

chlorophyll (klôr'ə fil') A green substance in plant cells that helps plants make food by trapping the Sun's energy. (pp. A7, A73)

chromosome (krō'mə sōm') One of the threadlike structures inside a cell's nucleus that control an organism's traits. (p. A9)

circuit (sûr'kit) A complete path through which electricity can flow. (p. F78)

circuit breaker (sûr'kit brā'kər) A reusable switch that protects circuits from dangerously high currents. (p. F84)

circulatory system (sûr′kyə lə tôr′ē sis′təm) The organ system that moves blood through the body. (p. B46)

cirrus cloud (sir′əs kloud) A high-altitude cloud with a featherlike shape, made of ice crystals. (p. D71)

class (klas) A smaller group within a phlyum, such as all those animals that produce milk for their young. Classes are made up of smaller groups called orders. (p. A22)

classify (klas′ə fī) To place things that share properties together in groups. (p. S7)

clone (klōn) An exact copy of its parent formed during asexual reproduction. (p. B60)

cloud (kloud) A mass of tiny droplets of condensed water in the atmosphere. (p. D17)

cnidarian (nī dâr′ē ən) An invertebrate with poison stingers on tentacles . (p. B17)

cold front (kōld frunt) A front where cold air moves in under a warm front. (p. D81)

cold-blooded (kōld′blud′id) Said of an animal that cannot control its body temperature. (p. B28)

comet (kom′it) A chunk of ice and rock that orbits the Sun in a long, narrow orbit. (p. C86)

communicate (kə mū′ni kāt′) To share information. (p. S7)

community (kə mū′ni tē) The living part of an ecosystem. (p. A40)

compound (kom′pound) A substance made when two or more elements are joined together and lose their own properties. (p. E36)

compound machine (kom′pound mə shēn′) A combination of two or more simple machines. (p. F29)

concave lens (kän kāv′ lenz) A lens that is thinner in the middle than at the edges, spreading light rays apart and making images appear smaller. (p. F47)

condensation (kon′den sa′shən) The process in which water particles change from a gas to a liquid. (p. D17)

conduction (kən duk′shən) The transfer of energy between two objects that are touching. (p. F36)

conductor (kən duk′tər) A material through which heat or electricity flows easily. (pp. F34, F72)

PRONUNCIATION KEY

a at; ā ape; ä far; âr care; ô law; e end; ē me; i it; ī ice; îr pierce; o hot; ō old; ôr fork; oi oil; ou out; u up; ū use; ü rule; u̇ pull; ûr turn; hw white; ng song; th thin; <u>th</u> this; zh measure; ə about, taken, pencil, lemon, circus

constellation (kon'stə lā'shən) A number of stars that appears to form a pattern. (p. C88)

consumer (kən sü'mər) Any organism that eats the food producers make. (p. A46)

contract (*v.,* kən trakt') To shrink or decrease in size, as most matter does when it cools. (p. F37)

convection (kən'vek'shən) The transfer of energy by the flow of liquids or gases, such as water boiling in a pot or warm air rising in a room. (p. F36)

convex lens (kän veks' lenz) A lens that bulges in the middle, bringing rays of light together and making images appear larger. (p. F46)

cornea (kôr'nē ə) The thin, clear tissue covering the eye. (p. F48)

crater (krā'tər) A hollow area or pit in the ground. (p. C71)

crest (krest) The highest part of a wave. (p. D32)

crust (krust) Solid rock that makes up the Moon's and Earth's outermost layers. (p. C58)

cumulus cloud (kū'myə ləs kloud) A puffy cloud that appears to rise up from a flat bottom. (p. D71)

current (kûr'ənt) An ocean movement; a large stream of water that flows in the ocean. (p. D28)

current electricity (kûr'ənt i lek tris'i tē) A moving electrical charge. (p. F78)

cytoplasm (sī'tə pla'zəm) A jellylike substance that fills a cell. (p. A9)

D

decomposer (dē'kəm pōz'ər) An organism that breaks down wastes and the remains of other organisms. (p. A46)

deep ocean current (dēp ō'shən kûr'ənt) A stream of water that flows more than 650 feet (200 meters) beneath the sea. (p. D28)

define based on observations (di fīn' bāst ôn ob'zər vā'shənz) To put together a description that relies on examination and experience. (p. S7)

density (den'si tē) The amount of matter in a given space. In scientific terms, density is the mass per unit of volume. (p. E20)

deposition (dep'ə zish'ən) The dropping off of soil and rock particles by waves, wind, running water, or glaciers. *See* **erosion**. (p. D34)

digestive system (di jes'tiv sis'təm) The organ system that breaks down food for fuel. (p. B49)

direct current (di rekt' kûr'ənt) Current that flows in one direction through a circuit. (p. F94)

discharge (*n.*, dis'chärj; *v.*, dis chärj') The sudden movement of an electric charge from the object where it built up onto another nearby object. (p. F72)

drought (drout) A long period of time with little or no precipitation. (pp. A56, D42)

drumlin (drum'lin) An oval mound of glacial till. (p. C35)

dry cell (drī sel) A battery that changes chemical energy into electrical energy. It is made of a carbon rod and a moist chemical paste. (p. F81)

E

earthquake (ūrth'kwāk) Movement or vibration in the rocks that make up Earth's crust. (p. C54)

echinoderm (i ki'nə dûrm') A spiny-skinned invertebrate. (p. B20)

ecology (ē kol'ə jē) The study of how living and nonliving things interact. (p. A40)

ecosystem (ek'ō sis'təm) The living and nonliving things in an environment and all their interactions. (p. A40)

efficiency (i fish'ən sē) The measure of how much useful work a machine puts out compared to the amount of work put into it. (p. F30)

effort force (ef'ərt fôrs) The amount of force needed to move something. (p. F22)

egg (eg) The female sex cell. (p. B61)

electric motor (i lek'trik mō'tər) A power source that transforms electrical energy into movement, or mechanical energy. (p. F93)

electrical charge (i lek'tri kəl chärj) The positive or negative property that particles are made of. (p. F70)

electrode (i lek'trōd) The negative or positive terminal of a wet cell. The positive electrode is made of copper, the negative electrode of zinc. (p. F81)

electromagnet (i lek'trō mag'nit) A temporary magnet created when current flows through wire wrapped in coils around an iron bar. (p. F92)

electromagnetic spectrum (i lek'trō mag net'ik spek'trəm) A range of all waves of varying wavelengths, including the visible spectrum. It ranges from radio waves, the longest waves with the lowest energy, to gamma waves, the shortest waves with the highest energy. (p. F43)

PRONUNCIATION KEY

a at; ā ape; ä far; âr care; ô law; e end; ē me; i it; ī ice; îr pierce; o hot; ō old; ôr fork; oi oil; ou out; u up; ū use; ü rule; u̇ pull; ûr turn; hw white; ng song; th thin; th this; zh measure; ə about, taken, pencil, lemon, circus

element (el′ə mənt) A substance that is made up of only one type of matter. (p. E32)

embryo (em′brē ō′) A developing organism that results from fertilization. (pp. A33, B61)

endoskeleton (en′dō skel′i tən) An internal supporting structure. (p. B20)

energy (en′ər jē) The ability to do work, either to make an object move or to change matter. (p. F14)

epidermis (e′pə dûr′mis) The outermost protective layer of a leaf. (p. A73)

erosion (i rō′zhən) The wearing away of soil and rock particles by waves, wind, running water, or glaciers. *See* **deposition**. (pp. C13, D34)

erratic (i rat′ik) An isolated boulder left behind by a glacier. (p. C37)

evaporation (i vap′ə rā′shən′) The process in which water particles change from a liquid to a gas. (pp. D16, E35)

evolution (ev′ə lü′shən) The change in living things over time. (p. A30)

excretory system (ek′skri tōr′ē sis′təm) The organ system that removes liquid wastes. (p. B47)

exoskeleton (ek′sō skel′i tən) A hard covering that protects an invertebrate's body. (p. B21)

expand (ek spand′) To increase in size, as most matter does when it is heated. (p. F37)

experiment (ek sper′ə ment′) To perform a test to support or disprove a hypothesis. (p. S7)

extinct (ek stingkt′) Said of an organism no longer alive on Earth. (p. A33)

F

family (fam′ə lē) A smaller group of organisms within a class. Families are made up of still smaller groups of very similar organisms called genuses. (p. A22)

fault (fôlt) A break in Earth's outer layer caused by the movement of rocks. (p. C56)

fertilization (fûr′tə lə zā′shən) The joining of a female sex cell, the egg, and a male sex cell, the sperm, to produce a fertilized egg. (pp. A85, B61)

fertilizer (fûr′tə lī′zər) Chemical or animal waste used to treat the soil. (p. D51)

fibrous root (fī′brəs rüt) One of the many hairy branching roots that is one of the two main types of plant roots. *See* **taproot**. (p. A71)

filter (fil′tər) A tool used to separate things by size. It works by means of a mesh or screen that retains the bigger pieces but allows smaller pieces to fall through the holes of the filter. (p. E35)

filtration (fil trā′shən) The passing of a liquid through materials that remove impurities. (p. D52)

food chain (füd chān) The set of steps in which organisms get the food they need to survive. (pp. A48, B7)

food web (füd web) The pattern that shows how food chains are related. (pp. A50, B7)

force (fôrs) Any push or pull that makes an object start moving, stop moving, speed up, slow down, or change direction. (p. F10)

form a hypothesis (fôrm ə hī poth'ə sis) To make a statement that can be tested to answer to a question. (p. S7)

fossil (fos'əl) Any evidence of an organism that lived in the past. (pp. A30, C14)

fossil fuel (fos'əl fū'əl) A substance such as coal or oil that was formed millions of years ago from the remains of plants and animals. These fuels are nonrenewable resources, and when burned for energy, are a major source of pollution. (p. F38)

frame of reference (frāme uv ref'ər əns) A description of the position of an object in terms of other objects that surround it. (p. F6)

freeze (frēz) The process in which moving particles in water slow down, lose heat, and change from a liquid to a solid. (p. D19)

frequency (frē'kwən sē) The number of times a sound source vibrates in one second. (p. F58)

friction (frik'shən) A force between surfaces that slows objects down or stops them from moving. (p. F11)

front (frunt) A boundary between air masses with different temperatures. (p. D80)

fulcrum (fùl'krəm) A fixed point that supports the bar of a lever and allows the bar to turn, or pivot. (p. F22)

fungi (fun'jī) *pl. n., sing.* **fungus** (fung'gəs) One- or many-celled organisms that absorb food from dead organisms. (p. A13)

fuse (fūz) A device that melts to keep too much electric current from flowing through wires. Once melted, a fuse cannot be reused. (p. F84)

gas (gas) A state of matter that does not take up a definite amount of space and has no definite shape. (p. E9)

gears (gîrz) Wheels with teeth that fit together, used for transmitting or changing motion. (p. F28)

PRONUNCIATION KEY

a at; ā ape; ä far; âr care; ô law; e end; ē me; i it; ī ice; îr pierce; o hot; ō old; ôr fork; oi oil; ou out; u up; ū use; ü rule; ù pull; ûr turn; hw white; ng song; th thin; <u>th</u> this; zh measure; ə about, taken, pencil, lemon, circus

generator (jen′ər rā′tər) A device that creates alternating current by spinning an electric coil between the poles of a powerful magnet. (p. F94)

genus (jēn′əs) A group made up of two or more very similar species. (p. A25)

germination (jûr′mə nā′shən) The sprouting of a seed into a new plant. (p. A82)

gizzard (giz′ərd) A muscular organ in birds that breaks down food with stored pebbles. (p. B49)

glacial till (glā′shəl til) An unsorted mixture of rock materials deposited as a glacier melts. (p. C35)

glacier (glā′shər) A large mass of snow and ice that slowly moves downward and outward over the land. (pp. D8, C34)

gneiss (nīs) A metamorphic rock composed of alternating light and dark layers. (p. C12)

gram (g) (gram) A unit used to measure the mass of small objects. There are 1,000 *grams* in one *kilogram*. *See* **kilogram.** (p. E8)

grounded (ground′əd) Said of an electric charge that flows into the ground, or surface of Earth. (p. F74)

groundwater (ground′wô′tər) Water stored in the cracks of underground rocks. (p. D10)

H

habitat (hab′i tat′) The home of an organism. (p. A40)

heat (hēt) The movement of thermal energy from warmer to cooler objects. (p. F34)

herbivore (hûr′bə vôr′) A consumer that eats only plants. (p. A48)

heredity (hə red′i tē) The passing of traits from parent to offspring. (p. B62)

horizon (hə rī′zən) A layer of soil differing from the layers above and below it. (p. C45)

humidity (hū mid′i tē) A measurement of how much water vapor is in air. (p. D66)

humus (hü′məs) Leftover decomposed plant and animal matter in the soil. (p. C44)

I

ice cap (īs kap) A thick sheet of ice covering a large area of land. (p. D8)

igneous rock (ig′nē əs rok) "Fire-made" rock formed from melted rock material. (p. C9)

imprint (*n.,* im′print′) A fossil created by a print or impression. (p. C18)

inclined plane (in klīnd′ plān) A straight, slanted surface, that is not moved when it is used. (p. F26)

inertia (i nûr′shə) The tendency of an object to remain in motion or to stay at rest unless acted upon by an outside force. (p. F11)

infer (in fûr′) To form an idea from facts or observations. (p. S7)

inherited behavior (in her′i təd bi hāv′yər) A behavior that is inborn, not learned. (p. B70)

inner core (in′ər kôr) A sphere of solid material at the center of the Moon or Earth. (p. C58)

instinct (in′stingkt′) A pattern of behavior that requires no thinking because it is programmed into an animal's brain. (p. B70)

insulator (in′sə lā′tər) A material through which heat or electricity does not flow easily. (pp. F34, F72)

interpret data (in tûr′prit dā′tə) To use the information that has been gathered to answer questions or solve a problem. (p. S7)

invertebrate (in vûr′tə brāt′) An animal without a backbone. (p. B8)

irrigation (ir′i gā′shən) A way to get water into the soil by artificial means. (p. D50)

kilogram (kg) (kil′ə gram′) The standard unit used to measure mass. *See* **gram**. (p. E8)

kinetic energy (ki net′ik en′ər jē) The energy an object has because it is moving. (p. F14)

kingdom (king′dəm) The largest group into which an organism can be classified. (p. A20)

L

larva (lar′və) A worm-like stage of some organisms that hatches from an egg during complete metamorphosis; a young organism with a form different from its parents. (p. B56)

law of reflection (lô uv ri flek′shən) When light strikes a surface such as a mirror, it is reflected at any outgoing angle equal to its incoming angle. (p. F45)

leaf (lēf) Any of the plant parts, usually green, that use sunlight to make food. (p. A70)

learned behavior (lûrnd bi hāv′yər) Behavior that is not inborn. (p. B71)

PRONUNCIATION KEY

a at; ā ape; ä far; âr care; ô law; e end; ē me; i it; ī ice; îr pierce; o hot; ō old; ôr fork; oi oil; ou out; u up; ū use;
ü rule; ù pull; ûr turn; hw white; ng song; th thin; <u>th</u> this; zh measure; ə about, taken, pencil, lemon, circus

length (lengkth) The number of units that fit along one edge of something. (p. E16)

lever (lev′ər) A simple machine made of a rigid bar or plank and a fixed point, called a fulcrum. (p. F22)

life cycle (līf sī′kəl) The stages of growth and change of an organism's life. (p. B58)

life span (līf span) How long an organism can be expected to live. (p. B59)

lightning (līt′ning) A discharge of static electricty from a thundercloud. (p. F73)

liquid (lik′wid) A state of matter that takes up a definite amount of space but has no definite shape. (p. E9)

load (lōd) The object being lifted or moved by a machine. (p. F22)

luster (lus′tər) The way a mineral reflects light. (p. C7)

M

magnetic field (mag net′ik fēld) A region of magnetic force around a magnet. (p. F91)

make a model (māk ə mod′əl) To make something to represent an object or event. (p. S7)

mammal (mam′əl) A warm-blooded vertebrate with hair or fur; female mammals produce milk to feed their young. (p. B34)

mantle (man′təl) The layer of rock lying below the crust. (p. C58)

mass (mas) The amount of matter making up an object. (p. E8)

matter (ma′tər) Anything that has mass and takes up space.

measure (mezh′ər) To find the size, volume, area, mass, weight, or temperature of an object, or how long an event occurs. (p. S7)

melt (melt) When water particles absorb heat energy and change from a solid to a liquid. (p. D19)

metamorphic rock (mət′ə môr′fik rok) Rock whose form has been changed by heat and/or pressure. (p. C12)

metamorphosis (met′ə môr′fə sis) A process of changes in form during an animal's development. (p. B56)

meteor (mē′tē ər) A fragment of rock, ice, or metal that glows as it collides with Earth's atmosphere. (p. C86)

meteorite (mē′tē ə rīt′) A chunk of rock from space that hit Earth. (p. C87)

metric system (met′rik sis′təm) A system of measurement based on units of 10. Metric units such as the meter, kilogram, and liter are used in most countries and in all scientific work. *See* **standard unit.** (p. E16)

microorganism (mī′krō ôr′gə niz′əm) An organism that is so small you need a microscope to see it. (p. A12)

mimicry (mim′i krē) When one organism imitates the traits of another. (p. B68)

mineral (min′ə rəl) A naturally occurring substance, neither a plant nor animal. (p. C6)

mixture (miks′chər) Two or more types of matter that are mixed together but keep their own properties. (p. E34)

mold (mold) A fossil clearly showing the outside features of the organism. (p. C18)

mollusk (mol′əsk) A soft-bodied invertebrate. (p. B20)

moraine (mə rān′) Rock debris carried and deposited by a glacier. (p. C35)

muscular system (mus′kyə lər sis′təm) The organ system made up of muscles that move bones. (p. B52)

N

nervous system (nûr′vəs sis′təm) The organ system that controls all other body systems. (p. B50)

neutron star (nü′tron stär) The remnant of a supernova that has become a very dense star. (p. E21)

newton (nü′tən) A metric unit for weight, measuring the pull of gravity between an object and Earth. (p. E19)

nucleus (nü′klē əs) A cell's central control station. (p. 9)

nymph (nimf) A stage of some organisms that hatch from an egg during incomplete metamorphosis; a *nymph* is a young insect that looks like an adult. (p. B57)

O

observe (əb sûrv′) To use one or more of the senses to identify or learn about an object or event. (p. S7)

omnivore (om′nə vôr′) A consumer that eats both plants and animals. (p. A48)

opaque (ō pāk′) Completely blocking light from passing through it. (p. F49)

orbit (ôr′bit) The path an object follows as it revolves. (p. C68)

order (ôr′dər) A smaller group within a class. Orders are made up of still smaller groups of similar organisms called families. (p. A22)

organ (ôr′gən) A group of tissues that work together to do a certain job. (p. A15)

PRONUNCIATION KEY

a at; ā ape; ä far; âr care; ô law; e end; ē me; i it; ī ice; îr pierce; o hot; ō old; ôr fork; oi oil; ou out; u up; ū use; ü rule; ù pull; ûr turn; hw white; ng song; th thin; <u>th</u> this; zh measure; ə about, taken, pencil, lemon, circus

organ system (ôr′gən sis′təm) A group of organs that work together to carry on life functions. (p. A15)

organism (ôr′gə niz′əm) A living thing that carries out five basic life functions on its own. (p. A6)

outer core (out′ər kôr) A liquid layer of Earth lying below the mantle. (p. C58)

outwash plain (out′wôsh plān) Gravel, sand, and clay carried from glaciers by melting water and streams. (p. C37)

ovary (ō′və rē) A structure containing egg cells. (p. A85)

overpopulation (ō′vər pop′yə la′shən) A depletion of resources that occurs when too many of at least one kind of living thing inhabits an ecosystem. (p. A57)

oxygen (ok′sə jən) A part of the air that is needed by most plants and animals to live. (p. A6)

P

parallel circuit (par′ə lel′ sûr′kit) A circuit in which each bulb is connected to the cell separately. (p. F82)

periodic (pîr′ē od′ik) Repeating in a pattern, like the periodic table of the elements. (p. E32)

permeability (pûr′mē ə bil′i tē) The rate at which water can pass through a material. Water passes quickly through porous soils with a high permeability. (p. C49)

petrified (pet′rə fīd′) Said of parts of plants or animals, especially wood and bone, that have been preserved by being "turned to stone." (p. C21)

phase (fāz) One of the different shapes the Moon appears to take as it travels around Earth. (p. C72)

photosynthesis (fō′tə sin′thə sis) A process in plants that uses energy from sunlight to make food from water and carbon dioxide. (p. A74)

phylum (fī′ləm), *pl.* **phyla** (fī′lə) A large group within a kingdom. Members share at least one major characteristic, like having a backbone. (pp. A22, B9)

physical change (fiz′i kəl chānj) A change that begins and ends with the same type of matter. *See* **chemical change.** (p. E44)

pistil (pis′təl) The part of the plant that produces the female sex cells, the eggs. (p. A84)

pitch (pich) The highness or lowness of a sound as determined by its frequency. (p. F59)

planet (plan′it) A satellite of the Sun. (p. C81)

plasma (plaz′mə) The liquid part of blood. (p. B46)

pole (pōl) One of two ends of a magnet; where a magnet's pull is strongest. (p. F90)

pollen (pol'ən) Powdery grains in a flower that contain its male sex cells. (p. A84)

pollination (pol'ə nā'shən) The transfer of a flower's pollen from anther to pistil. (p. A84)

pollution (pə lü'shən) The adding of harmful substances to the water, air, or land. (p. A58)

population (pop'yə lā'shən) One type of organism living in an area. (p. A40)

pore space (pôr spās) Any of the tiny gaps between soil particles, usually filled with water and air. *Porous* soils have large, well-connected pore spaces. (pp. C48, D38)

potential energy (pə ten'shəl en'ər jē) Energy that is stored or waiting to be used, giving an object the future ability to do work. (p. F14)

precipitation (pri sip'i tā'shən) Water in the atmosphere that falls to Earth as rain, snow, hail, or sleet. (p. D18)

predict (pri dikt') To state possible results of an event or experiment. (p. S7)

prism (pri'zəm) An object that separates white light into the colors that make it up. (p. F42)

producer (prə dü'sər) An organism, such as a plant, that makes food. (p. A46)

protist (prō'tist) Any of the one-celled organisms that live in water. Some are plantlike and make their own food. Some are animallike and are capable of motion. (p. A12)

pulley (pùl'ē) A machine made up of a rope, belt, or chain wrapped around a wheel with a groove in it. (p. F24)

pupa (pū'pə) A stage of some organisms that follows the larva stage; many changes take place as adult tissues and organs form. (p. B56)

R

radiation (rā'dē ā'shən) The transfer of energy through space. (p. F36)

reflection (ri flek' shən) The bouncing of light waves off a surface. (p. F45)

reflex (rē'fleks') The simplest inherited behavior that is automatic, like an animal scratching an itch. (p. B70)

refraction (ri frak'shən) The bending of light as it passes from one transparent material into another. (p. F46)

regeneration (rē jen'ə rā'shən) A form of asexual reproduction in simple animals where a whole animal develops from just a part of the original animal. (p. B60)

PRONUNCIATION KEY

a at; ā ape; ä far; âr care; ô law; e end; ē me; i it; ī ice; îr pierce; o hot; ō old; ôr fork; oi oil; ou out; u up; ū use; ü rule; ù pull; ûr turn; hw white; ng song; th thin; <u>th</u> this; zh measure; ə about, taken, pencil, lemon, circus

relative age (rel'ə tiv āj) The age of something compared to the age of another thing. (p. C11)

reproduction (rē'prə duk'shən) The making of offspring. (p. B60)

reptile (rep'təl') A cold-blooded vertebrate that lives on land and has a backbone, an endoskeleton, and waterproof skin with scales or plates. (p. B32)

resistor (ri zis'tər) A material through which electricity has difficulty flowing. (p. F80)

respiration (res'pə rā'shən) The release in plants of energy from their food. (p. A74)

respiratory system (res'pər ə tôr'ē sis'təm) The organ system that brings oxygen to body cells and removes waste gas. (p. B47)

retina (ret'ə nə) A tissue covering the back of the eye where light images are changed into signals that travel along the optic nerve to the brain. (p. F48)

revolve (ri volv') To move in a circular or nearly circular path around something else. (p. C68)

rock cycle (rok sī'kəl) A never-ending process by which rocks are changed from one type to another. (p. C13)

root (rüt) The part of a tree that takes in water and other materials a plant needs to make food. (p. A70)

root hair (rüt hâr) One of the threadlike cells on a root that take in water and minerals from the soil. (p. A71)

rotate (rō'tāt) To spin around. (p. C66)

runoff (run'ôf') The water that flows over Earth's surface but does not evaporate or soak into the ground. (p. D39)

S

scale (skāl) An instrument used to measure weight. (p. E19)

screw (skrü) An inclined plane that is wrapped around a pole. (p. F27)

sediment (sed'ə ment) Deposited rock particles and other materials that settle in a liquid. (p. C10)

sedimentary rock (sed'ə men'tə rē rok) Rock formed from bits or layers of rocks cemented together. (p. C10)

seed (sēd) An undeveloped plant with stored food sealed in a protective covering. (p. A82)

seismic wave (sīz'mik wāv) A vibration caused by rocks moving and breaking along faults. (p. C56)

seismograph (sīz'mə graf') An instrument that detects, measures, and records the energy of earthquake vibations. (p. C54)

septic tank (sep'tik tangk) An underground tank in which sewage is broken down by bacteria. (p. D53)

series circuit (sîr'ēz sûr'kit) A circuit in which the current must flow through one bulb in order to flow through the other. (p. F82)

sewage (sü'ij) Water mixed with waste. (p. D53)

sewer (sü'ər) A large pipe or channel that carries sewage to a sewage treatment plant. (p. D53)

short circuit (shôrt sûr'kit) A situation that allows too much current to flow through a conductor. (p. F80)

simple machine (sim'pəl mə shēn') A machine with few moving parts, making it easier to do work. The six types of simple machines are the lever, pulley, wheel and axle, inclined plane, wedge, and screw. (p. F20)

skeletal system (skel'i təl sis'təm) The organ system made up of bones. (p. B52)

soil profile (soil prō'fil) A vertical section of soil from the surface down to bedrock. The more horizons in a soil profile the greater the relative age of the soil. (p. C45)

soil water (soil wô'tər) Water that soaks into the ground. (p. D10)

solar system (sō'lər sis'təm) The Sun and all the objects that orbit around it. (p. C81)

solid (sol'id) A state of matter that has a definite shape and takes up a definite amount of space. (p. E8)

sound wave (sound wāv) An area of bunched-up and spread-out air particles that moves outward in all directions from a vibrating object. (p. F55)

species (spē'shēz') The smallest group into which an organism is classified. (p. A22)

spectrum (spek'trəm) A range of light waves with different wavelengths. (p. F42)

speed (spēd) The distance traveled in a certain amount of time (p. F8)

sperm (spûrm) The male sex cell. (p. B61)

sponge (spunj) The simplest kind of invertebrate. (p. B8)

spore (spôr) The cells in a seedless plant that grows into new organisms. (p. A88)

PRONUNCIATION KEY

a at; ā ape; ä far; âr care; ô law; e end; ē me; i it; ī ice; îr pierce; o hot; ō old; ôr fork; oi oil; ou out; u up; ū use; ü rule; ù pull; ûr turn; hw white; ng song; th thin; <u>th</u> this; zh measure; ə about, taken, pencil, lemon, circus

standard unit (stan′dərd ū′nit) A unit of measure that people all understand and agree to use. Units in the English system, such as the inch, pound, yard, and gallon are used mostly in the United States. *See* **metric system.** (p. E16)

star (stär) A hot sphere of gases that gives off energy. (p. C80)

state (stāt) Any of the three forms of matter—solid, liquid, or gas—that exist on Earth. (p. E8)

static electricity (stat′ik i lek tris′i tē) The buildup of an electric charge on a material. (p. F71)

stationary front (stā′shə ner ē frunt) An unmoving front where a cold air mass and a warm air mass meet. (p. D81)

stem (stem) The part of a tree that carries food, water and other materials to and from the roots and leaves. (p. A70)

stomata (stō′mə tə) *pl. n., sing.* **stoma** Pores in the bottom of leaves that open and close to let in air or give off water vapor. (p. A73)

stratus cloud (strā′təs kloud) A cloud that forms in a blanket-like layer. (p. D71)

streak plate (strēk plāt) A glass plate that a mineral can be rubbed against to find out the color of the streak it leaves. (p. C7)

subsoil (sub′soil′) A hard layer of clay and minerals that lies beneath topsoil. (p. C45)

surface current (sûr′fis kûr′ənt) The movement of the ocean caused by steady winds blowing over the ocean. (p. D29)

switch (swich) A device that can open or close an electric circuit. (p. F79)

symmetry (sim′ə trē) The way an animal's body parts match up around a point or central line. (p. B8)

T

taproot (tap′rüt′) A single, thick root that is one of the two main types of plant roots. *See* **fibrous root.** (p. A71)

temperature (tem′pər ə cher) A measure of how hot or cold something is. (p. F35)

terminus (tûr′mə nəs) The end, or outer margin, of a glacier where rock debris accumulates. (p. C35)

thermometer (thər mom′ə tər) An instrument used to measure temperature. (p. F35)

tide (tīd) The rise and fall of ocean water levels. (p. D30)

tissue (tish′ü) A group of similar cells that work together to carry out a job. (p. A14)

topsoil (top′soil′) The dark, top layer of soil, rich in humus and minerals, in which many tiny organisms live and most plants grow. (p. C45)

trait (trāt) A characteristic of a living thing. (p. A21)

translucent (trans lü'sənt) Letting only some light through, so that objects on the other side appear blurry. (p. F49)

transparent (trans pâr'ənt) Letting all light through, so that objects on the other side can be seen clearly. (p. F49)

transpiration (tran'spə rā'shən) A plant's release of excess water vapor through the stomata on the underside of its leaves. (pp. A73, D41)

trough (trôf) The lowest part of a wave. (p. D32)

use numbers (ūz num'bərz) To order, count, add, subtract, multiply, and divide to explain data. (p. S7)

use variables (ūz vâr'ē ə bəlz) To identify and separate things in an experiment that can be changed or controlled. (p. S7)

vacuole (vak'ū ōl') The cell's holding bin for food, water, and wastes. (p. A9)

vein (vān) One of the bundle of tubes in a stem that carry water to the leaf and take food from the leaf to the stem and roots. (p. A73)

vertebrate (vûr'tə brāt') An animal with a backbone. (p. B8)

vibration (vī brā'shən) The back-and-forth motion of an object. (p. F54)

virus (vī'rəs) Nonliving particles smaller than cells that are able to reproduce only inside living cells. (p. A16)

visible spectrum (viz'ə bəl spek'trəm) The seven colors of light that make up white light: red, orange, yellow, green, blue, indigo, violet. (p. F42)

volt (vōlt) A unit for measuring the force with which negative charges flow. (p. F96)

voltage (vōlt'tij') A measure of the force with which negative charges flow. (p. F96)

volume (vol'ūm) The amount of space an object takes up. (p. E17)

PRONUNCIATION KEY

a at; ā ape; ä far; âr care; ô law; e end; ē me; i it; ī ice; îr pierce; o hot; ō old; ôr fork; oi oil; ou out; u up; ū use; ü rule; ù pull; ûr turn; hw white; ng song; th thin; <u>th</u> this; zh measure; ə about, taken, pencil, lemon, circus

warm front (wôrm frunt) Gases that surround Earth. (p. D80)

warm-blooded (wôrm′blud′id) Said of an animal with a constant body temperature. (p. B28)

water conservation (wôtər kon′sər vā′shən) The use of water-saving methods. (p. D54)

water cycle (wô′tər sī′kəl)The continuous movement of water between Earth's surface and the air, changing from liquid to gas to liquid. (p. D20)

water table (wô′tər tā′bəl) The upper area of groundwater. (p. D39)

water treatment plant (wô′tər trēt′mənt plant) A place where water is made clean and pure. (p. D52)

water vapor (wô′tər vā′pər) A gas in Earth's atmosphere. (p. D6)

wave (wāv) An up-and-down movement of water. (p. D32)

wavelength (wāv′lengkth′) The distance from the top of one wave to the top of the next. (pp. D32, F42)

weathering (weth′ər ing) The process of breaking down rocks into smaller pieces that create sediment. (p. C13)

wedge (wej) A moving inclined plane. (p. F27)

weight (wāt) A measure of force that indicates the amount of gravity acting on an object. (p. F12)

weight (wāt) The measure of the pull of gravity between an object and Earth. (pp. E19, F12)

wet cell (wet sel) A device that produces electricity using two different metal bars placed in an acid solution. (p. F81)

wheel and axle (hwēl and ak′səl) A simple machine made of a handle or axis attached to the center of a wheel. (p. F25)

work (wûrk) The use of a force to move an object a certain distance (p. F13)

Index

A

Acceleration, F8
Acid rain, A59
Adaptations, B66–67, B69*, B73
Adult stage, B56, B57
Age, relative, C11
Air, D63*, D64, D66–69, D78
Air masses, D78–81
Air pollution, A59
Air pressure, D67, D69, D70*, D72
Air temperature, D66, D72
Al–Battani, C90–91
Algae, A12
Alligators, B32
Alloys, E38
Alternating current (AC), F94
Altitude, climate and, D87
Alvarez, Luis, A24
Alvarez, Walter, A24
Amber, C20
Ammeter, F78–79
Amoeba, A12
Amperes, F78–79
Amphibians, B28, B31, B45*, B47
Amplifier, F60
Amplitude, F59
Anemometer, D72
Animals, B4–41
  cells in, A7–11
  characteristics of, B5*–6
  development of, B54–59
  differences among, B8–10
  endangered, A36–37, B12–13
  energy sources for, B7
  helping people, B36, B71
  life cycle of, B58
  life span of, B59
  modeling cells of, A11*
  organ systems of, B44–53
  petrified, C21
  relationship to plants, A90–91
  reproduction in, B60–62
  soil formation and, C44
  survival by, B64–75
  tool use among, F21
  water in, D12
  with backbones. See Vertebrates.
  without backbones. See Invertebrates.
Anther, A84
Ant plant, A78–79
Apollo missions, C71
Arachnids, B21
Area, E17
Armadillos, B72
Arthropods, B16, B21–23
Aryabhata the First, C90–91
Ascaris, B18
Asteroids, C86
Atmosphere, D6, D11, D16–17, D64, D65
Atoms, E32, F70–71
Ax, F20
Axis of Earth, C67
Axles, wheels and, F20, F25

B

Bacteria, A13, C44
Bacteriologists, A94–95
Balance, E8, E19
Baleen whale, A33
Bar magnets, F88, F89*–90
Barometer, D70*, D72
Basalt, C9, C13
Bats, A32, B51
Batteries, F81
Beaches, D9
Beavers, F21
Bedrock, C44, C45
Berzelius, Jöns Jacob, E40–41
Bicycles, F28, F29
Bilateral symmetry, B9
Birds, B28, B33, B48, B49
Blackout, F76
Bladder, B47
Blind salamander, A33
Blood, B46
Body color, B65*–66, B67
Body plans, symmetrical, B8–10
Bones, A32, A33, C21
Bony fish, B28, B29, B30
Bottom dwellers, B30
Brains, comparison of, B50
Bryce Canyon, Utah, C4
Budding, B60
Buoyancy, E7
Butterflies, B9, B68

C

Cactus, A76
Calcite, C7, C8
California condor, B13
Camels, D4
Camouflage, B66
Canis familiaris, A25
Carbon, C21
Carbon dioxide, A70, A73, A74, D24, D25, D41, D64, D78
Carnivores, A48
Carrots, A71
Cartilaginous fish, B28, B29, B30
Cast (fossil), C19*
Caterpillars, A68, B6
Cell membrane, A9
Cells, A4–11, A14, A17
  chemical changes in, E56
  classifying organisms and, A20, A21
  definition of, A7
  in plant stem, A72
  jobs of, A10
  life span and division of, B59
  modeling, A11*
  of onion plant, A55*
  plant vs. animal, A7–11
  sex, A85, A87, A88
  shapes of, A10

*Indicates an activity related to this topic.

Cells, electric, F81
Cell wall, A8
Celsius scale, F35
Centipedes, B21, B22
CFCs, D74–75
Charge, electrical, F70–71
Cheetah, B34
Chemical changes in matter,
    E50–57, E51*
    causes of, E53
    characteristics of, E52–53
    in the real world, E56
    preventing, E55*
    products of, E54
Chemical energy, F15, F16
Chemists, E62–63
Chesapeake Bay cleanup, A60
Chitin, B21
Chlorine, D52
Chlorine gas, E53
Chlorophyll, A7, A73, A74
Chloroplasts, A8, A47
Chromosomes, A9
Cichlid, B30
Circuit breakers, F84
Circuits, F78–79
    kinds of, F82–83
    protection of, F84
    sizes of, F86–87
Circulatory system, B45*, B46
Cirrus clouds, D71
Classes, A22–23
Classification
    of matter, E31*–39
    of organisms, A18–35, A19*,
        B26, B28–35*
    skills in, A18, A24*, B14,
        B26, E30
Clean Air Act, A60
Clean Water Act, A60
Climate, D84–89
Clones, B60
Closed circuit, F78–79
Cloud cover, D71
Clouds, D17, D20, D21, D71,
    E56
Clovis point, F20
Cnidarians, B16, B17, B46
Coastlines, D34
Coconuts, A80

Cold–blooded animals, B28
Cold fronts, D81, D83
Comets, C86, C87*
Comet theory, A24
Communication skills, D46, E42,
    F88
Community, A40, A41
Compass, F8
Compound machines, F29
Compounds, E36–37, E54
Computer chips, F86–87
Concave lens, F47
Condensation, D17, D19, D20,
    D21
Conduction, F36
Conductors, F34–35, F72, F80*
Conglomerate, C10
Constellations, C88
Consumers, A46, A47, A48
Continental shelf, D7
Continental slope, D7
Contraction, F37
Convection, F36
Convex lens, F47
Copernicus, Nicolaus, C90–91
Copper acetate, E52
Copying behavior, B71
Coral reefs, B24
Cornea, F48
Crabs, B48
Craters, C71
Creep meter, C59
Crescent Moon, C72, C73
Crest of wave, D32, D33
Crocodiles, B32
Crustaceans, B21, B22
Crust of Earth, C58
Crystals, D22
Cumulus clouds, D71
Current electricity, F76–87
    circuits, F78–79, F82–84,
        F86–87
    delivery to homes, F96
    flow of, F80
    light bulbs, F77*–78
    safe use of, F98
    sources of, F81
    static electricity vs., F78*
Currents, ocean, D28–29
Cytoplasm, A9

Dams, D43
Damselflies, B57
Dandelions, A71, A86
Decomposers, A46, A47, A48, A49*
Deep ocean current, D28
Density, E20*–21
Deposition, D34
Desalination, D56–57
Deserts, A38, A44, A54
Development, B54–59
Diamond, C7
Diaphragm, B47
Digestive system, A15, B48–49
Dingos, A57
Dinosaurs, C14, C18
Direct current (DC), F94
Discharge, electrical, F72, F73–74
Diseases, A56
Dodo bird, A34
Dogs, B36, B71
Dolphins, B34
Dormant trees, A76
Dormouse, B70
Droughts, A56, D42
Drumlin, C34, C35
Dry cell, F81
Dry ice, D24, D25
Duckbilled platypus, B34
Dust storms, C40
Dusty seaside sparrow, A34

Eardrum, F57
Earle, Dr. Sylvia, D94–95
Ears, F57
Earth, C30–61, C53*, C82, C83
    as frame of reference, F7
    as magnet, F91
    earthquakes, C54–57, C59
    forces shaping, C33–41, D11
    Moon compared to, C70–71
    movement of, C65*–66, C68
    rotation of, D29

*Indicates an activity related to this topic.

seasons of, C68–69
soil, A42, C42–51, D37*–39
structure of, C58
Earthquakes, C54–57, C55*, C59
Echinoderms, B16, B20
Ecology, A40
Ecosystems, A40–61
    changes in, A54–61, A55*
    differences between, A42–43
    food chains in, A48, A49, A50, B7
    food webs in, A50
    kinds of, A44–45
    resources needed by, A56
    roles of organisms in, A46–49
Eels, B30
Efficiency of machines, F30
Effort force, F22
Egg, B61
Egg stage, B56, B57
Electrical charge, F70–71
Electrical discharge, F72, F73–74
Electrical energy, F15, F16
Electricity. *See also* Current elec-
    tricity; Static electricity.
    from magnets, F94–95
    produced by water, D50
Electric meter, reading, F97*
Electric motors, F93
Electrodes, F81
Electromagnetic spectrum, F42–43
Electromagnets, F92*–93
Electron microscope, A94–95
Elements, E32–36
El Niño, D87
Embryo, A33, A85, B61
Emerald tree boa, A26
Endangered animals, A36–37,
    B12–13
Endoplasmic reticulum, A8, A9
Endoskeleton, B20
Energy, F14–16
    forms of, A52–53, F14–16
    from lightning, F74
    light as, F42
English system of measurement,
    E16
Environment, A43, A47, C24, C71
Epidermis of leaves, A73
Equus, A30
Erosion, C47
    by glaciers, C33–37

by other agents, C38, C40–41
    by waves, D34
Erratics, C37
Esophagus, B49
Estuary, D9
Euglena, A12, A14
Evaporation
    heat energy and, E48*
    separating mixtures by, E35
    surface area and, D44*
    of water, D15*–17, D18*, D19,
        D20, D21, D44*
Evergreen, A76
Evolution, A30
Excretory system, B47
Exoskeleton, B21
Expansion, F37
Experience, learning from, B71
Experimentation skills, C32, D14,
    D26, D76, E14, E48*, E50, F40,
    F52
Extinction, A33, A34, C14
Exxon Valdez, A58
Eyes, B51*, F48–49

Fabrics, from plastics, E12
Fahrenheit scale, F35
Families, A22–23
Faraday, Michael, F99
Farming, water used in, D50
Fat, for warmth, F33*
Fault, C56
Feldspar, C6, C8
Ferris wheel, F25
Fertilization, A85, B61
Fertilizers, C47, D51
Fibrous roots, A71
Filters, E35
Filtration, D52
Finches, F21
Fins, B30, B67
Fire, ecosystem and, A57
First–class lever, F23
First Quarter Moon, C73
Fish, B28, B29–30, B44, B45*, B46,
    B51

Fixed pulley, F24
Flamingo, B33
Flatworms, B16, B18
Floods, D43
Flowering plants, A87
Fluorite, C7
Focus of earthquake, C56
Food, animal digestion of, B48
Food chains, A48, A49, A50, B7
Food web, A50, B7
Footprint, calculating animal size
    from, C23
Forces, F7–13
    effort, F22
    friction, F8, F11, F30
    gravity as, F12
    motion and, F7–13
    work and, F13
Forests, A26, A42–43, A45, A57
Fossil fuels, F38
Fossils, A30–31*, C14, C16–27
    formation of, C18–21
    learning from, C17*–18, C24
    processing, C22
    types of, C18–19
Frame of reference, F6–7
Frequency of sound wave, F58
Freshwater lakes and rivers, A45
Friction, F8, F11, F30
Frogs, B44, B48, B49, B50
Fronts, D80–81, D82
Fulcrum, F22
Full Moon, C72
Fungi, A13, C44
Fur, B67
Furrows, D50
Fuse, F84

Galena, C7, C8
Galileo, C76, C90–91
Gamma rays, F42–43
Gamma waves, F42–43
Garbage, managing, E11
Garbologists, E24–25
Gas, E9, E47
Gears, F28

Generators, F94–95
Genus, A22–23, A25
Geologists, C6
Geranium, A70
Germination, A82
Gibbous Moon, C72, C73
Gill flaps, B30
Gills, B29, B67
Giraffe, B67
Gizzard, B49
Glacial till, C35
Glaciers, C33*–37, D11
Glass, volcanic, C9
Global winds, D87
Gneiss, C12
Gobi Desert, C26
Goliath Bird Eater, B38–39
Grain beetle, B56
Grams, E8
Grand Canyon, C54
Granite, C6, C9
Grasshopper, B52
Grasslands, A44, A54
Gravity, C38, C70, D30, E19, F12
Gravity meter, C59
Great Barrier Reef, B24
Great Dark Spot, C85
Great Lakes, D83
Great Red Spot, C84
Greenhouse effect, D88
Green sea turtle, A37
Grid, electric, F86
Groundwater, D10, D11, D38,
    D40, D48, E24–25
Groups in periodic table, E33
Gulf, D9
Gypsy moths, A68

Habitat, A40, A41
Hail, D18, D22
Hailstones, D22
Half Moon, C73
Halley's comet, C87
Hawk, B33
Hearing aid, F60
Hearing, tools for, F60

Heart, B45*, B46
Heat, D21, F32–39
Heat energy, D16, D19, E47, E48*
Helping Hands program, B71
Henry, Joseph, F93, F99
Herbivores, A48
Heredity, B62*
Hibernation, B70
High Plains Climate Zone, D84–85
History of Science
    Berzelius, E40–41
    Views of the Universe, C90–91
Honeybees, B74–75
Hookworm, B18
Horizon, soil, C45
Hornblende, C6, C8
Horn tooth, B29
Horse, B34
Hot–air balloon, F62–63
Houston, Dr. Cliff, A94–95
Hubble Telescope, C77
Humans
    arms of, A32
    brain of, B50
    digestive system of, A15
    life cycle of, B58
    role in extinctions, A34
Humidity, D66, D72
Humpback whale flipper, A32
Humus, C44
Hurricanes, D34, D90–91
Hydra, B17, B60
Hydroelectric power plants, D50
Hydrogen, C80
Hygrometer, D72
Hypatia, C90–91
Hypothesis, forming, B69*
Hyracotherium, A30

Ice ages, C37
Icebergs, D8
Ice caps, D8, D11
Ice particles, D20
Igneous rocks, C9
Imprints, C18
Inclined plane, F20, F26, F27

Incoming angle, F45
Incoming rays, F45
Industry, water used in, D50
Inertia, F11
Inference–making skills, B4, B54,
    C4, C64, D4, D36, D62, D70*,
    E4, F32
Infrared light, F42–43
Inherited behavior, B70
Inner core of Earth, C58
Inner ear, F57
Inner planets, C82–83
Insects, B21, B23
    eyes of, B51
    incomplete metamorphosis in,
        B57
    pollination by, A84
Instinct, B70
Insulators, F34, F72
Interglacial periods, C37
International Space Station,
    F102–103
Interpreting data, C74
Interpretive skills, C16, C74
Invertebrates, B8, B14–25, B47
    budding in, B60
    characteristics of, B15*–16
    classifying, B16–23*, B24
    digestive system of, B49
    muscular system of, B52
Irrigation, D50

Jackson, Dionne, E62–63
Jawless fish, B28, B29
Jellyfish, B17
Joints, B52
Jones, Brian, F62
Jupiter, C84, C85

K

Kangaroos, A57
Kepler, Johannes, C90–91

*Indicates an activity related to this topic.

Kidneys, B47
Kilograms, E8
Kinetic energy, F14, F16
Kingdoms, A20–21, A22–23
Kittens, B54
Knife, F20, F27

L

Lakes, A45, D8, D11
Lampreys, B29
Landfills, E24–25
Land pollution, A59
Larva stage, B56
Lasers, F15, F50
Last Quarter Moon, C73
Lateral moraine, C34
Latitude, climate and, D86
Lava, C9, C13
Law of reflection, F45
Leaf cells, A10
Learning, B71
Leaves, A15, A24*, A69*, A70,
    A73, A83
Leeches, B19
"Leftover" structures of organisms,
    A33
Legs, B67
Length, E16
Lenses, F47
Levers, F22–23*
Life cycle, A87, B63
Life functions, A6–7
Life span, B59
Light, F40–51
    absorbing, F49*
    characteristics of, F42–43
    eyes and, F48–49
    lasers, F15, F50
    mixing colors of, F41*
    motion of, F44
    reflection, F45
    refraction, F46–47
Light energy, F15
Lightning, F73–74
Lightning rods, F74
Light pipes, F50
Limb bones, A32

Limestone, C10, C12, C14
Linnaeus, Carolus, A25
Liquids, E9, E17, E46
Liquid wastes, B47
Liters (L), E17
Littering, A59, A60
Liver, B49
Living things, A6–7. *See also*
    Animals; Plants; Organisms.
    interaction with nonliving
        things, A39*–40
    water in, D12
Lizards, B32, B48
Load, F22
Lobsters, B22, B48
Luster, C7

M

Machines, F20–31
    compound, F29
    efficiency of, F30
    simple. *See* Simple machines.
Magma, C9, C13
Magnetic field, F91
Magnetite, C8, F90
Magnets, F88–99
    bar, F88, F89*–90
    Earth as, F91
    electricity from, F94–95
    electromagnets, F92*–93
    properties of, F90
Magnifying glass, F47
Mammals, B28, B34–35
    fat in, F33*
    heart of, B46
Mammoths, A34, A62–63, C20
Manatees, B12
Mantle of Earth, C58
Maps, weather, D82–83
Marble, C12
Marshmallows, E56
Marianas Trench, D7
Marine sanctuaries, D94–95
Mars, C78, C82, C83
Marshes, D8
Mass, E8, E10
Mass extinctions, A24

Matter, E4–63
    changes in, E42–57, E43*, E51*
    characteristics of, E8–10*
    classifying, E31*–39, E36*
    definition of, E6
    identifying, E5*
    measuring, E14–26, E15*, E18*,
        E20*
    properties of, E6–7, E10
    states of, E8–9, E10, E45–47
Mealworms, B55*–56
Measuring skills, F9*
Mechanical energy, F15
Meet People in Science
    Earle, Dr. Sylvia, D94–95
    Houston, Cliff, A94–95
    Jackson, Dionne, E62–63
    Ochoa, Dr. Ellen, F102–103
    Patterson, Dr. Coretta, B78–79
    Sanchez, Dr. Pedro, C94–95
Melting, D19, D21
Mendeleyev, Dmitry, E33
Mercury, C82, C83
Merychippus, A30
Mesohippus, A30
Mesosphere, D65
Metamorphic rocks, C12–13
Metamorphosis, B56–57
Meteor Crater, C86
Meteorite, C87
Meteorologists, D94–95
Meteors, C86
Methane, E24–25
Metric system, E16, E22
Mica, C6, C8
Microorganisms, A12–13
Microscope, electron, A94–95
Microwaves, F42–43
Middle ear, F57
Mid–ocean ridge, D7
Midwest/Ohio Valley Climate
    Zone, D84–85
Migrating instinct, B70
Mild forest lands, A44
Milliliters (mL), E17
Millipedes, B21, B22
Mimicry, B68
Mina, E22
Minerals, C6–8*, C47
Mitochondria, A8, A9
Mixtures, E34–36*, E38

Modeling skills, A11, C78
Molds (fossils), C19*
Molds (organism), A49
Moles, F21
Mollusks, B16, B20
Molting, B21
Monarch butterflies, B68
Monkeys, Helping Hands, B71
Moon, the, C70–74
    movement of, C65*–66
    tides and, D30, D31
Moons, C83, C84, C85
Moraine, C34, C35
Moss plant, A88
Moths, B6, B66, B67
Motion, F4–13, F5*, F19*
    forces and, F7–13
    of light, F44
    position and, F6
    speed, F8
Motors, electric, F93
Mountains, D7, D86
Mouth, B49
Movable pulley, F24
Mummies, C20
Muscle tissue, A14
Muscular system, B52
Mushroom, A13

National Geographic Society
    Amazing Stories
    circling the globe in hot–air
        balloon, F62–63
    desalination, D56–57
    fossils, C26–27
    spider giants, B38–39
    woolly mammoth, A62–63
Neck, B67
Nectar, A84
Neptune, C84, C85
Nerve cells, A10
Nervous system, B50
Neutron star, E21
New England Climate Zone,
    D84–85
New Moon, C72, C73

Newt, B31
Newton, Sir Isaac, F10
Newton (unit of weight), E19, F10
Nitrogen, D64, D78
Nonwoody stems, A72
North Pole, C69
Northwestern Climate Zone,
    D84–85
Nuclear energy, F15, F95
Nucleus, A9
Numbers, using, C23, F97*
Nymph stage, B57

Observation skills, A38, B10, B44,
    C42, F18
Obsidian, C9
Ocean birds, D9
Oceanographers, D94–95
Oceans, D6, D7, D20, D27–35
    coastlines changed by, D34
    movement of, C38, D27*–34,
        D32*
Ochoa, Dr. Ellen, F102–103
Octopus, B14, B48
Oil spill, A58
Omnivores, A48
Onion plant, A55*
Opacity, F49
Open circuit, F78–79
Open sea ecosystems, A45
Orbit, C68
Orders, A22–23
Organisms, A6–7. See also Animals.
    classification of, A18–35, A19*,
        A24*, A31*
    roles in ecosystems, A46–49
Organs, A15
Organ systems, B44–53
    circulatory system, B45*, B46
    digestive system, A15, B48–49
    excretory system, B47
    muscular system, B52
    nervous system, B50
    respiratory system, B47
    skeletal system, B52
    special sense organs, B51

Ostrich, B33
Outer core of Earth, C58
Outer ear, F57
Outer planets, C84–85
Outgoing angle, F45
Outgoing rays, F45
Outwash plains, C37
Ovary, in plants, A85
Oxygen, A6, B47, D64, D78
Ozone layer, D74–75

Pangolins, B72
Panthera, A25
Parallel circuit, F83
Parasites, B18
Patterson, Dr. Coretta, B78–79
Penguin, B33
People. See Humans; Meet People
    in Science.
Peppered moths, B66, B67
Performance Assessment
    energy, F104
Periodic table, E32–33
Permeability of soil, C49
Pesticides, D51
Pet Partners, B36
Petrification, C21
Pharmacists, E62–63
Phloem cells, A72
Photosynthesis, A74, A75*
Phylum, A22–23, B16
Physical adaptations, B67
Physical changes in matter,
    E42–49, E43*
    in position or texture, E45
    in size or shape, E44, E45
    in state, E45–48*
    in the real world, E56
Piccard, Bertrand, F62
Pistil, A84
Pitch, F59
Pith cells, A72
Planarian, B15, B18, B60
Plane, inclined, F20, F26, F27
Planets, C81–85
    inner, C82–83

*Indicates an activity related to this topic.

outer, C84–85
Plants, A68–89
  cactus vs. evergreen, A76
  cells in, A7–11, A14
  dormant, A76
  incredible, A78–79
  leaves of, A15, A24*, A69*,
    A70, A73, A83
  life cycle of flowering plants, A87
  modeling cells of, A11*
  organs of, A15
  petrified, C21
  photosynthesis in, A74, A75*
  relationship to animals, A90–91
  respiration in, A74, A75*
  roots of, A70, A71, A83
  seeds of, A82–86, A91
  stems of, A70, A72, A83
  sunlight and, A41*
  water in, D12, D41
  with spores, A88
Plastics, recycled, E12
Pluto, C84, C85
Poles, magnetic, F90
Pollen, A84, A90–91
Pollen tube, A85
Pollination, A84, A90–91
Pollution, A58, A60, E56
  from fossil fuels, F38
  from landfills, E24–25
  of water, A58, A60, D51
Polyps, B24
Popcorn, E56
Populations, A40, A41
Porcupine, B72
Pore spaces, C48–49, D38, D43
Position, E45, F6
Potential energy, F14
Pouches, mammals with, B35
Pound, E22
Precipitation, D18–19, D21, D22, D24
  runoff from, D39*, D43
Predator fish, B30
Predicting skills, A75*, B64, C52, F76
Pressure, D67, D69, D70*, D72
Primary waves, C57
Prisms, F42–43
Process skills
  classifying, A18, A24*, B14,
    B26, E30

communicating, D46, E42, F88
experimenting, C32, D14, D26,
    D76, E14, E48*, E50, F40, F52
glacier flow, C36*
hypothesizing, B69*
inferring, B4, B54, C4, C64, D4,
    D36, D62, D70*, E4, F32
interpreting, C16, C74
measuring, F9*
modeling, A11, C78
observing, A38, B10, B44, C42,
    F18
predicting, A75*, B64, C52, F7
using numbers, C23, F97*
using variables, A80, D44*,
    D62, F4
Producers, A46, A47, A48
Project Lokahi, A36–37
Properties, E6
Protective resemblance, B66
Protists, A12
Ptolemy, C90–91
Puffer fish, B72
Pulleys, F19*, F20, F24
Pupa stage, B56
Pupil, F48
Pyrite, C7, C8

Quartz, C6, C8
Quills, B72

Radial symmetry, B9
Radiation, F36
Radio waves, F42–43
Rain, D18, D22, D72, D77*
Rain forests, A26, A45, A57
Rain gauge, D72
Rainmaking, D24–25
Ramp, F26
Rays (animal), B30
Rays (light), D74–75, F44–45

Receiver, F60
Rectangle, area of, E17
Recycling, E11, E12
Red blood cell, A10
Red–breasted toucan, A26
Red–eyed green tree frog, A26
Red giant, E21
Reef fish, B30
Reflection, F45
Reflex, B70
Refraction, F46–47
Regeneration, B60
Relative age, C11
Reproduction, B60–62
Reptiles, B28, B32
Resemblance, protective, B66
Resistors, F80
Respiration, A74, A75*
Respiratory system, B47
Retina, F48
Revolution of Earth, C68
Rivers, A45, C40, D8, D11, D20
Robotics, F102–103
Rock cycle, C13
Rock debris, C34–35
Rock layers, A31
Rocks, C4–15
  breakup of, C44
  igneous, C9
  interpreting, C5*–8
  layers, C14
  metamorphic, C12–13
  minerals, C6–8*, C47
  sedimentary, C10–11, C18
  water flow through, D37*–38
Rock salt, C10
Root hairs, A71
Roots of plants, A70, A71, A83
Rotation of Earth, C66, C67, D29
Roundworms, B16, B18
Runoff, D39*, D43
Rust, E37

Salamander, B31
Salt, E37
Saltwater communities, D9

Saltwater shores, A45
Sanchez, Dr. Pedro, C94–95
Sandstone, C10
Sandworms, B19
Satellites of the Sun, C81
Saturn, C84, C85
Schaefer, Vincent, D24
Science Magazine
    alternative forms of energy,
        A52–53
    circuits, F86–87
    dancing bees, B74–75
    endangered animals, A36–37,
        B12–13
    erosion, C40–41
    ozone layer, D74–75
    plant–animal relationship,
        A90–91
    plants around the world,
        A78–79
    rainmaking, D24–25
    telescopes, C76–77
    views of the universe, C90–91
    wild weather, D90–91
Scissors, F29
Scolopendra, B22
Scorpions, B21
Screwdriver, F25
Screws, F20, F27
Sea anemones, B17, D9
Seas, D6
Seasons, C68–69
Sea star, B9, B20, B48
Secondary waves, C57
Second–class lever, F23
Sedimentary rocks, C10–11, C18
Sediments, C10, C11*
Seed coat, A82, A83
Seedling, A82, A83
Seeds, A81–86, A91
    dispersal of, A86
    formation of, A84–85
    growth of, A81*, A82–84
    parts of, A83
Segmented worms, B16, B19, B49
Seismic waves, C56–57
Seismogram, C57
Seismographs, C54, C57
Sense organs, special, B51
Series circuit, F82

Sex cells, A85, A87, A88
Shadows, F44
Shale, C10
Shape, volume and, E18*
Shark brain, B50
Sharks, B30
Shekel, E22
Shell, B67
Shore, D7
Short circuit, F80, F84
Silver iodide, D25
Simple machines, F20–28
    gears, F28
    inclined plane, F20, F26, F27
    levers, F22–23*
    pulleys, F19*, F20, F24
    screws, F20, F27
    wedges, F20, F27
    wheels and axles, F20, F25
Size, heat and, F37
Skeletal system, B52
Skeletons, A29*–30
Skin, E56
Skin cells, A14
Skunks, B72
Sleet, D18, D22
Smog, A59
Snake, B32, B51
Snow, D18, D22
Sodium, E53
Soil, C42–51
    composition of, C43*–44
    effect on ecosystems, A42
    layering of, C45
    permeability of, C49
    runoff and, D39
    similarities and differences in,
        C46–49
    water flow through, C48*–49,
        D37*–38
Soil profile, C45
Soil water, D10, D11, D38
Solar system, C78–93, C79*
    asteroids, C86
    comets, C86, C87*
    meteors, C86
    moons, C83, C84, C85
    planets, C81–85
    sun, C80–81, F15
Solids, E8, E17, E46

Solid wastes, B49
Sound, F52–61
    differences among, F58–59
    ears and, F57
    tools for hearing, F60
    travel through different
        materials, F56
    vibrations and, F53*–55
Sound wave, F55, F58–59
Southeastern Climate Zone, D84–85
Southern Climate Zone, D84–85
Southwestern Climate Zone, D84–85
Sow bug, B72
Speakers, F60
Species, A22–23, A25
    endangered, A36–37
Spectrum, F42–43
Speed, F8
Sperm, B61
Spherical symmetry, B9
Spiders, B21, B38–39, B70
Spiny anteater, B34
Sponges, B9, B16, B17, B46, B60
Spores, A88
Squid, B20, B48, B72
Standard units of measurement,
    E16–18*, E22–23
Stars, C88, E21. See also Sun.
States of matter, E8–9, E10, E45–47
Static electricity, F68–74
    cause of, F70–71
    discharge of, F72
    from rubbed balloons, F69*
    lightning, F73–74
Stationary front, D81
Statue of Liberty, E50
Stem cells, A10
Stems of plants, A70, A72, A83
Stethoscope, F60
Stomach, B49
Stomata, A73
Stone plant, A78–79
Strain meter, C59
Stratosphere, D65
Stratus clouds, D71
Strawberry plant, A72
Streak plate, C7
Streams, D8, D11
Subsoil, C45
Sugar, A74, E37, E53, E54

*Indicates an activity related to this topic.

Sumerians, F20
Sun, C80–81, F15
   as heat source, F38
   as star, C80–81
   movement of, C65*–66
   satellites of, C81
   tides and, D30
Sunlight, A41*, A42
Supernova, E21
Surface area and evaporation,
   D44*
Surface currents, D29
Surface waves, C57
Survival, animal, B64–75
   adaptations for, B66–67, B69*
   behaviors for, B70–72
   body color and, B65*–66, B67
   mimicry, B68
Swamps, D8
Swift, B33
Switch, F78–79
Symmetry, animal, B8–10

Tadpole, B31
Taiga, A44
Talc, C7, C8
Tapeworm, B18
Taproot, A71
Tarantulas, B38–39
Tarnish, E53
Tar pits, fossils in, C20
Telescopes, C76–77
Temperature
   heat vs., F35
   of air, D66, D72
   precipitation and, D19
Terminals, electric, F81
Terminus, C34, C35
Texture, C46, E45
Thermal energy, F15
Thermometer, D72, F35
Thermosphere, D65
Third–class lever, F23
Thunderstorms, D90
Tides, D30–31
Tilt meter, C59

Tissues, A14, A15
Titan arum flower of Sumatra,
   A78–79
Titanic, C32
Toad, B31
Tools for hearing, F60. *See also*
   Machines.
Topsoil, C45
Tornadoes, D90–91
Tortoises, B32
Traits, A21, B62
Transformers, F96
Translucency, F49
Transparency, F49
Transpiration, A73, D41
Trenches, D7
Tropical rain forest. *See* Rain
   forests.
Troposphere, D65
Trough of wave, D32, D33
Trunk, B67
Tuataras, B32
Tube feet, B20, B48
Tundra, A44
Turbine, F95
Turtles, B32, B61
Twisters, D90–91
Tyrannosaurus rex, A28

Ultraviolet light, D74–75, F42–43
Underground water sources, D10,
   D11
Universe, views of, C90–91
Uranus, C84, C85

Vacuole, A9
Valleys under water, D7
Van de Graaf generator, F68
Variables, using, A80, D44*, D62, F4
Vegetation, D39
Veins, A73, A74
Venus, C82, C83

Venus flytrap, A78–79
Vertebrates, A33, B8, B16, B26–35
   amphibians, B28, B31, B45*,
      B47
   birds, B28, B33, B48, B49
   bony fish, B28, B29, B30
   cartilaginous fish, B28, B29, B30
   characteristics of, B27*–28
   classifying, B26, B28–35*
   jawless fish, B28, B29
   mammals, B28, B34–35
   muscular system of, B52
   reptiles, B28, B32
Veterinarians, B78–79
Vibrations, sound and, F53*–55
Viceroy butterfly, B68
Vinegar eel, B18
Viruses, A16
Visible spectrum, F42–43
Volcanic glass, C9
Volt, F96
Voltage, F96
Volume, E17–18*
Vonnegut, Bernard, D25

W

Walruses, F32
Warm–blooded animals, B28
Warm fronts, D80, D81, D83
Wastes, B49, D51
Water, D4–26, D36–61, E37
   cleaning up, D52
   climate and bodies of, D86
   condensation of, D17, D19,
      D20, D21
   conservation of, D54
   desalination of, D56–57
   effect on ecosystems, A42
   erosion by, C38, C40–41
   evaporation of, D15*–17,
      D18*, D19, D20, D21, D44*
   flow through rocks, D37*–38
   flow through soil, C48*–49,
      D37*–38
   freezing of, D19, D20
   fresh, D47*, D48–50, D55
   in an apple, D12*

in living things, D12
plants' role in moving, D12, D41
pollution of, A58, A60, D51
precipitation, D18–19, D21,
    D22, D24, D39*, D43
sources of, D5*–11, D16–17
states of, E46–47
turbines powered by, F95
volume of solid measured
    using, E17
wasted, D54*
water cycle, D20–21, D41
wells, D40
Water pressure, D67
Water table, D38
Water treatment plants, D52
Water vapor, D6, D17, D19, D64,
    D78
clouds and, D71
Wavelength, D32, F42–43
Waves

ocean, C38, D32*–34
sound, F55, F58–59
Weather, D66–69
air masses and, D79–81
describing, D72
predicting, D82–83
storms, D90–91
Weather maps, D82–83
Weather vane, D72
Wedges, F20, F27
Weight, E19, F12
Wells, D40
Westerlies, D87
Wet cells, F81
Wheels and axles, F20, F25
Wind, D67–69
cause of, D68–69
climate and, D87
erosion by, C38, C40–41
global, D87
measuring, D72

waves and, D33
Wind turbines, F95
Wood, as insulator, F34
Woodland forest, A42–43
Woody stems, A72
Woolly mammoths, A34, A62–63
Work, F13
Worms, B16, B18, B19, B49

X rays, F42–43
Xylem cells, A72

Yeast, A13

*Indicates an activity related to this topic.

Credits

Page placement key: (t) top, (tr) top right, (tl) top left, (tm) top middle, (tml) top middle left, (tmr) top middle right, (m) middle, (l) left, (ml) middle left,(r) right, (mr) middle right,(b) bottom, (br) bottom right,(bl) bottom left, (bm) bottom middle, (bml) bottom middle left, (bmr) bottom middle right, (bg) background, (i) inset, (ti) top inset, (bi) bottom inset

Cover Design and Illustration: Robert Brook Allen

Cover Photos: VCG/FPG, (bg) Ian Cartwright/PhotoDisc

Illustrations: Kenneth Batelman: pp. D16, D17, D33, E12; Dan Brown: pp. D11, D20, D21, D30, D38, D40; Frank Comito: p. R6; Barbara Cousins: pp. B50, R25, R27, (l) R28, R29; Steven Cowden: p. F73; Michael DiGiorgio: pp. (b) A48, B16, B28; Drew-Brook-Cormack Associates: p. A41; Jeff Fagan: p. F26; Howard S. Friedman: p. A46; Function Through Form: p. E32; Peter Gunther: pp. A72, A82, A83, A84, A85, C72, C73, C77, D48, D49, D67, E08, E09, E21, E46, E47, F35, F36, F42, F43, F45, F48, F55, F59, F70, F92; Colin Hayes: pp. F22, F22, F23, F24, F24, F24, F25,(b) F91, F94, F97, R05, R07, R07, R09, R16,(l) R17, R18, R18,(l) R19; Joe Justus: p. D45; John Karapelou: pp. R30, R32, R33; Virge Kask: p. (t) A83; Yuan Lee: pp. A50, A87, F57; Joe LeMonnier: pp. (b) A37, A44, A79, C67, D79 , D82, D83, D84 , D87, D89, E22, F91; Tom Leonard: pp. A06, (b) A14, A32, (b) A33, A34, B07, B19, B56, B57, (l) B60, (r) F81, F98, R20, R21, R22, R23; Steve Oh: pp. A15, R26, R27, (r) R28, R29, R31, R34; Olivia: pp. R02, R03, R09, R10, R11, R14, R15, (r) R19; Sharron O'Neil: pp. A16, A20, A23, (l) A31, C11, C44, C48, C49, C49, D10, D41; Vilma Ortiz-Dillon: pp. D18, D28, D29, D52, D53; Precision Graphics: pp. B46, B46, B47, B49, B53, (r) B60, C37; Molly Scanlon: pp. D86, E35, F44; Rob Schuster: p. F34; Ted Williams: pp. C56, C57, C58, D24, E07, (b) E35, E37; J/B Woolsey Associates: pp. A07, A08, A09, A73, C34, D07, D32, D64, D69, D80, D81, D88; Patricia Wynne: pp. R24,(t) R33; Josie Yee: pp. A52, C68 , C70, C80; Craig Zolman: pp. F77, (l) F81, F82, F83;

Photography Credits: All photographs are by the Macmillan/McGraw-Hill School Division (MMSD) and Dan Howell for MMSD except as noted below.

Contents: viii: Joseph Sohm/Chromosohm, Inc./Corbis ix: Mike Howell/All Sport USA.

National Geographic Invitation to Science: S1: (i) James L. Stanfield/National Geographic Image Collection; (bg) Image Bank. S2: (bg) Photodisc. S3: (i) Image Bank. S4: Tony Stone Images. S5: Jeffrey L. Rotman/Corbis. S8: (br) Photodisc.

National Geographic Unit Opener A: A00: Yvette Cardozo/Index Stock Imagery. A0: Thomas Nebbia. A1: P. Montoya/PITCH; **Unit A:** A2: Karl Weidmann/Photo Researchers, Inc. A4: (bg) Jim Sugar Photography/Corbis. A5: Stephen Ogilvy. A7: (ml) Biophoto Associate/Photo Researchers, Inc.; (mr) Barry Runk/Grant Heilman Photography, Inc. A10: (tl) Biophoto Associates/Photo Researchers, Inc.; (ml) Ken Edward/Photo Researchers, Inc.; (tr) Biophoto Associates/Photo Researchers, Inc.; (bl) Photodisc; (br) J.F. Gennaro/Photo Researchers, Inc.; (mr) Photodisc. A11: (t) Biophoto Associate/Photo Researchers, Inc.; (b) Barry Runk/Grant Heilman Photography, Inc. A12: (t) David M. Phillips/Photo Researchers, Inc.; (bl) Michael Abbey/Photo Researchers, Inc.; (m) Astrid & Hanns-Frieder/Photo Researchers, Inc.; (br) Edward R. Degginger/Bruce Coleman Inc. A13: (tl) M.I. Walker/Photo Researchers, Inc.; (r) Joy Spur/Bruce Coleman Inc.; (i) CNRI/Science Photo/Photo Researchers, Inc.; (ml) Biophoto Associates/Photo Researchers, Inc.; (bl) Eric V. Grave/Photo Researchers, Inc. A14: (t) Biophoto Associate/Photo Researchers, Inc. A15: (r) Dan Howell. A18: (bg) Cesar Llacuna. A19: (t) Gregory Ochocki/Photo Researchers, Inc.; (mr) Carl R. Sams II/Peter Arnold Inc.; (tr) Kjell Sandved; (b) J. Foott/Tom Stack & Associates; (tl) Charlie Heidecker/Visuals Unlimited; (ml) Richard Schiell/Animals Animals; (bm) Hans Pfletschinger/Peter Arnold Inc.; (br) Mike Bacon/Tom Stack & Associates. A21: M.I. Walker/Photo Researchers, Inc. A22: Gregory Ochocki/Photo Researchers, Inc.; (l) William H. Mullins/Photo Researchers, Inc.; (t) Jerome Wexler/Photo Researchers, Inc. A25: (bl) Strauss/Curtis/The Stock Market; (t) Photodisc; (tm) Photodisc; (m) Photodisc; (bm) Photodisc; (br) Photodisc. A26: (r) Richard R. Hansen/Photo Researchers, Inc.; (m) Jany Sauvanet/Photo Researchers, Inc.; (l) Kevin Schafer/Corbis. A27: (tr) Adam Jones/Photo Researchers, Inc.; (tl) Scott Camazine/Photo Researchers, Inc.; (bl) Stephen Dalton/Photo Researchers, Inc. A28: (bg) Bill Wassman/The Stock Market; (i) Francois Gohier/Photo Researchers, Inc. A29: (t) Edward R. Degginger/Photo Researchers, Inc.; (b) Biophoto Associates/Photo Researchers, Inc. A30: (tr) American Museum of Natural History; (tmr) American Museum of Natural History; (bmr) American Museum of Natural History; (bl) American Museum of Natural History; (tl) Sharron O'Neil; (tml) Sharron O'Neil; (bml) Sharron O'Neil; (bl) Sharron O'Neil. A31: (r) Stephen Ogilvy. A33: (t) Charles E. Mohr/Photo Researchers, Inc. A35: Tom McHugh/Photo Researchers, Inc. A36: (bg) Project Lokahi; (i) Project Lokahi. A38: (bg) Jonathan Blair/Corbis. A39: Stephen Ogilvy. A40: Stephen Ogilvy. A42: (l) Renee Lynn/Photo Researchers, Inc.; (b) Jim Steinberg/Photo Researchers, Inc.; (r) Stephen Krasemann/Photo Researchers, Inc. A43: F. Stuart Westmorland/Photo Researchers, Inc. A44: (tl) Richard A. Cooke/Corbis; (tr) Charlie Ott/Photo Researchers, Inc.; (tmr) Herb Levart/Photo Researchers, Inc;.(mr) Robert Alexander/Photo Researchers, Inc.; (bmr) Christine M. Douglas/Photo Researchers, Inc.; (br) Victor Englebert/Photo Researchers, Inc. A45: (m) Michael P. Gadomski/Photo Researchers, Inc.; (tm) St. Meyers/Okapia/Photo Researchers, Inc.; (t) Nancy Sefton/Photo Researchers, Inc.; (bm) Phillip Colla; (b) Jeffrey L. Rotman/Corbis. A47: (t) Microfield Scientific/Photo Researchers, Inc.; (b) Andrew J. Martinez/Photo Researchers, Inc. A49: (tl) Albert Visage/Peter Arnold Inc.; (ml) Charlie Ott/Photo Researchers, Inc.; (mr) Stephen Ogilvy. A51: Richard A. Cooke/Corbis. A53: Steve Allen/Peter Arnold Inc. A54: (bg) Clem Haagner/Gallo Images/Corbis. A55: (t) Richard Megna/Fundamental Photographs; (b) Stephen Ogilvy. A56: (r) Bill Bachmann/Photo Researchers, Inc.; (m) Judyth Platt/Corbis; (l) Jacques Jangoux/Photo Researchers, Inc. A57: Fritz Prenzel/Animals Animals. A58: (t) Simon Fraser/Photo Researchers, Inc.; (b) Bilderberg/The Stock Market. A59: (t) Ron Watts/Corbis; (b) John Eastcott/Photo Researchers, Inc. A60: (t) James L. Amos/Photo Researchers, Inc.; (i) Jean Lauzon/Photo Researchers, Inc. A61: Arthur Tilley/FPG International. A63: (i) Jonathan Blair/Corbis; (bg) Jonathan Blair/National Geographic Image Collection. A65: NASA. A66: Ed Reschke/Peter Arnold Inc. A68: Gregory G. Dimijian/Photo Researchers, Inc.; (i) John Burnley/Photo Researchers, Inc. A69: Dan Howell. A70: Runk/Schoenberger/Grant Heilman Photography, Inc. A71: (l) Michael Hewes/FPG; (r) Runk/Schoenberger/ Grant Heilman Photography, Inc. A72: (br) Runk/Schoenberger/Grant Heilman Photography, Inc.; (bl) Photodisc. A73: (r) Michael P. Gadomski/Photo Researchers, Inc. A74: Frank Nikolaus/Photo Researchers, Inc. A75: Dave Mager. A76: (b) Charlie Ott/Photo Researchers, Inc.; (t) David Weintraub/Photo Researchers, Inc.; (i) Photodisc. A77: Vanessa Vick/Photo Researchers, Inc. A78: (t) Darlyne A. Murawski/Peter Arnold Inc.; (b) Geoff Bryant/Photo Researchers, Inc. A79: (l) John Pontier/Earth Scenes; (r) N. et Perennou/Photo Researchers, Inc. A80: (bg) Craig Tuttle/The Stock Market; (i) Hans Reinhard/Photo Researchers, Inc. A81: Dan Howell. A82: (b) Kelly Culpepper/Transparencies, Inc. A84: (b) David Muench/Corbis. A85: (tl) N. Cattlin Holt Studios/Photo Researchers, Inc.; (mr) Cesar Llacuna. A86: (r) IPS/Index Stock photography Inc.; (m) John Colwell/Grant Heilman Photography, Inc.; (l) Gregory K. Scott/Photo Researchers, Inc. A88: (i) Runk/Schoenberger/Grant Heilman Photography, Inc.; (t) Runk/Schoenberger/Grant Heilman Photography, Inc.; (b) K. Van Nostrand/Photo Researchers, Inc. A89: (l) Barry L. Runk/Grant Heilman Photography, Inc. A90: (bg) Edward R. Degginger/Bruce Coleman Inc.; (i) Dieter & Mary Plage/Bruce Coleman Inc.; (t) Dieter & Mary Plage/Bruce Coleman Inc. A91: (b) Edward R. Degginger/Bruce Coleman Inc. A94: (l) University of Texas Medical Branch; (r) Dr. Immo Rantala/Photo Researchers, Inc. A95: Geoff Tompkinson/Photo Researchers, Inc. A96: (t) Fabio Colombini/Earth Scenes; (b) George Bernard/Earth Scenes.

National Geographic Unit Opener B: B0: Dorling Kindersley. B1 Friedrich Von Horsten /Animals Animals. **Unit B:** B2: Betty H. Press/Animals Animals. B4: (bg) Zefa/Index Stock Imagery. B6: (t) Biophoto Associate/Photo Researchers, Inc.; (bl) Mary Ann Frasier/Photo Researchers, Inc.; (br) Scott Smith/Animals Animals. B8: (l) M.H. Sharp/Photo Researchers, Inc.; (r) Kaj R. Svensson/Photo Researchers, Inc. B9: (t) Ray Coleman/Photo Researchers, Inc.; (bl) Stuart Westmorland/Photo Researchers, Inc.; (br) Charles V. Angelo/Photo Researchers, Inc. B10: (t) Joe McDonald/Bruce Coleman Inc.; (tm) James R. McCullagh/Visuals Unlimited; (m) Ron & Valerie Taylor/Bruce Coleman Inc.; (bl) John Chellmen/Animals Animals; (br) Neil S. McDaniel/Photo Researchers, Inc. B11: (l) David Doubilet. B12: Douglas Faulkner/Photo Researchers, Inc. B13: (l) Peter B. Kaplan/Photo Researchers, Inc.; (r) Kennan Ward/Bruce Coleman Inc. B14: (bg) Stuart Westmorland/Corbis. B15: (t) Kim Taylor/Bruce Coleman Inc.; (b) Ray Coleman/Photo Researchers, Inc. B17: (i) Marian Bacon/Animals Animals; (t) Sefton/Bruce Coleman Inc. B18: (t) J. H. Robinson/Photo Researchers, Inc.; (b) Carol Geake/Animals Animals. B20: (t) Joyce & Frank Burek/Animals Animals; (b) Zig Leszczynski/Animals Animals. B21: Doug Sokell/Photo Researchers, Inc. B22: (t) Ed Bishop/Index Stock Imagery; (b) Tom McHugh. B23: (i) Dwight Kuhn; (tl) Mary Snyderman/Visuals Unlimited; (tr) L. West/Bruce Coleman Inc.; (ml) Fabio Colombini/Animals Animals; (mr) Mary Beth Angelo/Photo Researchers, Inc.; (bmr) John D. Cunningham/Visuals Unlimited; (bml) Cabisco/Visuals Unlimited; (b) J. H. Robinson/Photo Researchers, Inc. B24: L. Newman A./Photo Researchers, Inc. B25: William J. Pohley/Visuals Unlimited. B26: (bg) Dr. E. R. Degginger/Bruce Coleman Inc. B27: Norman Owen Tomalin/Bruce Coleman Inc. B29: (t) Fred McConnaughey/Photo Researchers, Inc.; (b) Hans Reinhard/Bruce Coleman Inc. B30: (t) Jane Burton/Bruce Coleman Inc.; (b) Dave B. Fleetham/Visuals Unlimited. B31: (t) Suzanne L./Joseph T. Collins/Photo Researchers, Inc.; (m) L. West/Bruce Coleman Inc.; (b) Phil A. Dotson/Photo Researchers, Inc. B32: (t) Tom McHugh/Photo Researchers, Inc.; (tm) Christian Grzimek/Photo Researchers, Inc.; (bm) Jany Sauvanet/Photo Researchers, Inc. B32: (b) Jeffrey W. Lang/Photo Researchers, Inc. B33: (t) Frank Lane/Bruce Coleman Inc.; (tm) Eric & David Hosking/Corbis; (m) Jim Zuckerman/Corbis; (bm) Mark Carwardine/Peter Arnold Inc.; (b) Kevin Schafer/Corbis. B34: (t) Hugh Beebower/Corbis; (bm) Winifred Wisniewski/Corbis; (bl) Jean Phillipe Varin/Photo Researchers, Inc.; (br) Tom Brakefield/Corbis. B35: (t) Stuart Westmorland/Corbis; (tl) Dan Guravich/Photo Researchers, Inc.; (tr) Ron & Valerie Taylor/Bruce Coleman Inc.; (ml) Zig Leszczynski/Animals Animals; (mr) Jeff Lepore/Photo Researchers, Inc.; (bl) Wally Eberhart/Visuals Unlimited; (br) Dwight R. Kuhn. B36: Stephen Ogilvy. B37: (b) Nicolas Therond/Peter Arnold Inc. B38 : (bg) John Mitchell/Photo Researchers, Inc.; (i) Tom McHugh/Photo Researchers, Inc. B40: (t) Jane Burton/Bruce Coleman Inc.; (b) Christian Grzimek/Photo Researchers, Inc. B42: John Mitchell/Photo Researchers, Inc. B44: (bg) Douglas Peebles/Corbis; (i) J.C. Carton/Bruce Coleman Inc. B46: (l) Randy Faris/Corbis; (r) John Lemker/Animals Animals. B47: (t) O. S. F./Animals Animals; (b) Hutchings Photography. B48: (t) Ken Cole/Animals Animals; (m) Fred Bavendam/Peter Arnold Inc.; (b) Norman Owen Tomalin/Bruce Coleman Inc. B51: (t) Stephen Spotte/Photo Researchers, Inc.; (b) Kjell B. Sandved/Photo Researchers, Inc. B52: (t) Maresa Pryor/Animals Animals; (b) Dan Howell. B53: Dave Kingdon/Index Stock Imagery. B54: (bg) Fritz Prenzel/Animals Animals. B55: Stephen Ogilvy. B58: (i) Gary Meszaros/Photo Researchers, Inc.; (l) Norman Owen Tomalin/Bruce Coleman Inc.; (r) Kevin Schafer/Corbis. B60: (l) Biophoto Assoc./Photo Researchers, Inc.; (r) Michael Abbey/Photo Researchers, Inc. B61: (l) E.R. Degginger/Animals Animals; (r) David M. Phillips/Photo Researchers, Inc. B62: (t) Robert Landau/Corbis; (b) Joel Satore/Grant Heilman Photography, Inc. B63: Ken Glaser/Index Stock Imagery. B64: (bg) Grant Heilman Photography, Inc. B66: (t) Michael Fogden/Bruce Coleman Inc.; (b) Breck P. Kent/Animals Animals. B67: Jim Zuckerman/Corbis. B68: (l) John Shaw/Bruce Coleman Inc.; (r) John Shaw/Bruce Coleman Inc. B70: (t) Maria Zorn/Animals Animals; (b) W.J.C. Murray/Bruce Coleman Inc. B71: Jeffrey L. Rotman/Corbis. B72: (i) George Schaller/Bruce Coleman Inc.; (t) Jane Burton/Bruce Coleman Inc.; (bl) Galen Rowell/Corbis; (br) Vittoriano Rastelli/Corbis. B73: (b) Dan Guravich/Corbis. B74: (i) Thomas C. Boyden/Dembinsky Photo Associates; (t) Photodisc. B75: (b) Ralph A. Clevenger/Corbis. B78: (bg) Thomas Kitchin/Tom Stack & Associates; (i) Photodisc. B79: Larry Cameron/Photo Researchers, Inc. B80: (t) Gary Milburn/Tom Stack & Associates; (m) Arthur Gloor/Animals Animals; (b) Ken Karp.

National Geographic Unit Opener C: C0: Michael Frye/Tony Stone. C1: David Hiser/Tony Stone. **Unit C:** C2: Michael T. Sedam/Corbis. C4: (bg) Harvey Lloyd/Peter Arnold Inc. C5: Stephen Ogilvy. C6: (l) Ken Karp; (r) Stephen Ogilvy; (ml) Ken Karp; (mr) Ken Karp; (b) Joyce Photographics/Photo Researchers, Inc. C7: (tl) Stephen Ogilvy; (tr) Dr. D.R. Degginger; (bl) Stephen Ogilvy; (br) Stephen Ogilvy. C8:

Photodisc. C9: (l) Ken Karp; (m) Andrew J. Martinez/Photo Researchers, Inc.; (r) Andrew J. Martinez/Photo Researchers, Inc. C10: (l) Charles Winters/Photo Researchers, Inc.; (r) Andrew J. Martinez/Photo Researchers, Inc.; (ml) Stephen Ogllvy; (mr) Ken Karp. C11: Dan Howell. C12: (t) Dr. D.R. Degginger; (bl) Ken Karp; (br) Dr. D.R. Degginger. C13: (tl) Dr. D.R. Degginger; (tr) G. Carleton Ray/Photo Researchers, Inc.; (b) Philippe Bourseiller/Photo Researchers, Inc.; (bl) Dr. D.R. Degginger; (br) Andrew J. Martinez/Photo Researchers, Inc. C14: (t) J C Carton/Bruce Coleman Inc.; (b) Francois Gohier/Photo Researchers, Inc. C16: (bg) Schafer & Hill/David R. Frazier Photolibrary. C18: Francois Gohier/Photo Researchers, Inc. C19: (l) Charles R. Belinky/Photo Researchers, Inc.; (r) Stephen Ogilvy. C20: (l) Edward R. Degginger/Bruce Coleman Inc.; (r) A.J. Copley/Visuals Unlimited. C21: (l) Staffan Widstrand/Corbis; (r) Ed Bohon/The Stock Market. C22: Carlos Goldin/Photo Researchers, Inc. C23: A.J. Copley/Visuals Unlimited. C24: (t) A.J. Copley/Visuals Unlimited; (b) Tom McHugh/Photo Researchers, Inc. C26: Phil Degginger/Bruce Coleman Inc. C26: (bg) Joel Bennett/Peter Arnold Inc.; (i) Francois Gohier/Photo Researchers, Inc. C27: George Holton/Photo Researchers, Inc. C29: Edward R. Degginger/Bruce Coleman Inc. C30: Dave Bartuff/Corbis. C32: (bg) Tui De Roy/Bruce Coleman Inc. C35: Charlie Heidecker/Bruce Coleman Inc. C36: Dan Howell. C38: J. Serrano/Photo Researchers, Inc. C39: Joyce Photographics/Photo Researchers, Inc. C40: Ron Sanford/The Stock Market. C42: (bg) Isaac Geib/Grant Heilman Photography, Inc. C43: Stephen Ogilvy. C45: Bruce Coleman Inc. C46: (tl) Stephen Ogilvy; (ml) Stephen Ogilvy; (bl) Stephen Ogilvy. C47: Janis Burger/Bruce Coleman Inc. C48: Stephen Ogilvy. C50: M. Wendeer/Photo Researchers, Inc. C52: (bg) Gerald L. French/Panoramic Images. C53: Stephen Ogilvy. C54: (t) Tom McHugh/Photo Researchers, Inc.; (b) Grantpix/Index Stock Imagery. C55: Stephen Ogilvy. C61: Roger Ressmeyer/Corbis. C62: E.R. Degginger/Bruce Coleman Inc. C64: (bg) Fritz Henle/Photo Researchers, Inc. C65: John Sanford/Photo Researchers, Inc. C66: Arni Katz/Index Stock Imagery. C67: Debra P. Hershkowitz/Bruce Coleman Inc. C70: Lionel A Twill/Peter Arnold Inc.; NASA/Peter Arnold Inc. C72: John Sanford/Photo Researchers, Inc. C75: NASA. C76: (b) David Ducros/Photo Researchers, Inc.; (t) NASA/Corbis; (bl) Roger Ressmeyer/Corbis. C77: Roger Ressmeyer/Corbis. C78: (bg) NASA/Photo Researchers, Inc. C79: Dan Howell. C82: (t) US Geological Survey/Science Photo Library/Photo Researchers, Inc.; (m) NASA/Photo Researchers, Inc.; (b) DRA/Still Pictures/Peter Arnold Inc. C83: (t) US Geological Survey/Photo Researchers, Inc.; (l) Phil Degginger/NASA; (m) NASA/Photo Researchers, Inc.; (r) US Geological Survey/Photo Researchers, Inc.; (ml) US Geological Survey/Science Photo Library/Photo Researchers, Inc.; (mr) DRA/Still Pictures/Peter Arnold Inc. C84: (t) Ross Ressmeyer /NASA/Corbis; (m) NASA/Photo Researchers, Inc.; (r) Space Telescope Science Institute/NASA/Photo Researchers, Inc. C85: (tl) NASA /Phil Degginger; (tr) NASA /Phil Degginger; (l) NASA /Phil Degginger; (m1) NASA/Photo Researchers, Inc.; (m2) Space Telescope Science Institute/NASA/ Photo Researchers, Inc. C85: (r) NASA /Phil Degginger; (ml) Ross Ressmeyer /NASA/Corbis; (mr) NASA /Phil Degginger. C86: (t) Francois Gohier/Photo Researchers, Inc.; (b) Mike Agliolo/Index Stock Imagery. C87: Jerry Lodriguss/Photo Researchers, Inc. C88: John R. Foster/Photo Researchers, Inc. C89: David Nunuk/Photo Researchers, Inc. C90: (bg) Burstein Collection/Corbis; (l) Bettmann/Corbis; (r) Bettmann/Corbis. C91: (t) Michael Nicholson/Corbis; (b) Bettmann/Corbis. C93: NASA/Peter Arnold Inc. C94: (t) Kevin Horan/Stock • Boston; (b) David Muench/Corbis. C96: Eastcott/Momatiuk/Earth Scenes; (m) Ken Karp; (b) Ken Karp.

National Geographic Unit Opener D: D0: George D. Lepp/Photo Researchers, Inc. D1: Ron Thomas/FPG International. **Unit D:** D2: Dave G. Houser/Corbis. D4: (bg) JC Carton/Bruce Coleman Inc. D5: Stephen Ogilvy. D6: Planet Earth Pictures/FPG International. D8: Wolfgang Kaehler/Corbis. D9: (t) Jim Zipp/Photo Researchers, Inc.; (b) Jeffrey L. Rotman/Corbis. D10: Roy Morsch/The Stock Market. D12: (t) Stephen Ogilvy; (b) Joe McDonald/Bruce Coleman Inc. D14: (bg) Michael S. Yamashita/Corbis. D15: Stephen Ogilvy. D19: (i) Joe DiMaggio/The Stock Market; (b) Lee Rentz/Bruce Coleman Inc. D22: (tl) John Shaw/Bruce Coleman Inc.; (tr) John Shaw/Bruce Coleman Inc.; (b) Layne Kennedy/Corbis. D23: Adam Woolfitt/Corbis. D24: Library of Congress/Corbis. D25: (l) Barry L. Runk/Grant Heilman Photography, Inc.; (r) Charles D. Winters/Photo Researchers, Inc. D26: (bg) Zeta Visual Media/Index Stock Imagery. D27: Stephen Ogilvy. D30: (t) Andrew J. Martinez/Photo Researchers, Inc.; (b) Andrew J. Martinez/Photo Researchers, Inc. D31: (t) Martin Bond/Science Photo Library; (b) Gary Randall/FPG International. D32: Dan Howell. D34: (i) Courtesy of Bruce M. Richmond/USGS; (b) Courtesy of Bruce M. Richmond/USGS. D35: (t) Joe Mozdzen/Index Stock Imagery. D36: (bg) William H. Mullins/Photo Researchers, Inc. D37: Stephen Ogilvy. D39: (t) Michael S. Renner/Bruce Coleman Inc. D42: (i) J. Dermid/Bruce Coleman Inc.; (l) Photodisc. D43: Richard & Susan Day/Animals Animals. D44: Stephen Ogilvy. D46: (bg) Tom Van Sant/Photo Researchers, Inc. D47: NASA. D49: Richard Hutchings/Photo Researchers, Inc. D50: (i) Photodisc; (t) Photodisc; (b) Omni Photo Communications, Inc./Index Stock Imagery. D51: Blackstone R. Millbury/Bruce Coleman Inc. D53: Norman Owen Tomalin/Bruce Coleman Inc. D54: (l) John Elk III/Bruce Coleman Inc.; (r) Anthony Marsland/Tony Stone Images. D55: Stephen Ogilvy. D56: (bg) W. Wayne Lockwood/Corbis; (i) Yann Arthus-Bertrand/Corbis. D59: Bill Schild/Corbis. D60: D. Boone/Corbis. D62: (bg) Jay Syverson/Corbis. D63: Dan Howell. D66: (t) Christopher Talbot/Natural Selection Stock Photography; (b) Michael Schneider/Peter Arnold Inc. D67: (tl) David Muench/Corbis; (tr) John Sohm/Corbis; (b) Douglas Peebles/Corbis. D68: (t) David Muench/Corbis; (b) Grant Heilman Photography, Inc. D69: Sandy Felsenthal/Corbis. D71: (t) Grant Heilman Photography, Inc.; (m) Douglas Faulkner/Photo Researchers, Inc.; (b) G.R. Roberts/Photo Researchers, Inc. D72: (t) Dr. E.R. Degginger; (tl) John Kaprielian/Photo Researchers, Inc.; (tr) Jules Bucher/Photo Researchers, Inc.; (bm) Myron Wood/Photo Researchers, Inc.; (bl) Van Bucher/Photo Researchers, Inc.; (br) Fundamental Photographs. D74: NASA/Photo Researchers, Inc. D75: (t) Aaron Haupt/Photo Researchers, Inc.; (m) Richard Megna/Fundamental Photographs. D76: (bg) Francois Gohier/Photo Researchers, Inc. D77: Dan Howell. D78: Tom Van Sant/Photo Researchers, Inc. D80: Grant Heilman Photography, Inc. D86: Phil Degginger/Earth Scenes. D90: (t) L. Wantland/Tom Stack & Associates. D91: (t) Dr. E. R. Degginger; (b) Merrilee Thomas/Tom Stack & Associates. D92: (bg) Zefa Germany/The Stock Market; (i) Dr. Earle. D95: Bob Daemmrich/Stock • Boston. D96: (t) Dan Howell; (b) Ken Karp.

National Geographic Unit Opener E: E0: James Holmes/Science Photo Library/

Photo Researchers, Inc. E1: Mauritius/GMBH/Phototake. **Unit E:** E2: Raymond Gehman/Corbis. E4: (bg) Joseph Sohm/Chromosohm, Inc./Corbis. E5: Dan Howell. E8: Stephen Ogilvy. E9: (t) Photodisc. E10: (t) Stephen Ogilvy; (bl) Cesar Llacuna; (br) J.C. Carton/Bruce Coleman Inc. E11: Stephen Ogilvy. E12: Stephen Ogilvy. E13: Stephen Ogilvy. E14: (bg) Kevin R. Morris/Corbis. E15: Dan Howell. E16: Photodisc. E18: Stephen Ogilvy. E19: Stephen Ogilvy. E20: Stephen Ogilvy. E21: Craig Tuttle/The Stock Market. E22: (t) BIPM; (b) Stockbyte. E24: (bg) Maximilian Stock Ltd./Photo Researchers, Inc.; (i) Peter Beck/The Stock Market. E28: Gary Braasch/Corbis. E30: (bg) Charles & Josette Lenars/Corbis. E31: Stephen Ogilvy. E33: Bettmann/Corbis. E34: (tr) Ted Mahieu/The Stock Market; (ml) Stephen Ogilvy; (bl) Stephen Ogilvy; (br) Stephen Ogilvy. E36: Stephen Ogilvy. E38: (tl) Photodisc; (tr) Hutchings Photography; (bl) Photodisc; (br) Steven Needham/Envision. E40: (t) Science Photo Library; (b) Chris Collins/The Stock Market. E41: Science Photo Library. E43: Dan Howell. E44: (t) Jodi Jacobson/Jodi Jacobson; (b) Jodi Jacobson/Jodi Jacobson. E45: (i) Layne Kennedy/Corbis; (tl) Jon Feingersh/The Stock Market; (tr) Jodi Jacobson/Jodi Jacobson; (b) Warren Morgan/Corbis. E46: (l) Richard Megna/Fundamental Photographs; (r) Richard Megna/Fundamental Photographs. E47: (t) The Purcell Team/Corbis; (b) Richard Megna/Fundamental Photographs. E48: Stephen Ogilvy. E49: Photodisc. E50: (bg) Charles E. Rotkin/Corbis. E51: Stephen Ogilvy. E52: (t) Phil Degginger/Bruce Coleman Inc.; (br) Charles Winters/Photo Researchers, Inc. E53: (tl) Richard Megna/Fundamental Photographs; (tr) Michael Keller/FPG International; (tm) Richard Megna/Fundamental Photographs; (b) Photodisc. E54: Cesar Llacuna. E55: (l) R. B. Smith/Dembinsky Photo Associates; (m) Charles Winters/Photo Researchers, Inc.; (r) Stephen Ogilvy. E56: (tl) Gerald Zanetti/The Stock Market; (tr) Robert Jonathan Kligge/The Stock Market; (ml) Biophoto Associates/Photo Researchers, Inc.; (mr) Brownie Harris/The Stock Market; (bl) Philip James Corwin/Corbis; (br) Adam Hart-Davis/Photo Researchers, Inc. E57: (t) Stephen Ogilvy. E58: (t) Joel Arrington/Visuals Unlimited; (m) David McGlynn/FPG International; (b) Paul Bierman/Visuals Unlimited. E59: (m) Sylvan/Visuals Unlimited; (t) Mike Gibson/Index Stock Imagery. E61: (tl) John DeWaele/Stock • Boston; (tr) Photodisc; (ml) Tania Midgley/Corbis; (mr) Photodisc; (b) Ken Karp. E62: (bg) Dr. E.R. Degginger /NASA; (i) Kennedy Space Center. E63: Frank Rossotto/The Stock Market.

National Geographic Unit Opener F: F0: Ralph Wetmore/Tony Stone. F1: Keith Kent/Science Photo Library/Photo Researchers, Inc. **Unit F:** F2: Jeff Vanuga/Corbis. F4: (bg) Mike Howell/All Sport USA. F5: Dan Howell. F6: (l) Terry Wild Studio; (r) Terry Wild Studio. F7: Tim Davis/Photo Researchers, Inc. F8: Bob Daemmrich/Stock • Boston. F9: Dan Howell. F10: (t) Clive Brunskill/All Sport USA; (b) Tom Stewart/The Stock Market. F11: Rick Stewart/All Sport USA. F12: (t) Rob Matheson/The Stock Market; (b) NASA. F13: (t) Pete Saloutos/The Stock Market; (b) Tom & Dee Ann McCarthy/The Stock Market. F14: (t) Doug Martin/Photo Researchers, Inc.; (b) Adam Pretty/All Sport USA. F15: (t) Elizabeth Watt/The Stock Market; (tm) John Henry Williams/Bruce Coleman Inc.; (m1) Rosenfeld Images Ltd./Science Photo Library/Photo Researchers, Inc.; (m2) Margo Cristofori/The Stock Market; (bm) Dr. E. R. Degginger; (b) Phil Degginger/NASA. F16: (l) Alan Majchrowicz/Peter Arnold Inc.; (r) Phil Degginger/NASA. F17: Phil Degginger. F18: (bg) Index Stock Imagery. F19: Dan Howell. F20: (t) J. Fennell/Bruce Coleman Inc.; (b) Steve Elmore/Bruce Coleman Inc. F21: (i) Kenneth H. Thomas/Photo Researchers, Inc.; (t) Perry D. Slocum/Animals Animals. F21: (b) Jeff Foott/Bruce Coleman Inc. F22: (l) Richard Hamilton Smith/Corbis; (r) Ariel Skelley/The Stock Market. F23: (l) Michael Kevin Daly/The Stock Market. F25: Alan Schein/The Stock Market. F26: Jeff Greenberg/Photo Researchers, Inc. F27: (tl) Michael P. Gadomski/Photo Researchers, Inc.; (b) Rick Gayle/The Stock Market. F28: Michal Newman/PhotoEdit. F29: (t) Photodisc; (b) David Madison/Bruce Coleman Inc. F30: S. C. Fried/Photo Researchers, Inc. F32: (bg) Dotte Larsen/Bruce Coleman Inc. F33: Stephen Ogilvy. F34: Larry West/Bruce Coleman Inc. F35: Stephen Ogilvy. F36: (t) D. Donadoni/Bruce Coleman Inc.; (b) Dr. E. R. Degginger. F37: (l) Breck P. Kent/Earth Scenes; (r) Stephen Ogilvy. F38: Dr. E. R. Degginger. F39: Photodisc. F40: (bg) Dr. E. R. Degginger/Bruce Coleman Inc. F41: Dan Howell. F42: (t) Kunio Owaki/The Stock Market; (m) Tony Freeman/PhotoEdit; (r) Dr. E. R. Degginger/Earth Scenes. F43: (l) Ariel Skelley/The Stock Market; (m) Dr. E. R. Degginger; (r) Charles D. Winters/Photo Researchers, Inc. F44: (t) Dr. E. R. Degginger; (m) Alan Schein/The Stock Market; (b) Richard Megna/Fundamental Photographs. F45: Michael Sewell/Peter Arnold Inc. F46: Richard Megna/Fundamental Photographs. F47: (tl) Dr. D.R. Degginger; (tr) Dr. E. R. Degginger; (m) Dr. D.R. Degginger; (bl) Dr. E. R. Degginger; (br) Kent Wood/Photo Researchers, Inc. F48: Lennart Nilsson/Albert Bonniers Forlag AB. F49: (t) D. P. Hershkowitz/Bruce Coleman Inc.; (b) Will and Deni McIntyre/Photo Researchers, Inc. F51: Ellen B. Senisi/Photo Researchers, Inc. F52: (bg) Bob Daemmrich Photo, Inc.; F53: Dan Howell. F54: (t) Lew Long/The Stock Market; (b) Peter Arnold Inc. F55: Richard Hutchings/Photo Researchers, Inc. F56: (t) Michael Keller/The Stock Market; (r) Amos Nachoum/The Stock Market. F58: (tl) Lawrence Migdale; (tr) Joseph Nettis/Photo Researchers, Inc.; (b) D. P. Hershkowitz/Bruce Coleman Inc. F59: George Hall/Corbis. F60: (l) Tim Davis/Photo Researchers, Inc.; (r) Grant Pix/Photo Researchers, Inc. F61: Bob Daemmrich/Stock • Boston. F62: (bg) AFP/Corbis; (i) Bettmann/Corbis. F65: Ariel Skelley/The Stock Market. F68: (bg) Richard Megna/Fundamental Photographs. F69: Dan Howell. F71: Nance Trueworthy/Stock • Boston. F72: Stephen Ogilvy; Reinhard Eisele/Corbis. F74: Kent Wood/Photo Researchers, Inc. F75: Photodisc. F76: (bg) Richard Berenholtz/The Stock Market. F79: Stephen Ogilvy; (b) Dr. E. R. Degginger. F84: (t) Dr. E. R. Degginger; (m) Cesar Llacuna; (b) Norman Owen Tomalin/Bruce Coleman Inc. F86: (bg) Michael W. Davidson/Photo Researchers, Inc.; (b) Don Mason/The Stock Market. F87: David Parker/Seagate/Photo Researchers, Inc. F88: Janis E. Burger/Bruce Coleman Inc.; (i) Stephen Ogilvy. F89: Stephen Ogilvy. F90: (t) Stephen Ogilvy. F91: Charles D. Winters/Photo Researchers, Inc. F92: Stephen Ogilvy. F93: (t) AFP/Corbis; (b) Jeff Foott/Bruce Coleman Inc. F96: (t) Norbert Schafer/The Stock Market; (tm) Dr. E. R. Degginger; (bm) Lester Lefkowitz/The Stock Market; (b) Mary Ann Kulla/The Stock Market. F97: Michael Dalton/Fundamental Photographs. F99: (t) Culver Pictures, Inc. F102: (bg) David Ducros/Photo Researchers, Inc.

Science and Health Handbook: R4-R12: Stephen Ogilvy. R13: PhotoDisc. R28-R34: Hutchings Photography.